iPad®

FOR DUMMIES®

A Wiley Brand

8th Edition

by Edward C. Baig and
Bob "Dr. Mac" LeVitus

iPad® For Dummies®, 8th Edition

Published by: **John Wiley & Sons, Inc.,** 111 River Street, Hoboken, NJ 07030-5774, www.wiley.com

Copyright © 2016 by John Wiley & Sons, Inc., Hoboken, New Jersey

Published simultaneously in Canada

For general information on our other products and services, please contact our Customer Care Department within the U.S. at 877-762-2974, outside the U.S. at 317-572-3993, or fax 317-572-4002. For technical support, please visit www.wiley.com/techsupport.

Wiley publishes in a variety of print and electronic formats and by print-on-demand. Some material included with standard print versions of this book may not be included in e-books or in print-on-demand. If this book refers to media such as a CD or DVD that is not included in the version you purchased, you may download this material at http://booksupport.wiley.com. For more information about Wiley products, visit www.wiley.com.

Library of Congress Control Number: 2015957707

ISBN 978-1-119-13778-8 (pbk); ISBN 978-1-119-15047-3 (ebk); ISBN 978-1-119-15048-0 (ebk)

Manufactured in the United States of America

10 9 8 7 6 5 4 3 2 1

Contents at a Glance

Table of Contents

Introduction

A s Yogi Berra would say, "It was déjà vu all over again": front-page treatment, top billing on network TV and cable, and diehards lining up for days in advance to ensure landing a highly lusted-after product from Apple. The products generating the remarkable buzz this time around are the iPad Pro and its accessories, the Apple Pencil and Smart Keyboard. Every iPad is a magical device and the iPad Pro is no exception.

We hope you bought this book to find out how to get the most magic out of your iPad, regardless of its model. Our goal is to deliver the information you need in a light and breezy fashion. We expect you to have fun using your iPad and we hope you have fun spending time with us.

About This Book

We need to get one thing out of the way right from the get-go. We think you're pretty darn smart for buying a *For Dummies* book. That says to us that you have the confidence and intelligence to know what you don't know. The *For Dummies* franchise is built around the core notion that everyone feels insecure about certain topics when tackling them for the first time, especially when those topics have to do with technology.

As with most Apple products, iPads are beautifully designed and intuitive to use. And though our editors may not want us to reveal this dirty little secret (especially on the first page, for goodness' sake), the truth is you'll get pretty far just by exploring the iPad's many functions and features on your own, without the help of this (or any other) book.

Okay, now that we've spilled the beans, we'll tell you why you shouldn't run back to the bookstore and request a refund. This book is chock-full of useful tips, advice, and other nuggets that should make your iPad experience all the more pleasurable. We'll even go so far as to say that you won't find some of these nuggets anywhere else. So keep this book nearby and consult it often.

Foolish Assumptions

Although we know what happens when one makes assumptions, we've made a few anyway. First, we assume that you, gentle reader, know nothing about using an iPad or iOS — beyond knowing what an iPad is, that you want to use iOS, that you want to understand your iPad and its operating system without digesting an incomprehensible technical manual, and that you made the right choice by selecting this particular book.

And so, we do our best to explain each new concept in full and loving detail. Perhaps that's foolish, but . . . oh, well.

One last thing: We also assume that you can read. If you can't, please ignore this paragraph.

Icons Used in This Book

Little round pictures (or *icons*) appear in the left margins throughout this book. Consider these icons as miniature road signs, telling you something extra about the topic at hand or hammering a point home. Here's what the five icons used in this book look like and mean.

These juicy morsels, shortcuts, and recommendations might make the task at hand faster or easier.

This icon emphasizes the stuff we think you ought to retain. You may even jot down a note to yourself in the iPad.

Put on your propeller beanie hat and insert your pocket protector; this text includes the truly geeky stuff. You can safely ignore this material, but if it weren't interesting or informative, we wouldn't have bothered to write it.

You wouldn't intentionally run a stop sign, would you? In the same fashion, ignoring warnings may be hazardous to your iPad and (by extension) your wallet. There, you now know how these warning icons work, for you have just received your very first warning!

We put a New icon next to anything that's new or improved in iOS 9 or with the iPad.

Beyond the Book

We wrote a bunch of things that just didn't fit in the print version of this book. Rather than leave them on the cutting room floor, we've posted the most useful bits online for your enjoyment and edification.

Here's where you'll find them:

▶ **Online articles covering additional topics are at**

www.dummies.com/extras/ipad

You'll find the following: a fairly complete list of phrases Siri understands; how to make sense of the alphabet soup of cellular data networks (EDGE, 4G, LTE, HSDPA, GSM, CDMA, and more); why your computer offers a shopping mall for content while your iPad doesn't; info on international and third-party keyboards; an overview of Apple's iWork and iLife apps; and much more.

▶ The Cheat Sheet for this book is at

www.dummies.com/cheatsheet/ipad

Here, you'll find info on using the iPad's buttons and icons, tips for mastering multitouch, and where to find additional help if your iPad is acting contrary.

Where to Go from Here

Why, go straight to Chapter 1, of course (without passing Go).

In all seriousness, we wrote this book for you, so please let us know what you think. If we screwed up, confused you, left out something, or — heaven forbid — made you angry, drop us a note. And if we hit you with one pun too many, it helps to know that as well. Because writers are people too (believe it or not), we also encourage positive feedback if you think it's warranted. So kindly send email to Ed at Baigdummies@gmail.com and to Bob at iPadLeVitus@boblevitus.com. We do our best to respond to reasonably polite email in a timely fashion. Most of all, we want to thank you for buying our book. Please enjoy it along with your new iPad.

Note: At the time we wrote this book, all the information it contained was accurate for all Wi-Fi and Wi-Fi + 3G and 4G iPads with the exception of the first-generation iPad, which we no longer cover. The book is also based on version 9 of the iOS (operating system) and version 12.3 of iTunes. Apple is likely to introduce new iPad models and new versions of iOS and iTunes between book editions, so if the hardware or user interface on your new iPad or the version of iTunes on your computer looks a little different, be sure to check out what Apple has to say at www.apple.com/ipad. You'll no doubt find updates on the company's latest releases. When a change is substantial, we try to add an update or additional information at www.dummies.com/extras/ipad.

Part I
Getting to Know Your iPad

Visit www.dummies.com for great *For Dummies* content online.

In this part . . .

- ✔ Get basic training for getting along with your iPad.

- ✔ Enjoy a gentle introduction to your iPad.

- ✔ Take a peek at your iPad hardware and software and explore the way it works.

- ✔ Discover the joys of synchronization over USB or Wi-Fi and find out how to get your data — contacts, appointments, movies, songs, podcasts, books, and so on — from a computer onto your iPad, quickly and painlessly.

Unveiling the iPad

In This Chapter

▶ Looking at the big picture

▶ Touring the outside of the iPad

▶ Checking out the iPad's apps

*C*ongratulations! You've selected one of the most incredible handheld devices we've ever seen. Of course, the iPad is a combination of a killer audio and video iPod, an e-book reader, a powerful Internet communications device, a superb handheld gaming device, a still and video camera, and a platform for over 1.6 million apps at the time this was written — and probably a lot more by the time you read this.

Apple has produced 11 iPad models so far: The original iPad (2010), the iPad 2 (2011), the iPad third generation (Spring 2012), the iPad fourth generation (Fall 2012), the iPad mini (Fall 2012), the iPad Air and the iPad mini 2 (Fall 2013), the iPad Air 2 and iPad mini 3 (Fall 2014), and the iPad Pro and iPad mini 4 (Fall 2015). To avoid confusion, we refer to the four original full-sized iPads — the ones that don't have Air, mini, or Pro as their surname — as first-, second-, third-, and fourth-generation iPads, respectively.

Note that we're not covering the first-generation iPad in this book because the latest operating system (iOS 9) doesn't run on it. If you're the owner of an original iPad, you can still find a lot of handy information, but some things might look or work differently. You might want to rummage around for a previous edition of this book.

In this chapter, we offer a gentle introduction to all the pieces that make up your iPad, plus overviews of its revolutionary hardware and software features.

Exploring the iPad's Big Picture

The iPad has many best-of-class features, but perhaps its most notable feature is that there's no physical keyboard or stylus in the box. Instead, every iPad includes a super-high-resolution touchscreen that you operate using a pointing device you're already intimately familiar with: It's called your finger. (Apple did, however, introduce its first optional stylus and keyboard — the $149 Apple Pencil and $169 Smart Keyboard — for the iPad Pro.)

Every iPad ever built has a beautiful screen, and the third-generation and fourth-generation iPad, both iPad Airs, and all iPad minis except the first sport Apple's exclusive high-definition Retina display, which is easily the most beautiful screen we've ever seen on a tablet.

Other things we love include the iPad's plethora of built-in sensors. It has an *accelerometer* to detect when you rotate the device from portrait to landscape mode — and instantly adjust what's on the display accordingly.

The screen rotates — that is, unless the screen orientation lock is engaged. We tell you more about this feature shortly.

A light sensor adjusts the display's brightness in response to the current ambient lighting conditions.

In addition to the aforementioned sensors, iPads have a three-axis gyro sensor that works with the accelerometer and built-in compass.

The latest models — the iPad Air 2, iPad mini 4, and iPad Pro — also include Apple's Touch ID sensor, which lets you unlock your iPad with your fingerprint.

Last, but definitely not least, most iPads (third generation and newer), come with Siri, a voice-controlled personal assistant happy to do almost anything you ask (as long as your iPad is running iOS 6 or later).

In the following sections, we're not just marveling about the wonderful screen and sensors. Now it's time to take a brief look at the rest of the iPad's features, broken down by product category.

The iPad as an iPod

We agree with the late Steve Jobs on this one: The iPad is magical — and without a doubt the best iPod Apple has ever produced. You can enjoy all your existing iPod content — music, audiobooks, audio and video podcasts, iTunes U courses, music videos, television shows, and movies — on the gorgeous color display found on every iPad ever made (even the oldest iPads have gorgeous color displays).

Here's the bottom line: If you can get the content — be it video, audio, or whatever — into iTunes on your Mac or PC, you can synchronize it and watch or listen to it on your iPad. And, of course, you can always buy or rent content on your iPad in the iTunes Store.

Chapter 3 is all about syncing (transferring media from your computer to your iPad), but for now, just know that some video content may need to be converted to an iPad-compatible format, with the proper resolution, frame rate, bit rate, and file format to play on your iPad. If you try to sync an incompatible video file, iTunes alerts you that an issue exists.

If you get an error message about an incompatible video file, select the file in iTunes and choose File⇨Create New Version. When the conversion is finished, sync again. Chapter 8 covers video and video compatibility in more detail.

And here's another tip at no extra cost: The free HandBrake app (`http://handbrake.fr`) often provides better results than iTunes when converting movie files to an iPad-friendly format. It has presets for most iPad models, so it's simple to use, and it can often convert movie files and formats that would choke iTunes.

The iPad as an Internet communications device

But wait — there's more! Not only is the iPad a stellar iPod, but it's also a full-featured Internet communications device with — we're about to drop some industry jargon on you — a rich HTML email client that's compatible with most POP and IMAP mail services, with support for Microsoft Exchange ActiveSync. (For more on this topic, see Chapter 5.) Also onboard is a world-class web browser (Safari) that makes web surfing fun and easy on the eyes, unlike what's on many mobile devices. Chapter 4 explains how to surf the web using Safari.

Another cool Internet feature is Maps, a killer mapping app that's improved in iOS 9. By using GPS (3G or 4G models) or triangulation (Wi-Fi–only models), the iPad can determine your location, let you view maps and satellite imagery, and obtain driving directions and traffic information regardless of where you happen to be. (See Chapter 6 for the scoop on Maps.) You can also find businesses (such as gas stations, pizza restaurants, hospitals, and Apple Stores) with just a few taps. And in iOS 9, you can even use Maps to get directions for public transportation in a handful of U.S. cities (and China), with more cities in both countries coming soon.

Maps is useful over Wi-Fi but more useful and more accurate on cellular iPads with 3G or 4G.

We dare say that the Internet experience on an iPad is far superior to the Internet experience on any other handheld device.

The iPad as an e-book reader

Download the free iBooks app if you don't already have it, or any of the excellent (and free) third-party e-book readers such as the Kindle and Nook apps, and you'll discover a whole new way of finding and reading books. The iBooks Store and News app (covered in Chapter 10) are chock-full of good reading at prices that are lower than what you'd pay for a printed copy. Better still, when you read an e-book, you're helping the environment and saving trees. Furthermore, some (if not many) titles include audio, video, or graphical content not available in the printed editions. Plus, a great number of good books are free. And best of all, you can carry your entire library in one hand. If you've never read a book on your iPad, give it a try. We think you'll like (or love) it.

The iPad as a multimedia powerhouse

The spectacular screen found on second-generation iPads is superb for personal video viewing, and the Retina display on the third-generation and all later iPads makes the experience even more extraordinary. Add an adapter cable or Apple TV, as discussed in Chapter 17, and your iPad turns into a superb device for watching video on an HDTV (or even a non-HD TV), with support for output resolutions up to 1080p.

You won't need the (admittedly less expensive) adapter cable if you choose an Apple TV (from $69), which is a marvelous little device that, among other things, lets you stream audio and video to your HDTV wirelessly.

And iPads include a pair of cameras and the FaceTime video-chatting app, taking the iPad's multimedia acumen to new heights. Chapter 8 gets you started with FaceTime.

The iPad as a platform for third-party apps

At the time of this writing, more than 1.6 million apps were available in the App Store, with over 100 billion downloads to date in categories such as games, business, education, entertainment, healthcare and fitness, music, photography, productivity, travel, and sports. The cool thing is that most of them, even ones designed for the iPhone or iPod touch, also run flawlessly on the iPad.

Of those million+ apps, well over half are designed specifically for the iPad's larger screen, with more arriving daily.

Chapter 11 helps you fill your iPad with all the cool apps your heart desires. We share our favorite free and for-pay apps in Chapters 18 and 19, respectively.

What do you need to use an iPad?

To *use* your iPad, only a few simple things are required. Here's a list of everything you need:

- An iPad
- An Apple ID (assuming that you want to acquire content such as apps, videos, music, iBooks, and podcasts, which you almost certainly do)
- Internet access — broadband wireless Internet access is recommended

In previous editions of this book, we said you *needed* a computer with iTunes to sync your iPad. That's no longer true; you can activate, set up, update, back up, and restore an iPad wirelessly without a computer.

Although you don't technically *need* a computer, it's nice to have a symbiotic relationship between your iPad and your Mac or PC, because many common tasks are faster and easier using a computer with iTunes than they are on your iPad. If you decide to introduce your iPad to your computer (and we think you should), you need one of the following for syncing (which we discuss at length in Chapter 3):

- A Mac with a USB 2.0 or 3.0 port, Mac OS X version 10.8.5 or later, and iTunes 12.3 or later
- A PC with a USB 2.0 or 3.0 port, Windows 7 or later, and iTunes 12.3 or later

iTunes is a free download, available at `www.itunes.com/download`.

Touring the iPad Exterior

The iPad is a harmonious combination of hardware and software. In the following sections, we take a brief look at the hardware — what's on the outside.

On the top

On the top of your iPad, you find the headphone jack, microphone, and the sleep/wake button, as shown in Figure 1-1:

- **Sleep/wake button:** This button is used to put your iPad's screen to sleep or to wake it up. It's also how you turn your iPad on or off. To put it to sleep or wake it up, just press the button. To turn it on or off, press and hold down the button for a few seconds.

  Your iPad's battery will run down faster when your iPad is awake, so we suggest that you make a habit of putting it to sleep when you're not using it.

When your iPad is sleeping, nothing happens if you touch its screen. To wake it up, merely press the button again or press the Home button on the front of the device (as described in a moment).

If you use an Apple Smart Cover or Smart Case (or any of the third-party cases that use the Smart Cover mechanism), you can just open the cover to wake your iPad and close the cover to put it to sleep.

In Chapter 15, you can find out how to make your iPad go to sleep automatically after a period of inactivity.

✔ **Headphone jack:** This jack lets you plug in a headset. You can use the Apple headsets or headphones that came with your iPhone or iPod. Or you can use pretty much any headphones or headset that plugs into a 3.5-mm stereo headphone jack.

Throughout this book, we use the words *headphones, earphones,* and *headset* interchangeably. Strictly speaking, a headset includes a microphone so that you can talk (or record) as well as listen; headphones or earphones are for listening only. Either type works with your iPad, as do most wireless Bluetooth headsets.

✔ **Microphone:** The tiny dot in the middle of the top is actually a pretty good microphone.

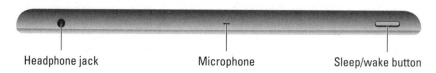

Headphone jack   Microphone   Sleep/wake button

Figure 1-1: The top of the iPad.

On the bottom

On the bottom of your iPad are the speaker and dock connector, as shown in Figure 1-2:

✔ **Speaker:** The speaker plays monaural (single-speaker) audio — music or video soundtracks — if no headset is plugged in.

✔ **30-pin dock connector (second and third generation) or Lightning connector (fourth generation, iPad Airs, iPad minis, and iPad Pro).** This connector has three purposes:

 • *Recharge your iPad's battery:* Simply connect one end of the included dock connector–to–USB cable to the dock or Lightning connector and the other end to the USB power adapter.

 • *Synchronize your iPad:* Connect one end of the same cable to the dock connector and the other end to a USB port on your Mac or PC.

- *Connect your iPad to cameras or televisions using adapters:* Such connectors include the camera connection kit or the other adapter cables discussed in Chapter 17. Make sure to use an adapter that is appropriate for your dock or Lightning connector.

If you connect the USB cable to USB ports on your keyboard, USB hub, display, or other external device, or even the USB ports on an older Mac or PC, you may be able to sync, but more than likely you can't charge the battery. For the most part, only your computer's built-in USB ports (and only recent-vintage computers at that) have enough juice to recharge the battery. If you use an external USB port on a hub, you'll probably see a *Not Charging* message next to the battery icon at the top of the screen (unless the hub has its own AC power source).

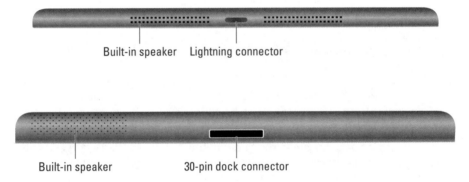

Built-in speaker   Lightning connector

Built-in speaker   30-pin dock connector

Figure 1-2: The bottom of the second- and third-generation iPad (bottom) and the iPad Air (top).

On the right side

On the right side of your iPad are the volume up and volume down buttons and the ring/silent switch, as shown in Figure 1-3:

✓ **Ring/silent switch:** When the switch is set to silent mode — the down position, with an orange dot visible on the switch — your iPad doesn't make any sound when you receive new mail or an alert pops up on the screen. Note that the ring/silent switch doesn't silence what you think of as *expected* sounds, which are sounds you expect to hear in a particular app. Therefore, it doesn't silence the iTunes or Videos apps, nor does it mute games and other apps that emit noises. About the only thing the ring/silent switch mutes are unexpected sounds, such as those associated with notifications from apps or the iPad operating system (iOS).

If the switch doesn't mute your notification sounds when engaged (that is, you can see the little orange dot on the switch), look for a little screen orientation icon (shown in the margin) to the left of the battery icon near the top of your screen.

When you flick the ring/silent switch, if you see this icon, it means you've selected the Lock Rotation option in the Settings app's General pane.

✔ **Volume up and volume down buttons:** These buttons are just below the ring/silent switch. Press the upper button to increase the volume; press the lower button to decreases the volume.

The Camera app uses the volume up button as an alternative shutter release button to the on-screen shutter release button. Press either one to shoot a picture or start and stop video recording.

Volume up and volume down buttons

Ring/silent switch

Figure 1-3: The right side has two buttons.

On the front and back

On the front and back of your iPad, you find the following (labeled in Figure 1-4):

✔ **Touchscreen:** You find out how to use the iPad's gorgeous high-resolution color touchscreen in Chapter 2. All we have to say at this time is: Try not to drool all over it.

✔ **Home button/Touch ID sensor (iPad Air 2 and iPad mini 3 only):** No matter what you're doing, you can press the Home button at any time to display the Home screen, as shown in Figure 1-4. If you have an iPad Air 2 or iPad mini 3, your Home button doubles as a Touch ID sensor, and you can use your fingerprint (or a passcode) to unlock your phone and authenticate purchases.

✔ **Front camera:** The front camera is serviceable and delivers decent-enough video for video chats and such, but it's not particularly good for taking still photos.

✔ **App icons:** Each of the 20 icons shown on the screen (see Figure 1-4) launches an included iPad app. You read more about these apps later in this chapter and throughout the rest of the book.

✔ **Rear camera:** iPads have a better camera (than the one in front) on the backside, just below the sleep/wake button. The iPad 2's rear camera captures decent video at 720p and shoots fair-to-middling stills; all other iPads have better rear cameras that shoot nice HD video at 1080p and very nice stills.

App icon

Front camera

Rear camera

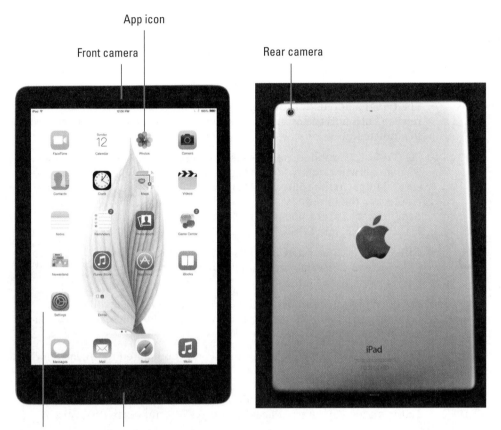

Touchscreen   Home button

Figure 1-4: The front and back of the iPad: a study in elegant simplicity.

Status bar

The status bar, which is at the top of the screen, displays tiny icons that provide a variety of information about the current state of your iPad:

 ✔ **Airplane mode:** Airplane mode should be enabled when you fly. It turns off all wireless features of your iPad — the cellular, 4G, 3G, GPRS (General Packet Radio Service), and EDGE (Enhanced Datarate for GSM Evolution) networks; Wi-Fi; and Bluetooth — so you can enjoy music, video, games, photos, or any app that doesn't require an Internet connection while you're in the air.

Tap the Settings app and then tap the Airplane Mode switch on (so green is displayed). The icon shown in the margin appears on the left side of your status bar whenever airplane mode is enabled.

Disable airplane mode when the plane is at the gate before takeoff or after landing so you can send or receive email and iMessages.

There's no need to enable airplane mode on flights that offer onboard Wi-Fi. On such flights it's perfectly safe to use your iPad's Wi-Fi while you're in the air (but not until the captain says so).

LTE   ✔ **LTE (Wi-Fi + 4G models only):** This icon lets you know that your carrier's 4G LTE network is available and your iPad can use it to connect to the Internet.

3G   ✔ **3G (Wi-Fi + 3G models only):** This icon informs you that the high-speed 3G data network from your wireless carrier (that's AT&T, Verizon, Sprint, and T-Mobile in the United States) is available and that your iPad can connect to the Internet via 3G. (Wondering what 3G, 4G, and these other data networks are? Check out the nearby sidebar, "Comparing Wi-Fi, 4G, LTE, 3G, GPRS, and EDGE.")

O   ✔ **GPRS (Wi-Fi + 3G and 4G models only):** This icon says that your wireless carrier's GPRS data network is available and that your iPad can use it to connect to the Internet.

E   ✔ **EDGE (Wi-Fi + 3G and 4G models only):** This icon tells you that your wireless carrier's EDGE network is available and you can use it to connect to the Internet.

 🛜   ✔ **Wi-Fi:** If you see the Wi-Fi icon, your iPad is connected to the Internet over a Wi-Fi network. The more semicircular lines you see (up to three), the stronger the Wi-Fi signal. If your iPad has only one or two semicircles of Wi-Fi strength, try moving around a bit. If you don't see the Wi-Fi icon on the status bar, Internet access with Wi-Fi is not currently available.

 ☺   ✔ **Personal hotspot:** You see this icon when you're sharing your Internet connection with computers or other devices over Wi-Fi. Personal hotspot is available for every iPad except the iPad 2 and may not be available in all areas or from all carriers. Additional fees may apply. Contact your wireless carrier for more information.

 ↻   ✔ **Syncing:** This icon appears on the status bar when your iPad is syncing with iTunes on your Mac or PC.

 ☀   ✔ **Activity:** This icon tells you that some network or other activity is occurring, such as over-the-air synchronization, the sending or receiving of email, or the loading of a web page. Some third-party apps use this icon to indicate network or other activity.

VPN   ✔ **VPN:** This icon shows that you're currently connected to a virtual private network (VPN).

 🔒   ✔ **Lock:** This icon tells you when your iPad is locked. See Chapter 2 for information on locking and unlocking your iPad.

Comparing Wi-Fi, 4G, LTE, 3G, GPRS, and EDGE

Wireless (that is, cellular) carriers may offer one of three data networks relevant to the iPad as of this writing. For now anyway, only the third-generation and later iPads can take advantage of the speediest 4G or LTE networks, which carriers are rolling out as fast as they can. The second-fastest network is called 3G, and there are older, even slower data networks called EDGE and GPRS. Your iPad starts by trying to connect to the fastest network it supports. If it makes a connection, you see the 4G or 3G icon on the status bar. If it can't connect to a 4G or 3G network, it tries to connect to a slower EDGE or GPRS network, and you see EDGE or GPRS icons on the status bar.

Most Wi-Fi networks, however, are faster than even the fastest 4G cellular data network — and much faster than 3G, EDGE, or GPRS. So, because all iPads can connect to a Wi-Fi network if one is available, they do so, even when a 4G, 3G, GPRS, or EDGE network is also available.

Last but not least, if you don't see one of these icons — 4G, 3G, GPRS, EDGE, or Wi-Fi — you don't currently have Internet access. Chapter 4 offers more details about these different networks.

✔ **Screen orientation lock:** This icon appears when the screen orientation lock is engaged.

✔ **Location Services:** This icon appears when an app (such as Maps; see Chapter 6 for more about the Maps app) is using Location Services (GPS) to establish your physical location (or at least to establish the physical location of your iPad).

✔ **Do Not Disturb:** This icon appears whenever Do Not Disturb is enabled, silencing incoming FaceTime calls and alerts. See Chapter 15 for details on Do Not Disturb.

✔ **Play:** This icon informs you that a song is currently playing. You find out more about playing songs in Chapter 7.

✔ **Bluetooth:** This icon indicates the current state of your iPad's Bluetooth connection. If you see this icon on the status bar, Bluetooth is on, and a device (such as a wireless headset or keyboard) is connected. If the icon is gray, Bluetooth is turned on, but no device is connected. If the icon is white, Bluetooth is on, and one (or more) devices are connected. If you don't see a Bluetooth icon, Bluetooth is turned off. Chapter 15 goes into more detail about Bluetooth.

- **Bluetooth Battery:** Displays the battery level of supported Bluetooth devices (while paired). Only certain devices — mostly headsets and speakers — support this feature. If you see this icon in your status bar, it's telling you the approximate battery level of whichever supported device is currently paired with your iPad.

- **Battery:** This icon shows the level of your battery's charge, and also indicates when you're connected to a power source. It's completely filled when you aren't connected to a power source and your battery is fully charged (as shown in the margin). It then empties as your battery becomes depleted. You see an on-screen message when the charge drops to 20 percent or below, and another when it reaches 10 percent.

Discovering the Delectable Home Screen and Dock Icons

The iPad Home screen and dock display 20 icons, with each icon representing a different built-in app or function. Because the rest of the book covers each and every one of these babies in full and loving detail, we merely provide brief descriptions here.

To get to your Home screen, tap the Home button. If your iPad is asleep when you tap, the unlock screen appears. After your iPad is unlocked, you see whichever page was on the screen when it went to sleep. If that happens to have been the Home screen, you're golden. If it wasn't, merely tap the Home button again to summon your iPad's Home screen.

In the following sections, we tell you briefly about the icons preloaded on your iPad's first Home screen page, as well as the icons you find on the dock that are always accessible from each Home screen.

Home is where the screen is

If you haven't rearranged your icons, you see the following apps on the first Home screen, starting at the top left:

- **FaceTime:** Use this app to participate in FaceTime video chats, as you discover in Chapter 8.

- **Calendar:** No matter what calendar program you prefer on your Mac or PC (as long as it's iCal, Calendar, Microsoft Entourage, or Microsoft Outlook or online calendars such as Google or iCloud), you can synchronize events and alerts between your computer and your iPad. Create an event on one device, and the event is automatically synchronized with the other device the next time the two devices are connected. Neat stuff.

✔ **Photos:** This app is the iPad's terrific photo manager, which just keeps getting better. It lets you view pictures from a camera or SD card (using the optional camera connection kit), screen shots of your iPad screen, photos synced from your computer, saved from an email or web page, or saved from one of the myriad third-party apps that let you save your handiwork in the Photos app. You can zoom in or out, create slideshows, email photos to friends, crop, do a bit of image editing, and much more. And it's where you'll find the Camera Roll album with photos and videos you've taken with your iPad. To get started, see Chapter 9.

✔ **Camera:** You use this app to shoot pictures or videos with your iPad's front- or rear-facing camera. You find out more in Chapters 8 (videos) and 9 (camera).

✔ **Contacts:** This handy little app contains information about the people you know. Like the Calendar app, it synchronizes with the Contacts app on your Mac or PC (as long as you keep your contacts in Address Book, Contacts, Microsoft Entourage, or Microsoft Outlook), and you can synchronize contacts between your computer and your iPad. If you create a contact on one device, the contact is automatically synchronized with the other device the next time your devices are connected. Chapter 12 explains how to start using the Calendar and Contacts apps.

✔ **Clock:** The Clock app includes alarm clocks, timers, and more. You hear more about this nifty app in Chapter 13.

✔ **Maps:** This app is among our favorites. View street maps or satellite imagery of locations around the globe, or ask for directions, traffic conditions, or even the location of a nearby pizza joint. You can find your way around the Maps app with the tips you find in Chapter 6.

✔ **Videos:** This handy app is the repository for your movies, TV shows, and music videos. You add videos via iTunes on your Mac or PC or by purchasing them from the iTunes Store with the iTunes app on your iPad. Check out Chapter 8 to find out more.

✔ **Photo Booth:** This one is a lot like those old-time photo booths, but you don't have to feed it money. You discover details about Photo Booth in Chapter 9.

✔ **Notes:** This program enables you to type notes while you're out and about. You can send the notes to yourself or to anyone else through email, or you can just save them on your iPad until you need them. For help as you start using Notes, flip to Chapter 13.

✔ **Reminders:** This app may be the only to-do list you ever need. It integrates with iCal, Calendar, Outlook, and iCloud, so to-do items and reminders sync automatically with your other devices, both mobile and desktop. You'll hear much more about this great app, but you have to wait until Chapter 13.

- ✔ **News:** This app is new in iOS 9; it's where you'll find news culled from magazines, newspapers, and websites. You read more about News in Chapter 10.

- ✔ **iTunes Store:** Tap this puppy to purchase music, movies, TV shows, audiobooks, and more. You find more info about iTunes (and the Music app) in Chapter 7.

- ✔ **App Store:** This icon enables you to connect to and search the iTunes App Store for iPad apps that you can purchase or download for free over a Wi-Fi or cellular data network connection. Chapter 11 is your guide to buying and using apps from the App Store.

- ✔ **iBooks:** If you wanted iBooks under iOS 7, you had to download it (it's free). iOS 8 corrected this shortcoming, so if you're running iOS 8 or iOS 9, the latest and greatest version of iOS, you have it already. You use iBooks to read books, which you can buy in the iTunes Store.

- ✔ **Settings:** Tap this icon to change settings for your iPad and its apps. With so many settings in the Settings app, you'll be happy to hear that Chapter 15 is dedicated exclusively to Settings.

Now, swipe from right to left across the first Home screen to make the second Home screen appear. Its icons include the following:

- ✔ **Game Center:** This app is the Apple social networking app for game enthusiasts. Compare achievements, boast of your conquests and high scores, or challenge your friends to battle. You hear more about social networking and Game Center in Chapter 13.

- ✔ **Tips:** This app offers tips from Apple on doing more with your iPad. And here's a tip about Tips: Apple pushes new tips to the app every week, so if you haven't looked at the app lately, consider doing so to see what's new.

- ✔ **Podcasts:** Use the Podcasts app to (d'oh!) listen to your favorite podcasts, which you download and subscribe to (let's all say it together this time) in the iTunes Store.

- ✔ **Find Friends:** See the locations of friends and family who opt in.

- ✔ **Find iPhone:** If your iPad (or iPhone or iPod touch) goes missing, use this app to determine its last known location.

- ✔ **iCloud Drive:** This app (if enabled in Settings⇨iCloud⇨iCloud Drive) contains all documents you've saved to your iCloud Drive. Apple apps as well as many third-party apps know how to use it.

Sittin' on the dock of the iPad

At the bottom of the iPad screen are the final four icons, sitting on a special shelf-like area called the *dock*.

The thing that makes the icons on your dock special is that they're available on every Home screen page.

By default, the dock icons are

- **Messages:** This app provides to iPads, iPhones, iPod touches, and Macs a unified messaging service dubbed iMessage. You can exchange unlimited free text or multimedia messages with any other device running iOS 5 or later (the iPad, iPhone, and iPod touch) or Mac OS X Mountain Lion or later. Find out more about iMessage in Chapter 5.

- **Mail:** This app lets you send and receive email with most POP3 and IMAP email systems and, if you work for a company that grants permission, Microsoft Exchange, too. Chapter 5 helps you start emailing everyone you know from your iPad.

- **Safari:** Safari is your web browser. If you're a Mac user, you know that already. If you're a Windows user who hasn't already discovered the wonderful Safari for Windows, think Internet Explorer on steroids. Chapter 4 shows you how to start using Safari on your iPad.

- **Music:** Last but not least, this icon unleashes all the power of an iPod right on your iPad so that you can listen to music or podcasts. You discover how the Music app works in Chapter 7.

The dock on all iPads can hold up to six icons. Feel free to add icons to or remove icons from the dock until it feels right to you. Press and hold down on an icon until all the icons wiggle. Then drag the icon to where you want it. Press the Home button to save your arrangement.

Two last points:

- iOS 5 introduced the totally useful Notification Center, which became better and better with each new version of iOS. We wanted to mention it even though it doesn't have an icon of its own. You hear much more about it in Chapter 13; to see it now (we know you can't wait), swipe your iPad screen from top to bottom to make it appear. Then swipe from bottom to top to put it away again.

- We'd be remiss not to mention the even more useful Control Center, with controls for Wi-Fi, Bluetooth, audio playback, and more, all available from any screen in any app. You discover much more about Control Center in Chapter 14, but if you just can't stand the suspense, put your finger at the very bottom of your iPad screen and swipe upward to check out Control Center (and then swipe downward or tap the Home button to put it away).

iPad Basic Training

In This Chapter

▶ Getting going

▶ Setting up the iPad

▶ Locking your iPad

▶ Mastering multitouch

▶ Cutting, copying, and pasting

▶ Multitasking with your iPad

▶ Watching video through a picture-in-picture function

▶ Spotlighting search

*B*y now you know that the iPad you hold in your hands is very different from other computers.

You also know that these slate-style machines are rewriting the rule book for mainstream computing. How so? For starters, iPads don't come with a mouse or any other kind of pointing device. They lack traditional computing ports or connectors, such as USB. And they have no physical or built-in keyboard, though Apple will sell you a Smart Keyboard accessory for the large-display iPad Pro model.

iPads even differ from other so-called tablet PCs, some of which feature a pen or stylus and let you write in digital ink. As we point out (pun intended) in Chapter 1, the iPad relies on an input device that you always have with you: your finger. Okay, so the iPad Pro you meet in this book also breaks that longstanding iPad rule, at least if you spring for the Apple Pencil accessory.

Tablet computers of one form or another have actually been around since the last century. They just never captured the fancy of Main Street. Apple's very own Newton, an ill-fated 1990s personal digital assistant, was among the machines that barely made a dent in the market.

What's past is past, of course, and technology — not to mention Apple itself — has come a long way since Newton. And suffice it to say that in the future, tablets — led by the iPad brigade, of course — promise to enjoy a much rosier outlook. Indeed, since the iPad burst onto the scene, numerous tech titans (as well as smaller companies) have introduced their own touch-enabled tablets; many rely on the Google Android mobile operating system, some on versions of the Microsoft Windows operating system, and a few on other operating systems. Some solid machines are among them, but the iPad remains the market leader and a true pioneer in the space.

If you were caught up in the initial mania surrounding the iPad, you probably plotted for weeks about how to land one. After all, the iPad, like its close cousin the iPhone, rapidly emerged as the hippest computer you could find. (We consider you hip just because you're reading this book.) You had to plot to get subsequent versions as well.

Speaking of the iPhone, if you own one or its close relative, the Apple iPod touch, you already have a gigantic start in figuring out how to master the iPad multitouch method of navigating the interface with your fingers. If you've been using iOS 9 on those devices, you have an even bigger head start. You have our permission to skim the rest of this chapter, but we urge you to stick around anyway because some things on the iPad work in subtly different ways than on the iPhone or iPod touch. If you're a total novice, don't fret. Nothing about multitouch is painful.

Getting Started on Getting Started

We've always said that you needed the following four things to enjoy your new iPad, but starting with iOS 5, you don't *need* a computer (and the connection to iTunes and whatever program you use to store your contacts) to use an iPad. You see, iOS 5 was the first operating system to allow you to activate, set up, and apply iOS updates to an iPad wirelessly, without having to connect it to a computer. And iOS 6, iOS 7, iOS 8, and iOS 9 continue the tradition. We show you how to get your iPad set up without a computer in the next section; in Chapter 3, we show you how to set up your iPad with your computer.

Because even though you don't *need* a computer, we think you'll prefer using your iPad with one rather than without one.

In our experience, many tasks — such as iOS software updates and rearranging app icons — are faster and easier to do using iTunes on a Mac or PC than on the iPad. Having a backup for your data helps too.

Now, here are those four things you need to use your iPad:

- **A computer:** As we point out, you don't really need a computer, though it's helpful to use your iPad with one just the same. The computer can be a Macintosh running Mac OS X version 10.5.8 or later, or a PC running Windows 10, Windows 8, Windows 7 (or Windows Vista or Windows XP Home or Professional Edition with Service Pack 3 or later if you still have such a machine).

  The iCloud service has higher requirements: Mac OS X Mountain Lion, Lion (10.7), Mavericks, Yosemite, or El Capitan for Macs; or Windows Vista, Windows 7, Windows 8, or Windows 10 for PCs. Flip to Chapter 3 for details about iCloud.

- **iTunes software:** More specifically, you need version 10.7 or later of iTunes — emphasis on the *later* because by the time you read this, it will be later. After all, iTunes was up to version 12.3 by the time we were preparing this book.

  Apple constantly tweaks iTunes to make it better. You can go to www. itunes.com/download to fetch a copy. Or launch your current version of iTunes and then choose iTunes⇨Check for Updates.

  The uninitiated might want to know that *iTunes* is the nifty Apple jukebox software that owners of iPods and iPhones, not to mention PCs and Macs, use to manage music, videos, apps, and more. iTunes is at the core of the iPad as well, because an iPod is built into the iPad, as part of the Music app. You can use iTunes to synchronize a bunch of stuff from your Mac or PC to and from an iPad, including (but not limited to) apps, photos, movies, TV shows, podcasts, iTunes U lectures, and of course, music.

  Syncing is such a vital part of this process that we devote an entire chapter (Chapter 3) to the topic.

- **An Apple ID account:** Read Chapter 7 for details on how to set up an account. Like most things Apple, the process isn't difficult. You'll want an account to download content from iTunes, the App Store, or to take advantage of iCloud.

- **Internet access:** Your iPad can connect to the Internet in either of two ways: Wi-Fi or cellular (if you bought an iPad with 3G or 4G capabilities). You can connect your iPad to cyberspace via Wi-Fi in your home, office, school, favorite coffeehouse, bookstore, or numerous other spots.

At press time, 3G (third-generation) and 4G (fourth-generation) wireless data connections were available from many carriers in countries too numerous to mention; in the United States, you can choose among AT&T, Sprint, Verizon Wireless, and T-Mobile. Those wireless carriers are pretty far along building the zippier *4G* (fourth-generation) networks across the United States, with Verizon in the lead rolling out the fastest variety, called *LTE* (Long Term Evolution). While the others play catch-up on LTE, the latest iPad on AT&T and T-Mobile makes nice with other pretty fast networks, including something known as *HSPA+*.

As this book goes to press, data rates (no contract required) are reasonably priced as long as you don't stream or download a lot of movies or watch tons of videos while connected over 3G or 4G. For as little as $5 in some instances, you can purchase a day pass for data instead of opting for a monthly plan.

Figuring out how much data you need beforehand isn't always easy, but it's simple enough to adjust along the way. If you're streaming a lot of music, T-Mobile for one provides a nice benefit: the capability to stream free on most major services, including Spotify and Apple's own Apple Music.

The following are some of the offerings from the major U.S. carriers when we published this book. Keep in mind that all the rate plans cited are subject to change and sometimes tied to shareable family plans that include smartphones. In some instances, you must pay activation or other fees. Promotions are also common:

- AT&T: $14.99 a month for 250MB, 3GB for $30, and 5GB for $50
- Sprint: $10 a month for 100MB, 3GB for $35, and 6GB for $50
- T-Mobile: $20 a month for 1GB, 3GB for $30, and 5GB for $40
- Verizon: $20 for 2GB, $30 a month for 4GB, $40 for 6GB.

A friendly warning pops up on your iPad when you get close to your limit. At that point, you can pay more to add to your data bucket or start from scratch next month. Keep in mind that with 4G, you're likely to consume more data in a hurry. And prices of course are subject to change.

Find a Wi-Fi network if you want to buy, rent, or watch movies.

Turning On and Setting Up the iPad

Unless your iPad is brand-spanking new and fresh out of the box, chances are good that you've already performed the steps that follow. We cover them here because if you choose to use your iPad computer-free, these steps make up the entire setup process.

Apple has taken the time to partially charge your iPad, so you get some measure of instant gratification and can go ahead and set it up right away by following these steps:

1. **After taking your iPad or iPad mini out of the box, press and hold down the sleep/wake button on the upper-right edge.**

    You'll see the Apple logo, followed by the word *hello* and similar greetings in a bunch of other languages. An arrow appears near the bottom of the screen, alongside another message in many languages. We're pretty sure they all say, "Slide to Set Up," or some variation, because that's what the English rendition says.

2. **Swipe the Slide to Set Up arrow to the right.**

3. **Tap to choose your language, followed by your country or region preferences.**

4. **Tap to choose an available Wi-Fi network, provide a password (if necessary), and then tap the blue Join button.**

   On certain models you may choose a cellular network, if available, and set up or change your Wi-Fi network later. (If you do wait to set up your Wi-Fi network, turn to Chapter 15 to find out how to do so via Settings.)

   It may take a few minutes to activate your iPad. Next, the Location Services screen appears.

5. **Tap to enable or disable Location Services.**

   Location Services is your iPad's way of knowing where you are geographically. The Maps app, for example, relies on Location Services to determine where in the world you are.

   Location Services can be turned on or off globally or for individual apps in Settings, as you discover in Chapter 15.

   The Touch ID screen appears on compatible models; the passcode key on other models.

6. **Do one of the following:**

   • *If you see the Touch ID screen:* Place your finger or thumb on the Home button to enable Touch ID.

     Touch ID lets you get past the lock screen by using your fingerprint. Read about it in the sidebar that follows. Just know that if you don't set up Touch ID now, you can always set it up later.

   • *If you see a passcode key:* Type a passcode to unlock this iPad. When the Re-enter Your Passcode screen appears, type your passcode again.

   If you choose a common passcode (such as 1111, 1234, or 0000) before the Re-enter Your Passcode screen appears, your iPad will warn you that the code you typed can be easily guessed. You can either change it or use it anyway — it's your choice. However, we suggest that you change it if you're at all concerned about keeping what's on your iPad safe from prying eyes. You'll be able to go with a longer passcode as well. If you have an iPad Air 2, iPad mini 3, iPad mini 4, or iPad Pro, read the sidebar on using the Touch ID fingerprint scanner.

   The Apps & Data screen for setting up your iPad appears.

7. **Tap one of the following: Restore from iCloud Backup, Restore from iTunes Backup, Set Up as New iPad, or Move Data from Android.**

   See Chapter 16 for the scoop on restoring from iCloud or iTunes backups. For these steps, tap Set Up as New iPad. The Apple ID screen appears.

8. **Tap an option to sign in with your Apple ID or create a new one.**

   If you have an Apple ID, enter your credentials here. If you don't have one or forget it, tap the Don't Have an Apple ID or Forget It? button. Through your Apple ID, you can take advantage of iCloud. See the end of this chapter for an introduction to this service.

   Meantime, if you use a different Apple ID for iCloud than you do for iTunes, you can enter both at this stage. Tap the Use Different Apple IDs for iCloud & iTunes? button, and you'll get the opportunity to enter your credentials for both.

   Note that if you skip this step now, you can sign in later by tapping Settings⇨iCloud⇨Account.

   The Terms and Conditions screen appears.

9. **Tap the blue Agree button in the lower-right corner, and then tap the Agree button in the Terms and Conditions alert box that appears in the middle of the screen.**

   What happens if you disagree? You don't want to know. And, of course, you won't be able to use your iPad.

   The Apple Pay screen appears on Air 2, mini 3, mini 4, and iPad Pro.

10. **Tap Next to proceed.**

11. **Supply your credit card credentials.**

    If you already have a credit card on file with iTunes or the App Store, Apple may already prepopulate certain info on the card to get you started.

    Why use Apple Pay? We have to say the feature is pretty cool and convenient. You can add numerous credit, debit, or store cards and employ Apple Pay with the finger you just used to authenticate Touch ID to make purchases with any of the cards you've added. (Again, read the "Pointing a finger at Touch ID" sidebar if you have a Touch ID-capable iPad.) We discuss Apple Pay in greater detail in Chapter 15.

    The iCloud Keychain screen appears.

12. **Tap Approve from Other Device, Use iCloud Security Code, or Don't Restore Passwords.**

    iCloud Keychain is an iOS 7 (and later) feature that stores usernames, passwords, credit card numbers, and other web data in the cloud. When you've finished deciding what to do with iCloud Keychain, you see the screen for Siri, the loquacious digital assistant living inside your iPad.

13. **Tap either Turn On Siri or Turn On Siri Later.**

    If your iPad is third generation or later, it offers the desirable option (at least in our humble opinion) of using your voice to control the device, as well as the capability to use dictation in any app that displays an on-screen keyboard.

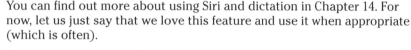

You can find out more about using Siri and dictation in Chapter 14. For now, let us just say that we love this feature and use it when appropriate (which is often).

If you choose not to enable Siri at this time, you can switch on this feature later in the Settings app's General pane.

The next couple of screens address Diagnostics Apple uses to improve its products, and App Analytics you can share (or not) with app developers.

14. **Tap either Automatically Send or Don't Send. Then tap to respond to a similar request to share app analytics.**

The first tap is to send or not send, respectively, anonymous diagnostic and usage data to Apple. The second tap is to share or not share data with app developers to help cut down on crashes.

Pointing a finger at Touch ID

Apple wants you to give the iPad Air 2, iPad mini 3, iPad mini 4, or iPad Pro the finger. But only in a good way. All four devices are equipped with Touch ID, a fingerprint scanner cleverly embedded in the Home button. With a gentle press of any designated finger, you bypass your passcode. (Setting up passcode safeguards is a good idea, and it's something we also touch on in the chapter on Settings, Chapter 15.)

What's more, you can use your own digit (not the numerical kind) to authenticate iTunes and App Store purchases. (Go to Settings⇨Touch ID & Passcode and make sure that the iTunes & App Store switch is turned on.)

On the iPhone or Apple Watch you get another benefit through Touch ID: the capability to purchase stuff in physical retail stores by using a payment technology known as Apple Pay. But Apple Pay on the iPad works only through participating online merchants, at least as of this writing.

To set up Touch ID, you must first let your compatible iPad get chummy with at least one of your fingers, though the system can handle up to five individual fingers, yours or anyone else's with whom you share the tablet.

The iPad instructs you to press and lift your finger against the Home button repeatedly and from different orientations. Red lines fill an animated drawing of a generic fingerprint on the screen, giving you a sense of how far along you are. The process doesn't take long, and if all goes smoothly, the iPad will soon enough declare your efforts to be a success.

What could go wrong? Well, your designated digit must be dry. The iPad needs to see your entire fingerprint, so don't try this with a bandaged finger or one that has open wounds.

To add fingers after the initial setup, tap Settings⇨Touch ID & Passcode. Type your passcode, and then tap Add a Fingerprint. Then repeat the setup drill we just described.

Whether you choose to set up fingerprint authentication now, later, or not at all, you should still establish an old-fashioned four-digit (or longer) passcode as well. In fact, if you do opt to go with Touch ID, you must set up a passcode as a backup should the iPad fail to recognize your paw three times in a row. Hey, it happens. Maybe you're sweating profusely, or you have a cut in the wrong place, or you're wearing gloves.

The Welcome to iPad screen appears.

15. Tap Get Started and let the fun begin.

Your iPad's Home screen appears in all its glory.

If you're using the iPad, the setup story ends here. Instead of using iTunes on your Mac or PC as described in Chapter 3, you have to make do with the available options in specific apps and in the Settings app (covered extensively in Chapter 15).

If you ever need to restore your iPad to factory condition, follow the same steps, as described in Chapter 16.

Locking the iPad

We can think of several sound reasons for locking your iPad:

- ✔ You won't inadvertently turn it on.
- ✔ You keep prying eyes at bay.
- ✔ You spare the battery some juice.

Apple makes locking the iPad a cinch.

You don't need to do anything to lock the iPad; it happens automatically as long as you don't touch the screen for a minute or two. As you find out in Chapter 15, which is all about settings, you can also set the amount of time your iPad must be idle before it automatically locks.

Can't wait? To lock the iPad immediately, press the sleep/wake button.

If you have an iPad with a Smart Cover or Smart Case (or a third-party equivalent), opening and closing the cover locks and unlocks your iPad, but the Smart Cover has the advantage of awakening your iPad without making you drag the slider (though you may still have to enter a passcode).

Unlocking the iPad is easy, too. Here's how:

1. Press the sleep/wake button, or press the Home button on the front of the screen.

Either way, the on-screen slider appears.

2. Drag the slider to the right with your finger.

3. Enter a passcode, or press the Home button on a Touch ID-capable iPad if you need to.

See Chapter 15 to find out how to password-protect your iPad.

Mastering the Multitouch Interface

The iPad, like the iPhone, dispenses with a physical mouse and keyboard, in favor of a virtual keyboard — a step that seemed revolutionary just a few years ago. Nowadays, a virtual keyboard doesn't seem as novel.

Neither does the fact that the designers of the iPad (and iPhone and iPod touch) removed the usual physical buttons in favor of a *multitouch display*. This beautiful and responsive finger-controlled screen is at the heart of the many things you do on the iPad.

In the following sections, you discover how to move around the multitouch interface with ease. Later, we home in on how to make the most of the keyboard.

Training your digits

Rice Krispies have *Snap! Crackle! Pop!* Apple's response for the iPad is *Tap! Flick! Pinch!* Oh yeah, and *Drag!*

Fortunately, tapping, flicking, pinching, and dragging are not challenging gestures, so you can master many of the iPad's features in no time:

- **Tap:** Tapping serves multiple purposes. Tap an icon to open an app from the Home screen. Tap to start playing a song or to choose the photo album you want to look through. Sometimes, you *double-tap* (tapping twice in rapid succession), which has the effect of zooming in (or out) of web pages, maps, and emails.

- **Flick:** Flicking is just what it sounds like. A flick of the finger on the screen lets you quickly scroll through lists of songs, emails, and picture thumbnails. Tap the screen to stop scrolling, or merely wait for the scrolling list to stop.

- **Pinch/spread:** Place two fingers on a web page, map, or picture, and then spread your fingers apart to enlarge the images. Or pinch your fingers together to make the map or picture smaller. Pinching and spreading (or what we call *unpinching*) are cool gestures that are easy to master and sure to wow an audience.

- **Drag:** Here's where you slowly press your finger against the touchscreen without lifting it. You might drag to move around a web page or map that's too large for the iPad's display area.

- **Drag downward from the top of the screen:** This special gesture displays Notification Center (which you find out about in Chapter 13). Press your finger at the very top of the screen and drag downward.

- **Drag downward from any Home screen without starting at the very top of the screen:** This action summons Spotlight search, a discussion for later in this chapter.

✔ **Drag upward from the bottom of the screen:** This time, you're calling up Control Center, a handy repository for music controls, airplane mode (see Chapter 15), Wi-Fi, Bluetooth, do not disturb, mute, volume, orientation lock, timer (Clock app), camera, AirPlay, and brightness controls. Check out Figure 2-1 for one view of Control Center.

Figure 2-1: We think you'll call on Control Center a lot.

✔ **Four- or five-finger swipes and pinches:** To quickly multitask or switch among or view running apps (see the later section, "Multitasking"), use four or five fingers to swipe upward. Swipe left or right (only one finger required) to switch between recently used apps. Pinch using four or five fingers to jump to your Home screen. Swipe up (one finger will do the trick) on an app's thumbnail to quit it. The four- or five-finger swipes and pinches require you to enable Multitasking Gestures in the Settings app's General pane.

Later in this chapter, you read about a couple of new ways to employ your digits, at least on certain models: slide over and split view.

Navigating beyond the Home screen

The Home screen, which we discuss in Chapter 1, is not the only screen of icons on your tablet. After you start adding apps from the iTunes App Store (which you discover in Chapter 11), you may see a row of two or more tiny dots just above the main apps parked at the bottom of the screen. Those dots denote additional Home screens each containing up to 20 additional icons, not counting the 4 to 6 separate icons docked at the bottom of each of these Home screens. You can have up to 15 Home screens. You can also have fewer docked icons at the bottom of the Home screen, but we can't think of a decent reason why you'd want to ditch any of them. In any case, more on these in a moment.

Here's what you need to know about navigating among the screens:

✔ To navigate between screens, flick your finger from right to left or left to right across the middle of the screen, or tap directly on the dots. The number of dots you see represents the current number of screens on your iPad. The all-white dot denotes the screen that you're currently viewing.

You can also drag your finger in either horizontal direction to see a different screen. Unlike flicking — you may prefer the term *swiping* — dragging your finger means keeping it pressed against the screen until you reach your desired page.

✔ Make sure you swipe and not just tap, or you'll probably open one of the app icons instead of switching screens.

✏ Press the Home button to jump back to the Home screen. Doing so the first time takes you back to whatever Home screen you were on last. Tapping Home a second time takes you to the first Home screen.

✏ The dock — which contains the Messages, Mail, Safari, and Music icons in the bottom row — stays put as you switch screens. In other words, only the first 20 icons on the screen change when you move from one screen to another.

You can add one or two more icons to the dock. Or move one of the four default icons into the main area of the Home screen to make space for additional app icons you may use more often, as described later in this chapter.

Select, cut, copy, and paste

Being able to select and then copy and paste from one place on a computer to another has seemingly been a divine right since Moses, and that's the case on the Apple tablet as well. You can copy and paste (and cut) with pizzazz.

On the iPad, you might copy text or a URL from the web and paste it into an email or a note. Or you might copy a bunch of pictures or video into an email.

Suppose you're in the Notes app, jotting down ideas that you'll eventually copy to an email. Here's how you would exploit the copy-and-paste feature:

1. **Double-tap or press against a word to select it.**

2. **Tap Select All to grab everything.**

   You can also drag the blue *grab points* (handles) to select a larger block of text or to contract the text you've already selected, as shown in Figure 2-2. Dragging grab points may take a little practice.

   Figure 2-2: Drag the grab handles to select text.

3. **After you select the text, tap Copy. If you want to delete the text block, tap Cut instead.**

4. **Open the Mail program (see Chapter 5) and start composing a message.**

5. **When you decide where to insert the text you just copied, tap the cursor.**

   Up pop the Select, Select All, Paste, Quote Level, Insert Photo or Video, and Add Attachment commands, as shown in Figure 2-3. (We get to the last three options in Chapter 5.)

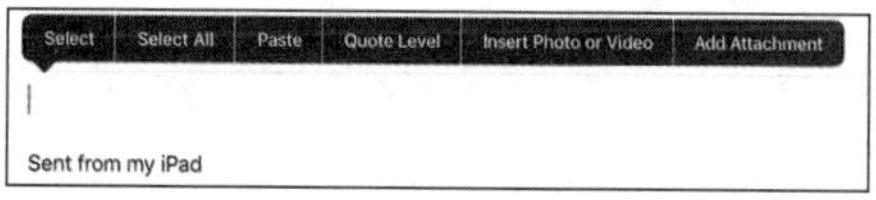

   Figure 2-3: Tap Paste and text will appear.

6. **Tap Paste to paste the text into the message.**

Here's the pizzazz part. If you made a mistake when you were cutting, pasting, or typing, shake the iPad. Doing so undoes the last edit (provided that you tap the Undo Paste or Undo option when it appears and keep the feature enabled in Settings).

You also see these options:

- *Auto-Correct:* If you happen to select a word with a typo, the iPad might underline that word. If you tap the underlined work, the iPad might show you the word it thinks you meant to spell. Tap that suggested word to accept it.

- *Predict:* A predictive word feature reveals up to three word or phrase options in buttons just above the keyboard. If one of these words or phrases is what you had in mind, tap the appropriate button.

- *Replace:* The iPad may show you possible replacement words. For example, replacement words for *test* might be *fest, rest,* or *text.* Tap the word to substitute it for the word you originally typed.

- *Define:* Tap your selected word for a definition, courtesy of the *New Oxford American Dictionary,* the *Oxford Dictionary of English,* an Apple dictionary, or a foreign language dictionary if you've downloaded any dictionaries onto your iPad.

Multitasking

Multitasking on the iPad was introduced way back in iOS 4, and it has become better ever since, most dramatically with the iOS 7, iOS 8, and iOS 9 upgrades. Through multitasking, you can run numerous apps in the background simultaneously and easily switch from one app to another. The following examples illustrate what multitasking enables you to do on your iPad:

- A third-party app, such as Slacker Personal Radio, continues to play music while you surf the web, peek at pictures, or check email. Without multitasking, Slacker would shut down the moment you opened another app.

- A navigation app can update your position while you're listening to, say, Pandora Internet radio. From time to time, the navigation app will pipe in with turn-by-turn directions, lowering the volume of the music so that you can hear the instructions.

- If you're uploading images to a photo website and the process is taking longer than you want, you can switch to another app, confident that the images will continue to upload behind the scenes.

- Leave voice notes in the Evernote app while checking out a web page.

Multitasking couldn't be easier — and as noted it's become pretty smart through the various iOS upgrades. Now your iPad can anticipate your needs. For example, if it detects, over time, that you tend to turn to your social networking apps around the same time every morning, it will make sure the feeds are ready for you.

Double-press (not double-tap) the Home button. You see preview pages with icons just above them for any open apps, as shown in Figure 2-4. Scroll to the right or left to see more apps. Tap the preview screen for the app you want to switch to: The app remembers where you left off. (Scroll all the way to the left, and you'll also see a preview screen for the last Home screen you opened, which was the preview all the way on the right.) If you hold the tablet sideways in landscape mode, the previews for your apps appear sideways, too.

Figure 2-4: Scroll to see the apps you've recently used or are still running.

Apple insists that multitasking will not overly tax the battery or exhaust system resources. The iPad conserves power and resources by putting apps in a state of suspended animation. And your iPad will schedule updates only during power-efficient times, such as when your device is connected to Wi-Fi.

Still, we think it's a good idea to shut down apps you're not using because you'll see a battery hit over time. To remove an app from the multitasking rotation, swipe up the app's preview. Poof — it's gone.

You can use the four- or five-finger gesture to swipe upward to reveal your multitasking options and to swipe left or right to switch between apps. From this multitasking view, you can pinch with four or five fingers to return to the Home screen. It's a cool gesture.

Now lets take a look at some newer tricks that make multitasking even more powerful.

Splitting the screen

Of course, all the iPads have larger screens compared to their iOS cousin, the iPhone. (We're talking a really larger screen with iPad Pro.) And with iOS 9, you can exploit the extra screen real estate to make multitasking even more productive.

For starters, there's a new feature called *slide over*. Launch the first app you want to use and then press your finger against the right edge of the iPad screen. Swipe left and you can drag a second running app into a sidebar area that extends out roughly one-third the way across the entire display.

We bet you can think of all sorts of reasons to run two apps at the same time. Maybe you're composing a message to a friend in the Mail app while scrolling through Safari in the smaller panel to find a place to have lunch. Maybe you're sketching in one app while using a photo in another as a reference point.

You can switch the app that appears in the sidebar by swiping down from the top of the sidebar and tapping the icon for the alternative app.

When you're done with that secondary app, just slide it away. The slide over feature works with Apple's own apps as well as some third-party apps.

Useful as slide over is, you may want that secondary app to get equal billing with the first app you opened. To make that happen, press your finger in the short line that appears on the sidebar border and slide toward the center of the iPad display. Now each running app will automatically claim half the screen. Apple refers to this extension of the slide over feature as *split view*.

Split view works only on the iPad Air 2, iPad mini 4, and iPad Pro models.

Figure 2-5 shows slide over and split view, side by side.

Picture-in-picture

There's a good possibility that your television at home has a picture-in-picture feature that enables you to watch one channel in the main portion of the TV screen while checking out a second channel in a small window on the screen. You don't really want to miss any of the action in the big game now, do you?

Figure 2-5: Turning a slide over view (left) into a split view.

With iOS 9, your iPad gains the same feature. You're not necessarily watching live TV shows in this smaller window, but you might be. The picture-in-picture feature on the iPad works when you're on a FaceTime video call or watching a video via the Videos app. Both topics are reserved for Chapter 8.

Picture-in-picture couldn't be simpler. While watching a video, press (not tap) the Home button. The video picture shrinks into a small window hanging out in the lower-right corner of the display.

You can pause the video or shut it down by tapping the controls that appear in this diminutive video window. (Tap the window if you don't see the controls.) If you want the video to take over the entire iPad screen, the way it started out before you pressed Home, tap the leftmost picture control inside the video window, shown in Figure 2-6.

Figure 2-6: Like your TV, the iPad has a picture-in-picture feature.

Meanwhile, if the video window is blocking a portion of the screen that you want to see, you can drag it to another space.

Picture-in-picture works on the iPad Air, iPad Air 2, iPad mini 2, iPad mini 3, iPad mini 4, and iPad Pro.

Organizing icons into folders

Finding the single app that you want to use among apps spread out over 15 screens may seem like a daunting task. But Apple felt your pain and added a handy organizational tool: folders. The Folders feature lets you create folder icons, each containing apps that pertain to the name that Apple assigned or you gave to that folder.

To create a folder, follow these steps:

1. **Press your finger against an icon until all the icons on the screen wiggle.**

2. **Decide which apps you want to move to a folder and then drag the icon for the first app on top of the second app.**

   The two apps now share living quarters inside a newly created folder. Apple names the folder according to the category of apps inside the folder.

3. **(Optional) Change the folder name by tapping the X on the bar where the folder name appears and typing a new name.**

To launch an app inside a folder, tap that folder's icon and then tap the icon for the app that you want to open.

You have plenty of room for all your apps on the iPad. Indeed, you can put as many as 16 apps inside a folder, stash up to 20 apps or folders per page (not counting up to 5 apps in the dock), and have as many as 15 pages.

When you drag all the apps from a folder, the folder automatically disappears. You can also drag apps on or off the dock.

Printing

Apple didn't include built-in printer functionality with the original iPad. A variety of third-party apps helped fill the bill to some degree, but still the faithful waited for Apple to come up with a solution. The AirPrint feature that subsequently arrived provided just such a remedy — to a point. You can print wirelessly from the iPad to an AirPrint-capable printer. The first of these compatible features emerged on more than a dozen HP printers; now you have offerings from Epson, Canon, and others.

AirPrint works with Mail, Photos, Safari, and iBooks (PDF files). You can also print from apps in Apple's iWork software suite, as well as third-party apps with built-in printing.

An AirPrint printer doesn't need any special software, but it does have to be connected to the same Wi-Fi network as the iPad.

To print, follow these steps:

1. **Tap the share icon, and then tap the Print command.**

   The icon is shown in the margin.

2. **In the Printer Options bubble that appears, tap Select Printer to select a printer, which the iPad locates in short order.**

3. **Depending on the printer, specify the number of copies you want to print, the number of double-sided copies, and a range of pages to print.**

   Graphics that appear may even show you how much ink the printer has left.

4. **When you're happy with your settings, tap Print.**

If you display the preview pages while a print job is underway, the Print Center icon appears with all your other recently used apps. A badge indicates how many documents are in the print queue, along with the currently printing document.

Proactive search

Using the Safari browser (see Chapter 4), you can search the web via Google, Yahoo!, Bing, or DuckDuckGo. If you've added a foreign language keyboard, other options may present themselves. For example, with a Chinese keyboard enabled, you can summon the Baidu search engine.

You can search also for people and programs across your iPad and within specific apps, using a combination of Spotlight and Siri. We show you how to search within apps in the various chapters dedicated to Mail, Contacts, Calendar, and Music.

Searching across the iPad is based on the powerful Spotlight feature familiar to Mac owners. Spotlight can search for news and trending topics, local restaurants, movie times, and content in Apple's own iTunes Store, App Store, and iBooks Store.

Moreover, with Siri teaming up with the Spotlight feature (familiar to Mac owners), you'll also see circled icons representing the contacts you engage with the most, the people you are next scheduled to meet, as well as nearby eateries, shops, and other nearby places of possible interest.

The searches with the iOS 9 update are also proactive, meaning that the device gets to know you over time and makes suggestions accordingly. It attempts to read your mind. The tablet might surface the News app for example, if it learns that you turn to it every morning (while enjoying your coffee).

Or if you're in a particular area, you may see the news that's trending in your location.

Here's how the search feature works:

1. **Swipe down from any Home screen to access search.**

   A bar slides into view at the top of the screen.

2. **Tap the bar and use the virtual keyboard to enter your search query.**

   The iPad spits out results the moment you type a single character; the list narrows as you type additional characters.

   The results are pretty darn thorough. Say that you entered *Ring* as your search term, as shown in Figure 2-7. Contacts whose last names have *Ring* in them show up, along with friends who might do a trapeze act in the Ringling Bros. circus. All the songs on your iPad by Ringo Starr show up too, as do such song titles as Tony Bennett's "When Do the Bells Ring for Me," if that happens to be in your library. The same goes for apps, videos, audiobooks, events, and notes with the word *Ring*.

3. **Tap any listing to jump to the contact, ditty, or app you seek.**

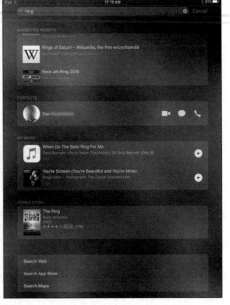

Figure 2-7: Putting the Spotlight on search.

 At the bottom of the Spotlight results list, you can tap to move your search query to the web (using your designated search engine) or to Wikipedia, the online encyclopedia. You can search the Maps app too.

The Incredible, Intelligent, and Virtual iPad Keyboard

As you know by now, instead of a physical keyboard, several soft, or virtual, English-language or (depending upon what you chose during setup) foreign-language keyboard layouts slide up from the bottom of the iPad screen, including variations on the alphabetical keyboard, the numeric and punctuation keyboard, the more punctuation and symbols keyboard, and the emoji keyboard.

Indeed, the beauty of a software keyboard is that you see only the keys that are pertinent to the task at hand. The layout you see depends on the app.

The keyboards in Safari differ from the keyboards in Mail. For example, in Mail, you'll see a Return key. The similarly placed key in Safari is labeled Go. Figure 2-8 displays the difference between the Mail (top) and Safari (bottom) keyboards.

Before you consider how to actually *use* the keyboard, we want to share a bit of the philosophy behind its so-called *intelligence*. Knowing what makes this keyboard smart can help you make it even smarter when you use it. The keyboard

Figure 2-8: The keys on the Mail (top) and Safari (bottom) keyboards.

✔ Has a built-in English dictionary that even includes words from today's popular culture. Dictionaries in other languages are automatically activated when you use a given international keyboard, as described in the sidebar "A keyboard for all borders," later in this chapter.

✔ Adds your contacts to its dictionary automatically.

✔ Uses complex analysis algorithms to predict the word you're trying to type.

✔ Suggests corrections as you type. It then offers you the suggested word just below the misspelled word. When you decline a suggestion and the word you typed is *not* in the iPad dictionary, the iPad adds that word to its dictionary and offers it as a suggestion if you mistype a similar word in the future.

Decline incorrect suggestions (by tapping the characters you typed as opposed to the suggested words that appear below what you've typed). This extra step helps your intelligent keyboard become even smarter.

✔ Reduces the number of mistakes you make as you type by intelligently and dynamically resizing the touch zones for certain keys. The iPad increases the zones for keys it predicts might come next and decreases the zones for keys that are unlikely or impossible to come next, although you can't see this behavior.

Anticipating what comes next

The keyboards on your iPad became even more useful with the arrival of iOS 8. Now the keyboard takes an educated stab at the next word you mean to type and presents what it surmises to be the best possible word choices front and center. Say you're in the Messages app and the last message you received was an invitation to lunch or dinner. Above the row of keys on the iPad keyboard, you'd see buttons with three word suggestions: *Dinner, Lunch,* and *Not sure* (as shown in Figure 2-9). If one of those was the appropriate response, you could tap the button to insert its text into your reply.

If you wanted to respond with something different than the three options presented by Apple, you'd just type your response with the regular QWERTY keys. As you type additional letters and words, the three suggested word choices above the keyboard change in real time. For instance, if you start by typing *That is a* in your message, the new trio of word choice buttons that show up might be *great, good,* and *very.*

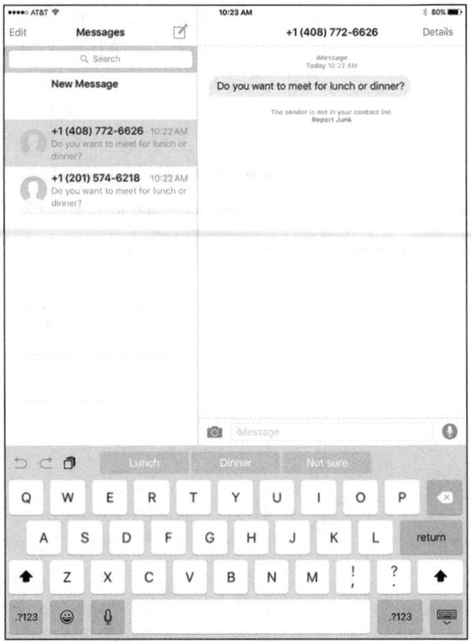

Such QuickType keyboard predictions vary by app and even according to the person with whom you are communicating. So the predictive text choices that show up in Messages when you're involved in an exchange with a friend are likely to be more casual than those in an email to your boss.

Figure 2-9: The iPad keyboard predicts what you might want to type next.

To exploit the predictive typing feature, make sure the Predictive setting is turned on (as it is by default). Go to Settings⇨General⇨Keyboard, and slide the Predictive switch to on.

Such suggestions don't appear only in English. If you're using an international keyboard, suggestions are presented in the appropriate language.

Discovering the special-use keys

The iPad keyboard contains several keys that don't actually type a character. Here's the scoop on each of these keys:

- ✔ **Shift:** If you're using the alphabetical keyboard, the shift key switches between uppercase and lowercase letters. You can tap the key to change the case, or hold down shift and slide to the letter you want to be capitalized.

- ✔ **Caps lock:** To turn on caps lock and type in all caps, you first need to enable the Caps Lock setting (if it's not already enabled) by tapping Settings⇨General⇨Keyboard and then tapping the Enable Caps Lock item to turn it on. After the Caps Lock setting is enabled, double-tap the shift key to turn on caps lock. (The arrow will be underlined in black.)

Tap the shift key again to turn off caps lock. To disable caps lock, just reverse the process by turning off the Enable Caps Lock setting (tap Settings➪General➪Keyboard).

✓ **Typewriter:** Enable the Split Keyboard option (tap Settings➪General➪Keyboard), and you can split the keyboard in a thumb-typist-friendly manner, as shown in Figure 2-10. When you're ready to split your keyboard, press and hold down the typewriter icon key, and tap Split on the menu. From that

Figure 2-10: Press and hold down the typewriter icon key to split the keyboard.

menu you can also dock the keyboard to the bottom of the screen. When you want to bring the keyboard back together, press and hold down the typewriter icon key again and choose either Merge or Dock and Merge from the menu. You can also tap this key to hide the keyboard and then tap the screen in the appropriate app to bring back the keyboard.

✓ **#+= or 123:** If you're using a keyboard that shows only numbers and symbols, the traditional shift key is replaced by a key labeled #+= or 123 (sometimes shown as .?123). Pressing that key toggles between keyboards that just have symbols and numbers.

✓ **Emoji:** Tap this key and you can punctuate your words by adding smiley faces and other emoticons or emojis.

✓ **International keyboard:** You see this key only if you've turned on an international (or third-party) keyboard, as explained in the nearby sidebar "A keyboard for all borders." From this key, you can also pull up an emoji keyboard with numerous smiley faces and pictures.

✓ **Delete:** Tapping this key (otherwise known as the backspace key) erases the character immediately to the left of the cursor.

✓ **Return:** This key moves the cursor to the beginning of the next line. You might find this key labeled Go or Search, depending on the app you're using.

✓ **Dictation:** Tap the microphone icon and start talking. The iPad listens to what you have to say. Tap the key again, and the iPad attempts to convert your words into text. You can use this dictation feature in many of the instances in which you can summon the keyboard, including the built-in Notes and Mail apps, as well as many third-party apps. See Chapter 14 for more on dictation.

When you use dictation, the things you say are recorded and sent to Apple, which converts your words into text. Just make sure to proofread what you've said because the process isn't foolproof. Apple also collects other information, including your first name and nickname, the names and nicknames of folks in your Contacts list, song names in Music, and more. Apple says it does this to help the Dictation feature perform its duties. If any of this freaks you out, however, tap Settings⇨General⇨Keyboard and slide the Enable Dictation switch to off. You can also restrict the use of dictation in Settings, as explained in Chapter 15.

The addition of iOS 9 brought a few fresh options to some of the keyboards on your iPad. On the top row of the keyboards that pop up in certain apps — Mail and Notes, for instance — you'll find dedicated **B**, *I,* and U keys to the right of the three suggested word alternatives. These permit you to bold, italicize, or underline selected text. Consult Figure 2-8 (top) to take a peek.

To the left of the three alternative word suggestions on various iOS 9 keyboards, you'll see icons for undoing or redoing your last steps, plus a third icon that pastes the last selected word or passage that you copied. Such options are visible in both images that make up Figure 2-8.

Choosing an alternative keyboard

Good as the keyboards that Apple supplies to your iPad are, you can choose an alternative keyboard from a third-party app developer, a welcome iOS 8 change to the producers of the SwiftKey, Swype, and Fleksy keyboards, among others, which debuted on the rival Android mobile operating system. You can fetch new keyboards in the App Store. Some are free; some require a modest sum.

After you've downloaded a keyboard, visit Settings⇨General⇨Keyboard⇨Keyboards⇨Add New Keyboard and select the keyboard of choice. Then press and hold down on the international keyboard key (globe icon) on the iPad's own keyboard, and select your new keyboard from the list that appears. Alternatively, keep tapping the globe icon until the keyboard you want takes over.

Finger-typing on the virtual keyboards

The virtual keyboards in Apple's multitouch interface just might be considered a stroke of genius. Or they just might drive you nuts.

If you're patient and trusting, in a week or so, you'll get the hang of finger-typing — which is vital to moving forward, of course, because you rely on a virtual keyboard to tap a text field, enter notes, type the names of new contacts, and so on.

As we note earlier in this chapter, Apple has built intelligence into its virtual keyboard, so it can correct typing mistakes on the fly or provide helpful word choices by predicting what you're about to type next. The keyboard isn't exactly Nostradamus, but it does an excellent job of coming up with the words you have in mind. We've found that tapping one of the predictive buttons appears to speed things up as well as bolster our typing accuracy.

A keyboard for all borders

Apple is expanding the iPad's reach globally with international keyboard layouts for dozens of languages. To access a keyboard that isn't customized for Americanized English, tap Settings ⇨General⇨Keyboard⇨Keyboards⇨Add New Keyboard. Then flick through the list to select any keyboard you want to use. Up pops the list shown in the figure, with custom keyboards for German, Italian, Japanese, and so on. Apple even supplies four versions of French (including keyboards geared to Belgium, Canadian, and Swiss customers) and several keyboards for Chinese. Heck, you can even find Australian, Canadian, Indian, Singapore, and U.K. versions of English.

A note about the Chinese keyboards: You can use handwriting character recognition for simplified and traditional Chinese, as shown here. Just drag your finger in the box provided. We make apologies in advance for not knowing what the displayed characters here mean. (We neither speak nor read Chinese so can only assume what we've produced is gibberish.)

Have a multilingual household? You can select as many of these international keyboards as you might need by tapping the language in the list. (You can call upon only one language at a time.)

When you're in an app that summons a keyboard, tap the international keyboard key (globe icon) in the lower left until the keyboard you want to call on shows up. (The globe key sometimes shows up as an emoji key with a smiley face; you have to tap the emoji key to see the globe icon.) Tap again to choose the next keyboard in the corresponding list of international keyboards that you turned on in Settings. If you keep tapping, you come back to your original keyboard. Or press against the globe icon until you see the list of all the keyboards you've added. You'll also see the aforementioned Predictive switch above the list of keyboards that you've added to your iPad.

To remove a keyboard that you've already added to your list, tap the Edit button in the upper-right corner of the Settings screen showing your enabled keyboards and then tap the red circle with the white horizontal line that appears next to the language to which you want to say *adios.*

As you start typing on the virtual keyboard, we think you'll find the following additional tips helpful:

✓ **See what letter you're typing.** As you press your finger against a letter or number on the screen, the individual key you press darkens until you lift your finger, as shown in Figure 2-11. That way, you know that you struck the correct letter or number.

✓ **Slide to the correct letter if you tap the wrong one.** No need to worry if you touched the wrong key. You can slide your finger to the correct key because the letter isn't recorded until you release your finger.

✓ **Tap and hold down to access special accent marks, alternative punctuation, or URL endings.** Sending a message to an overseas pal? Keep your finger pressed against a letter, and a row of keys showing variations on the character for foreign alphabets pops up, as shown in Figure 2-12. This row lets you add the appropriate accent mark. Just slide your finger until you're pressing the key with the relevant accent mark and then lift your finger.

Figure 2-11: The ABCs of virtual typing.

Figure 2-12: Accenting your letters.

Meanwhile, if you press and hold down the .? key in Safari, it offers you the choice of .us, .org, .edu, .com, or .net with additional options if you also use international keyboards. Pretty slick stuff, except we miss the dedicated .com key that was on the keyboard prior to iOS 7. You can bring the key back by holding down the period key and then releasing your finger when .com is highlighted.

✓ **Tap the space bar to accept a suggested word, or tap the suggested word to decline the suggestion.** Alas, mistakes are common at first. Say that you meant to type a sentence in the Notes app that reads, "I am typing an important . . . " But because of the way your fingers struck the virtual keys, you actually entered "I am typing an *importsnt* . . . " Fortunately, Apple knows that the *a* you meant to press is next to the *s* that showed up on the keyboard, just as *t* and *y* and *e* and *r* are side by side. So the software determines that *important* was indeed the word you had in mind and, as Figure 2-13 reveals, places it front and center among the three predictive text buttons. You'll note that the suspect word is highlighted.

Figure 2-13: Fixing an *important* mistake.

To accept the suggested word, merely tap the space bar. And if for some reason you actually did mean to type *importsnt,* tap that word instead among the predictive buttons that appear.

If you don't appreciate these features, you can turn off Auto-Correction and Predictive in Settings. See Chapter 15 for details. Visit `www.wiley.com/extras/ipad` for autocorrection tricks.

Because Apple knows what you're up to, the virtual keyboard is fine-tuned for the task at hand, especially when you need to enter numbers, punctuation, or symbols. The following tips help you find common special characters or special keys that we know you'll want to use:

- **Putting the @ in an email address:** If you're composing an email message (see Chapter 5), a dedicated @ key pops up on the main Mail keyboard when you're in the To: field choosing whom to send a message to. That key disappears from the first view when you tap the body of the message to compose your words. You can still get to the @ by tapping the .?123 key.

- **Switching from letters to numbers:** When you're typing notes or sending email and want to type a number, symbol, or punctuation mark, tap the .?123 key to bring up an alternative virtual keyboard. Tap the ABC key to return to the first keyboard. This toggle isn't hard to get used to, but some may find it irritating.

- **Adding apostrophes and other punctuation shortcuts:** If you press and hold down the exclamation mark/comma key, a pop-up offers the apostrophe. If you press and hold down the question mark/period key, you'll see the option to type quotation marks.

If you buy the iPad Pro, you'll likely want to consider purchasing the optional iPad Pro Smart Keyboard cover accessory. It's kind of pricey at $169, but the large screen might just tempt you go with a physical keyboard. You'll be tempted also by the $99 accessory stylus know as Apple Pencil. For more on iPad accessories, let us direct you to Chapter 17.

Of course, we already mentioned that other iPads, unlike some tablets from the past (and a few in the present), eschew a pen or stylus. But sometimes you might want to call upon a digital pen, and third-party companies fill the bill. For example, Wacom sells various Bamboo Stylus models, starting around $8 and going well up from there. It's a potentially useful tool for those with too broad, oily, or greasy fingers, or those who sketch, draw, or jot notes. You can find lower-priced styluses as well.

Editing mistakes

We think typing with abandon, without getting hung up over mistyped characters, is a good idea. The self-correcting keyboard can fix many errors (and occasionally introduce errors of its own). That said, plenty of typos are likely to turn up, especially in the beginning, and you have to correct them manually.

A neat trick for doing so is to hold your finger against the screen to bring up the magnifying glass. Use the magnifying glass to position the pointer on the spot where you need to make the correction. Then use the delete key (also called the backspace key) to delete the error and press whatever keys you need to type the correct text.

And with that, you are hereby notified that you've survived basic training. The real fun is about to begin.

Synchronicity: Getting Stuff to and from Your iPad

In This Chapter

▸ Getting your head around iCloud

▸ Starting your first sync

▸ Disconnecting during a sync

▸ Synchronizing contacts, calendars, email accounts, and bookmarks

▸ Synchronizing music, podcasts, videos, photos, books, and applications

▸ Synchronizing manually

*W*e have good news and . . . more good news. The good news is that you can easily set up your iPad so that your contacts, appointments, reminders, events, mail settings, bookmarks, books, music, movies, TV shows, podcasts, photos, and apps are synchronized between your computer and your iPad (or other iDevices). And the more good news is that after you set it up, your contacts, appointments, events, and everything else we just mentioned can be kept up to date automatically in multiple places — on one or more of your computers and iPad, iPhone, and iPod touch devices.

Here's more good news: Whenever you make a change in one place, it's reflected almost immediately in all the other places it occurs. So if you add or change an appointment, an event, or a contact on your iPad while you're out and about, the information is automatically updated on your computers and iDevices. And if no Wi-Fi or cellular network is available at the time, the update syncs the next time your iPad encounters a wireless network, all with no additional effort on your part.

This communication between your iPad and computer is called *syncing* (short for *synchronizing*). Don't worry: It's easy, and we walk you through the entire process in this chapter.

But wait. We have even more good news. Items that you choose to manage on your computer, such as movies, TV shows, podcasts, and email account settings, are synchronized only one way — from your computer to your iPad, which is the way it should be.

The information in this chapter is based on iTunes 12.3 and iOS 9, the latest and greatest when these words were written. If your screens don't look exactly like ours, you probably need to upgrade to iTunes 12.3 or higher (choose iTunes⇨Check for Updates), or iOS 9 or higher (on your iPad, tap Settings⇨General⇨Software Update), or both. Both upgrades — iTunes and iOS — are free, and offer useful new features not found in their predecessors.

Because Apple updates iTunes and iOS often, having the latest and greatest version is a double-edged sword. Sometimes you'll see something in the book that looks different on your iPad because you're using a *newer* version of iOS than we had when we wrote this. If you encounter a figure or an instruction that conflicts with what you're seeing on your iPad (and you're certain you're using the latest and greatest versions of both iTunes and iOS), please drop us a note so that we can make any necessary changes; our email addresses appear at the end of this book's introduction.

iOS 9 does let you set up your iPad computer-free (and as such, you're not *required* to sync your iPad with a computer running iTunes). Turn to Chapter 2 if you really want to set up your iPad computer-free. But some things are easier with a computer than without.

In this chapter, you find out how to sync all the digital data your iPad can handle, right after this short interlude about Apple's iCloud service.

A Brief iCloud Primer

Apple's iCloud service is more than just a wireless hard drive in the sky. iCloud is a complete data synchronization and wireless storage solution. In a nutshell, iCloud stores and manages your digital stuff — your music, photos, contacts, events, and more — and makes it available to all your computers and iDevices automatically.

iCloud pushes information such as email, calendars, contacts, reminders, and bookmarks to and from your computer and to and from your iPad and other iDevices, and then keeps those items updated on all devices wirelessly and without any effort on your part. iCloud also includes nonsynchronizing options, such as photo stream and iCloud photo sharing (see Chapter 9) and email (see Chapter 5).

Your free iCloud account includes 5GB of storage, which is all many users will need. If you have several devices (including Macs and PCs) or like saving data in the cloud, you'll probably find yourself needing more storage; 20- and 200-gigabyte upgrades are available for $1 and $4 a month, respectively.

A nice touch is that music, apps, periodicals, movies, and TV shows purchased from the iTunes Store, as well as your photo stream and iTunes Match content (see Chapter 7), don't count against your 5GB of free storage. iBooks don't count against your 5GB either, but audiobooks do. You'll find that the things that do count — such as mail, documents, photos taken with your iPad camera, account information, settings, and other app data — don't use much space, so 5GB may last a long time.

If you're not using iCloud photo library, you might want to sync your iPad photos with a computer every so often and then delete the photos from the iPad. Otherwise, over time, those photos will take up a lot of space.

If you plan to go PC-free but still want to have your email, calendars, contacts, and bookmarks synchronized automatically and wirelessly (and believe us, you do) between computers and other iDevices, here's how to enable iCloud syncing on your iPad:

1. **On your Home screen, tap Settings.**

2. **In the list of settings on the left, tap iCloud.**

3. **Tap Account, and then provide your Apple ID and password (if you haven't provided it previously).**

4. **Tap Done.**

A list of apps appears. Tap any individual on/off switch to enable or disable iCloud sync for Mail, Contacts, Calendars, Reminders, Safari (Bookmarks), Notes, and News.

In the same list are five items that don't have switches:

- ✔ **iCloud Drive:** This feature lets iCloud-savvy apps open and save documents and data in iCloud. Your options follow:

  - *iCloud Drive:* Allow apps to use iCloud Drive.

  - *Show on Home Screen:* This new option creates an iCloud Drive icon on your Home screen. Tap it and you'll see all the documents all your apps have ever saved to iCloud Drive.

  - *Look Me Up by Email:* Tap to see a list of apps that allow other people to look you up by your Apple ID. When enabled, users of the app will be able to look for you by your first and last names.

- *Use Cellular Data:* Use cellular data for sending and receiving data from your iCloud Drive. This option is enabled only on Wi-Fi + cellular iPads, of course. We suggest that you enable this option only if you are fortunate enough to have an unlimited data plan.

✔ **Photos:** Enable or disable four iCloud services with the by now familiar on/off switches (see Chapter 9 for details). The options are:

- *iCloud Photo Library:* Automatically upload and store your entire photo library in iCloud. The benefit is that you can access all your photos and videos on all your Macs and iDevices. One possible downside: This option could put you over iCloud's free 5GB limit.

  If you enable iCloud photo library, a pair of mutually exclusive options appear. If you choose Optimize iPad Storage, whenever your iPad runs low on space, your full-resolution photos and videos will automatically be replaced with lower-resolution versions that use less space. Or if you choose Download and Keep Originals, your iPad will download full-resolution versions of every photo and video in your iCloud photo library.

- *Upload to My Photo Stream:* Automatically upload photos you shoot with your iPad camera and send them to all your devices when connected to Wi-Fi.

  When Upload to My Photo Stream is enabled, the Upload Burst Photos option appears. Enable it to upload all photos taken in burst mode; disable to upload only favorites from bursts.

- *iCloud Photo Sharing:* Create and share albums with other iCloud users, or subscribe to other iCloud users' shared albums.

✔ **Backup:** Enable or disable iCloud backup, which backs up your photo library, accounts, documents, and settings whenever your iPad is plugged in, locked, and connected to Wi-Fi. Tap the Back Up Now button to initiate a backup, well, now.

✔ **Keychain:** Keep passwords and credit card information you save up to date on all devices you approve. The info is encrypted and can't be read by Apple (or, we hope, by anyone else).

✔ **Find My iPad:** Tap this option to reveal two choices. The first is Find My iPad, so you can locate, lock, or erase your iPad and prevent anyone else from erasing or reactivating it without your password. The second option, Send Last Location, tells the iPad to send its location when the battery gets critically low.

Tap Storage (near the top of the screen) to manage iCloud storage or upgrade your storage plan. Tap Family (also near the top) to add or remove family members and shared payment methods from your Family Sharing plan (which you read more about in Chapter 15).

You find out much more about iCloud in the rest of this chapter and several other chapters, so let's move on to syncing your iPad.

Syncing with iTunes

Synchronizing your iPad with iTunes on a Mac or PC provides three main benefits over computer-free iPad use:

- ✔ iTunes makes it easier to manage your media — your music, movies, apps, and so on — than managing it directly on your iPad.

- ✔ Managing your iPad's contents with iTunes provides numerous options that you won't find anywhere on your iPad.

- ✔ Managing your iPad's apps and Home screen layouts is much easier in iTunes than on your iPad.

Synchronizing your iPad with your computer is a lot like syncing an iPod or iPhone with your computer. If you're an iPod or iPhone user, the process will be a piece of cake. But even if you've never used an iPod, an iPhone, or iTunes, the process isn't difficult. Follow these steps:

1. **Start by connecting your iPad to your computer with the USB cable that came with your iPad.**

   When you connect your iPad to your computer, iTunes should launch automatically. If it doesn't, chances are that you plugged the cable into a USB port on your keyboard, monitor, or hub. Try plugging it into one of the USB ports on your computer instead. Why? Because USB ports on your computer supply more power to a connected device than USB ports on a keyboard, monitor, or most hubs, and the iPad requires a lot of that power — even more than an iPod or an iPhone.

   You may see an alert asking whether you want iTunes to open automatically when you connect this iPad. Click Yes or No, depending on your preference. You have the opportunity to change this setting later if you like, so don't give it too much thought.

   If iTunes still doesn't launch automatically, try launching it manually.

2. **Click the iPad icon (shown in the margin), which is near the top left of the iTunes window.**

   If you use more than one iDevice with this computer and you hover the pointer over the iPad icon, you'll see the number of devices (for example, *3 Devices*). If you have multiple devices, clicking the button displays a drop-down list with all your devices.

If you don't see the iPad icon and you're positive that it's connected to a USB port *on your computer* (not the keyboard, monitor, or hub), try restarting your computer.

The Welcome to Your New iPad screen appears.

3. **Click Set Up as New iPad or select a backup from the Restore from This Backup drop-down menu and then click Continue.**

   See Chapter 16 for the scoop on restoring from iCloud or iTunes back-ups. For this example, we tap Set Up as New.

   The Sync with iTunes screen appears.

4. **Click the Get Started button.**

   The iPad screen appears, as shown in Figure 3-1.

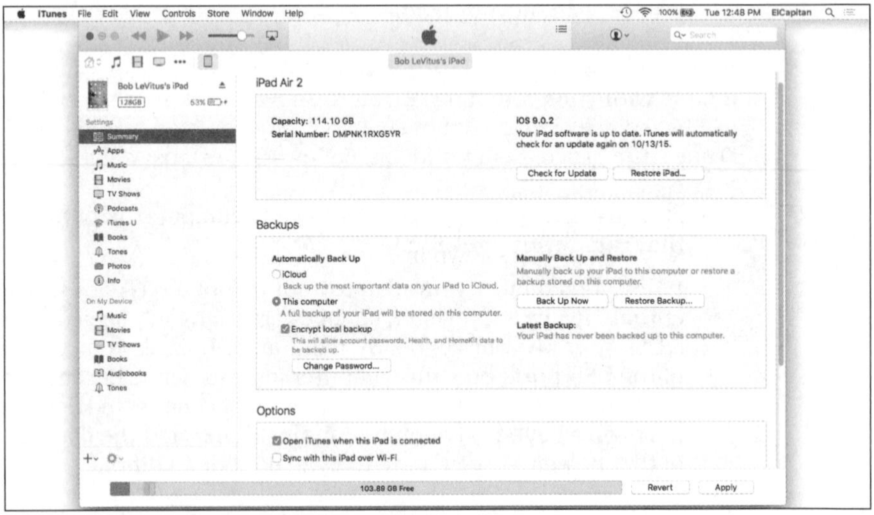

Figure 3-1: The Summary pane is pretty painless.

5. **Click the Summary tab near the top of the window on the left, as shown in Figure 3-1.**

   If you don't see a Summary tab, make sure your iPad is still connected. If you don't see your iPad's name near the top-left corner of the iTunes window, as shown in Figure 3-1, go back to Step 1 and try again.

6. **(Optional) If you want to rename your iPad, click its name and type a new one.**

   We renamed the one in Figure 3-1 *Bob LeVitus's iPad.*

From the Summary pane, you can set any options that you want from the Options area:

- ✔ **Open iTunes When This iPad Is Connected check box:** Select this option if you want iTunes to launch automatically whenever you connect your iPad to your computer. Why might you choose not to enable this option? If you intend to connect your iPad to your computer to charge it, for example, you might not want iTunes to launch every time you connect it. If you do choose to enable it, iTunes launches and synchronizes automatically every time you connect your iPad.

  Don't worry about this setting too much right now. As usual, if you change your mind, you can always come back to the Summary pane and deselect the Open iTunes When This iPad Is Connected check box.

  If you do select the Open iTunes When This iPad Is Connected check box but don't want your iPad to sync automatically every time it's connected, launch iTunes and choose iTunes⇨Preferences (Mac) or Edit⇨Preferences (PC). Click the Devices tab at the top of the window and select the Prevent iPods, iPhones, and iPads from Syncing Automatically check box. This method prevents your iPad from syncing automatically, even if the Open iTunes When This iPad Is Connected option is selected. If you choose this option, you can sync your iPad by clicking the Sync or Apply button that appears in the lower-right corner of the iTunes window when your iPad is selected in the sidebar. (The Apply button is shown in Figure 3-1.)

- ✔ **Sync with This iPad Over Wi-Fi:** If you want to sync automatically over your Wi-Fi connection, select this check box.

  If you choose to sync wirelessly, your iPad and computer must be on the same Wi-Fi network and your iPad must be plugged into a power source for syncing to occur.

  You may need to scroll down to see the following options (which are not visible in Figure 3-1).

- ✔ **Sync Only Checked Songs and Video:** If you want to sync only items that have check marks to the left of their names in your iTunes library, select this check box. If you choose to use Apple's iTunes Match cloud-based storage (described in Chapter 7), as we have in Figure 3-1, this option will appear dimmed and be unavailable.

- ✔ **Prefer Standard Definition Videos:** If you want high-definition videos you import to be automatically converted into smaller standard-definition video files when you transfer them to your iPad, select this check box.

  Standard-definition video files are significantly smaller than high-definition video files. You'll hardly notice the difference when you watch the video on your iPad (unless it's an iPad with a Retina display, in which case you'll almost certainly notice), but you can have more video files on your iPad because they take up less space.

The conversion from HD to standard definition takes a *long* time, so be prepared for very long sync times when you sync new HD video and have this option selected.

If you plan to use Apple's digital AV adapter (choose the dock version or Lightning version, as appropriate), or Apple TV ($99) to display movies on an HDTV, consider going with high definition. Although the files will be bigger and your iPad will hold fewer videos, the HD versions look spectacular on a big-screen TV. There's more info on these accessories in Chapter 17.

✔ **Convert Higher Bit Rate Songs to 128/192/256 Kbps AAC:** If you want songs with bit rates higher than 128, 192, or 256 Kbps converted into smaller AAC files when you transfer them to your iPad, select this check box and choose the lower bit rate from the drop-down menu (which reads 128 kbps in Figure 3-1).

A *higher* bit rate means that the song will have better sound quality but use a lot of storage space. Songs that you buy at the iTunes Store or on Amazon, for example, have bit rates of around 256 Kbps. So a four-minute song with a 256-Kbps bit rate is around 8MB; convert it to 128-Kbps AAC, and it's roughly half that size (that is, around 4MB) while sounding almost as good.

Most people don't notice much (if any) difference in audio quality when listening to music on most consumer audio gear. So unless you have your iPad hooked up to a great amplifier and superb speakers or head-phones, you probably won't hear much difference, but your iPad can hold roughly twice as much music if you choose this option. Put another way, we're picky about our audio, and we both used to select this option to allow us to carry more music around with us on our iPads before we subscribed to iTunes Match and Apple Music. Neither of us has noticed the lower bit-rate songs sounding much different (or worse) with the types of headphones and speakers we use with our iPads. Finally, using higher bit rates may increase the time it takes to sync.

✔ **Manually Manage Videos:** To turn off automatic syncing in the Video panes, select this check box.

One more thing: If you decide to select the Prevent iPods, iPhones, and iPads from Syncing Automatically check box on the Devices tab in iTunes Preferences (that's iTunes⇨Preferences on a Mac and Edit⇨Preferences on a PC), you can still synchronize manually by clicking the Sync or Apply button in the lower-right corner of the window.

Why the Sync *or* Apply button? Glad you asked. If you've changed *any* sync settings since the last time you synchronized, the Sync button instead says Apply. When you click that button — regardless of its name — your iPad will start to sync.

Backing Up Your iPad

Whether you know it or not, your iPad backs up your settings, app data, photos and videos you shoot, and other information whenever you connect to a computer and use iTunes to sync with, update, or restore your iPad.

Every time you sync your iPad and computer, most (but not all) of your iPad content, including (but not limited to) photos in the Camera Roll album, text messages, notes, contact favorites, and sound settings is backed up to either your computer's hard drive or to iCloud before the sync begins. Most of your media, including songs, TV shows, and movies, *isn't* backed up in this process. This shouldn't be a problem; these files should be restored when you sync with iTunes again.

Backups are saved automatically and stored on your computer by default, or you can choose to back up to iCloud by clicking the appropriate button in the iTunes Summary pane.

To switch to backing up to iCloud using iTunes on your computer, follow these steps:

1. **Connect the iPad to the computer.**

   If iTunes doesn't launch automatically when you connect the iPad, launch it now.

2. **Click the iPad icon near the top of the window on the left.**

   If you use more than one iDevice with this computer, select the device from the drop-down list that appears when you click the iPad icon.

3. **On the left, click the Summary tab.**

4. **In the Automatically Back Up section, click iCloud.**

If anything goes wonky, or you get a new iPad, you can restore most (if not all) of your settings and files that aren't synced with iCloud or iTunes on your computer. Or, if you've backed up an iPhone, an iPod touch, or another iPad, you can restore the new iPad from the older device's backup.

Regardless of whether you back up locally or to iCloud, you should encrypt your backups. Unless you enable encryption, important data such as website and Wi-Fi passwords won't be backed up. Because backups to iCloud are encrypted by default with the Apple ID password associated with the account, you don't have to do anything else if you choose iCloud backups. But if you back up to your computer, encryption is turned off by default. So enable the Encrypt Local Backup check box (refer to Figure 3-1).

Trust us, you want your backups encrypted; just select the box, type a password (and don't forget it), and you'll never have to think about it again.

If you're using an iPad computer-free, here's how to enable backing up to iCloud from your iPad (if it's not already enabled), which we strongly suggest computer-free iPad users do without further delay:

1. **Tap Settings⇨iCloud.**

2. **Tap Backup.**

3. **Tap iCloud Backup to switch it on (green).**

Choosing this option means your iPad no longer backs up automatically if you connect it to a computer.

If you are a computer-free iPad user, you don't care because you never connect your iPad to a computer. But if you sync your iPad with your computer like many folks do, give some thought to which option suits your needs. Restoring from a computer backup requires physical or Wi-Fi access to that computer, but you don't need Internet access. Restoring from iCloud requires Internet access — and can happen anywhere on Earth that has it.

Backups are good; select one or the other and move on.

One last thing: Many users maintain both types of backup: iCloud and computer. To do this, merely enable This Computer instead of iCloud (or iCloud instead of This Computer) and click the Back Up Now button. When the backup is finished, switch it back (or not). Either way, you now have a backup on your hard disk and a second backup in iCloud (and redundancy is a good thing when it comes to backups).

Disconnecting the iPad

When an iPad is connected to your computer, you see the eject icon to the right of its name in the devices drop-down menu (Bob LeVitus's iPad in Figure 3-2). If your iPad is connected and syncing, you'll instead see the sync icon next to the device (Bob LeVitus's Other iPad in Figure 3-2). At the same time, a message appears at the top of the iTunes window to inform you that your iPad is syncing, as shown at the top of Figure 3-2.

Click to cancel sync   Sync icon

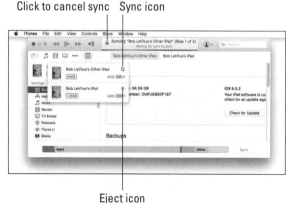

When the sync is finished, the sync icon in Figure 3-2 stops spinning and morphs back into an eject icon, and the message at the top of the window disappears.

Eject icon

Figure 3-2: During a sync, the eject icon turns into a sync icon; click the x-in-a-circle to cancel the sync.

If you disconnect your iPad before the sync finishes, all or part of the sync may fail. Although early termination of a sync isn't usually a problem, it's safer to cancel the sync and let it finish gracefully than to yank the cable out while a sync is in progress. So just don't do that, okay?

To cancel a sync properly and disconnect your iPad *safely* from your Mac or PC, click the little *x*-in-a-circle to the left of the sync message in iTunes, as shown in Figure 3-2.

Synchronizing Your Data

Your next order of business is to tell iTunes what data you want to synchronize between your iPad and your computer.

To get started, first select your iPad by clicking the iPad icon (or the devices drop-down menu, if you have more than one iDevice) near the top left of the iTunes window. Then click the Info tab, which is the last tab in the Settings list on the left.

If you're using iCloud to sync contacts, calendars, bookmarks, or notes, you won't be able to enable these items in iTunes, as we're about to describe. Turn off iCloud syncing on your iPad (Settings⇨iCloud) for items you want to sync with your Mac or PC.

On some displays you may see only one or two sections at any time and have to scroll up or down to see the others.

The Info pane has five sections: Sync Contacts, Sync Calendars, Sync Mail Accounts, Other, and Advanced. The following sections look at them one by one. One last thing: To use your iPad with your Google or Yahoo! account, you must first create an account on your iPad, as described in Chapter 5. After you've created a Yahoo! or Google account on your iPad, you can enable contact or calendar syncing with it in the Settings app's Mail, Contacts, Calendars section.

Contacts

In Figure 3-3, note that the section is named Sync Contacts because this image was captured on a Mac. Contacts (formerly known as Address Book) is the Mac application that syncs with your iPad's Contacts app.

If you use a PC, you see a drop-down list that gives you the choices of Outlook, Google Contacts, Windows Address Book, or Yahoo! Address Book. Don't worry — the process works the same on either platform.

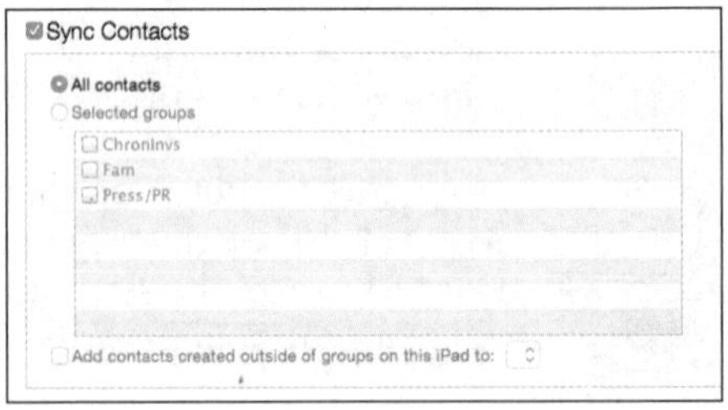

The iPad syncs with the following address book programs:

Figure 3-3: Want to synchronize your contacts? This is where you set up things.

- ✓ **Mac:** Contacts and other address books that sync with Contacts, such as Microsoft Outlook 2011 or the discontinued Microsoft Entourage

- ✓ **PC:** Windows Contacts (Vista, Windows 7 or later), Windows Address Book (XP), Microsoft Outlook, and Microsoft Outlook Express

- ✓ **Mac and PC:** Yahoo! Address Book and Google Contacts

You can sync contacts with multiple apps.

Here's what each option does:

- ✓ **All Contacts:** One method is to synchronize all your contacts, as shown in Figure 3-3. This will synchronize every contact in your Mac or PC address book with your iPad's Contacts app.

- ✓ **Selected Groups:** You can synchronize any or all groups of contacts you've created in your computer's address book program. Just select the appropriate check boxes in the Selected Groups list, and only those groups will be synchronized.

If you sync with your employer's Microsoft Exchange calendar and contacts, it's possible that all personal contacts and calendars already on your iPad will be wiped out. You might want to check with the administrator of your Exchange server or other iPad users before you enable syncing with Exchange.

Calendars

The Calendars section of the Info pane determines how synchronization is handled for your appointments, events, and reminders. You can synchronize all your calendars, as shown in Figure 3-4. Or you can synchronize any or all individual calendars you've created in your computer's calendar program. Just select the appropriate check boxes.

The iPad syncs with the following calendar programs:

- **Mac:** iCal or Calendar
- **PC:** Microsoft Exchange and Outlook 2003, 2007, and 2010
- **Mac and PC:** Google and Yahoo! Calendars

You can sync calendars with multiple apps.

Figure 3-4: Set up sync for your calendar events here.

Advanced

Every so often, the contacts, calendars, mail accounts, or bookmarks on your iPad get so screwed up that the easiest way to fix things is to erase that information from your iPad and replace it with information from your computer.

If that's the case, go to the Advanced section of the Info pane and click to select the Contacts or Calendars check boxes (or both). Then, the next time you sync, that information on your iPad will be replaced with the contacts or calendars from your computer.

Because the Advanced section is at the bottom of the Info pane and you have to scroll down to see it, you can easily forget that the Advanced section is there. Although you probably won't need to use this feature very often (if ever), you'll be happy you remembered that it's there if you do need it.

One last thing: Check boxes in the Advanced section are disabled for items not selected. If you're using iCloud and you want to replace any of these items on your iPad, you must first enable that item as discussed in the previous sections of this chapter. In other words, to replace contacts or calendars we had to disable iCloud syncing before we could enable the check boxes to replace the Contacts and Calendars on this iPad.

Synchronizing Your Media

If you chose to let iTunes manage synchronizing your data automatically, welcome. This section looks at how you get your media — your music, podcasts, videos, and photos — from your computer to your iPad.

Podcasts and videos (but not photos) from your computer are synced only one way: from your computer to your iPad. If you delete a podcast or a video that got onto your iPad via syncing, the podcast or video will not be deleted from your computer when you sync.

That said, if you buy or download any of the following items from the Apple iTunes, iBooks, or App Store *on your iPad,* the item *will* be copied back to your computer automatically when you sync:

- ✔ Songs
- ✔ Ringtones
- ✔ Podcasts
- ✔ Videos
- ✔ iBooks, e-books, and audiobooks
- ✔ Apps
- ✔ Playlists that you create on your iPad

And if you save pictures from email messages, the iPad camera, web pages (by pressing and holding down on an image and then tapping the Save Image button), or screen shots (which can be created by pressing the Home and sleep/wake buttons simultaneously), these too can be synced using your favorite photo application (as long as it's Photos, Aperture, or Adobe Photoshop Elements).

You use the Apps, Music, Movies, TV Shows, Podcasts, iTunes U, Books, Audiobooks, Tones, and Photos panes to specify the media that you want to copy from your computer to your iPad. The following sections explain the options you find in each pane.

To view any of these panes, make sure that your iPad is still selected and then click the appropriate tab in the list of Settings on the left.

The following sections focus only on syncing. If you need help acquiring apps, music, movies, podcasts, or anything else for your iPad, just flip to the most applicable chapter for help.

The last step in each section is "Click the Sync or Apply button in the lower-right corner of the window." You have to do this only when selecting that item for the first time and if you make any changes to the item after that.

Sharp-eyed readers may notice that we aren't covering syncing iPad *apps* in this chapter. Apps are so darn cool that we've given them an entire chapter, namely Chapter 11. In that chapter, you discover how to find, sync, rearrange, review, and delete apps, and much, much more.

Music, music videos, and voice memos

To transfer music to your iPad, select the Sync Music check box in the Music pane. You can then select the option for Entire Music Library or Selected Playlists, Artists, and Genres. If you choose the latter, select the check boxes next to particular playlists, artists, and genres you want to transfer. You also can choose to include music videos or voice memos or both by selecting the appropriate check boxes at the top of the pane (see Figure 3-5).

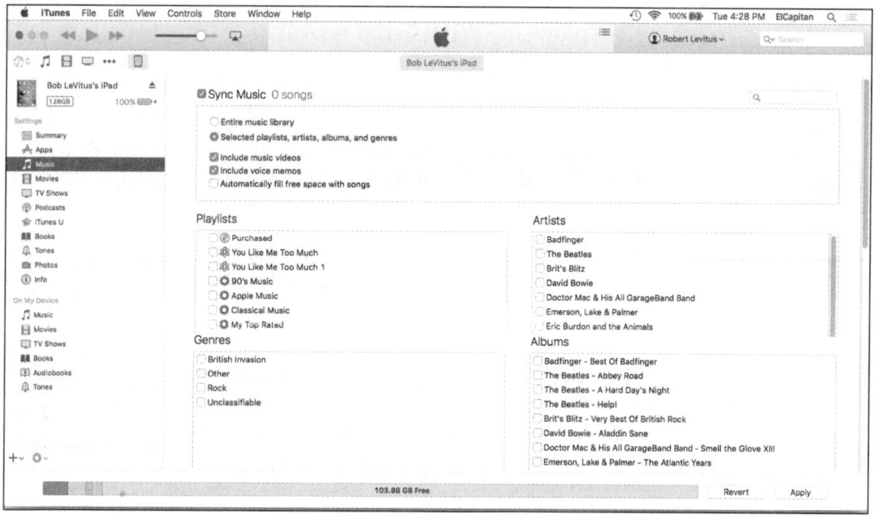

Figure 3-5: Use the Music pane to copy music, music videos, and voice memos from your computer to your iPad.

How much space did I use?

If you're interested in knowing how much free space is available on your iPad, look near the bottom of the iTunes window while your iPad is connected. You'll see a chart that shows the contents of your iPad, color-coded for your convenience. As you can see in the figure, this iPad has a whopping 103.88GB of free space. Hover your cursor over any color to see a bubble with info on that category, as shown for Documents and Data in the figure.

> Documents & Data
> 1.40 GB
>
> 103.88 GB Free

You can find similar information about space used and space remaining on your iPad by tapping Settings⇨General⇨Usage. The iPad's display isn't as pretty as the one pictured here, but it is useful when you need that info and you're not near your computer.

If none of the options just mentioned sounds just right (pun intended), you may prefer using the On This iPad tab, which is covered in some detail later in this chapter.

If you choose Entire Music Library and have more songs in your iTunes library than storage space on your iPad, you'll see an error message when you try to sync. You'll also see a yellow alert on the right side of the capacity chart at the bottom of the screen, along with how much over your iPad's capacity adding the entire music library would make you. To avoid such errors, select playlists, artists, and genres that total less than the free space on your iPad, which is also displayed in the capacity chart at the bottom of the iTunes screen.

Music, podcasts, and video are notorious for using massive amounts of storage space on your iPad. If you try to sync too much media content, you see lots of error messages. Forewarned is forearmed.

One solution is to create one or more iPad-specific playlists and sync only those. Or listen to podcasts with the Podcasts app, which can stream episodes (in addition to letting you download them).

Finally, if you select the Automatically Fill Free Space with Songs check box, iTunes fills any free space on your iPad with music. Think long and hard about enabling this option. We recommend against it because when it's enabled, you can easily run out of space for pictures and videos you shoot or documents you save (to name just a few of the possible consequences of filling your iPad with songs).

Movies

To transfer movies to your iPad, select the Sync Movies check box and then choose an option for movies you want to include automatically from the pop-up menu, as shown in Figure 3-6. If you choose an option other than All, you can optionally select individual movies and playlists by selecting the boxes in appropriate sections.

Figure 3-6: Your choices in the Movies pane determine which movies are copied to your iPad.

TV shows

The procedure for syncing TV shows is slightly different from the procedure for syncing movies. First, select the Sync TV Shows check box to enable TV show syncing. Then choose how many episodes to include and whether you want all shows or only selected shows from the two pop-up menus, as shown in Figure 3-7. If you want to also include individual episodes or episodes on playlists, select the appropriate check boxes in the Shows, Episodes, and Include Episodes from Playlists sections of the TV Shows pane.

Regardless of the choices you make in the pop-up menus, you can always select individual episodes by selecting their check boxes.

Podcasts, iTunes U, and books

You can also sync podcasts, educational content from iTunes U, two types of books — e-books for reading and audiobooks for listening — and photos.

If you like to read e-books or watch or listen to podcasts or iTunes U courses, visit the App Store (see Chapter 11) and grab copies of Apple's free Podcasts, iBooks, and iTunes U apps. Audiobooks, on the other hand, don't require a special app; you can listen to them using the Music app (see Chapter 7).

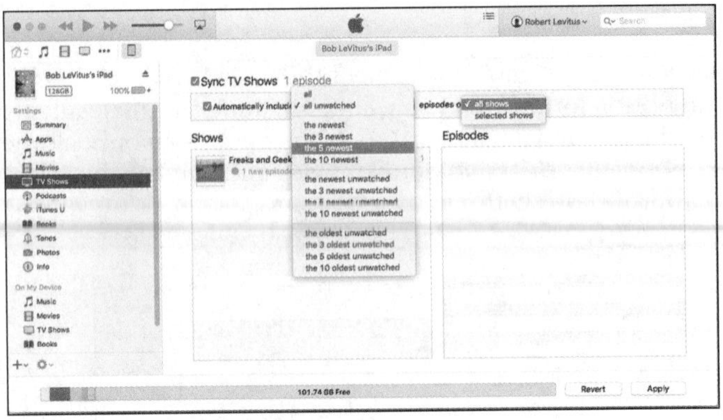

Figure 3-7: These menus determine how TV shows are synced with your iPad.

Podcasts

To transfer podcasts to your iPad, select the Sync Podcasts check box in the Podcasts pane. Then you can automatically include however many podcasts you want by making selections from the two pop-up menus, the same way you did for TV Shows. If you have podcast episodes on playlists, you can include them by selecting the appropriate check box in the Include Episodes from Playlists section.

iTunes U

To sync educational content from iTunes U, first select the Sync iTunes U check box to enable iTunes U syncing. Then choose how many episodes to include and whether you want all collections or only selected collections from the two pop-up menus. If you want to also include individual items or items on playlists, select the appropriate check boxes in the Items section and Include Items from Playlists section of the iTunes U pane.

Books

By now we're sure you know the drill: You can sync all your e-books and audiobooks as well as just sync selected titles by choosing the appropriate buttons and check boxes in the Books pane.

To sync e-books, you need the free iBooks app; if you don't already have it, you can download it from the App Store. For more information on apps and the App Store, read Chapter 11. To start using iBooks, see Chapter 10.

Tones

If you have custom ringtones in your iTunes library, select the Sync Tones check box in the Tones pane. Then you can choose either all ringtones or individual ringtones by selecting their check boxes. These tones can be used also as text tones and alarms.

Photos

Syncing photos is a little different from syncing other media because your iPad has a built-in camera — two cameras, actually — and you may want to copy pictures or videos you take with the iPad to your computer, as well as copy pictures stored on your computer to your iPad.

You won't see syncing options if you've enabled iCloud photo library. But if you haven't, you can sync your iPad photos and videos with the following programs:

- **Mac:** Aperture version 3.2 or later, Photos version 1.2 or later, or Image Capture (included with Mac OS X), which can import photos only from your iPad to your Mac (and not from your Mac to your iPad).

  Apple ended development of Aperture in 2014. Although you can't buy a new copy, if you already own Aperture, it still works. That said, it will probably stop working someday, so you might want to start thinking about a different solution.

- **PC:** Adobe Photoshop Elements or Adobe Photoshop Album (or any other app that recognizes the iPad as a camera when you connect it).

You can also sync photos with any folder on your Mac or PC that contains images.

In the Photos pane, select the Sync Photos From check box, and then choose an application or folder from the pop-up menu (which says Photos in Figure 3-8).

If you choose an application that supports photo albums (such as Photoshop Elements, Aperture, or Photos), projects (Aperture), events (Photos), facial recognition and places (Aperture or Photos), or any combination thereof, you can automatically include recent projects (Aperture), events (Photos), or faces (Aperture and Photos) by making a selection from the same pop-up menu.

Note that although Photoshop Elements includes features called Places and Faces, those features are not supported by your iPad.

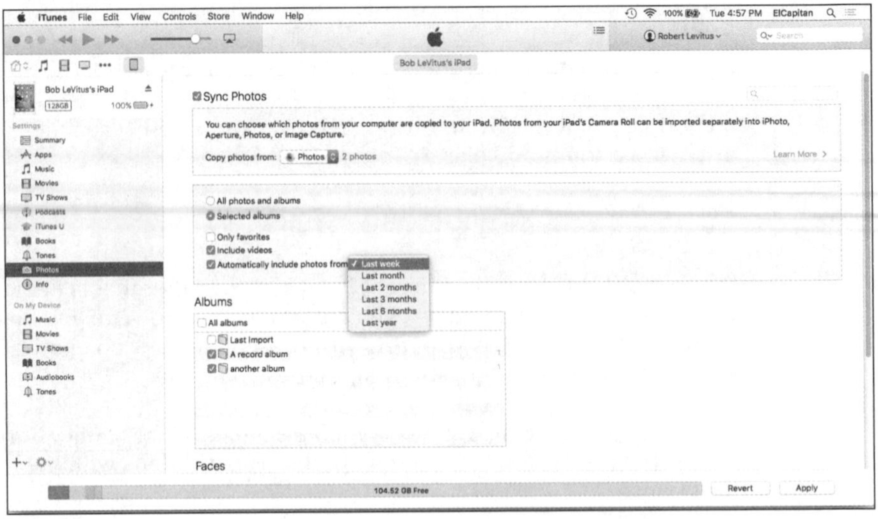

Figure 3-8: The Photos pane determines which photos will be synchronized with your iPad.

TIP

You can also type a word or phrase in the search field (in the upper right) to search for a specific event or events.

If you choose a folder full of images instead of Photos or another app, you can create subfolders inside it that will appear as albums on your iPad. But if you choose an application that doesn't support albums or events, or a single folder full of images with no subfolders, you have to transfer all or nothing.

Because we selected Photos in the Sync Photos From menu, and Photos 1.2 (the version installed on our Mac) supports projects and faces in addition to albums and photos, we have the option of syncing any combination of photos, projects, albums, and faces.

If you've taken any photos with your iPad or saved images from a web page, an email, an MMS message, or an iMessage since the last time you synced, the appropriate program launches (or the appropriate folder is selected), and you have the option of uploading the pictures to your computer.

Manual Syncing

This chapter has focused on automatic syncing thus far. Automatic syncing is great; it selects items to sync based on criteria you've specified, such as genre, artist, playlist, and album. But it's not efficient for transferring a few items — songs, movies, podcasts, or other files — to your iPad.

The solution? Manual syncing. With automatic syncing, iTunes updates your iPad automatically to match your criteria. Changes to your iTunes library since your last sync are synced automatically to your iPad. With manual syncing, you merely drag individual items to your iPad.

Automatic and manual sync aren't mutually exclusive. If you've set up automatic syncing, you can still sync individual items manually.

You can manually sync music, movies, TV shows, podcasts, and iTunes U lessons but not photos and info such as contacts, calendars, and bookmarks.

To configure your iPad for manual syncing:

1. **Connect your iPad to your computer via USB or Wi-Fi.**

   If iTunes doesn't open automatically, open it manually.

2. **Click the iPad icon.**

   If you have more than one iDevice, the iPad icon becomes a drop-down menu listing all your connected iDevices. Click the icon to display the menu with your devices, and then select the device you want.

3. **(Optional) Click the Summary tab. In the Options section, select Manually Manage Music and Videos.**

   This step disables automatic syncing for music and videos.

   If you're happy with automatic syncing and just want to get some audio or video from your computer to your iPad, feel free to skip this step.

To add items from iTunes to your iPad without using the syncing controls or performing an actual sync, first click the icon for the type of media you want to copy to your iPad — music, movies, or TV shows — or click the ellipsis (. . .) to select podcasts, iTunes U, audiobooks, or tones. Then start dragging the media to the left. As you do, a new pane appears on the left side of the iTunes window. Drag the media to this pane, as shown in Figure 3-9, and the media will be copied to your iPad immediately.

In Figure 3-9, we dragged an album called "The Art of McCartney" from the My Music tab, using the Album view. You can just as easily drag media from the other items in the menu: Song List, Artists, Genres, or Composers. And you can add other types of content, such as movies, TV shows, podcasts, and books. Just click the appropriate icon or the ellipsis. (We selected the music icon in the figure.)

You can add a media file to your iPad without syncing at least one other way. As before, your iPad has to be connected to your computer via Wi-Fi or USB, so you have to see the iPad icon above the picture of your iPad or this (as well as the previous method) won't work.

Figure 3-9: Drag and drop to copy media to your iPad.

The other way to add media to your iPad without syncing is to click the little ellipsis (. . .) in a circle next to songs, albums, movies, TV shows, books, and other media. Choose Add To Playlist from the pop-up menu and then choose your iPad in the list to add the file to your iPad.

And that's pretty much all you need to know to sync files automatically or manually. And if you haven't figured out how to watch movies or listen to audio on your iPad yet, it's only because you haven't read Part III on multimedia, where watching and listening to your iPad are made crystal clear.

Part II
The Internet iPad

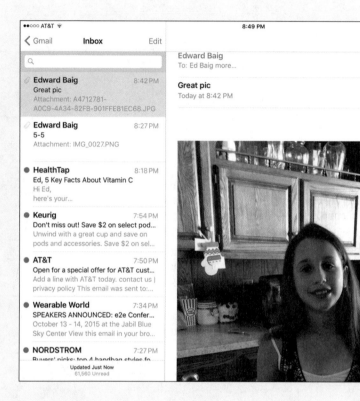

Check out your options for getting online (whether with Wi-Fi, 3G, or 4G) at www.dummies.com/extras/ipad.

In this part . . .

✔ Explore Safari, the best web browser to ever to grace a hand-held device. Take advantage of links and bookmarks and find out how to open multiple web pages at the same time. And view on your iPad every open web page on any of your other Apple devices.

✔ See how easy it is to set up email accounts and send and receive real honest-to-goodness email messages and attachments.

✔ Marvel at the Maps app's unerring capability to show you where you are. Discover the joys of step-by-step driving directions and real-time traffic info.

Going on a Mobile Safari

In This Chapter

▶ Surfing the Internet with Safari

▶ Navigating the web

▶ Having fun with bookmarks and reading and history lists

▶ Sharing websites

▶ Searching the World Wide Web

▶ Securing Safari

"*Y*ou feel like you're actually holding the web right in the palm of your hand."

When an Apple marketer says such a thing to describe surfing the web on the iPad, a lot of truth is behind it. The spectacular Retina display that was introduced with the third-generation iPad, in combination with the snappy Apple-designed A5X chip (third generation) or A6X chip (fourth generation) with quad-core graphics inside the machine, makes browsing on Apple's tablets an absolute delight. The iPad minis with the Retina display and the original iPad Air got ever-more-powerful A7 chips. The iPad Air 2 gets an A8X processor. And the newest member of the iPad stable, the large-screen iPad Pro, gets an A9X chip (and M9 motion processor).

In this chapter, you discover the pleasures — and the few roadblocks — in navigating cyberspace on your iPad.

Surfin' Dude

A version of the Apple Safari web browser is a major reason that the Net on the iPad is very much like the Net you've come to expect on a more tra-ditional computer. Come to think of it, the Internet often looks a lot better on iPads with the striking Retina display. And the screens on iPad models without the Retina display aren't too shabby either. Safari for the Mac and for Windows are two of the very best web browsers in the business. In our view, Safari on the iPhone has no rival as a cellphone browser. As you might imagine, Safari on the iPad is even more appealing.

Through older iterations of iOS, Apple revved up Safari's performance with what the company refers to as a *Nitro JavaScript engine.* Even a consumer-friendly company like Apple can't help but rely on geeky terms every now and then.

Exploring the browser

We start our cyberexpedition with a quick tour of the Safari browser. Take a gander at Figure 4-1. Not all browser controls found on a Mac or a PC are present, but Safari on the iPad still has a familiar look and feel. We describe these controls and others throughout this chapter.

Before plunging in, we recommend a little detour. Find out more about the wireless networks that enable you to surf the web on the iPad in our web extras at www.dummies.com/extras/ipad.

Blasting off into cyberspace

Surfing the web begins with a web address, of course.

Here are a few tips for using the keyboard in Safari (and see Chapter 2 for more help with using the virtual keyboard):

- ✔ Because so many web addresses end with the suffix .com (pronounced *dot com*), the virtual keyboard has a few shortcuts worth noting. Press and hold your finger against the .? key, and you'll see that .com option. You'll see other common web suffixes as well — .edu, .net, .org, .us, .ro, and .eu. Some options appear only if you've selected an international keyboard (as discussed in Chapter 2).

- ✔ The moment you tap a letter, you see a list of web addresses that match those letters. For example, if you tap the letter *E* (as we did in the example shown in Figure 4-2), you see web listings for eBay, ESPN, and others. Tapping *U* or *H* instead may display listings for *USA TODAY* or the *Houston Chronicle* (shameless plugs for the newspapers where we're columnists).

Models with Siri can lend a hand, um, voice, as you surf. If you call upon Siri and ask the voice genie inside the iPad to open the Safari app, Siri obliges. If you mention a specific website to Siri — "ESPN.com," say — Siri opens your designated search engine (Google, Bing, or Yahoo!), as discussed later in this chapter. And if Siri heard you right, the site you mentioned appears at the top of the search results.

Previous page

Next page

Bookmarks/reading list/shared links

Smart search field

View open tabs

Add tab

Share

Figure 4-1: The iPad's Safari browser.

When you tap certain letters, the iPad has three ways to determine websites to suggest:

- **Bookmarks:** The iPad suggests websites you've bookmarked from the Safari or Internet Explorer browser on your computer (and synchronized, as we describe in Chapter 3). More on bookmarks later in this chapter.

- **History:** The iPad suggests sites from the history list — those cyberdestinations where you recently hung your hat. Because history repeats itself, we also tackle that topic later in this chapter.

✔ **Smart search field:** When you type an address in the search field, you see icons for sites you frequent most often, and you can tap any of those icons to jump immediately to those sites.

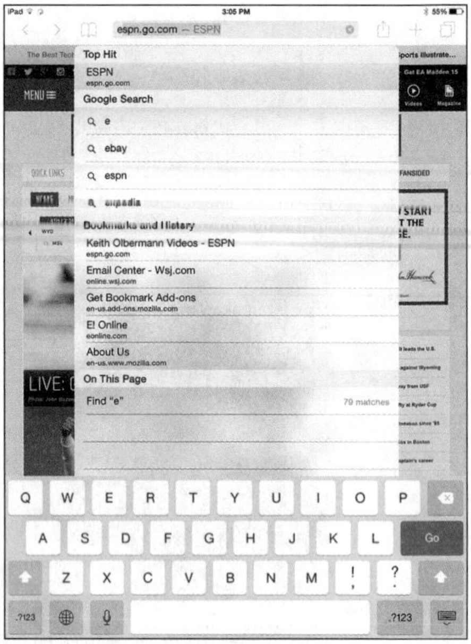

You might as well open your first web page now — and it's a full *HTML* page, to borrow from techie lingo:

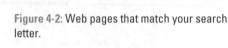

1. **Tap the Safari icon docked at the bottom of the Home screen.**

   If you haven't moved it, it's a member of the Fantastic Four on the dock (along with Messages, Mail, and Music). Chapter 1 introduces the Home screen.

2. **Tap the smart search field (refer to Figure 4-1).**

Figure 4-2: Web pages that match your search letter.

3. **Begin typing the web address, or *URL,* on the virtual keyboard that slides up from the bottom of the screen.**

4. **Do one of the following:**

   • *To accept one of the bookmarked (or other) sites that show up in the list, merely tap the name.*

     Safari automatically fills in the URL in the address field and takes you where you want to go.

   • *Keep tapping the proper keyboard characters until you enter the complete web address for the site you have in mind and then tap the Go key on the right side of the keyboard.*

You don't need to type **www** at the beginning of a URL. So if you want to visit `www.theonion.com` (for example), typing **theonion.com** is sufficient to transport you to the humor site. For that matter, Safari can take you to this site even if you type **theonion** without the .com.

Because Safari on the iPad runs a variation of the iPhone mobile operating system, every so often you may run into a site that serves up the light, or mobile, version of a website, sometimes known as a *WAP site.* Graphics may be stripped down on these sites. Alas, the producers of these sites may be unwittingly discriminating against you for dropping in on them by using an iPad. In fact, you may be provided a choice of which site you want — the light or the full version. Bravo! If not, you have our permission to berate these site producers with letters, emails, and phone calls until they get with the program. Fortunately, such a scenario is increasingly rare.

Zoom, zoom, zoom

If you know how to open a web page (if you don't, read the preceding section in this chapter), we can show you how radically simple it is to zoom in on pages so that you can read what you want to read and see what you want to see, without enlisting a magnifying glass.

Try these neat tricks for starters:

- ✓ **Double-tap the screen so that the area of the display that you make contact with fills the entire screen.** It takes just a second before the screen comes into focus. By way of example, check out Figure 4-3, which shows two views of the same *Sports Illustrated* web page. In the first view, you see what the page looks like when you first open it. In the second one, you see how the menu of stories box takes over much more of the screen after you double-tap it. The area of the screen you double-tapped is the area that swells. To return to the first view, double-tap the screen again.

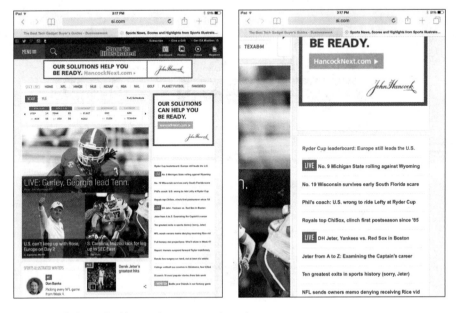

Figure 4-3: Doing a double-tap dance zooms in and out.

- ✔ **Pinch the page.** Sliding your thumb and index finger together and then spreading them apart (or, as we like to say, *unpinching*) also zooms in and out of a page. Again, wait just a moment for the screen to come into focus.

- ✔ **Press down on a page and drag it in all directions, or flick through a page from top to bottom.** You're panning and scrolling, baby.

- ✔ **Rotate the iPad to its side.** This action reorients from portrait view to a widescreen landscape view. The keyboard is also wider in this mode, making it a little easier to enter a new URL. However, this little bit of rotation magic won't happen if you set and enabled the screen orientation lock feature, which we describe in Chapter 1.

Reading clutter-free web pages

It's all too easy to get distracted reading web pages nowadays, what with ads, videos, and other clutter surrounding the stuff you want to take in. So pay attention to the horizontal lines that often appear in the smart search field, as shown in Figure 4-4 (left). Tap those lines to view the same article without the needless diversions, as shown in Figure 4-4 (right). Tap the lines again to return the standard web view.

Tap for clutter-free reading

Figure 4-4: Reducing clutter when reading a web story.

Finding Your Way around Cyberspace

In this section, we discuss ways to navigate the Internet on your iPad by using links and tabs.

Looking at lovable links

Because Safari functions on the iPad the same way that browsers work on your Mac or PC, links on the device behave in much the same way.

Text links that transport you from one site to another typically are underlined, are shown in blue, red, or bold type, or appear as items in a list. Tap the link to go directly to the site or page.

Tapping other links leads to different outcomes:

- **Open a map:** Tapping an address may launch the Maps app that is, um, addressed in Chapter 6.

- **Prepare an email:** Tap an email address, and the iPad opens the Mail program (see Chapter 5) and prepopulates the To field with that address. The virtual keyboard is also summoned so that you can add other email addresses and compose a subject line and message. Note that this shortcut doesn't always work.

To see the URL for a link, press your finger on the link and hold it there until a list of options appears, as shown in Figure 4-5.

Use this method also to determine whether a picture has a link. Just hold your finger down on the picture; if it's linked, you see the web address to which the link points.

Figure 4-5: Press and hold down on a link, and a list of options appears.

As for the link options shown in Figure 4-5, here's what two of them do:

- **Open:** Opens the page in this tab.

- **Copy:** Copies the link's URL to your iPad's Clipboard so that you can paste it elsewhere.

You read more about the other two options — Open in New Tab and Add to Reading List — a little later in this chapter.

Not every web link cooperates with the iPad because it doesn't support some common web standards — most notably, Adobe Flash video. If you see an incompatible link, nothing may happen — or a message may appear, asking you to install a plug-in.

This lack of support for Adobe Flash video is a void that is (frankly) unlikely to ever get addressed. Even Adobe is no longer embracing Flash for mobile devices. Apple does support the ever-popular HTML 5 standard for audio and video, which Adobe, too, is now backing.

Tabbed browsing

When we surf the web on a Mac or PC, we rarely go to a single web page and call it a day. In fact, we often have multiple web pages open at the same time. Sometimes we choose to hop around the web without closing the pages we visit. Sometimes a link automatically opens a new page without shuttering the old one. (If these additional pages are advertisements, this behavior isn't always welcome.)

Safari on the iPad lets you open multiple pages simultaneously, via a brilliant rendition of tabbed browsing similar to the desktop version of browsers such as Safari.

After you have one page open, you have two ways to open additional web pages in Safari so that they appear on the tab bar at the top of the screen (rather than replace the page you're currently viewing):

New tab

✔ **Tap the + icon (see Figure 4-6) near the top-right corner of the browser.** A tab named Favorites appears, as shown in Figure 4-6. Now type a URL, tap a book-mark or an icon for a favorite or frequently visited site, or initi-ate a search, and the result will appear in this tab.

Figure 4-6: A new tab, ready to display any page you choose.

✔ **Hold your finger on a link until a list of options appears (refer to Figure 4-5), and then tap Open in New Tab.**

To switch tabs, just tap the tab. To close a tab, tap the gray X that appears on the left edge of the active tab.

You can manage tabs in one other way. Tap the view open tabs icon in the top-right corner of the browser (refer to Figure 4-1) to summon thumbnail views of your open web pages, as shown in Figure 4-7. You can tap the X on any thumbnail to close it. From here you can also go into private browsing mode (discussed later in this chapter) or check out iCloud tabs, the topic we're about to dive into.

iCloud tabs

Although the iPad is your likely traveling companion just about everywhere you go, we know that you also browse the web from your smartphone or personal computer. If that smartphone happens to be an iPhone and the computer is a Macintosh (or a Windows PC running Safari), you can take advantage of iCloud tabs, a feature that lets you resume reading web pages that you started looking at on those other devices. The feature works with the iPod touch, too. If you read the preceding section, you already know how to access iCloud tabs: Tap the View Open Tabs icon to bring up tab view, which is shown in Figure 4-7. In this example, there are open tabs on Edward's MacBook Air and on his iPhone. Tap a link to open the page on your tablet.

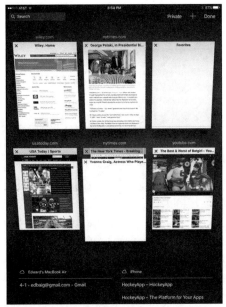

Figure 4-7: A thumbnail view of all your open tabs.

Revisiting Web Pages Time and Again

Surfing the web would be a drag if you had to enter a URL every time you wanted to navigate from one page to another. So you can find those favorite websites in the future, the iPad provides bookmarks, web clips, reading lists, and history lists.

Book (mark) 'em, Dano

You already know how useful bookmarks are and how you can synchronize bookmarks from the browsers on your computer. It's equally simple to bookmark a web page directly on the iPad. Follow these steps:

1. **Make sure that the page you want to bookmark is open, and then tap the share icon (shown in the margin) at the top of the screen.**

   You have many options beyond bookmarking when you tap the share icon (refer to Figure 4-1, though not all the options are visible in the figure). You can tap Message, Mail, Notes, Twitter, or Facebook. Sina Weibo and Tencent Weibo (Chinese variations of Twitter) are also available, provided you added a Chinese keyboard in Settings (see Chapter 2). You can tap Save PDF to iBooks. Or you can tap Add to

Favorites, Add Bookmark, Add to Reading List, Add to Home Screen, Copy, Print, Find on Page, or Request Desktop Site, as we show you here. You can also use the wireless feature called AirDrop to share the page with people nearby via Wi-Fi or Bluetooth, provided they have a fourth-generation iPad or later, the iPad mini, or a Mac with OS X Yosemite, or OS X El Capitan. See Chapter 13 to find out how to use AirDrop.

2. **Tap Add Bookmark.**

   A new Add Bookmark window opens with a default name for the bookmark, its web address, and its folder location.

3. **Give it a name and folder location:**

   • *Accept the default bookmark name and default bookmark folder:* Tap Save.

   • *Change the default bookmark name:* Tap the *x*-in-a-circle next to the name, enter the new title (using the virtual keyboard), and then tap Save.

   • *Change the location where the bookmark is saved:* Tap the > symbol to the right of the suggested location (likely Favorites), tap the folder where you want the bookmark to be kept so that a check mark appears, and then tap Save.

To open a bookmarked page after you set it up, tap the bookmarks icon, which is to the left of the smart search field. (Refer to Figure 4-1.)

If you don't see bookmarks right away, make sure that the leftmost of the three tabs at the top of the screen is highlighted in blue. The other tabs are for the reading list and for shared links — those shared by your contacts from selected social networks.

If the bookmark you have in mind is buried inside a folder, tap the folder name first and then tap the bookmark you want.

Altering bookmarks

If a bookmarked site is no longer meaningful, you can change it or get rid of it:

✔ **To remove a bookmark (or folder),** tap the bookmarks icon and then tap Edit. Tap the red circle next to the bookmark you want to toss off the list, and then tap Delete.

To remove a single bookmark or folder, swipe its name from right to left and then tap the red Delete button.

✔ **To change a bookmark name or location,** tap Edit at the bottom-right corner of the Bookmarks window. Tap a given bookmark, and an Edit Bookmark window appears, with the name, URL, and location of the bookmark already filled in. Tap the fields you want to change. In the Name field, tap the X in the gray circle and then use the keyboard to enter a new title. In the Location field, tap the location name and scroll up or down the list until you find a new home for your bookmark.

✔ **To create a new folder for your bookmarks,** tap Edit and then tap New Folder. Enter the name of the new folder, and choose where to put it.

✔ **To move a bookmark up or down in a list,** tap Edit and then drag the three bars to the right of the bookmark's name to its new resting place.

If you take advantage of iCloud, the web pages you've bookmarked on your Mac and on your other iOS devices will be available on the iPad, and vice versa.

Saving to your reading list

When you visit a web page you'd like to read, but just not now, the reading list feature is sure to come in handy, including when you're offline. Here's how it works:

✔ **Saving a page for later:** Tap the share icon and then tap Add to Reading List. Or, if you see a link to a page you'd like to read later, press on the link until a list of options appears (refer to Figure 4-5) and then tap Add to Reading List.

✔ **Reading a page on your reading list:** Tap the bookmarks icon and tap the page in the reading list, as shown in Figure 4-8.

✔ **Keeping track of what you've read:** Tap Show Unread to display only those items that you haven't read yet. Tap Show All to show all the items in the reading list.

✔ **Removing items from the reading list:** Swipe the item from right to left, and then tap its red Delete button.

Figure 4-8: Tap a page in the reading list to read it.

The reading list feature used to require an active Internet connection, which is why we always admired the superb save-to-read-later Instapaper app — and still do. It's now free in the App Store, though there are also premium subscription options that add functionality separate from the Safari reading list.

In Safari Settings, you can choose to use your cellular network (if available) to save reading list items from iCloud so you can read them offline.

Finally, don't forget that you can share your reading list (and bookmarks) among your computers and iOS devices with iCloud, as described in Chapter 3.

Clipping a web page

You frequent lots of websites, some way more than others. For example, perhaps you consult the train schedule several times during the day. In their infinite wisdom, the folks at Apple let you bestow special privileges on frequently visited sites, not just by bookmarking pages but also by affording them their unique Home screen icons. Apple used to call these *web clips,* and we still like the term. Creating one is dead simple. Follow these steps:

1. **Open the web page in question, and tap the share icon (shown in the margin).**

2. **Tap Add to Home Screen.**

   Apple creates an icon out of the area of the page that was displayed when you saved the clip, unless the page has its own custom icon.

3. **Type a new name for your web clip or leave the one that Apple suggests.**

4. **Tap Add.**

   The icon appears on your Home screen.

As with any icon, you can remove a web clip by pressing and holding down on its icon until it starts to wiggle. Tap the X in the corner of the icon, and then tap Delete. You can also move the web clip to a more preferred location on one of your Home screens or on the dock.

Letting history repeat itself

Sometimes you want to revisit a site that you failed to bookmark, but you can't remember the darn destination or what led you there in the first place. Good thing you can study the history books.

Safari records the pages you visit and keeps the logs on hand for several days. Here's how to access your history:

1. **Tap the bookmarks icon and then tap History.**

   The History option is at the top of the bookmarks list.

2. **Tap the day you think you hung out at the site.**

   Sites are listed under such headings as "This Morning," "Thursday Evening," or "Thursday Morning," or segregated by a specific date.

3. **When you find the listing, tap it.**

   You're about to make your triumphant return.

To clear your history so that nobody else can trace your steps — and just what is it you're hiding? — tap Clear at the bottom-right corner of the history list. You can clear the last hour, clear only the day that you tapped Clear, clear today and yesterday, or clear all your history. Alternatively, starting on the Home screen, tap Settings ➪ Safari ➪ Clear History and Website Data. In both instances, per usual, you have a chance to back out without wiping the slate clean.

When you clear your history from settings, your history, cookies and browsing data will be removed from all the devices you have signed into iCloud. If that is not your intention, tap Cancel.

Saving web pictures

You can capture most pictures you come across on a website — but be mindful of any potential copyright violations, depending on what you plan to do with the images. To copy an image from a website, follow these steps:

1. **Press your finger against the image.**

2. **Tap the Save Image button that appears, as shown in Figure 4-9.**

   Saved images end up in your Photos library in the All Photos album, from which they can be synced back to a computer.

   Figure 4-9: Hold your finger against a picture in Safari to save it to the iPad.

Tap Copy instead, and you can paste the image into an email or as a link in a program such as Notes.

In some cases, typically advertisements, you also see an Open button or an Open in New Tab button, which takes you to the ad image.

Sharing Your Web Experiences

When you find a great website that you just must share, use Safari to tweet it, post it to Facebook, or — go old-school — print it.

To make Twitter and Facebook work, of course, the iPad must know your username and password, which you can fill add in Settings (see Chapter 15).

Tap the share icon (shown in the margin), and you find these sharing options:

- ✔ **AirDrop:** Share the page with other people who have compatible devices and AirDrop. You'll need to turn on AirDrop in Control Center (just drag upward from the bottom of the screen). Then you can choose whether to make your iPad discoverable to everyone or only to people in your contacts. AirDrop works only with fourth-generation iPads or later, the iPad mini, or Mac computers with OS X Yosemite or OS X El Capitan.

- ✔ **Message:** Send a link to the web page in a text or an iMessage.

- ✔ **Mail:** The Mail program opens with a link for the page in the message and the name of the site or page in the Subject line.

- ✔ **Notes:** Sure you can bookmark pages. But sometimes it's even more convenient to reserve space in the Notes app for a web page you want to refer to later. Aren't you glad to know that you can?

- ✔ **Twitter:** The iPad adds to an outgoing tweet a link to the web page. You must fill in the rest of the actual post.

- ✔ **Facebook:** Post the page — and whatever comments you choose to add — to the popular social network.

- ✔ **Sina Weibo** and **Tencent Weibo:** If available, you post via these Chinese blogging services. You need to activate a Chinese keyboard or language to see these options.

- ✔ **Save PDF to iBooks:** To do just that, tap here.

- ✔ **Reminders:** You can add a page to the Reminders app. If you tap Options, you can be reminded on a given day or at a location.

- ✔ **Print:** The iPad searches for an AirPrint printer. If you have one, you can choose the number of copies you want. Tap Print to complete the job.

- ✔ **Find on Page:** Tap this option and use the virtual keyboard that slides up to type in the field above the keyboard the word that you want to find. Highlighted words appear in yellow. Use the up and down arrows to find each mention of the word. Tap Done when you're done.

- ✔ **Request Desktop Site:** If such a page is available (and different from the mobile site), tapping here delivers that page.

- ✔ **More:** Tap More to summon a list of activities. You can change the order of the activities by dragging the three horizontal lines to the right of each activity. (By pressing down on an icon, you can drag it to a new position without tapping More.)

Launching a Mobile Search Mission

Most of us spend a lot of time using search engines. And the ones we summon most often are Google, Yahoo!, and Microsoft Bing, at least in the United States. If you're in China, chances are you search using Baidu. All these search options are available on the iPad, along with DuckDuckGo, a search engine that doesn't track your web footsteps.

With iOS 7, Apple brought the previously separate address bar and search fields together into a single convenient, unified strip called the *smart search field,* following the path taken on most popular web browsers for PCs and Macs. Although you can certainly use the virtual keyboard to type *google. com, yahoo.com, bing.com,* or other search engines into this field, Apple doesn't require that tedious effort. Instead, just type your search query directly in the box.

To conduct a web search on the iPad, tap the smart search field. You immediately see icons for your favorite web destinations, with Apple betting on your frequent return visits. But when you start typing in the smart search field, a Google (or other) search mission commences, with top hits — an educated guess, really — shown at the top.

You see other search suggestions as you start tapping additional letters. In Figure 4-10, for example, typing the letters **le** yields such suggestions as Lexmark, LeBron James, and league of legends. Tap any search results that look promising, or tap Go on the keyboard to immediately land on the top hit. Or keep tapping out letters until you generate the search result you want.

 You can also find a search word or phrase on the web page you have on-screen. Just look in the list for On This Page. You're informed of the number of matches;

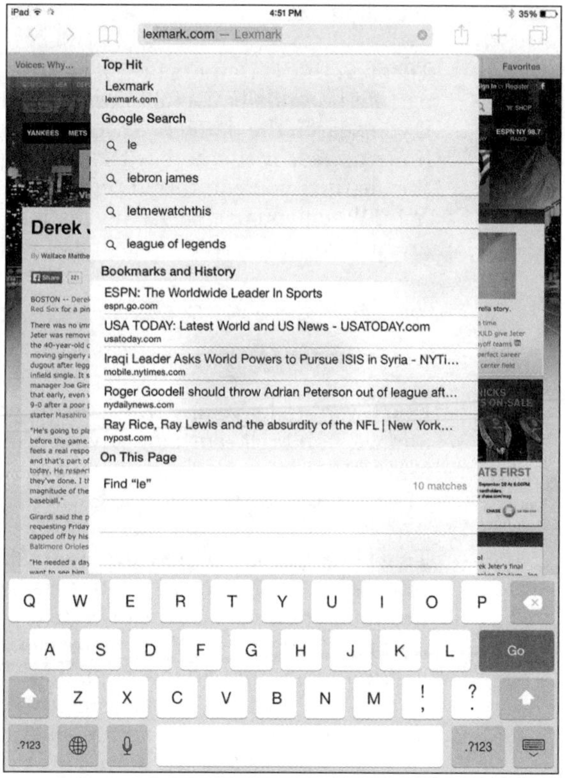

Figure 4-10: Running a search on the iPad.

if it's more than one, you can move back and forth through them with the up-pointing and down-pointing arrows, respectively, at the bottom of the screen.

To switch the search field from the current search engine to another search engine choice on your iPad, check out the "Smart Safari Settings" section, later in this chapter.

As mentioned earlier in this chapter, Siri can open Safari — all you have to do is ask. We also mentioned that Siri can (in some cases, anyway) take you to your favorite search engine, just by you uttering the name of a website. Of course, much of what Siri can do is web-centric. So now is as good a time as any to recommend Chapter 14, where you get an excellent sense of all that Siri can do.

You conduct a web search also by initiating a Spotlight search. To summon the Spotlight search field, swipe down from any Home screen. Type (or dictate) your search term and then scroll to the bottom of the list below any search results that point to the use of the term on the iPad itself (meaning inside messages, notes, apps, and so on). Tap Search Web to search the web with the term you entered, or tap Search Wikipedia to run that search inside Wikipedia, the online encyclopedia. You can also tap Search Maps to, well, search maps.

Through the Search Engine Suggestions and Safari Suggestions features, you can get potentially useful information even if you don't explicitly search for it. If you search the name of a movie, for example, Safari will also provide showtimes at nearby theaters without being asked. If you're not comfortable with this feature, you can turn it off in Settings. And why wouldn't you be comfortable? When you use Safari Suggestions, your search queries and related data are shared with Apple. Speaking of which . . .

Private Browsing

Don't want to leave any tracks while you surf? Don't worry — we won't ask and we won't tell. Turn on private browsing for a "what happens in Safari stays in Safari" tool. Those truly bent on staying private will also want to tap Clear History, as we mention earlier in this chapter.

To go incognito, tap the view open tabs icon (refer to Figure 4-1), and then tap the Private button at the upper-right corner of the screen. After private browsing is on, any traces of your visit to nonono.com (or wherever) are nowhere to be found. Your history is wiped clean, open tabs don't appear in iCloud tabs, and your autofill information is not stored anywhere. To remind you that you're browsing privately, the Safari interface takes on a darker shade — a not-so-subtle message here, we suppose, that you might be engaging in a shady or naughty activity. We don't pass judgment. Besides, we assume that you're just a private soul, and we certainly respect that.

To come out of hiding, tap the view open tabs icon again and then tap Private again.

The history of pages you've visited can be useful and a huge timesaver, so don't forget to disable this option again when you're finished doing whatever it is you don't want people to know you're doing.

You can separately turn on a Do Not Track setting in Settings. Speaking of which, kindly move on to the next section.

Be mindful of your settings on other machines. If you run Safari on both an iPad and a Mac, but choose to go private only on Apple's tablet, your Mac browsing history will still show up in your history listings on the iPad.

Smart Safari Settings

Along with the riches galore found on the Internet are places in cyberspace where you're hassled. You might want to take action to protect your privacy and maintain your security.

To get started, tap the Settings icon on the Home screen and then tap Safari.

The following settings enable you to tell your iPad what you want to be private and how you want to set your security options:

- ✔ **Search Engine:** Tap the search engine you desire — just as long as that search engine happens to be Google, Yahoo!, Bing, DuckDuckGo, or, if you've enabled a Chinese keyboard, Baidu. Other settings found here let you determine whether the iPad can make Search Engine Suggestions and Safari Suggestions, features touched on earlier in this chapter.

- ✔ **Passwords:** Use a finger to authorize Touch ID, and you can view and edit the passwords you use all over the Internet.

- ✔ **AutoFill:** Safari can automatically fill out web forms by using your personal contact information, usernames, and passwords, or information from your other contacts. Tap AutoFill and then tap the on/off switch to enable or disable AutoFill.

  - Tap Use Contact Info if you're comfortable using the information found about your Contacts.

  - Tap My Info to select yourself in your contacts so that Safari knows which address, phone numbers, email addresses, and other information to use when it fills in a form.

- Tap the Names and Passwords on/off switch to enable or disable, respectively, Safari's capability to remember usernames and passwords for websites. You also get to decide whether credit card information can be used and saved.

- Tap Credit Cards to manage and enter the credit card numbers you're comfortable sharing.

Turning on AutoFill can compromise your security if someone gets hold of your iPad.

✔ **Open New Tabs in Background:** If you enable this setting, new tabs that you open in Safari will load even if you're reading a different page in another tab.

✔ **Favorites:** Apple lets you quickly access favorite bookmarks when you enter an address, search, or create a tab. Tap the category of sites for which you'd like to see icons in that category (News, Business, Technology, whatever). A check mark appears next to your selection. Or if you're cool with it, leave the default category setting as Favorites.

✔ **Show Favorites Bar:** If you enable the Show Favorites Bar option, you'll be able to see Safari's bookmarks bar between the smart search field and tab bar.

✔ **Show Tab Bar:** You can display the open tab buttons in a bar near the top of the Safari display or not, another matter of personal preference.

✔ **Block Pop-ups:** *Pop-ups* are those web pages that appear whether or not you want them to. Often, they're annoying advertisements. But on some sites, you welcome the appearance of pop-ups, so remember to turn off blocking under such circumstances.

✔ **Quick Website Search:** Determine whether or not to use website shortcuts when you're searching within a website. For example, you can type **wiki FDR** to show Wikipedia entries for Franklin Roosevelt.

✔ **Preload Top Hit:** We talk about the smart search field throughout this chapter. Here you get to choose whether the iPad can preload the top hit, or both.

✔ **Block Cookies:** We're not talking about crumbs you may have accidentally dropped on the iPad. *Cookies* are tiny bits of information that a website places on the iPad when you visit so that the site recognizes you when you return. You need not assume the worst; most cookies are benign.

If this concept wigs you out, you can take action and block cookies from third parties and advertisers: If you tap the Always Block option, you will theoretically never again receive cookies on the iPad. Or you can choose to accept cookies only from the website you're currently visiting or only from the websites you happen to visit. You can also tap Always to accept cookies from all sites. Tap Safari to return to the main Safari Settings page.

If you set the iPad so that it doesn't accept cookies, certain web pages won't load properly, and other sites such as Amazon won't recognize you or make any of your preferred settings or recommendations available.

✔ **Do Not Track:** As the name suggests, if you turn this setting on, the iPad will not trace your cyberfootsteps.

✔ **Clear History and Website Data:** You met this option earlier. Tap it to erase everything in Safari's history, leaving nary a trace of the pages you've visited.

✔ **Fraudulent Website Warning:** Safari can warn you when you land on a site whose producers have sinister intentions. The protection is better than nothing, but don't let down your guard because the Fraud Warning feature isn't foolproof. The setting is on by default.

✔ **JavaScript:** Programmers use JavaScript to add various kinds of functionality to web pages, from displaying the date and time to changing images when you drag over them. However, some security risks have also been associated with JavaScript. If you do turn it off, though, some things might not work as you expect. But this setting is found under the Advanced topic for a reason, meaning that Apple doesn't think too many of us should mess with this setting. We generally leave things as they are, but go with whatever makes you comfortable.

✔ **Advanced:** Although the Advanced settings are indeed advanced (see the preceding bullet), you might want to drop by if you're curious about how much data you're consuming at different sites. Developers might also want to check out Advanced settings to turn on a Web Inspector feature that most readers need not concern themselves with.

5

The Email Must Get Through

*O*n any computing device, emails come and go with a variety of emotions. Messages may be amusing or sad, frivolous or serious. Electronic missives on the iPad are almost always touching.

The reason, of course, is that you're touching the display to compose and read messages. Okay, so we're having a little fun with the language. But the truth is, the bundled Mail app on the iPad is a modern program designed not only to send and receive text email messages but also to handle rich HTML email messages — formatted with font and type styles and embedded graphics. If someone sends you mail with a picture, it's quite likely that the picture is visible right in the body of the message. (That's the default behavior, but your results may vary depending on the sender's email capabilities and your iPad's mail settings.)

Furthermore, your iPad can read several types of file attachments, including (but not limited to) PDFs, JPG images, Microsoft Word documents, PowerPoint slides, and Excel spreadsheets, as well as stuff produced through Apple's own productivity software, notably Pages, Keynote, and Numbers. (As you'll discover, you can mark up attachments too, those you receive or those you send out.) Better still, all this sending and receiving of text, graphics, and documents can happen in the background, so you can surf the web or play a game while your iPad quietly and efficiently handles your email behind the scenes.

Apple even lets you grant VIP status to important senders so that there's almost no chance you'll miss mail from the people who matter most. Let's see, there's your spouse, your kids, your boss . . . are we missing anybody?

Prep Work: Setting Up Your Accounts

First things first. To use Mail, you need an email address. If you have broadband Internet access (that is, a cable modem, FiOS, or DSL), you probably received one or more email addresses when you signed up. If you're one of the handful of readers who doesn't already have an email account, you can get one for free from Yahoo! (http://mail.yahoo.com), Google (http://mail.google.com), Microsoft Outlook (http://www.microsoft.com/en-us/outlook-com/), AOL (www.aol.com), or numerous other service providers.

Or you can get a free premium email account (for example, *yourname@iCloud.com*) from Apple as part of iCloud. From your Home screen, just tap Settings➪Mail, Contacts, Calendars➪iCloud.

Many free email providers add a bit of advertising at the end of your outgoing messages. If you'd rather not be a billboard for your email provider, either use the address(es) that came with your broadband Internet access (*yourname*@comcast.net or *yourname*@att.net, for example) or pay a few dollars a month for a premium email account that doesn't tack advertising (or anything else) onto your messages.

Finally, while the rest of the chapter focuses on the Mail app, you can also use Safari to access most email systems, if that's your preference.

Setting up your account the easy way

Chapter 3 explains the option of automatically syncing the email accounts on your Mac or Windows PC with your iPad. If you chose that option, your email accounts should be configured already on your iPad. And if you signed in with an iCloud account while setting up your iPad (read Chapter 2), you should already be good to go with your iCloud email account. You may proceed directly to the later section "See Me, Read Me, File Me, Delete Me: Working with Messages."

If you haven't yet chosen that option but want to set up your account the easy way now, go to Chapter 3, read about syncing email accounts, and then sync your iPad with your Mac or PC. Then you, too, can proceed directly to the section "See Me, Read Me, File Me, Delete Me: Working with Messages," later in this chapter.

Remember that syncing email accounts doesn't have any effect on your email messages; it merely synchronizes the *settings* for email accounts so you don't have to set them up manually on your iPad.

Setting up your account the less-easy way

If you don't want to sync the email accounts on your Mac or PC, you can set up an email account on your iPad manually. It's not quite as easy as clicking a box and syncing your iPad, but it's not rocket science either. Here's how you get started:

- **If you have no email accounts on your iPad:** The first time you launch Mail, you see the Welcome to Mail screen. Your choices are iCloud, Microsoft Exchange (business email), Google (Gmail), Yahoo!, AOL, Microsoft Outlook.com, and Other.

    Merely tap the account type you want to add to the iPad and follow the steps in the upcoming "Setting up an account with another provider" or "Setting up corporate email" section.

- **If you have one or more email accounts on your iPad and want to add a new account manually:** Tap Settings on the Home screen and then tap Mail, Contacts, Calendars ⇨ Add Account.

    You see an Add Account screen, shown in Figure 5-1, with the same account options that appear on the Welcome to Mail screen. Proceed to one of the next three sections, depending on the type of email account you selected.

Figure 5-1: Tap a button to set up an account.

Setting up an email account with iCloud, Gmail, Yahoo!, AOL, or Microsoft Outlook

If your account is with iCloud, Gmail (Google), Yahoo!, AOL, or Outlook, follow these steps:

1. **Tap the appropriate button on the Welcome to Mail screen (refer to Figure 5-1).**

2. **Enter your name, email address, password, and optional description, as shown in Figure 5-2.**

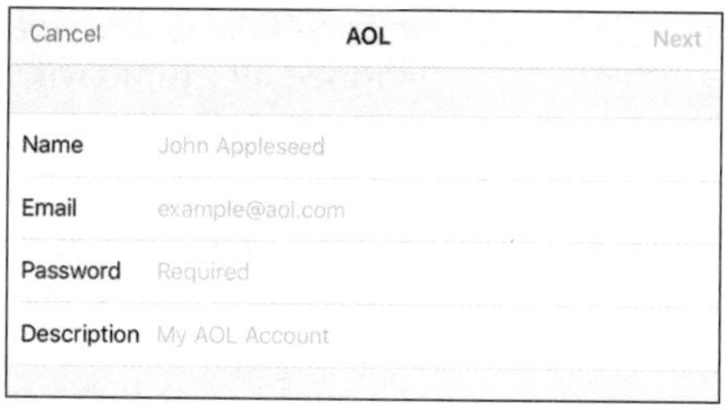

Figure 5-2: Just fill 'em in and tap Next, and you're ready to rock.

If you don't add a description (such as Work or Personal), the field usually fills in automatically with the contents of the Address field. Some accounts don't have space for a description or even your name. In other words, all that is required is an email address and password.

3. **Tap the Next button in the upper-right corner of the screen.**

   You're finished. That's all there is to setting up your account. You can now proceed to "See Me, Read Me, File Me, Delete Me: Working with Messages."

Setting up an account with another provider

If your email account is with a provider other than iCloud, Gmail (Google), Yahoo!, AOL, or Microsoft Outlook, you have a bit more work ahead of you. You need a bunch of information about your email account that you may not know or have handy.

We suggest that you scan the following instructions, note the items you don't know, and go find the answers before you continue. To find the answers, look at the documentation you received when you signed up for your email account or visit the account provider's website and search there.

Here's how you set up an account:

1. **Starting at the Home screen, tap Settings⇨Mail, Contacts, Calendars⇨Add Account⇨Other.**

2. **Under Mail, tap Add Mail Account.**

3. **Fill in the name, address, password, and description in the appropriate fields, and then tap Next.**

   With any luck, that's all you'll have to do. The iPad will look up and retrieve your account credentials. If that doesn't happen, continue with Step 4.

4. **Tap the button at the top of the screen that denotes the type of email server this account uses, IMAP or POP, as shown in Figure 5-3.**

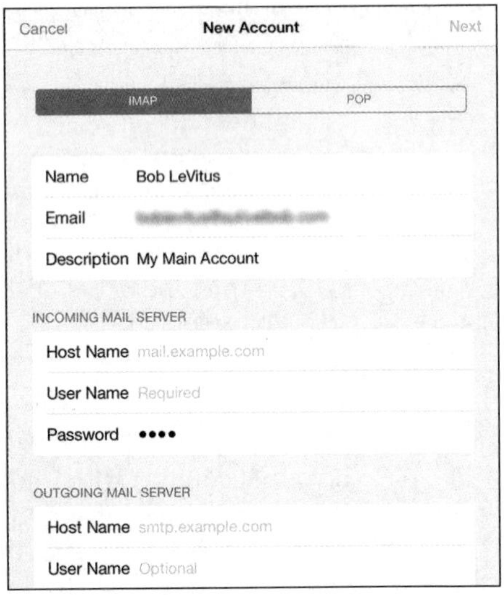

Figure 5-3: If you set up an IMAP or a POP email account, you may have a few more fields to fill in before you can rock.

5. **Fill in the Internet hostname for your incoming mail server, which looks something like mail.*providername*.com.**

6. **Fill in your username and password.**

7. **Enter the Internet hostname for your outgoing mail server, which looks something like smtp.*providername*.com.**

8. **Enter your username and password in the appropriate fields.**

9. **Tap the Next (or Save) button in the upper-right corner to create the account.**

    You're now ready to begin using your account. See the section "See Me, Read Me, File Me, Delete Me: Working with Messages."

 Some outgoing mail servers don't need your username and password. The fields for these items on your iPad note that they're optional. Still, we suggest that you fill them in anyway. Doing so saves you from having to add them later if your outgoing mail server does require an account name and a password, which almost all do these days.

Setting up corporate email

The iPad makes nice with the Microsoft Exchange servers that are a staple in large enterprises, as well as many smaller businesses.

What's more, if your company supports Microsoft Exchange ActiveSync, you can exploit push email so that messages arrive pronto on the iPad, just as they do on your other computers. (To keep everything up to date, the iPad also supports push calendars and push contacts.) For push to work with an Exchange Server, your company must be simpatico with one of the last several iterations of Microsoft Exchange ActiveSync (most companies are). If you run into a problem, ask your company's IT or tech department.

Setting up Exchange email isn't particularly taxing, and the iPad connects to Exchange right out of the box. However, you might have to consult your employer's techie-types for certain settings.

Start setting up your corporate email on your iPad by following these steps:

1. **Tap the Exchange listing on the Welcome to Mail or Add Account screen. (Refer to Figure 5-1.)**

2. **Fill in what you can: your email address, domain, username (sometimes domain\user), and password. Or call on your IT staff for assistance. Tap Next when you're done.**

3. **On the next screen, as shown in Figure 5-4, enter the Server email address, assuming that the Microsoft Autodiscover service didn't already find it. Tap Next when you're done.**

   That server address may begin with exchange.*company*.com.

4. **Choose which information you want to synchronize through Exchange by tapping each item you want.**

   You can choose Mail, Contacts, Calendars, Reminders, and Notes. When one of these switches is turned on, it turns green, as in Figure 5-5; otherwise, what you see appears dimmed.

5. **Tap Save.**

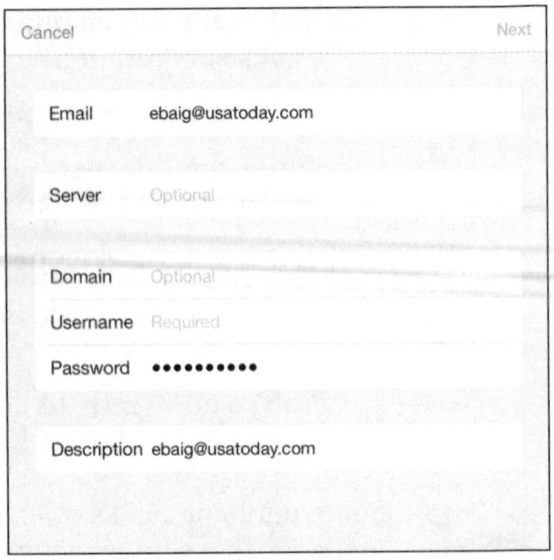

The company you work for doesn't want just anybody having access to your email — heaven forbid if your iPad is lost or stolen. So your bosses may insist that you change the passcode lock in Settings on your iPad. (The passcode lock is different than your email account password.) Skip over to Chapter 15 to find instructions for adding or changing a passcode. (We'll wait for you.) Now if your iPad ends up in the wrong hands, your company can remotely wipe the contents clean.

You can choose how long you want the iPad to keep email synchronized. Head to Settings; tap Mail, Contacts, Calendars; and then tap the email account that uses ActiveSync. Tap Mail Days to Sync, and tap No Limit or choose another time frame (1 day, 3 days, 1 week, 2 weeks, or 1 month).

If you're moonlighting at a second job, you can configure more than one Exchange ActiveSync account on your iPad; prior to iOS 5, there was a limit of just one such account per device.

Figure 5-4: You're on your way to a corporate email account.

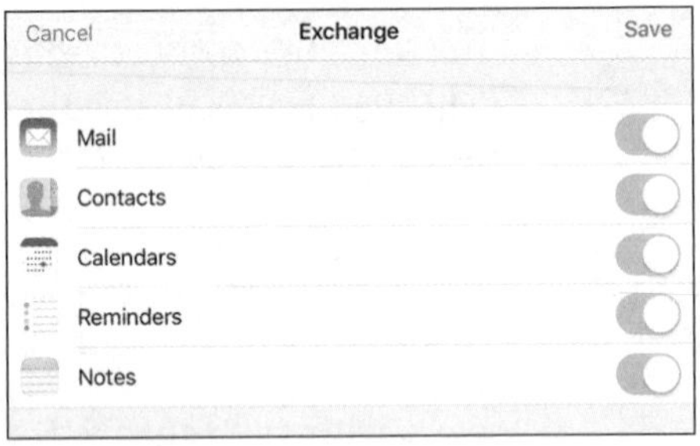

Figure 5-5: Keeping your mail, contacts, calendars, and reminders in sync.

See Me, Read Me, File Me, Delete Me: Working with Messages

Now that your email accounts are all set up, it's time to figure out how to receive and read the stuff. Fortunately, you've already done most of the heavy lifting when you set up your email accounts. Getting and reading your mail are a piece of cake.

You can tell when you have unread mail by looking at the Mail icon at the bottom of your Home screen. The cumulative number of unread messages across all your email inboxes appears in a little red badge in the upper-right area of the icon. If you have many unread messages, you may see the number appear as 6. . .23 (signifying, say, 62,523 messages — yes, we get lots of mail).

The badge display is the default behavior. If you don't care for it, you can turn it off in the Settings app's Notifications pane.

In the following sections, you find out how to read messages and attached files and send messages to the trash or maybe a folder when you've read them. Or, if you can't find a message, check out the section on searching your email messages. Reading email on an iPad versus a desktop or notebook computer is similar, except you have the advantage of the iPad's touchscreen.

Reading messages

To read your mail, tap the Mail icon on the Home screen. Remember that what appears on-screen depends on whether you're holding the iPad in landscape or portrait mode as well as what was on the screen the last time you opened the Mail app:

- ✔ **Landscape:** With the iPad in landscape mode, you see All Inboxes at the top of the Mailboxes section (see Figure 5-6), which, as its name suggests, is a repository for all the messages across all your accounts. The number to the right of All Inboxes (64,136 in Figure 5-6) matches the number (or abbreviated shortcut) on the Mail icon on your home page. Again, it's the cumulative tally of unread messages across all your accounts.

  Below the All Inboxes listing are the inboxes for your individual accounts. The number to the right of them, as you'd expect, is the number of unread messages in those accounts (981 in iCloud and 63,155 in Gmail, inthe example shown in Figure 5-6).

  If you tap an account, you see the available subfolders for that account (Drafts, Sent Mail, Trash, and so on).

  One of these accounts is the VIP mailbox. The VIP mailbox lists all the messages from senders you deem the most important. We tell you how to give someone VIP status in the later section, "More things you can do with messages."

See all records

Move message

Flag/mark/move to junk/notify me   Trash

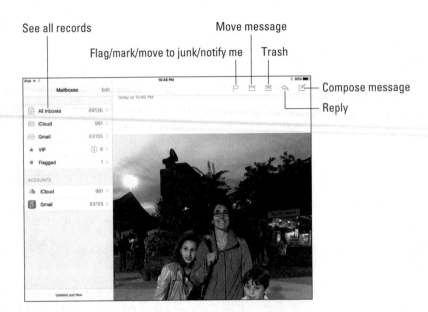

Compose message

Reply

Figure 5-6: When you're holding the iPad sideways, Mail looks something like this.

REMEMBER

Depending on the last time the Mail app was open, you may alternatively see previews of the messages in your inbox in the left panel. Previews show the name of the sender, the time the message arrived, the subject header, and the first two lines of the message. (In Settings, you can change the number of lines shown in the preview from one line to five or to no preview lines.)

✔ **Portrait:** When you hold the iPad in portrait mode, as shown in Figure 5-7, the last incoming message fills the entire screen. You have to tap the Inbox button (in the upper-left corner of the screen) to summon a panel that displays other accounts or mes-sage previews. You can summon the panel also by swiping from the left edge of the screen to the right. The panel overlays the message that otherwise fills the screen.

Figure 5-7: When you're holding the iPad in portrait mode, the message fills the screen.

Messages display in *threads,* or conversations, making them easy to follow. Of course, you can still view accounts individually. Follow these steps to read your email:

1. **If the email mailbox you want to see isn't front and center, tap the Mailboxes button in the upper-left corner of the screen to summon the appropriate one.**

   Again, this button may say All Inboxes, Mailboxes, or some other folder name, or it may say the name of the email account that is currently open. Within an email account, you can see the number of unread messages in each mailbox.

2. **(Optional) To summon new messages, swipe down the left panel that lists your accounts or mailboxes and immediately release.**

   If you see a spinning gear, the iPad is searching for new mail.

3. **Swipe down one of the inboxes or accounts to refresh that specific mailbox. To summon the unified inbox, tap All Inboxes instead.**

   If a blue dot appears next to a message, the message hasn't been read.

4. **Tap a message to read it.**

5. **When you've finished reading, tap the Mailboxes button in the upper-left corner of the message.**

   The button carries a different name, depending on which account you have open. For example, it may say Exchange, Inbox, or something else.

6. **Read additional messages.**

   When a message is on-screen, the buttons for managing incoming messages appear at the top, most of which you're already familiar with.

   - *In portrait mode:* Tap the up/down arrow that corresponds to the next or previous message, respectively. (Refer to Figure 5-7.)

   - *In landscape mode (and from within an account):* Tap a preview listing to the left of a message to read the next or previous message or any other visible message on the list. Scroll up or down to find other messages you may want to read.

Threading messages

Apple lets you *thread* messages, or have Mail automatically group related missives. The beauty of this arrangement is that you can easily trace an email conversation. When you organize messages by thread, the related messages appear as a single entry in the mailbox, with a double right-pointing arrow cluing you in that the message is indeed part of a larger ongoing exchange. If a message is not part of a thread, you just see the time, day, or date that that single message arrived. Figure 5-8 (left) shows that Bob and Melisa are hanging together by a thread — tapping the listing reveals underlying messages that make up the conversation. When you tap the message preview, you see previews of those underlying messages, as shown in Figure 5-8 (right).

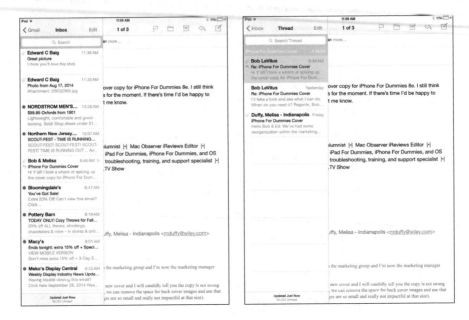

Figure 5-8: Your emails are hanging together by a thread.

When you look at a message that's part of a thread, the numbers at the top of the screen (visible in portrait mode) tell you the message's location in the conversation. For example, in Figure 5-8 (right), the message we chose to read is number 1 of 3 in this thread.

To turn on threading, go to the Home screen and tap Settings ➪ Mail, Contacts, Calendars, and then tap on Organize by Thread so that green is visible, as shown in Figure 5-9. You may have to scroll down to see the Organize by Thread setting.

Figure 5-9: Organize by Thread keeps related messages together.

 TIP You can search for an item in the thread by scrolling to the top of the thread's Mail listing and typing your query in the search thread box. Consider this a prelude to an upcoming section on searching email messages.

Managing messages

Managing messages typically involves either moving the messages to a folder or deleting them. To herd your messages into folders, you have the following options:

- ✒ **To create a folder to organize messages you want to keep:** Tap an account under the Accounts listings on the left side of the screen, and tap Edit. Tap New Mailbox, and type a name for the mailbox and location for it.

- ✒ **To file a message in another folder:** Tap the move message icon (labeled in Figure 5-6). When the list of mailboxes appears, tap the folder where you want to file the message. Watching the message fly and land in the designated new folder is cool.

- ✒ **To read a message that you've filed:** Tap the folder where the message now resides and then tap the header or preview for the message in question.

- ✒ **To delete, move, or mark multiple messages:** Tap Edit. In both portrait and landscape, Edit appears at the top of your inbox or another mailbox when those mail folders are selected. Tap Edit, and it becomes a Cancel button, and Mark All, Move All, and Trash All buttons appear at the bottom of the list. Tap each message you want to select so that a check mark appears at that point; Mark All becomes Mark, Move All becomes Move, and Trash All becomes Trash, as shown in Figure 5-10.

  - *Tap Trash* to delete all selected messages.

  - *Tap Move* to move all selected messages to another folder in the same or another Mail account, and then tap the new folder or mailbox (or both) in which you want those messages to hang out.

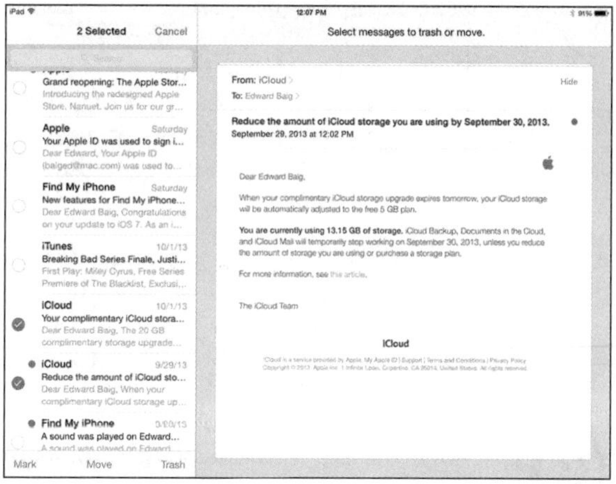

Figure 5-10: Wiping out, moving, or marking messages, en masse.

  - *Tap Mark* to mark all selected messages as Read (and Unread) and Flagged (and Unflagged).

- ✒ **To delete a single message:** Tap the delete message (trash can) icon. In case you tap the delete message icon by mistake, you have a chance to cancel, provided the Ask Before Deleting switch is turned on in Settings.

✔ **To delete a single message without opening it:** Swipe one finger to the left across the message in the mailbox list, and then tap the red Delete button that appears to the right of the message. (In some accounts, such as Gmail, you might see an Archive button instead.) You'll also see a Flag option and a More button. Tapping More gives you, well, more options: reply, forward, or flag the message (yes, flag is still an option here); mark it as unread, move it to junk or elsewhere, or have the iPad send a notification when someone replies to the message or thread.

In certain Mail accounts, Gmail being one, the Trash option may be replaced by an Archive option, depending on your preference. That means you're not getting rid of a message but stashing it, or to be precise, saving the message in your All Mail folder. If the Archive message option does present itself, you can turn the feature on or off in Settings.

Searching emails

With Spotlight search, you can quickly and easily search through a bunch of messages to find the one you want to read — such as that can't-miss stock tip from your broker. In the search box at the top of a mailbox preview pane, type *stock* or whichever search term seems relevant. All matching emails that have already been downloaded appear. And you can run a search to find words within the body of an email message from the Mail app. (For more on search, see Chapter 2.)

Search within Mail is quite powerful. For example, you can search by time frame by typing something along the lines of *March meetings.* Those search terms will find all the appropriate messages having to do with meetings that month. You can also search to find just flagged messages from your VIPs *(flag unread VIP).*

Via the iPad, you can also search just the current mailbox or across all your mailboxes. Just scroll to the top of the mailbox previews pane and tap either the All Inboxes tab or the tab for a given mailbox account. Then enter your search query in the box at the top of the preview pane.

Siri can also find emails on your behalf. For example, you can ask the iPad's voice assistant to find all the emails from a particular person in a particular month.

If you're using Exchange, iCloud, or certain IMAP-type email accounts, you may even be able to search messages stored on the server.

Keeping files in order

In simple terms, computers of any type, including tablets like the iPad — and the software that runs on them — must have some way to recognize the files that run on the system and to act appropriately upon them. Long ago, the bright minds in technology cooked up standard ways to organize the layout of data so files that serve a particular purpose adhere to a similar structure. You recognize such files by the *filename extension*, the suffix that is separated by a dot, or period, after its name. Many more file formats exist than most folks will ever need to become familiar with. But you — or, more precisely, the hardware and software you're working with — will encounter some popular file types repeatedly. Such formats include .doc for Microsoft Word documents and .jpg for images. If any computer you're using encounters files that don't seem to open or respond, it's likely because the machine doesn't have the software to recognize such files. The good news is that the iPad supports most common file types it encounters.

Don't grow too attached to attachments

Your iPad can even receive email messages with attachments in a wide variety of popular file formats. (See the nearby sidebar "Keeping files in order" if you're not sure what file formats are.) Which file formats does the iPad support? Glad you asked:

- **Images:** .jpg, .tiff, .gif, .png
- **Microsoft Word:** .doc, .docx
- **Microsoft PowerPoint:** .ppt, .pptx
- **Microsoft Excel:** .xls, .xlsx
- **Web pages:** .htm, .html
- **Apple Keynote:** .key
- **Apple Numbers:** .numbers
- **Apple Pages:** .pages
- **Preview and Adobe Acrobat:** .pdf
- **Rich Text:** .rtf
- **Text:** .txt
- **Contact information:** .vcf

If the attachment is a file format that the iPad doesn't support (for example, an Adobe Photoshop .psd file), you see the name of the file, but you can't open it on your iPad, at least without an assist from a third-party app that you may have installed.

Here's how to read a supported attachment:

1. **Open the email that contains the attachment, which you can identify by a little paper clip icon.**

2. **Tap the attachment.**

   The attachment typically appears at the bottom of the message, so you might need to scroll down to see it.

   In some cases, the attachment downloads to your iPad and opens automatically. In other instances, you may have to tap the button representing the attachment to download it.

3. **Read or (in the case of a picture) eyeball the attachment.**

4. **Tap the attachment you're reading (in the case of a document), and tap Done to return to the message text.**

   Or you can (again, for a document) open the Pages word processor if you've purchased it or downloaded it free if you bought a device with iOS 7, iOS 8, or iOS 9. You can also open the doc in certain other apps you may have. Incidentally, the documents you create in the Pages app are automatically saved to your iPad. With the latest version of Pages, you can also save a document to iCloud, where it can be made available automatically to the version of Pages for Mac computers. If you have a Windows PC, you can work with an iCloud version of Pages.

You can open an attachment from a different app than the one summoned to duty. Just touch and hold down on the attachment in the email, and then tap the app from the options that present themselves. You may also be able to tap Quick Look to peek at the attachment. Or tap Markup and reply to add your comments to a document before whisking it back to the sender.

Later in this chapter, we show you a new way Apple cooked up in iOS 9 to help you send an attachment as part of an outgoing message.

More things you can do with messages

Wait! You can do even more with your incoming email messages:

- ✔ **To see all recipients of a message:** Tap More, which appears to the right of the recipients' names, assuming you cannot already see all the names of the people receiving the message. You might see a number next to More, indicating the number of other people in the recipient list.

If all recipients are displayed, you'll see Hide instead of More; tap Hide to hide all names except the sender's.

- **To add an email recipient or sender to your contacts:** Tap the name or email address at the top of the message and then tap Create New Contact, Add to Existing Contact, or Update Contact.

- **To make a sender a VIP:** Tap the name or email address at the top of the message and then tap Add to VIP. You may want to give VIP status to the important people in your life, such as your significant other, family members, boss, or doctor. A star appears next to any incoming messages from a VIP. You can summon mail from all your VIPs by tapping the VIP folder in the list of Mailboxes. To demote a VIP to an NVIP (not very important person), tap the name or email at the top of the message and then tap Remove from VIP.

- **To mark a message as unread, flag it, move it to junk, or arrange to receive a notification when someone replies:** Tap the flag icon at the top of a message. These options appear:

  - *Mark as Unread:* Choose Mark as Unread for messages that you may want to revisit at some point but which don't necessarily have special significance. The message is again included in the unread message count on the Mail icon on your Home screen, and its mailbox again has a blue dot next to it in the message list for that mailbox. You can tap Mark as Read if the message loses its significance. As an alternative, you can mark a message as unread by swiping from right to left in the preview pane.

  - *Flag:* Choose Flag for those messages that deserve special status or that you want to find again in a hurry.

  - *Move to Junk:* We all get crap email. This option moves those messages to your junk pile.

  - *Notify Me:* Tap to receive notifications whenever anyone replies to this email thread.

- **To zoom in on and out of a message:** Use the pinch and unpinch gestures, at which we suspect you now excel. See Chapter 2 if you need help with your touchscreen moves.

- **To follow a link in a message:** Tap the link. Links are typically displayed in blue, but they sometimes appear in other colors, or underlined, or both. If the link is a URL, Safari opens and displays the web page. If the link is a phone number, the iPad gives you the chance to add it to your contacts, copy it, call it using FaceTime Audio or your iPhone (through a Handoff feature added with iOS 8), or send a message. If the link is an address, the Maps app opens and displays the location. If you tap a date, you can create an event on that date or show it in Calendar. And, last but not least, if the link is an email address, a new preaddressed blank email message is created.

✔ If the link opens Safari, Contacts, or Maps and you want to return to your email, press the Home button on the front of your iPad and then tap the Mail icon. Or double-press the Home button and select the Mail icon from the gallery of running apps.

Darling, You Send Me (Email)

Sending email on your iPad is a breeze. You'll encounter several subspecies of messages: pure text, text with a photo, a partially finished message (a *draft*) that you want to save and complete later, or a reply to an incoming message. You can also forward an incoming message to someone else — and in some instances print messages. The following sections examine these message types one at a time.

Sending an all-text message

To compose a new email message, tap Mail on the Home screen. As before, what you see next depends on how you're holding your iPad. In landscape mode, your email accounts or email folders are listed in a panel along the left side of the screen, with the actual message filling the larger window on the right.

Now, to create a message, follow these steps:

1. **Tap the compose new message icon (labeled in Figure 5-6).**

   The New Message screen appears, like the one shown in Figure 5-11.

2. **Type the names or email addresses of the recipients in the To field, or tap the + symbol to the right of the To field to choose a contact(s) from your iPad's contacts list.**

   If you start typing an email address, email addresses that match what you typed appear in a list below the To or Cc field. If the correct one is in the list, tap it to use it.

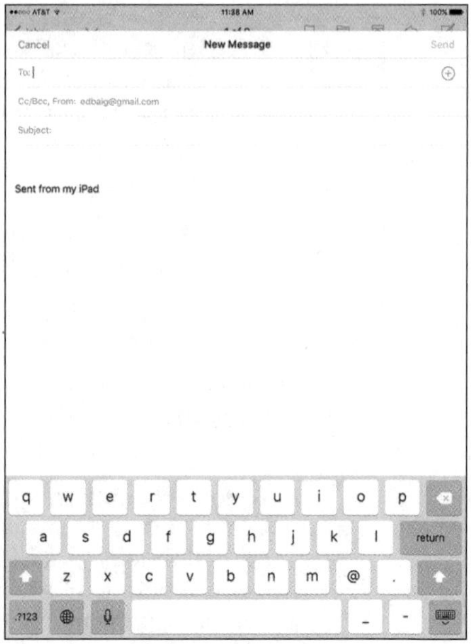

Figure 5-11: The New Message screen appears, ready for you to start typing the recipient's name.

As part of the more intelligent and proactive iOS 9 operating system, your iPad may suggest people that you typically include when starting to address a message.

3. **(Optional) Tap the field labeled Cc/Bcc, From.**

Doing so breaks the field into separate Cc, Bcc, and From fields (refer to Figure 5-11).

The Cc/Bcc label stands for *carbon copy/blind carbon copy. Carbon copy* (a throwback term from another era) is kind of an FYI to a recipient. It's like saying, "We figure you'd appreciate knowing this, but you don't need to respond."

When using Bcc, you can include a recipient on the message, but other recipients can't see that this recipient has been included. Bcc is great for those secret agent emails! Tap the respective Cc or Bcc field to type names. Or tap the + symbol that appears in those fields to add a contact.

4. **(Optional) If you tap From, you can choose to send the message from any of your email accounts on the fly — assuming that you have more than one account set up on the iPad.**

5. **In the subject field, type a subject.**

The subject is optional, but it's considered poor form to send an email message without one.

6. **In the message area, type your message.**

The message area is immediately below the Subject field. You have ample space to get your message across.

With iOS 8 or iOS 9, you can go with an optional third-party keyboard.

7. **Tap the Send button in the upper-right corner of the screen.**

Your message wings its way to its recipients almost immediately. If you aren't in range of a Wi-Fi network or a cellular network when you tap Send, the message is sent the next time you're in range of one of these networks.

Formatting text in an email

One of the goodies in Mail is the capability to format email text by underlining, bolding, or italicizing it. First you select the text by pressing your finger against the screen until you see the options to select some or all of the text. After making your selection, you'll have various other options: Cut, Copy, Paste, BIU, Replace, Define, Share, Quote Level, Insert Photo or Video, or Add Attachment. To format text, tap the BIU button. Then apply whichever style (bold, italics, underline) suits your fancy.

If you tap Quote Level — another option that appears when you tap the right-pointing arrow after selecting a word — you can quote a portion of a message you're responding to. ***Note:*** Increase Quote Level must be turned on in Settings. You can also increase or decrease the indentation in your outgoing message.

If you tap Replace, you are provided with alternative word choices to the word that you selected. Tap one of the alternative options to select it.

If you tap Define, you can summon a definition from the *New Oxford Dictionary* or another available dictionary.

Sending a photo with an email message

Sometimes a picture is worth a thousand words. When that's the case, here's how to send an email message with a photo attached:

1. **Tap the Photos icon on the Home screen.**

2. **Find the photo you want to send.**

3. **Tap the share icon in the bottom-left corner of the screen (and shown in the margin).**

4. **Tap the Mail button.**

   An email message appears on-screen with the photo already attached. The image may appear to be embedded in the body of the message, but the recipient receives it as a regular email attachment.

   On the Cc/Bcc line of your outgoing message, you see the size of the attached image. If you tap the size of the image shown, a new line appears, giving you the option to choose an alternative size among Small, Medium, Large, or Actual Size (in other words, keeping what you have). Your choice affects both the visible dimensions and file size of the photo (with the actual size of the file as measured in kilobytes or megabytes reported for each possible choice).

5. **Choose what size photo you want to send.**

6. **Address the message and type whatever text you like, as you did for an all-text message previously, and then tap the Send button.**

You have an alternative way of inserting pictures (or videos) into your outgoing mail messages. In the preceding "Formatting text in an email" section, we mention an Insert Photo or Video option that appears after you press your finger against the body of a message that you're composing. Tap Insert Photo or Video, tap the album in which the photo (or video) you want to send exists, and then tap that photo or video. Tap Use to embed the image and proceed with composing.

Adding attachments

You've seen how you can attach photos and videos to your outgoing messages. In iOS 9, Apple supplies a new way to add an attachment. Press your finger against the body of the message in the same way you just did to format text. Tap the arrow to the right of Quote Level and tap the new Add Attachment option. You're immediately ushered to an iCloud Drive screen, where you can choose the attachment you would like to add from the likes of the Pages app, Keynote, Preview, QuickTime Player, and TextEdit. Tap the file to add it to the body of your soon-to-be sent email.

You can also select among other options, depending on the apps you have installed on your iPad.

Marking up attachments

If you're attaching a photo or a PDF document, you can take advantage of the Markup feature added with iOS 9. With the picture attachment or PDF embedded in your outgoing message, tap and hold down or double-tap the attachment, and from the share menu that appears, tap Markup.

You can summon the Markup feature also when you receive a PDF or picture attachment. Tap on the attachment and then tap the briefcase icon, which appears in the lower-right corner.

Now that you're in markup mode, you can draw on that image or PDF, tapping the simple annotation tools just below. The tools are represented by icons: one for a pen tool (unless you use an optional stylus, your finger will be that pen), one for a magnification loupe so that you can zoom in on the document or pic, one for writing text (you can summon the keyboard), and one for drawing your signature, which we get to in a moment.

If you draw a shape such as an arrow and the iPad recognizes that that was the shape you had in mind, it will give you the option to draw it for you. You can leave your own imperfect arrow (or other symbol) if you prefer to use that one instead of Apple's. One piece of advice on that arrow business that we discovered: Draw with a single stroke and do not lift your finger.

Within Markup, you have the option to change the color and thickness of the lines and symbols that you draw.

Lastly, you can write your signature in script, a potential boon for lawyers or folks needing to get a John Hancock on a contract or lease. Just choose the fourth icon at the bottom of the Markup screen and tap Add or Remove Signature. Then tap the + and sign your name with your finger.

Saving an email to send later

Sometimes you start an email message but don't have time to finish it. When that happens, you can save it as a draft and finish it some other time. Here's how:

1. **Start an email message, as described in one of the previous sections.**

2. **When you're ready to save the message as a draft, tap the Cancel button in the upper-left corner of the screen.**

3. **Tap the Save Draft button if you want to save this message as a draft and complete it another time.**

   If you tap the Delete Draft button, the message disappears immediately without a second chance. Don't tap Delete Draft unless you mean it.

To work on the message again, tap the Drafts mailbox. A list of all messages you saved as drafts appears. Tap the draft you want to work on, and it reappears on the screen. When you're finished, you can tap Send to send it or tap Cancel to save it as a draft again.

The number of drafts appears to the right of the Drafts folder, the same way that the number of unread messages appears to the right of other mail folders, such as your inbox.

Replying to, forwarding, or printing an email message

When you receive a message and want to reply to it, open the message and then tap the reply icon (the curved arrow at the upper-right corner of the screen, as shown in Figure 5-12). Then tap Reply, Reply All, Forward, or Print, as described next:

- ✔ **Reply and Reply All:** The Reply button creates an email message addressed to the sender of the original message, with the content of that original message embedded in your reply. The Reply All button creates an email message addressed to the sender and all other recipients of the original message, plus Ccs. (The Reply All option appears only if more than one recipient was on the original email.) In both cases, the subject is retained with a *Re:* prefix added. So if the original subject were *iPad Tips,* the reply's subject would be *Re: iPad Tips.*

Figure 5-12: Reading and managing an email message.

✓ **Forward:** Tapping the Forward button creates an unaddressed email message that contains the text of the original message. Add the email address(es) of the person or people you want to forward the message to, and then tap Send. In this case, rather than a *Re:* prefix, the subject is preceded by *Fwd:*. So this time, the subject would be *Fwd: iPad Tips.* If the email you're forwarding has an attachment, you'll be given the option to forward the attachment along with the message.

✓ **Print:** Tap Print if you want to print using an AirPrint-capable printer.

It's considered good form to leave the subject lines alone (with the *Re:* or *Fwd:* prefix intact), but you may want to change them sometimes. You can edit the subject line of a reply or a forwarded message or edit the body text of a forwarded message the same way you'd edit any other text. Worth noting: When the Re: is modified, a new email thread is created and the modified message won't be included in the old thread listing.

To send your reply or forwarded message, tap the Send button as usual.

Settings for sending email

You can customize the mail you send and receive in lots of ways. In this section, we explore settings for sending email. Later in this chapter, we show you settings that affect the way you receive and read messages. In each instance, start by tapping Settings on the Home screen.

You can customize your mail in the following ways:

✓ **To hear an alert when you successfully send a message:** From the main Settings screen, tap Sounds. Make sure that the Sent Mail setting is turned on. You'll know because you'll see a sound type listed (among alert sounds and ringtones), Swoosh by default. If you tap Sent Mail in Settings, you can select another sound besides Swoosh or choose None if going silent is your preference.

If you want to change other settings, tap the Sounds button at the top of the screen. If you're finished setting the settings, tap the Home button on the front of your iPad.

✓ No matter what setting you've just accessed, if you want to continue using Settings, tap whichever left-pointing button appears at the top of the right Settings pane — General, Mail, Contacts, or something else. After you return to the previous screen, you can change other settings. Similarly, you can tap the Home button on the front of your iPad when you're finished setting any setting. That action always saves the changes you just made and returns to the Home screen.

✔ **To add a signature line, phrase, or block of text to every email message you send:** Tap Settings ⇨ Mail, Contacts, Calendars, and then tap Signature in the right pane. The default signature is *Sent from my iPad.* You can add text before or after it, or delete it and type something else. Your signature is affixed to the end of all your outgoing email. You can choose a signature that is the same across all your accounts or select different signatures for each account.

✔ **To have your iPad send you a copy of every message you send:** Tap Settings ⇨ Mail, Contacts, Calendars and then turn on the Always Bcc Myself setting. This step isn't always necessary because your Sent folder typically captures all such messages.

✔ **To set the default email account for initiating email from outside the Mail application:** Tap the Settings icon on the Home screen and then tap Mail, Contacts, Calendars ⇨ Default Account. Tap the account you want to use as the default. This designated email account is the one that's used when you want to email a picture directly from the Photos app, for example. Note that this setting applies only if you have more than one email account on your iPad. Also, if you choose one default account, you can dispatch mail from another account at send time.

Setting Your Message and Account Settings

This final discussion of Mail involves more settings that deal with your various email accounts.

Checking and viewing email settings

Several settings affect the way you can check and view email. You might want to modify one or more, so we describe what they do and where to find them:

✔ **To specify how often the iPad checks for new messages:** Tap the Settings icon on the Home screen; tap Mail, Contacts, Calendars ⇨ Fetch New Data. You're entering the world of *fetching* or *pushing.* Check out Figure 5-13 to glance at your options. If your email program (or, more precisely, the email server behind it) supports push and the Push setting is enabled on your iPad, fresh messages are sent to your iPad automatically as soon as they hit the server. If you turned off push or your email program doesn't support it, the iPad fetches data instead. Choices for fetching are Every 15 Minutes, Every 30 Minutes, Hourly, and Manually. Tap the one you prefer. With push email, messages can show up on the lock screen and in Notification Center. This setting might be relevant for those using the iPad with a cellular connection but is less so if you rely on Wi-Fi.

✔ **To hear an alert sound when you receive a new message:** Tap Sounds on the main Settings screen and then tap the New Mail setting. The Ding sound is there by default. Do nothing if you're satisfied with the Ding you hear each time a new message arrives. If you aren't satisfied, tap New Mail and select an alternative sound from the list, or tap None if you don't want to hear any such alert.

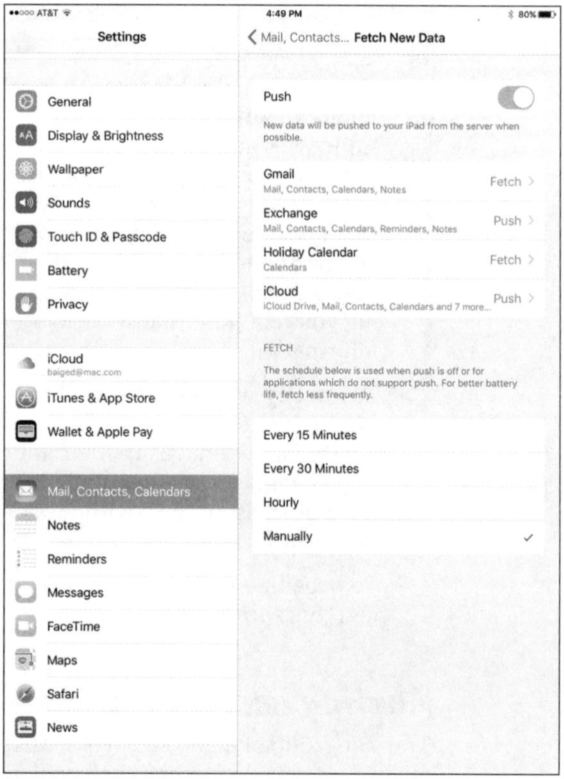

✔ **To set the number of lines of each message to be displayed in the message list:** From the main Settings screen, tap Mail, Contacts, Calendars ⇨ Preview;

Figure 5-13: Fetch or push? It's your call.

then choose a number. Your choices are None, 1, 2, 3, 4, and 5 lines of text. The more lines of text you display in the list, the fewer messages you can see at a time without scrolling. Think before you choose 4 or 5.

✔ **To specify whether the iPad shows the To and Cc labels in message lists:** From the main Settings screen, tap Mail, Contacts, Calendars and turn on or off the Show To/Cc Label setting.

✔ **To turn on or off the Ask before Deleting warning:** From the main Settings screen, tap Mail, Contacts, Calendars; then turn on or off the Ask before Deleting setting. If this setting is turned on, you need to tap the trash icon at the bottom of the screen and then tap the red Delete button to confirm the deletion. When the setting is turned off, tapping the trash icon deletes the message, and you never see a red Delete button.

✔ **To change swipe options:** From the main Settings screen, tap Mail, Contacts, Calendars and then tap Swipe Options. You can choose whether swiping left (on the preview pane) flags messages and whether swiping right marks messages as unread.

- **To change the flag style from a color to a shape:** Tap Settings ⇨ Flag Style and make your determination.

- **To mark email addresses that originate or are received from a designated mail server:** Tap Settings ⇨ Mail, Contacts, Calendar ⇨ Mark Addresses and flip the switch on. Enter the email address from your company (or wherever) that you do *not* want marked. From then on, when you're composing a message, all email addresses sent to or from that specified address will appear in blue, while all other mail addresses will be shaded red. Why do this? The idea is that you can more easily identify mail dispatched to addresses outside your organization, alerting you to a potential security risk if you're exchanging, say, sensitive information.

- **To specify whether the iPad will automatically display images that are embedded in an email:** Tap Mail, Contacts, Calendars and then tap Load Remote Images in the right pane so that the switch is green (on). If it's off, you can still manually load remote images. Certain security risks have been associated with loading remote images, and they can also hog bandwidth.

- **To organize your mail by thread:** Tap Organize by Thread so that the setting is on.

Altering account settings

The last group of email settings we explore in this chapter deals with your email accounts. You most likely will never need most of these settings, but we'd be remiss if we didn't at least mention them briefly. So here they are, whether you need 'em or not:

- **To stop using an email account:** Tap the Settings icon on the Home screen; tap Mail, Contacts, Calendars ⇨ *Account Name* and flip the switch so that Mail is turned off. As a reminder, when Mail is on, you see green by the Mail switch. Otherwise, the switch is gray.

This setting doesn't delete the account; it only hides it from view and stops it from sending or checking email until you turn it on again. (You can repeat this step to turn off calendars, contacts, reminders, and notes in a given account.)

- **To delete an email account:** Tap the Settings icon on the Home screen; tap Mail, Contacts, Calendars ⇨ *Account Name* ⇨ Delete Account ⇨ Delete. Tap Cancel if you change your mind and don't want your account blown away, or tap Delete to proceed.

Deleting an email account will also remove calendar entries, contact names, and notes from the given account.

You can find still more advanced Mail settings, reached the same way: Tap the Settings icon on the Home screen; tap Mail, Contacts, Calendars; and then tap the name of the account with which you want to work.

The settings you see under Advanced (sometimes shown as Advanced Settings under a specific email account) and how they appear vary by account. This list describes some of the settings you might see:

- **To specify how long until deleted messages are removed permanently from your iPad:** Tap Advanced ⇨ Mail ⇨ Advanced ⇨ Remove. In iCloud Mail, your choices are Never, After One Day, After One Week, and After One Month. Tap the choice you prefer. Other mail accounts may give you different time frame options or not present this setting at all.

- **To choose whether drafts, sent messages, archived, and deleted messages are stored on your iPad or on your mail server:** Tap Advanced and then choose the setting under Mailbox Behaviors Stored on My iPad or Stored on the Server. You can decide for drafts, sent messages, and trash. If you choose to store any or all of them on the server, you can't see them unless you have an Internet connection (Wi-Fi or cellular). If you choose to store them on your iPad, they're always available, even if you don't have Internet access. Under Mailbox Behaviors, in certain circumstances, you also get to determine whether to delete or archive discarded messages.

We strongly recommend that you don't change the next two items unless you know exactly what you're doing and why. If you're having problems with sending or receiving mail, start by contacting your ISP (Internet service provider), email provider, or corporate IT person or tech department. Then change these settings only if they tell you to. Again, these settings and exactly where and how they appear vary by account.

- **To reconfigure mail server settings:** In the Incoming Mail Server or Outgoing Mail Server section of the account settings screen, tap Host Name, User Name, or Password and make your changes.

- **To adjust Use SSL, Authentication, IMAP Path Settings, or Server Port:** Tap Advanced and then tap the appropriate item and make the necessary changes.

And that, as they say in baseball, retires the side. You're now fully qualified to set up email accounts and send and receive email on your iPad. But, as the late Apple cofounder Steve Jobs was wont to say, there is one more thing . . .

Getting the iMessage

The Messages app lets you exchange iMessages, pictures, contacts, videos, audio recordings, and locations with anyone using an Apple iDevice with iOS 5 or higher or with a Mac running OS X Mountain Lion, OS X Mavericks, OS X

Yosemite, or OS X El Capitan. In the following sections, find out how each of the iMessages features works.

Sending iMessages

To start a new message, tap the Messages icon on the Home screen to launch the Messages app and then tap the compose new message icon, the little pencil-and-paper icon in the left pane of the screen (on the Messages list).

At this point, with the To field active and awaiting your input, you can do three things:

- ✔ **If the recipient *is* in your contacts list, type the first few letters of the name.** A list of matching contacts appears. Scroll through it if necessary and tap the name of the contact.

  The more letters you type, the shorter the list becomes. And after you've tapped the name of a contact, you can begin typing another name so that you can send this message to multiple recipients at once.

- ✔ **Tap the blue circled + icon on the right side of the To field to select a name from your contacts list.**

- ✔ **If the recipient *isn't* in your contacts list, type his or her phone number or email address.**

You have a fourth option if you want to compose the message first and address it later. Tap inside the text-entry field (the narrow rectangular area just above the keyboard and to the left of the Send button or microphone icon) to activate the field and then type or dictate your message. When you've finished typing, tap the To field and use one of the preceding techniques to address your message.

You aren't limited to sending an iMessage to a single person. To initiate a group message, type the names or phones numbers of everyone you want to include in the To field.

When you've finished addressing and composing, tap the Send button to send your message on its merry way. And that's all there is to it.

Group messages

The Messages app on your iPad is all-inclusive — that is, an iMessage need not be one to one. Instead, a group of folks can communicate. Start by preparing a message with a single recipient, and then tap the circled + in the To field to add people to the conversation from your contacts or manually.

Adding voice to an iMessage

With iOS 8 or iOS 9, you can record an audio message and send it along to a recipient. Apple calls this Tap to Talk and here's how to take advantage of it. Press and hold down the microphone icon to the right of the text-entry field (not the microphone icon on the iPad keyboard) and start speaking. Your voice appears as a waveform at the bottom of the screen, as shown in Figure 5-14. When you've finished speaking, keep your finger pressed down and swipe up to send the message. You can listen to the audio before sending it by tapping the play icon, which appears after you release the button you held down to record. If you're not thrilled with what you've just recorded, swipe left instead to cancel.

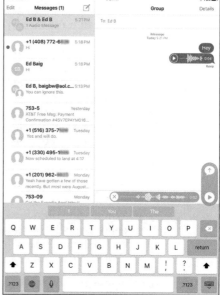

Figure 5-14: Lending your voice to an iMessage.

The recipient of your recorded iMessage will be able to tap a Play button to listen to what you had to say. But in some cases, he or she had best listen right away because you can set things (in Settings) so that audio messages expire after two minutes. Your only other option is for the message to never expire.

Keep in mind that the microphone icon that lets you record your voice will be enabled only if you're sending an iMessage to a chat partner.

Being a golden receiver: Receiving iMessages

When determining your settings for receiving iMessages, first things first. Decide whether you want to hear an alert when you receive a message:

✔ **If you want to hear an alert sound when you receive a message:** Tap the Settings icon on your Home screen, tap Sounds ⇨ Text Tone, and then tap an available sound. You can audition the sounds by tapping them. If you have a Mac, you can create your own text tones in GarageBand.

You hear the sounds when you audition them in the Settings app, even if the ring/silent switch is set to Silent. After you exit the Settings app, however, you *won't* hear a sound when a message arrives if the ring/silent switch is set to Silent.

✓ **If you *don't* want to hear an alert when a message arrives:** Instead of tapping one of the listed sounds, tap None, which is the first item in the list of alert tones.

✓ **If you don't want any messages:** Turn off iMessages. If you won't want iMessages (or other interruptions) for a designated period, consider the Do Not Disturb feature. It lives up to its name. Turn on the feature in Settings, and you'll see a moon icon in the status bar. Even easier, turn on Do Not Disturb in Control Center, and you won't be inundated with messages. You can also tap Details in a given message thread to summon and turn on Do Not Disturb, which mutes notifications for this particular conversation. For more about the Do Not Disturb feature and other settings, head to Chapter 15.

The following pointers explain what you can do with iMessages that you receive:

✓ **When your iPad is asleep:** All or part of the text and the name of the sender appear on the unlock screen. Slide to the right to reply to a specific message (you'll have to get past any passcodes first).

✓ **When your iPad is awake and unlocked:** All or part of the message and the name of the sender appear at the top of the screen in front of whatever's already there. If what's already there is your Home screen, as shown in Figure 5-15, the Messages icon displays the number of unread messages.

These notifications are on by default; turn them off in the Settings app's Notifications pane if you don't care for them. You'll also see any notifications for messages you've received in Notification Center.

✓ **Reading or replying to a message:** Tap the Messages icon on your Home screen, swipe

Figure 5-15: This is what a notification looks like when your iPad is awake.

downward from the top of the screen to display Notification Center, or tap the notification if you can be quick about it (the notification fades away in a few seconds).

✔ **Following the conversation:** Each conversation you have is saved as a series of text bubbles. Your messages appear on the right side of the screen in blue bubbles; the other person's messages appear in gray ones. When your message has been delivered, that fact will be noted just below the last bubble in your exchange, as shown in Figure 5-16. If there was a problem delivering the message, you'll see Not Delivered instead. If at first you don't succeed, try again.

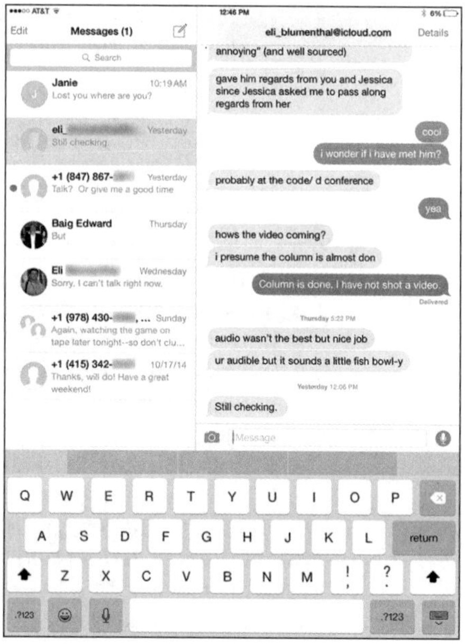

✔ **Forwarding a conversation:** If you want to forward all or part of a conversation to another iMessage user, press against a text bubble and tap the More button. Tap additional text, photo, or video bubbles that you want to forward (the one you pressed to summon the More button is already selected) so that a check mark appears in a circle to the left of each. Then tap the forward (curved arrow) icon at the lower right of the screen. The contents of the selected text bubbles are copied to a new text message; specify a recipient and then tap Send.

✔ **Deleting part of a single conversation thread:** Press against a text bubble and tap More. Tap each text bubble that you want to delete; a check mark appears in the circle next to each one. Then tap the delete (trash can) icon at the bottom of the pane, and tap Delete Message(s). Or, to delete the entire conversation in one fell swoop, tap the Delete All button at the top of the screen and then tap Delete Conversation.

Figure 5-16: This is what an iMessage conversation looks like.

✔ **Deleting an entire conversation thread:** Tap the Edit button at the upper left of the Messages list, tap the circle that appears to the left of the person's name, and then tap the Delete button at the bottom of the pane. Or swipe from right to left on the message in the Messages pane and then tap the red Delete button.

Sending pix and vids in a message

To send a picture or video in a message, follow the instructions for sending a text message and then tap the camera icon to the left of the text-entry field at the bottom of the screen. You'll then have the option of using an existing picture or video or taking a new one. You can also add text to photos or videos. When you're finished, tap the Send button.

But just as you can send an audio message by using the Tap to Talk feature, you can record and send a video message through a similar shortcut. (And as with audio messages, go to Settings to make a video message go away after two minutes or to arrange so it doesn't automatically expire.) To record a video message in this manner, press and hold down on the camera icon to the left of the text-entry box, and then tap the red video button that appears instead of the white photo button. Tap the button again after you have finished recording. If you'd rather take a still image, tap the photo button instead. Tap the circled x if you change your mind and don't want to take a still image or capture video.

If you *receive* a picture or video in a message, it appears in a bubble just like text. Tap the play icon to play it right in Messages. Tap again to have the video take over the full screen.

In full-screen mode, tap the share icon in the upper-right corner of a received video or picture for additional options, such as sharing the image on Facebook or Twitter, assigning it to a contact, or more. If you don't see the icon, tap the picture or video once, and the icon will magically appear.

Smart messaging tricks

Here are some more things you can do with messages:

✔ **Search your messages for a word or phrase.** Type the word or phrase in the search field at the top of the Messages screen.

✔ **Send Read Receipts to allow others to be notified when you have read their missives.** Tap Settings ➪ Messages, and slide the switch so that Send Read Receipts is on.

In iMessages, you can see when your own message has been delivered and read, and when the other person is readying a response.

✔ **Use a Bluetooth keyboard for typing instead of the on-screen keyboard.** Follow the instructions in Chapter 15 to pair your Bluetooth keyboard with your iPad.

The Apple Wireless Keyboard ($69) works with the iPad and the iPhone. Find out more in Chapter 17.

✔ **Dictate a message (third-generation iPads or later).** Tap the microphone key on your keyboard and start talking. Tap the microphone key again when you're done. This method isn't as quick or as much fun as Tap to Talk, but it works.

✔ **Open a URL included in an iMessage.** Tap the URL to open that web page in Safari.

✔ **Send an email to an address included in an iMessage.** Tap the email address in a message to open a preaddressed email message in Mail.

✔ **See an address included in an iMessage.** Tap the address to see it on a map in Maps.

✔ **Choose how you can be reached via iMessage.** Tap Settings ➪ Messages ➪ Send & Receive. Then add another email address or remove any existing addresses. You can also select the email address (or phone number) from which to start new conversations.

✔ **Show the Subject field.** Flip the switch to show a Subject field with your messages.

✔ **Filter Unknown Senders.** Flip this switch to turn off notifications for iMessages from folks who are not among your contacts. You can sort such unknown senders into a separate list.

✔ **Block a sender.** Block someone who is harassing you or has left your good graces. Tap Settings ➪ Messages ➪ Blocked and select a name from your contacts. You will no longer receive messages or FaceTime calls from this person.

✔ **Share your location.** Meeting a recipient in an unfamiliar place? In the middle of your conversation, you can share your location on a map. Tap the Details button at the upper-right corner and then tap either Send My Current Location or Share My Location. Choosing the latter gives you the option to share your whereabouts indefinitely, until the end of the day or for one hour. In Details, you can monitor how much time is left before your location will no longer be shared.

✔ **See all the message attachments at once.** Tap Details and you can browse in one place all the photos and videos from your conversation.

✔ **Keep Messages history.** You can keep your entire Messages history on the iPad permanently, for one year, or for 30 days. Tap Settings ➪ Messages ➪ Keep Messages and make your choice.

And that's all there is to it. You are now an official iMessage maven.

6

Maps Are Where It's At

In This Chapter

▶ Finding out where you're at

▶ Searching

▶ Navigating around by viewing, zooming, and panning

▶ Bookmarking favorites

▶ Getting to where you want to go fast: routes and real-time traffic

*W*ith Maps on the iPad, you can quickly and easily discover exactly where you are, find nearby restaurants and businesses, get turn-by-turn driving instructions from any address to any other address, and see real-time traffic information and a photographic street view of many locations as well.

Apple says Maps is "beautifully designed from the ground up (and the sky down)," and we have to agree. But beyond its good looks, zooming in and out is faster than ever, and the spoken turn-by-turn navigation with real-time traffic updates actually works in most places. Plus it has a cool 3D flyover view.

Maps in iOS 9 now offers directions for public transit in several U.S. and Chinese cities, with more cities promised soon. The free Google Maps app (available in the iTunes App Store), on the other hand, has directions for using public transportation in far more cities than Apple Maps, at least for now. We keep both apps on our iPhones and iPads; you might want to do so as well.

You can't use the Maps app unless you're connected to the Internet via Wi-Fi, 3G, or 4G. See Chapter 2 to find out how to connect.

Finding Your Current Location with Maps

We start with something supremely simple yet extremely useful — determining your current location. At the risk of sounding like self-help gurus, here's how to find yourself:

1. **Tap the Maps icon on your Home screen.**

2. **Tap the Location Services icon in the lower-left corner of the screen.**

If you haven't used Maps previously, an alert will ask if you want to allow Maps to access your location while you use the app. You do, so tap Allow. (Tapping the other option, Don't Allow, renders Maps all but useless.)

The icon's background turns blue, as shown in the margin, which assures you that Location Services

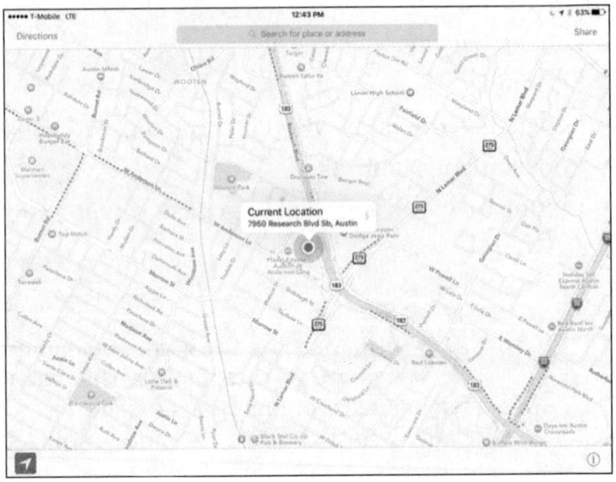

Figure 6-1: A blue marker shows your GPS location.

is doing its thing. You'll soon see a blue circle on the map (see Figure 6-1), which indicates your approximate location.

If you tap, drag the map, or zoom in or out, your iPad continues to update your location, but it doesn't continue to center the marker. When you tap the Location Services icon, it turns dark blue (refer to Figure 6-1) to indicate that your current location is in the middle of the screen. If you tap, drag, rotate, or zoom the map (that is, do anything that moves the current location indicator from the center of the screen), the icon turns white with a blue outline. So, if the icon is all blue, your current location is currently in the middle of the screen; if the icon is white with a blue outline, your current location is anywhere except the middle of the screen.

Unless, that is, you're using the satellite view, in which case you'll see gray instead of blue. You find out more about these views shortly.

How does Maps do that?

Maps uses iPad's Location Services to determine your approximate location using available information from your wireless data network. Wi-Fi–only models use local Wi-Fi networks; iPad Wi-Fi + 3G and 4G models use assisted GPS plus cellular data. If you're not using Location Services, turning it off conserves the battery.

(To turn it off, tap Settings⇨General⇨Location Services.) Don't worry if Location Services is turned off when you tap the arrow icon — you're prompted to turn Location Services on. Keep in mind that it may not be available in all areas at all times.

Searching

The Maps app wouldn't be very useful if you couldn't use it to find things. In the following sections, we show you how to search for places you want to go and people you want to see — including people stored as contacts.

Finding a person, place, or thing

To find a person, place, or thing with Maps, follow these steps:

1. **Tap the search field at the top of the screen to make the keyboard appear, and then type what you're looking for.**

   You can search for addresses, zip codes, intersections, towns, landmarks, and businesses by category and by name, or in combinations such as *New York, NY 10022; pizza 60645;* or even *BBQ Lockhart TX.*

2. **If the letters you type match names in your contacts list, the matching contacts appear in a list below the search field; tap a name to see a map of that contact's location.**

   Maps is smart about it, too; it displays only the names of contacts that have a street address. See the section "Connecting maps and contacts," later in this chapter, for details.

3. **When you finish typing, tap Search.**

   After a few seconds, a map appears. If you searched for a single location, it's marked with a pushpin. If you searched for a category (*BBQ Lockhart TX,* for example), you see multiple pushpins, one for each matching location, as shown in Figure 6-2.

When you tap the search field, a handy drop-down list shows the search terms you've used recently. Tap any item in the list to search for it again.

Connecting maps and contacts

Maps and contacts go together like peanut butter and jelly. In this section, you discover two helpful tasks that illustrate maps and contacts at work.

To see a map of a contact's street address, follow these steps:

1. **Tap in the search field, tap Favorites, and then tap the Contacts tab at the bottom of the overlay.**

   A list of your contacts appears.

2. **Scroll through the list, or tap in the search field and begin typing the contact's name.**

   The list is updated as you type.

3. **Tap the contact's name whose address you want to see on the map.**

   A pin appears on the map at that contact's address.

If you find a location by typing an actual street address in the search field, you can add that location to one of your contacts or create a contact with a location you've found. To do either one, follow these steps:

1. **Tap the location's pushpin on the map.**

2. **Tap the little gray right arrow to the right of the location's name (labeled in Figure 6-2).**

   That contact's info overlay appears, as shown in Figure 6-3.

3. **Scroll to the bottom of the info overlay and tap Create New Contact or Add to Existing Contact, whichever is applicable.**

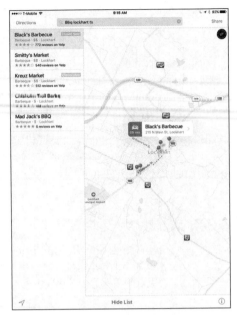

Figure 6-2: If you search for BBQ Lockhart TX, you see pushpins for all BBQ joints near Lockhart, Texas.

Figure 6-3: The info screen for Black's Barbecue appears as an overlay.

4. Fill in the new contact information and tap Done. Or select an existing contact from the list that appears.

You work with your contacts by tapping the Contacts icon on your Home screen. Go to Chapter 12 to find out more about the Contacts app.

Don't forget that you can swipe across your iPad screen with four or five fingers to switch apps. So if you're in Contacts, a four- or five-finger swipe from right to left should bring you back to the Maps app. If you have a lot of open apps, you might need more than one swipe to find the Maps app.

And don't forget that you can also use a four-finger swipe upward or double-press the Home button to reveal the multitasking screen and switch between Contacts and Maps (or any open apps, for that matter).

If nothing happens when you swipe with four or five fingers, tap Settings⇨ General, scroll down to the Multitasking Gestures On/Off switch, and make sure it's on.

You can also use the Slide Over or Split Screen feature with Maps, to see two apps at once on iPads that support those features.

You can also get driving or walking directions from most locations, including a contact's address, to any other location, including another contact's address. You see how to do that task in the "Smart Map Tricks" section, later in this chapter.

Viewing, Zooming, and Panning

The preceding section talks about how to find just about anything with Maps. Now here's a look at some ways that you can use what you find. First, you need to know how to work with what you see on the screen. Three views are available at any time: standard, transit, and satellite. Select a view by tapping the little *i*-in-a-circle in the lower-right corner of the screen; an overlay appears with the view buttons and several other options, as shown in Figure 6-4.

In standard, transit, or satellite view, you can zoom to see either more or less of the map — or scroll (pan) to see what's above, below, or to the left or right of the current screen, as follows:

  ✏ **Zoom out:** Pinch the map or tap using *two* fingers. To zoom out even more, pinch or tap using two fingers again.

Map	Transit	Satellite
	Hide Traffic	
	3D Map	
	Drop a Pin	
	Report an Issue	
	Data from TOMTOM others ›	

Figure 6-4: Tap the little *i*-in-a-circle to see these options.

The two-finger tap may be new to you. Simply tap with two fingers touching the screen simultaneously (rather than the usual one finger).

✓ **Zoom in:** Unpinch the map or double-tap (the usual way — with just one finger) the spot you want to zoom in on. Unpinch or double-tap with one finger again to zoom in even more. An *unpinch* (some people refer to this gesture as a *spread*) is the opposite of a pinch. Start with your thumb and a finger together and then spread them apart.

You can unpinch also with two hands (using two fingers or two thumbs), but you'll probably find that a single-handed pinch and unpinch are handier.

✓ **Scroll:** Flick or drag up, down, left, or right to pan your view of the map.

Tap the little *i*-in-a-circle in the lower-right corner and then tap Show 3D Map to see the map from a three-dimensional bird's-eye view.

Saving Time with Favorites, Recents, and Contacts

In Maps, three tools can save you from typing the same locations repeatedly: favorites, recents, and contacts. You access them on the overlay displayed when you tap in the search field at the top of the screen. The following sections give you the lowdown on these tools.

Favorites

Favorites in the Maps app work like bookmarks in Safari. When you have a location you want to save as a favorite so that you can reuse it later without typing a single character, follow these steps:

1. **Tap the right arrow to the right of the location's name or description.**

   The info overlay for that location appears. (Refer to Figure 6-3.)

2. **Tap the heart icon at the top-right of the overlay.**

   The heart icon, which is hollow until you tap it, will turn solid blue to indicate that this is a favorite (also shown in Figure 6-3).

After you add a favorite, you can recall it at any time. To do so, tap the search field as though you were going to search for a location, and then tap Favorites at the top of the overlay that appears. You can then tap the favorite's name to see it on the map.

The first things you should make favorites are your home and work addresses and their zip codes. You'll use these all the time with Maps, so you might as well add them to Favorites now to avoid typing them over and over.

Use zip code favorites to find nearby businesses. Choose the zip code favorite, and then type what you're looking for, such as *78729 pizza, 60645 gas station,* or *90201 Starbucks.*

To manage your favorites, tap the Edit button in the upper-left corner of the favorites overlay. Then:

- **To move a favorite up or down in the list:** Drag the little icon with three gray bars that appears to the right of the favorite. Drag upward to move the favorite higher in the list or downward to move the favorite lower in the list.

- **To delete a favorite from the Favorites list:** Tap the – sign in a red circle to the left of the favorite's name and then tap the red Delete button.

When you've finished using Favorites, tap Done in the upper-right corner of the overlay to return to the map.

By the way, you can drop a pushpin anywhere on a map even if you don't know an exact address or zip code. Think of a *pushpin* as a temporary favorite.

Dropping a pushpin is simple: Press the location where you want the pin to appear, and hold down for two or three seconds until the pin appears with either *Dropped Pin,* the street address, or both along with a little right arrow. Tap the right arrow to see the info overlay, or press and drag the pin to a new location.

To save a dropped pin as a favorite, either tap the heart icon at the top-right of the info overlay or tap the Share button at the top-right of the screen and then tap Add to Favorites.

The Share button also lets you share a location via AirDrop, Messages, Mail, FaceBook, and more.

Finally, to remove a dropped pin, tap the little right arrow and then tap Remove Pin.

Recents

The Maps app automatically remembers locations you've searched for and directions you've viewed in its recents list. To see this list, just tap in the search field, tap Favorites, and then tap the Recents tab at the bottom of the overlay.

To see a recent item on the map, tap the item's name.

To clear the recents list, first tap in the search field, then tap Favorites, and finally tap the Recents tab at the bottom of the overlay. Now tap the Clear button in the upper-left corner of the overlay, and then tap the big red Clear

All Recents button at the bottom of the overlay (or tap Cancel if you change your mind). Note that you can't clear an individual item — clearing the recents list is an all-or-nothing proposition.

When you're finished using the recents list, tap the Done button in the top-right corner of the overlay to return to the map.

Contacts

To see a list of your contacts, tap in the search field, tap Favorites, and then tap the Contacts button at the bottom of the overlay. A list of all your contacts appears. You can swipe to scroll up or down, and you can search for a contact by name by tapping in the search field and typing.

To see a map of a contact's location, tap the contact's name in the list.

To limit the contacts list to specific groups (assuming that you have some groups in your contacts list), tap the Groups button in the upper-left corner of the overlay and then tap the name of the group. Now only contacts in this group are displayed in the list.

When you've finished using the contacts list, tap the Done button in the upper-right corner of the overlay to return to the map.

Smart Map Tricks

The Maps app has more tricks up its sleeve. Here are a few nifty features that you may find useful.

Getting route maps and driving directions

You can get route maps and driving directions to any location from any location (within reason; a former tech editor tried to get driving directions from 1600 Pennsylvania Ave. in Washington, DC, to 10 Downing Street in London, but that didn't work). Just follow these steps:

1. **Tell your iPad to get directions for you.**

   You can do so in a few ways:

   - *When you're looking at a map screen:* Tap the Directions button in the upper-left corner of the screen. The search field transforms into Start and End fields.

   - *If a pushpin is already on the screen:* Tap the pushpin and then tap the little *i*-in-a-circle to the right of the name or description. This action displays the item's info screen. Tap the Directions to Here or Directions from Here button to get directions to or from that location, respectively.

- *Ask Siri for directions:* Press and hold the Home button, and ask Siri, "How do I get to *(fill in the blank)*?" (This, of course, works only if your iPad includes Siri. See Chapter 14 for more on Siri.)

2. **Tap in the Start or End field to designate the starting or ending point of your trip.**

   You can either type the start or end point or choose it from a list of your favorites, recent maps, or contacts.

3. **(Optional) If you need to swap the starting and ending locations, tap the little swirly arrow button between the Start and End fields.**

4. **When the start and end locations are correct, tap the Route button in the upper-right corner of the Directions overlay.**

   Suggested routes appear on the map, as shown in Figure 6-5.

   If multiple routes exist, Maps shows you up to three, as in Figure 6-5. To switch routes, just tap the route you want to switch to. Note that the text at the bottom of the list on the left updates to tell you the time and distance of the selected route (40 minutes – 30 miles – US Highway 183 S in Figure 6-5).

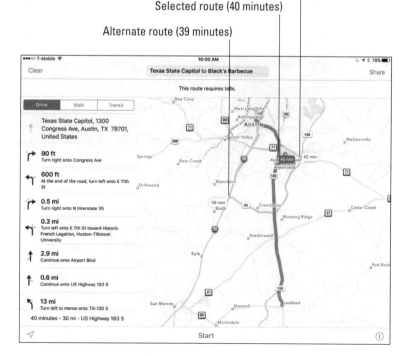

Figure 6-5: Three routing options for travel from the State Capitol in Austin, Texas, to Black's Barbecue in Lockhart, Texas.

5. **(Optional) Tap the Drive, Walk, or Transit tab (upper left) to choose driving, walking, or public transportation directions.**

The transit view, not shown, is just the map view with added information about bus and train routes and stations. At present, it's available in only a handful of cities in the U.S. and China, with the promise of additional cities soon.

6. **If Maps suggests several routes, select one by tapping its light blue line or balloon.**

In Figure 6-5, the 40-minute route is selected.

Tap the little *i*-in-a-circle in the lower-right corner of the map you're viewing and then tap the Show Traffic button to help you decide which route will be most expedient.

7. **Tap the Start button at the bottom of the screen to begin your directions.**

When you tap the Start button, a series of stark white road signs appear across the top of the map, one for each step in the directions, as shown in Figure 6-6.

Figure 6-6: The road signs show you each step of your route.

8. **Navigate your directions by swiping the road signs to the left or right or by choosing from a list:**

   • *Road signs:* Swipe right or left on the road signs to see the next or previous step in your route. Or just drive, and the map directions will update automatically as you proceed.

   • *List:* If you prefer to see your driving directions displayed as a list, tap the Overview button near the top-right corner of the screen and then tap the List button at the bottom of the screen, dead center. The steps appear in an overlay, as shown in Figure 6-7.

Tap any step in the list to see that leg of the trip displayed on the map. Tap outside the list to return to the map.

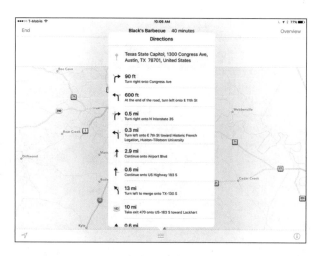

Figure 6-7: Step-by-step driving directions displayed as a list.

Getting traffic info in real time

You can find out the traffic conditions for the map you're viewing by tapping the little *i*-in-a-circle in the lower-right corner of the map and then tapping Show Traffic. If it says Hide Traffic, don't tap — the option is already on.

Major roadways are color-coded to inform you of the current traffic speed, as shown in Figure 6-8. Here's the key: Orange dots show slowdowns, and red dashes show stop-and-go traffic.

To report an incident, tap the little *i*-in-a-circle, then tap Report a Problem. To see an incident report, tap a marker on the map (none appear in Figure 6-8).

Traffic info doesn't work in every location. The only way to find out is to give it a try and see whether color codes appear. And because Maps works only when you have a network connection, you won't see traffic info if you're not connected.

Getting more info about a location

If a location has a little right arrow to the right of its name or description (refer to Figure 6-2), you can tap it to see additional information about that location.

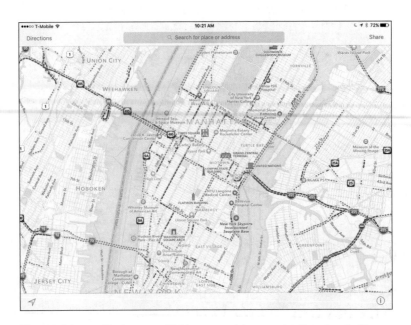

Figure 6-8: Lower Manhattan at 10:21 on a weekday morning has more traffic than most other cities at the peak of rush hour.

As we explain earlier in this chapter, you can get directions to or from that location, add the location to your favorites or contacts, or create a contact from it. With some locations, you can do two more things from the location's info screen:

✔ Tap the location's email address to launch the Mail app and send an email to the location.

✔ Tap the location's URL to launch Safari and view the location's website.

Part III
The Multimedia iPad

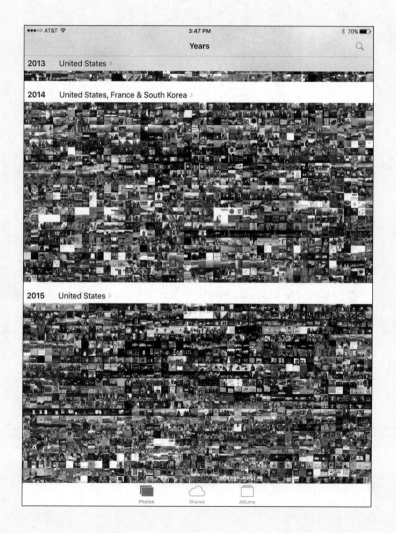

See www.dummies.com/extras/ipad to find out about international and third-party keyboards.

2013   United States >

2014   United States, France & South Korea >

2015   United States

In this part . . .

- ✔ Enjoy listening to music, podcasts, and audiobooks, plus get tips and hints for making your listening even more enjoyable.

- ✔ Everyone loves movies; learn how to capture good video with your iPad, watch video on your iPad, and share video with others with (what else?) your iPad.

- ✔ Find out how to shoot photos with your iPad, store them, sync them, and do all kinds of other interesting things with them.

- ✔ Join the e-book craze: Download and read a good book right on your iPad with the nifty iBooks app and store.

7

Get in Tune(s): Audio on Your iPad

In This Chapter

▶ Checking out your iPad's inner iPod

▶ Bossing your tunes around

▶ Having it your way: Tailoring your audio experience

▶ Shop 'til you drop with the iTunes Store app

*Y*our iPad is one of the best iPods ever — and it's especially adept at playing audio and video. In this chapter, we show you how to use your iPad to listen to music and other audio content; in Chapter 8, we cover video.

We start with a quick tour of the iPad's Music app. Then we look at how to listen to music on your iPad. After you're nice and comfy with using it this way, we show you how to customize your listening experience so that it's just the way you like it. Then we offer a few tips to help you get the most out of using your iPad as an audio player. Finally, we show you how to use the iTunes app to buy music, audiobooks, videos, and more, and how to download free content.

We assume that you already synced your iPad with your computer or with iCloud and that your iPad contains audio content — songs, podcasts, or audiobooks. If you don't have any audio on your iPad yet, we humbly suggest that you get some (flip to Chapter 3 and follow the instructions for syncing, or launch the iTunes Store app and buy a song or download a free podcast) before you read the rest of this chapter.

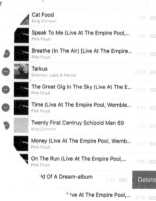

Okay, now that you have some audio content on your iPad to play with, are you ready to rock?

Introducing Your iPad's Music Player

To use your iPad to listen to music, just tap the Music icon on the Home screen. Then, at the bottom of the screen that appears, you should see five icons: For You, New, Radio, Connect, and My Music.

If you don't see these icons, tap the back icon in the upper-left corner of the screen (the one that looks like a little arrow pointing to the left).

Apple Music and iTunes Match Rock

iTunes Match and Apple Music are a pair of subscription music services offered by Apple.

iTunes Match is the older of the two, designed to let you store all your music in iCloud so you can stream all your songs to any Mac, PC, or iDevice. It performs its magic by first determining which songs in your iTunes library are available in iCloud. And because tens of millions of songs are up there already, chances are that most of your music is already in iCloud. Then, iTunes proceeds to upload a copy of every song it *can't* match (which is much faster than uploading your entire music library). The result is that you can stream any song in your iTunes library on any of your Macs, PCs, or iDevices, regardless of whether the song files are available on the particular device.

As a bonus, all the music that iTunes matches plays back from iCloud at 256-Kbps AAC DRM-free quality even if your original copy was lower quality. (You can even replace your lower bit-rate copies by downloading higher-quality versions.)

You can store up to 25,000 songs in iCloud — songs you purchased from the iTunes Store don't count. The result is that only tracks or albums you specify are stored locally on your devices, saving gigabytes of precious storage space.

At just $24.99 a year, iTunes Match is a bargain, but Apple Music, introduced in early 2015, may be a better (albeit more expensive) option. For $9.99 a month (or $14.99 a month for you and up

to five family members), your subscription provides access to more than 30 million songs on demand. That's good, but what's even better is that Siri now knows more about music than most people. Of course she can play songs, albums, artists, or genres by name, but you can also ask her to play things such as the number-one song in October of 1958 or music by a particular artist; in a few seconds, you'll be listening to whatever your heart desires.

Both services require Internet access, but as long as you're connected you can have your whole music library (iTunes Match) or access to over 30 million songs (Apple Music) on your iPad or other device, which means you won't have to worry about filling up your iDevice with music.

We'd be remiss if we didn't warn you that unless you have an unlimited data plan (on your cellular-equipped iPad), you might want to disable iTunes Match and Apple Music over cellular by tapping Settings⇨Music, and then turning off the Use Cellular Data switch. Both subscription services are reasonably priced, but data surcharges could cost you a lot if you're not careful.

Finally, here's our favorite tip for subscribers to either service: Before you go off the grid — say, on a plane flight or a cruise — tap the iCloud download button next to all the songs, albums, and playlists you want to have available when you're at 30,000 feet or out on the ocean.

You're welcome.

If you're used to the previous version of the Music app, you're surely wondering where your songs, playlists, artists, and everything else went. Don't worry; everything has been moved to the My Music tab, which we get to a little later in the chapter.

Before we can tell you about the Music app, you'll need to know about the new Apple Music and the not-so-new iTunes Match subscription services, because almost everything in the Music app works differently if you subscribe to one or both. So, to avoid confusion, read the nearby "Apple Music and iTunes Match Rock" sidebar before you do anything else.

It's music, just not YOUR music

Before we look at managing and listening to *your* music, let's take a quick look at the other tabs in the all-new Music app.

If you're not an Apple Music subscriber, you'll see four tabs: My Music, Playlists, Radio, and Connect. If you're an Apple Music subscriber, you'll see two additional tabs — For You and New — filled with music that's *not* technically yours, though you can listen to it as much as you care to for $9.99 ($14.99 for a family up to six people) per month.

Apple Music subscribers can listen to (almost) any song, album, or playlist that they discover; nonsubscribers can listen to a preview and purchase (almost) any song, album, or playlist they discover.

Here's a quick rundown of what you'll find in each tab:

- ✓ **Playlists:** If you've made any playlists — on your iPad or in iTunes on your computer — this is where you'll find them.
- ✓ **Radio:** If you've ever listened to the radio, you will grok the Radio tab immediately.
- ✓ **Connect:** This tab offers news and gossip direct from artists you choose to "follow" (by tapping the Follow button on their artist page). Or tap the See Who You're Following link near the top of the page to enable Automatically Follow Artists (when you add their songs to your music library). Not every artist "connects" at this time, but new artists appear regularly. If you can't connect with your favorite artist now, try again in a few weeks or months.

Apple Music subscribers see two additional tabs:

- ✓ **For You:** Many would say the first tab — For You — is the best thing about the new Music app, and we have to agree. Here you'll finds music that iTunes thinks you'll enjoy: playlists, albums, artists, and songs that (mostly) aren't part of your iTunes library. It's scary how often iTunes suggests music we enjoy; most days we listen to things we find in the For You tab more than we listen to the music we already own.

✔ **New:** Here you'll find the latest releases, plus song and album charts for dozens of musical genres as well as curated playlists featuring new songs and artists.

The Radio, Connect, For You, and New tabs all operate in the same fashion; each is a long page filled with content. Scroll down to see more, and then tap any item to see additional information.

While you're browsing these tabs, you'll encounter several small icons; here's what each of them does:

✔ Tap the + icon to add this song, album, or playlist to My Music (available only to Apple Music subscribers).

✔ Tap the heart icon to tell iTunes you love this artist, song, album, or playlist, which helps the For You tab suggest music it thinks you'll enjoy.

✔ Tap the ellipsis icon to see additional options, which may include Play Next, Add to Up Next, Add to a Playlist, create Genius Playlist, Make Available Offline, and Show in iTunes Store.

✔ Tap the Play icon to listen to this song, album, or playlist.

By now we're sure you're ready to start listening to some music. We begin with some radio because we know every one of you has Radio (and some of you may *not* have anything in your My Music tab yet).

To get started, tap the Music icon on your Home screen and then tap the Radio icon at the bottom of the screen.

The first thing you see at the top of the screen is Beats 1, Apple's new live radio station. It's on the air worldwide 24 hours a day, 7 days a week, with world-class programming, interviews, and music. To listen, tap the Listen Now button.

If Beats 1 isn't your cup of tea, scroll down the page for additional radio stations organized by

✔ **Recently Played:** These are stations that — you guessed it — you've played recently. Tap one to listen to it now.

✔ **Featured Stations:** This handful of stations has been hand-picked for your enjoyment by the nice folks at Apple. Tap one to listen to it.

✔ **Genres:** These stations are organized by genre, with stations as sub-genres, as shown in Figure 7-1. Tap a subgenre to listen to it.

Genres   Stations (sub-genres)

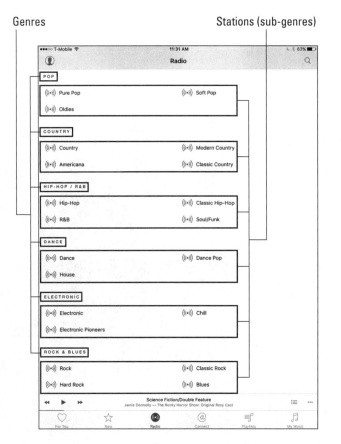

Figure 7-1: Scroll down past Recently Played and Featured
Stations to find stations organized by genre.

Did we mention that iTunes Radio is available on your iPhone, iPad, iPod
touch, Mac, PC, and Apple TV for free? You'll hear the occasional ad, but you
can listen without ads if you subscribe to iTunes Match.

So that's how you find a station; tap a station to start listening to it.

When a station is playing, the name of the current song appears near the
bottom of the screen (*"Science Fiction/Double Feature"* in Figure 7-1); tap it
for additional options, as shown in Figure 7-2.

If you want stations to play more songs you'll like, tap the heart icon to the left of the play/pause icon whenever a song you love is playing. The more you do this the better the suggestions in the For You tab will be.

And that, friends, is pretty much all you need to know to use and enjoy radio stations in the Music app.

My Music Is Your Music

Moving right along, let's look at how to listen to music you already own, which is to say the music in your iTunes library. If you haven't already launched the Music app, do so now, and then tap My Music at the bottom of the screen.

A library without library cards

Music in the My Music tab becomes available by syncing with iTunes (as

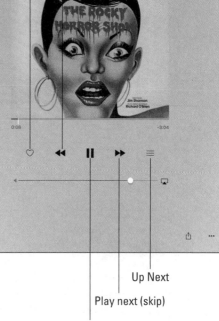

Love it (play more like this)

Play previous
(Apple Music subscribers only)

Up Next

Play next (skip)

Play/Pause

Figure 7-2: Tap the song's name to see these options.

described in Chapter 3), subscribing to iTunes Match, subscribing to Apple Music, buying music as described near the end of this chapter, or any combination of the four.

Note that a music file doesn't have to be stored on your iPad to be available on the My Music tab. You must have Internet access to play songs that aren't on your device. If you want to ensure that you'll be able to listen to a song, an album, or a playlist anytime you like, even without an Internet connection, you'll have to tap the ellipsis button (. . .) and choose Make Available Offline.

Readers with older devices surely remember previous versions of the Music app, which served up Artist, Album, Song, and Playlist buttons at the bottom of the main screen. You'll be happy to know that those useful features and many more are right here in My Music, albeit hidden in the drop-down menu at the top of the screen.

Below the Shuffle All and Shuffle buttons is a section with recently added songs or albums, as shown in Figure 7-3. Two of its five items are obscured by the drop-down menu in Figure 7-3; to see a longer list, tap Recently Added.

Tap to see more recently added items   Drop-down menu   Alphabet

The drop-down menu at the top of the screen lets you choose how your music is displayed. Tap Artists to see your music arranged by Artists, Albums, Songs, Genres, Composers, and more. If Songs isn't currently selected, tap the menu and select it to view your songs displayed in alphabetical order, as shown in Figure 7-3.

Figure 7-3: To see more of the songs or albums you've listened to lately, tap Recently Added.

If the list is longer than one screen (which it probably is), flick upward to scroll down or flick downward to scroll up. An easier way to find a song is to tap one of the little letters on the right side of the screen to jump directly to artists whose names start with that letter. In Figure 7-3, for example, that letter is *A*. The letters on the right are extremely small, so unless you have tiny fingers, you may have to settle for a letter close to the one you want or tap several times until you select the correct one.

Our technical editor for previous editions, the late Dennis Cohen, suggested that using a stylus instead of your finger may help. He was probably right.

But there's an even easier way to find an artist — or a song, an album, or a music compilation, for that matter. Tell Siri what you want to hear. All you have to do is ask (see "Using your voice to control your music," later in this chapter, for details).

If Siri isn't a viable option for you, you can achieve the same effect by typing your query. Tap the magnifying glass in the upper-right corner and then tap in the search field at the top of the screen to activate the virtual keyboard. Now type the name of the artist (or song or album) you're looking for, tap the Search button, and enjoy.

So choosing Songs from the drop-down menu displays a list of your songs; just tap any song in the list to hear it. But if you choose Artists, you see a Recently Added section and a list of artists.

When you tap an artist's name in the main list (or in a list of search results), one of two things occurs:

- ✔ **If you have songs from more than one album by an artist in your music library:** A list of albums and the songs they contain appears. Tap a song to play it or tap the first item in the list of songs on a particular album — Shuffle — to hear all songs on that album at random.

- ✔ **If all songs in your music library by that artist are on the same album or aren't associated with a specific album:** A list of all songs by that artist appears.

Either way, tap a song and the music starts.

Now for the good news: All the other items in the pop-up menu — Albums, Music Videos, Genres, Composers, and Compilations — work just like Artists. And, of course, Songs is nothing more than a long list of every song in your library. So you now know how to display and browse your library seven ways!

Play it again, list

Tap the Playlists tab at the bottom of the screen to view your playlists. If you don't have any playlists on your iPad, or don't know what a playlist is, don't sweat it. If you had any, you'd find them here; if you don't know what they are, let us tell you.

Playlists let you create and organize collections of songs around a particular theme or mood: opera arias, romantic ballads, British invasion, or whatever. Or you can make playlists of your favorite albums, favorite songs of all times, or greatest hits collections. (Younger folks sometimes call playlists *mixes;* older folks think of them as the digital equivalent of a *mix tape.*)

Tap a playlist and a list of the songs it contains appears. If the list is longer than one screen, flick upward to scroll down. Tap a song in the list and it plays. Or tap Shuffle (above the list of songs) to hear a song at random from the playlist; all subsequent songs will then play at random.

That's all there is to selecting and playing songs from your playlists.

It's easier to create playlists in iTunes on your computer than in the Music app on your iPad.

As you see in Chapter 3, you can sync playlists with iTunes on your computer. Or if you're an Apple Music subscriber, all your playlists are always available on all your devices.

Although it may be easier to create playlists in iTunes on your computer, this is an iPad book, so we show you how to create playlists in the Music app on your iPad:

1. **Tap the Music icon.**

2. **Tap the Playlists icon at the bottom of the screen.**

   If you're an Apple Music subscriber, the drop-down menu at the top offers All Playlists, My Playlists, and Apple Music Playlists, plus a switch to show Only Offline Music (music stored on this iPad).

   If you don't subscribe to Apple Music, you'll see all your playlists but will not see a drop-down menu.

3. **Tap New at the top of the screen on the right.**

4. **In the Title field, type a name for your new playlist.**

5. **(Optional) Type a description of your new playlist in the Add Description field.**

6. **Tap Add Songs (below the Add Description field).**

7. **Tap Artists, Albums, Songs, Music Videos, Genres, Composers, Compilations, or Playlists to choose songs for this playlist.**

   If you chose Songs, an alphabetical list of songs appears.

   If you chose any of the other options, a list of whatever you selected — Genres, Composers, Albums, and such — appears. You need to tap an Album, Genre, Composer, or whatever before you see a list of songs.

   Or tap the Search Music field and type the name of the song, artist, album, or whatever.

   Finally, note the little + that appears to the right of each song in the list.

8. **Tap the + next to a song name to add the song to your playlist.**

   Repeat this process until you've added all the songs you want on this playlist.

9. **Tap the Done button in the upper-right corner.**

If you create a playlist on your iPad and then sync with your computer, that playlist remains on the iPad and will also appear in iTunes on your computer. Or if you're an Apple Music subscriber, the playlist will appear on all your other devices within a few minutes.

The playlists remain until you delete them — in iTunes or on your iPad. To remove a playlist in iTunes, select the playlist's name in the source list and then press Delete or Backspace. To remove a playlist on your iPad, tap the Edit button (at the top of the list of playlists on the left), tap the red minus sign to the left of its name, and then tap the big red Delete button that appears to the right of its name.

You can also edit playlists on your iPad. To do so, tap the playlist you want to edit and then tap the Edit button near the top of the screen on the right to do any (or all) of the following:

- **Move a song up or down in the playlist:** A little icon with three gray bars appears to the right of each song, as shown in Figure 7-4. Drag the icon up to move the song higher in the list or drag down to move the song lower in the list.

- **Add more songs to the playlist:** Tap the + Add Songs button above the list.

- **Delete a song from the playlist:** Tap the – sign to the left of the song name. Note that deleting a song from the playlist doesn't remove the song from your iPad or your iTunes library; it removes it only from this particular playlist.

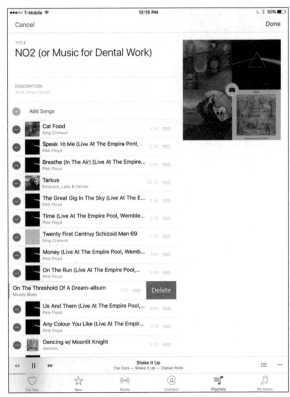

Figure 7-4: Tap the red – sign and then tap the red Delete button to remove a song.

When you finish editing, tap the Done button in the top-right corner of the screen. That's all there is to creating and managing playlists on your iPad.

Share and share alike

One of our favorite features on the iPad has always been Home Sharing, which lets you use your iPad to stream music, movies, TV shows, and other media content from the iTunes library on your Mac or PC.

iOS 8 introduced a new kind of sharing called Family Sharing, which lets you share purchases from iTunes, iBooks, and the App Store with up to six people in your family without having to share account information. Now you can pay for family purchases with the same credit card and approve kids' spending right from your iPad or iPhone. Here's the scoop on both types of sharing: Home and Family.

Home Sharing feature

Turn on Home Sharing to stream music, movies, TV shows, and other media from your computer to your iPad. The big gotcha here is that Home Sharing is available only if your iPad and your computer are on the same Wi-Fi network and use the same Apple ID.

To make Home Sharing work for you, first enable it on your computer, and then enable it on your iPad. To set up Home Sharing on your computer, launch iTunes and then Choose File⇨Home Sharing⇨Turn on Home Sharing. Type your Apple ID and password in the appropriate fields and click the Turn On Home Sharing button. From now on, as long as iTunes is open, your iTunes library will be available for Home Sharing on your Wi-Fi network.

Once Home Sharing is enabled on your computer (and your iPad and computer are on the same Wi-Fi network), enable Home Sharing on your iPad by tapping My Music at the bottom of the screen and then tapping the drop-down menu (which says Songs in Figure 7-3). Tap the last item on the menu, Home Sharing; if any shared libraries are available, you'll see them listed; tap one or more to make their contents available on your iPad for as long as you're connected to this Wi-Fi network.

Here's where it gets cool: Now, when you look at My Music, rather than just seeing the playlists, artists, and songs you've synced with your iPad (and your Apple Music), you'll now see all the playlists, artists, songs, albums, and everything else in the iTunes libraries on the Home Sharing computers as well. And you'll continue to see the shared content in your Music app as long as your iPad remains connected to this Wi-Fi network.

To switch back to seeing just your music, reverse the process and disable Home Sharing for all other libraries.

Movies and TV shows shared via Home Sharing don't appear in the Music app. Look for them in the Videos app, as described in Chapter 8.

Home Sharing is simple, elegant, and free. If you've never used this feature, what are you waiting for?

Family Sharing feature

Introduced in iOS 8, Family Sharing lets up to six members of the same family share everything they buy at the iTunes, iBooks, and App Stores. It also provides sharing of family photos and a family calendar, location sharing, and more. Finally, if you have a family subscription to Apple Music, up to five additional family members can use Apple Music at no additional cost.

To set up Family Sharing, one adult in the household (known as the family organizer) invites up to five family members to join and agrees to pay for all iTunes, iBooks, and App Store purchases those family members initiate while part of Family Sharing.

When any family member buys an app, a song, an album, a movie, or an iBook, it is billed directly to the family organizer's account. The item is then added to the purchaser's account and shared with the rest of the family. The organizer can turn on Ask to Buy for any family member to require approval for any purchase. When a purchase is initiated, a notification is sent to the family organizer, who can review the item and approve or decline the request from his or her iPad.

The fine print says: You can be part of only one family group at a time and may switch to a different family group only twice per year. The features of Family Sharing may vary based on country and content eligibility.

Family Sharing requires iCloud, and works with the following software and operating systems: iOS 8 or later, OS X 10.10 Yosemite or later, Find My Friends 3.0, Find My iPhone 3.1, and iCloud for Windows 4.0.

To become the family organizer, open Settings, tap iCloud, and then tap Set Up Family Sharing.

After you enable Family Sharing and invite your family members to join, everyone will have immediate access to other members' music, movies, TV shows, books, and apps, so you can download whatever you want to your iPad with a tap anytime you like without having to share an Apple ID or password.

Taking Control of Your Tunes

Now that you have the basics down, take a look at some other things you can do with the Music app, starting with the controls you see when a song is playing.

If you don't see the controls when a song is playing, tap the song name near the bottom of the screen.

Now, here's how to use those controls:

- ✏ **Back icon:** Tap to return to whichever list you used last — Playlists, Artists, Songs, and so on.

- ✏ **Scrubber bar:** Drag the little white line (the playhead) along the scrubber bar to skip to any point within the song. Note that the white line is near the left end of the bar in Figure 7-5, which means the person has heard roughly 5 percent of the song so far.

- ✏ **Time elapsed and remaining:** Just below the scrubber bar on the left is the amount of time this song has played already (0:38 in Figure 7-5) and how much of this song remains to be played (-3:58 in the figure).

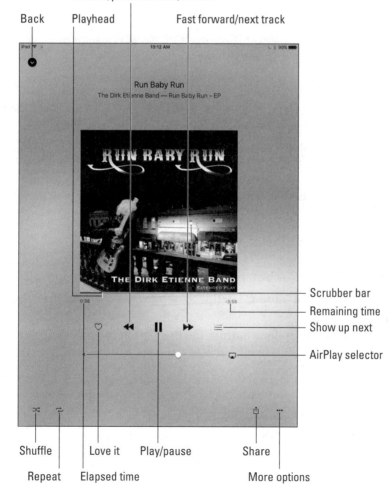

Restart/previous track/rewind

Back   Playhead   Fast forward/next track

Scrubber bar
Remaining time
Show up next

AirPlay selector

Shuffle   Love it   Play/pause   Share

Repeat   Elapsed time   More options

Figure 7-5: These are the controls that appear when a song is playing.

- ✔ **Song name, artist, and album:** Near the top of the screen see the name of the currently playing song, artist, and album. Tap it once and it will turn into 5 stars; tap to rate this song from one to five stars.

- ✔ **Love It button:** If you love this song, tapping the heart button will help the Music app choose more appropriate tracks in the For You tab.

- ✔ **Restart/previous track/rewind icon:** Tap once to go to the beginning of the track. Tap twice to go to the start of the preceding track in the list. Touch and hold down this icon to rewind the song at double speed.

- ✔ **Play/pause icon:** Tap to play or pause the song.

- ✔ **Next track/fast forward icon:** Tap to skip to the next track in the list. Touch and hold down this icon to fast-forward through the song at double speed.

- ✔ **Show up next:** Tap to switch to a list of upcoming songs. Tap Done when you're finished to return to the song controls.

- ✔ **Volume control:** Drag the little dot left or right to reduce or increase, respectively, the volume level.

- ✔ **AirPlay selector icon:** You may or may not see the AirPlay selector icon (shown in the margin and visible in Figure 7-5). AirPlay lets you stream content wirelessly over Wi-Fi from your iPad to any AirPlay-enabled device. Check out the "Playing with AirPlay" sidebar for the details.

- ✔ **Share button:** Tap to share this song with others via AirDrop, Message, Mail, Twitter, Facebook, or any of the other options in your iOS 9 Share sheet.

- ✔ **Shuffle button:** Tap once to shuffle songs and play them in random order. The button turns dark gray when shuffling is enabled. Tap it again to play songs in order again. The button goes back to its original color — light gray.

  You can also shuffle tracks in any list of songs — such as playlists or albums — by tapping Shuffle, which appears at the top of the list.

- ✔ **Repeat button:** Tap this button to hear the song that's currently playing again when it finishes.

- ✔ **More Options button:** Tap this button to add this song to a playlist or delete it from My Music.

If you're using the headset included with your iPad, you can squeeze the mic to pause, and squeeze it again to play. You can also squeeze it twice in rapid succession to skip to the next song. Sweet!

And that, gentle reader, is all you need to know to enjoy listening to music (and podcasts and audiobooks) on your iPad. But wait! There's more! Although you now know all you need to know about listening to music, you can customize your listening experience to make it even better.

Playing with AirPlay

AirPlay is a wicked cool bit of technology baked into every copy of iOS. It enables you to wirelessly stream music, photos, and video to AirPlay-enabled devices such as Apple's AirPort Express Wi-Fi base station and second-generation (and later) Apple TVs, plus certain third-party devices that have AirPlay technology, including (but not limited to) speakers and receivers.

The AirPlay Selector icon (shown here), which is available in some apps and Control Center, can be quite shy. It will appear only if your iPad detects an AirPlay-enabled device on the same Wi-Fi network. Bob has two Apple TVs at his house, so he sees both when he taps his AirPlay selector icon.

Tapping one Apple TV or the other sends whatever is playing on the Music app to that Apple TV. The Apple TV, in turn, is connected to an HDTV via HDMI (an optical audio cable would suffice if you want to stream only audio, not video).

But wait — there's more! If you use an Apple TV as your AirPlay-enabled device, in addition to streaming music, video, or photos from your iPad to your HDTV, you can also stream from your Mac, PC, iPad, or iPod touch. Bob just loves his Apple TV and says it is one of his favorite Apple inventions and would be a bargain at twice the price.

Customizing Your Audio Experience

In this section, we cover some Music features designed to make your listening experience more enjoyable.

Setting preferences

You can change a few preference settings to customize your iPad-as-an-iPod experience.

Play all songs at the same volume level

The iTunes Sound Check option automatically adjusts the level of songs so that they play at the same volume relative to each other. That way, one song never blasts out your ears even if the recording level is much louder than that of the song before or after it. To tell the iPad to use these volume settings, you first have to turn on the feature in iTunes on your computer. Here's how to do that:

1. **Choose iTunes⇨Preferences (Mac) or Edit⇨Preferences (PC).**

2. **Click the Playback tab.**

3. **Select the Sound Check check box to enable it.**

Now, to tell the iPad to use the Sound Check settings from iTunes: On the iPad's Home screen, tap Settings⇨Music⇨Sound Check.

Choose an equalizer setting

An *equalizer* increases or decreases the relative levels of specific frequencies to enhance the sound you hear. Some equalizer settings emphasize the bass (low end) notes in a song; other equalizer settings make the higher frequencies more apparent. The iPad has more than a dozen equalizer presets, with names such as Acoustic, Bass Booster, Bass Reducer, Dance, Electronic, Pop, and Rock. Each one is ostensibly tailored to a specific type of music.

The way to find out whether you prefer using equalization is to listen to music while trying out different settings. To do that, first start listening to a song you like. Then, while the song is playing, follow these steps:

1. **On the Home screen, tap Settings⇨Music⇨EQ.**

2. **Tap different EQ presets (Pop, Rock, R&B, or Dance, for example), and listen carefully to the way they change how the song sounds.**

3. **When you find an equalizer preset that you think sounds good, press the Home button and you're finished.**

If you don't like any of the presets, tap Off at the top of the EQ list to turn off the equalizer.

According to Apple's iPad battery information page (www.apple.com/batteries/ipad.html), applying an equalizer setting to song playback on your iPad can decrease battery life. So you need to decide which is more important to you: using equalization or maximizing battery life.

Set a volume limit for music (and videos)

You can instruct your iPad to limit the loudest listening level for audio or video. To do so, here's the drill:

1. **On the Home screen, tap Settings⇨Music⇨Volume Limit.**

2. **Drag the slider to adjust the maximum volume level to your liking.**

The Volume Limit setting limits the volume of only music and videos. It doesn't apply to podcasts or audiobooks. And, although the setting works with any headset, headphones, or speakers plugged into the headset jack on your iPad, it doesn't affect sound played on your iPad's internal speaker.

Setting a sleep timer

If you like to fall asleep with music playing but don't want to leave your iPad playing music all night long, you can turn on its sleep timer.

Here's how:

1. **On the Home screen, tap the Clock icon.**

2. **In the lower-right corner, tap the Timer icon.**

3. **Set the number of hours and minutes you want music to play, and then tap the When Timer Ends button.**

4. **Tap the last item in the list, Stop Playing.**

   If you don't see the Stop Playing item, don't be alarmed (semi-clever wordplay intended). You're simply looking at the middle (or the beginning) of the list of available alert sounds. To scroll to the bottom of the list and find the elusive Stop Playing item, flick upward on the list a few times.

5. **In the upper-right corner, tap the Set button.**

6. **Tap the Start button.**

That's it! If you have music playing already, you're finished. If not, press the Home button, tap the Music icon, and select the music you want to listen to as you fall asleep. When the specified time period elapses, the music stops playing and your iPad goes to sleep. By then, we hope you're in slumberland as well.

Using your voice to control your music

Here's something cool: You can boss around your music by using nothing but your voice. Just press and hold down the Home button (or the equivalent button on a headset) and, after you hear the tone, you can:

- **Play an album, an artist, or a playlist:** Say "Play" and then say "album," "artist," or "playlist," and the name of the album, artist, or playlist, respectively. You can issue these voice commands at any time except when you're on a phone call or having a FaceTime video chat. In other words, you don't have to have music playing for these voice commands to work.

- **Shuffle the current playlist:** Say "Shuffle." This voice command works only if you're listening to a playlist.

- **Find out more about the song that's playing:** Ask "What's playing?" "What song is this?" "Who sings this song?" or "Who is this song by?" Again, these commands work only if you're already listening to music.

- **Get creative:** In iOS 9, Siri has a much better grasp on music than before, so try asking her to do things like these:

  - Play songs popular in 1973.

  - Play music by The Beatles.

- Play the playlist "Music I Love."
- Play James Taylor's first album.
- Play some classic rock.

Siri can usually interpret commands such as these, and within seconds you'll be listening to exactly what you want to hear. Plus, if you're an Apple Music subscriber, you can ask Siri to play virtually any song in the iTunes Store (30 million plus at last count). Finally, because you're listening to this music on your iPad, you won't look stupid when you're talking to it!

Although we found that controlling your music by speaking works most of the time, in noisy environments the iPad may mishear your verbal request and start playing the wrong song or artist or try to call someone on the phone. Using the wired headset helps. And syntax counts, so remember to use the exact wording in the list.

Siri can also identify songs playing in the background, just like the Shazam app we rave about in Chapter 18. Just ask Siri, "What song is playing?" and let her listen for a moment. She'll identify the song if she can — and she even has a sense of humor about it. When we asked her to identify "Come Together" by The Beatles, she replied, "This is The Beatles playing 'Come Together.' Right now."

By the way, Siri's newfound song-identification prowess is powered by Shazam but doesn't require you to install the Shazam app. That said, we like all the other bells and whistles that the Shazam app brings to the party enough that we still recommend it.

Shopping with the iTunes Store app

Last but certainly not least, the iTunes Store app lets you use your iPad to download, buy, or rent just about anything you can download, buy, or rent with the iTunes application on your Mac or PC, including music, audiobooks, and videos. And, if you're fortunate enough to have an iTunes gift card or gift certificate in hand, you can redeem it directly from your iPad.

If you want to do any of those tasks, however, you must first sign in to your iTunes Store account. Tap Settings⇨iTunes and App Store⇨Sign In. Type your username and password, and then tap OK. Or, in the unlikely event that you don't have an iTunes Store account, tap Settings⇨Store⇨Create New Account, and follow the on-screen instructions.

After the iTunes Store knows who you are (and, more importantly, knows your credit card number, gift card balance, or PayPal info), tap the iTunes Store icon on your Home screen and shop until you drop.

iPad Videography

*P*icture this scene: The smell of popcorn permeates the room as you and your family congregate to watch the latest Hollywood blockbuster. A motion picture soundtrack swells up. The images on the screen are stunning. And all eyes are fixed on the iPad.

Okay, here comes the reality check. The iPad is not going to replace a wall-sized high-definition television as the centerpiece of your home theater, even if you have the comparatively mammoth 12.9-inch Retina display on the iPad Pro. Then again, it's worth pointing out that the gorgeous near-10-inch Retina displays on third-generation and later iPads has a higher-resolution screen than even the high-definition television in your living room. But you shouldn't have an inferiority complex if you have one of the displays on an iPad 2. Those screens look terrific, too, even when you're not viewing them head-on. And now that the recent iPad minis have also graduated to a Retina display, even a small-screen iPad is going to grab your attention.

Meantime, as you will discover, you can watch material that originates on the iPad on the bigger screen TV, too.

Bottom line: No matter which iPad you own, watching movies and other videos on Apple's prized tablet is a cinematic treat. What's more, you have front and rear cameras that can help turn you, under certain circumstances, into a filmmaker — right from the device.

And video on the iPad ventures into another area: video chat. You can keep in touch with friends and loved ones by gazing into each other's pupils.

It's all done through a version of *FaceTime,* a clever video chat program that comes with your iPad. In the interest of equal time, we'd also like to point out that you can do video chats on your iPad by downloading a popular third-party app such as Skype — and do clever group chats via another app called Spin from Net Power & Light.

We get to FaceTime later in this chapter. For now, and without any further ado, we get on with the show!

Finding Stuff to Watch

You have a few main ways to find and watch videos on your iPad. You can fetch all sorts of fare from the iTunes Store, whose virtual doors you can open directly from the iPad. Or you can sync content that already resides on your Mac or PC. (If you haven't done so yet, now is as good a time as any to read Chapter 3 for all the details on syncing.)

The videos you can watch on the iPad generally are in one of the following categories:

Figure 8-1: Buying and watching TV on the iPad is deadly fun.

✔ **Movies, TV shows, and music videos from the iTunes Store:** You can watch these by tapping the Videos icon on the Home screen.

The iTunes Store features dedicated sections for purchasing or renting episodes of TV shows, as shown in Figure 8-1, and for buying or renting movies, as shown in Figure 8-2.

Pricing varies, but it's not atypical (as of this writing) to fork over $1.99 to pick up an episode of a popular TV show in standard definition or $2.99 for a high-def version. And a few shows are free. You can also purchase a complete season of a favorite show. The final season of a classic show such as *Lost* costs $24.99 in standard-def and $29.99 in high-def.

A new release feature film typically costs $19.99 in high definition or $14.99 in standard def. But you can find HD movies for as little as $9.99 and sometimes even less.

You can also rent many movies, typically for $2.99, $3.99, or $4.99, though Apple usually serves up a juicy 99-cent rental as well, and we've seen rentals as high as $6.99. Not all movies can be rented, and we're not wild about current rental restrictions — you have 30 days to begin watching a rented flick and a day to finish watching after you've started, though you can watch as often as you want during the 24-hour period. But that's showbiz for you. Such films appear in their own Rented Movies section in the video list, which you get to by tapping Videos. The number of days before your rental expires is displayed.

In some instances, *World War Z* being one example, purchasing a movie also affords you so-called iTunes Extras for your Mac or PC, featuring the kind of bonus content that is sometimes reserved for DVDs.

Tap a movie listing in iTunes, and you can generally preview a trailer before buying (or renting) and check out additional tidbits: the plot summary, credits, reviews, and customer ratings, as well as other movies that appealed to other buyers of this one. See Figure 8-3. And you can search films by genre or top charts (the ones other people are buying or renting), or rely on the Apple Genius feature for recommendations based on stuff you've already watched. (Genius works for movies and TV much the way it works for music, as we explain in Chapter 7.) Apple also groups

Figure 8-2: You can spend hours watching movies on the iPad.

Figure 8-3: Bone up on a movie before buying or renting it.

movies by various themes — Family-Friendly Superheroes and Notable Indies are two examples.

- **The boatload of video podcasts and courseware, featured in the free Podcasts and iTunes U apps, both from Apple:** Podcasts started out as another form of Internet radio, although instead of listening to live streams, you downloaded files onto your computer or iPod to take in at your leisure. Lots of audio podcasts are still available, but the focus here is on video. You can watch free episodes that cover *Sesame Street* videos, sports, investing, political shows, and much more. And you can take a seminar at Harvard, Stanford, and other prestigious institutions, as shown in Figure 8-4. Indeed, iTunes U boasts more than 800,000 free lectures and other educational resources from around the world, many of them videos. And iTunes U now has content for younger students too, from K-12.

Figure 8-4: Get smart. iTunes U offers a slew of lectures on diverse topics.

Now the bad news, at least for some students in some courses: Some teachers can add homework and grade you (though that's still not typical). You might also have private discussions with your professor through the app; let us assume that part of it isn't bad news. And here's unqualified good news: at least there's still no tuition.

- **Videos that play via entertainment apps:** For example, Netflix offers an app that enables you to use your Netflix subscription, if you have one, to stream video on your iPad. Amazon's appealing Amazon Instant Video streaming app for members of its service is also available. Various TV networks offer their own apps so that you can catch up on favorite shows on your iPad. The Hulu Plus subscription app also lets you tap into current and past shows. And if you're an HBO subscriber, go for the HBO Go app. If you're a Showtime subscriber, go for Showtime Anytime. And these days, HBO, Showtime, and other content providers have streaming apps that effectively cut the cord of your cable provider, albeit for a separate subscription fee.

- **The movies you've created in iMovie software or other software on the Mac or, for that matter, other programs on the PC:** Plus you can view all the other videos you may have downloaded from the Internet, though sometimes you must convert these to a format that the iPad recognizes.

✔ **Videos you've given birth to using the rear- or front-facing camera:** A version of iMovie is made for iPads (and iPhones). The optional app costs $4.99 but is free for anyone running an iOS 7, iOS 8, or iOS 9 device, and a free upgrade is available if you have an earlier version. Check out the "Shooting Your Own Videos" section, later in this chapter, for direction on creating movies with the iPad.

You may have to prepare some videos so that they'll play on your iPad. To do so, highlight the video in question after it resides in your iTunes library. In iTunes, choose File➪Create New Version➪Create iPad or Apple TV Version. Alas, creating an iPad version of a video doesn't work for all the video content you download from the Internet, including video files in the AVI, DivX, MKV, Flash, WMV, and Xvid formats.

For a somewhat technical work-around without potential conversion hassles, try the $3.99 Air Video HD app from InMethod s.r.o. The utility app can deliver AVI, DivX, MKV, and other videos that wouldn't ordinarily play on your iPad. You have to download the free Air Video Server software to your Mac or PC to stream content to your iPad, even across the Internet. Or, for converting from a broader range of formats, try the excellent (and free) HandBrake app from `http://handbrake.fr/`.

For more on compatibility, check out the nearby "Are we compatible?" sidebar (but read it at your own risk).

Are we compatible?

The iPad works with a whole bunch of video, although not everything you'll want to watch will make it through. Several Internet video standards — notably Adobe Flash — are not supported. The absence of Flash is a bugaboo because Flash has been the technology behind much of the video on the web, though that landscape is changing. Even Adobe is pulling support for mobile versions of Flash.

Fortunately, Apple backs other increasingly popular standards — HTML 5, CSS 3, and JavaScript. But the company was apparently sensitive enough to the issue that in the early days of the iPad, Apple made mention of several sites where video *would* play on the iPad. The list included CNN, The New York Times, Vimeo, Time, ESPN, Major League Baseball, NPR, The White House, Sports Illustrated, TED, Nike, CBS, Spin, and National Geographic. By now, of course, most popular videos are readily accessible, but know that on increasingly rare occasions you may still run into a snag.

With the appropriate utility software, you might also be able to convert some nonworking video to an iPad-friendly format on your computer. But if something doesn't play now, it may in the future because Apple has the capability to upgrade the iPad through software.

Playing Video

Now that you know what you want to watch, here's how to watch it:

1. **On the Home screen, tap the Videos icon.**

   You see a tabbed interface for Movies, TV Shows, and Music Videos. If Home Sharing is running on your computer through iTunes, a Shared tab will also be visible. Depending on available content, you may also see a Home Videos tab.

2. **Tap the Movies tab.**

   For these steps, we walk you through watching a movie, but the steps for TV shows and music videos are similar.

   As Figure 8-5 shows, you see poster thumbnails for any movies you previously purchased through iTunes — even for those movies you haven't downloaded yet. (Some posters may reveal only a dimmed box, showing the title of the movie and a filmstrip icon.)

Figure 8-5: Choosing the movie, TV show, or music video to watch.

If you see the iCloud symbol on the video thumbnail, you can stream the movie, provided you have a decent Internet connection.

Tap Settings⇨Videos⇨Show iTunes Purchases to choose whether to see thumbnails for all the videos you have stored in iCloud or on the device, or show only those that have been downloaded to your iPad.

3. **Tap the poster that represents the movie or other video you want to watch.**

You're taken to a movie summary page that reveals a larger movie poster, a play icon, and tabs for Details, Chapters, and Related, as shown in Figure 8-6.

- Tap *Details* (if you're not already in that view) to see the plot summary, the run time, and sundry other details about the movie in question.

- Tap *Chapters* to jump to particular scenes or chapters in the movie and watch from that scene on. (If you're watching a TV show, you see the Episodes tab here instead.)

- Tap *Related* to see posters representing movies that are similar to this one and are (not so coincidentally) available to rent or buy in iTunes.

Figure 8-6: Getting a description of the movie you're about to watch.

4. **To start playing a movie (or resume playing from where you left off), tap the play icon.**

   Alternatively, from the Chapters view (see Figure 8-7), tap any chapter to start playing from that point.

   Want to start playing from where you left off rather than from the beginning (or vice versa)? Visit the Settings app, tap Videos, and make your selection.

5. **(Optional) Rotate your iPad to landscape mode to maximize a video's display on a movie you shot.**

   Hollywood movies and other content from iTunes can be watched only in landscape mode. Video you've shot can be viewed in portrait or landscape mode.

Figure 8-7: Start playing from any chapter.

The iPad 2 doesn't give you a full high-definition presentation because that requires at least 1,280-by-720-pixel resolution. Instead, the images are scaled down slightly. Having said that, we don't think you'll even notice the reduced quality of the images — unless, that is, you place them beside an iPad with a Retina display, which now includes versions of the iPad mini, along with the svelte full-sized iPad Air and Air 2 and the large-display iPad Pro.

Finding and Working the Video Controls

While a video is playing, tap the screen to display the controls shown in Figure 8-8. Here's how to work the controls:

- ✔ **To play or pause the video:** Tap the play/pause icon.

- ✔ **To adjust the volume:** Drag the volume slider to the right to raise the volume and to the left to lower it. The volume adjusts relative to how the physical Volume buttons are controlling audio levels.

- ✔ **To restart or go back:** Tap the restart/rewind icon to restart the video, or tap and hold down the same icon to rewind.

Figure 8-8: Controlling video.

✔ **To skip forward:** Tap and hold down the fast forward icon to advance the video. Or skip ahead by dragging the playhead along the scrubber bar.

✔ **To set how the video fills the screen:** Tap the scale icon, which toggles between filling the entire screen with video and fitting the video to the screen. Alternatively, you can double-tap the video to go back and forth between fitting and filling the screen.

Fitting the video to the screen displays the film in its theatrical aspect ratio. You may see black bars above and below the video (or to its sides), which some people don't like. The bars on the top and bottom are an example of *letterboxing;* on the sides, it's *pillarboxing. Filling* the entire screen with the video may crop or trim the sides or top of the picture, so you don't see the complete scene that the director shot.

✔ **To select subtitle settings:** Tap the audio and subtitles icon. You see options to select a different language, turn on or hide subtitles, and turn on or hide closed captioning. The control appears only if the movie supports any of these features. You can change certain subtitle styles by visiting Settings⇨General⇨Accessibility⇨Subtitles & Captioning and then turning on the Closed Captions + SDH switch.

✔ **To take advantage of the picture-in-picture feature:** Tap the picture-in-picture icon (labeled in Figure 8-8) to continue to watch the video in a small window, which you can drag around the screen while using a sepavrate app on your tablet.

✔ **To make the controls go away:** Tap the screen again (or just wait for them to go away on their own).

✔ **To access bonus features in some commercial movies:** Tap the Special Features button, which is shown at the bottom of Figure 8-8. You won't see this button in every movie.

✔ **To tell your iPad you've finished watching a video:** Tap Done. You return to the last videos screen that was visible before you started watching the movie.

Watching Video on a Big TV

We love watching movies on the iPad, but we also recognize the limitations of a smaller screen, even one as stunning as the Retina display. Friends won't crowd around to watch with you, as good as it is, so Apple offers two ways to display video from your iPad to a TV:

✔ **AirPlay:** Through the AirPlay feature, you can wirelessly stream movies — commercial flicks or videos you shot — as well as photos and music from the iPad to an Apple TV box connected to an HDTV. Start watching the movie on the iPad and tap the AirPlay in Control Center. You can watch only one screen at a time. Tap Apple TV to stream to the TV through the Apple TV box. Tap iPad to watch on the iPad.

You can multitask while streaming a video. Therefore, while the kids are watching a flick on the TV, you can surf the web or catch up on email.

Although you can stream from an iPad to an Apple TV and switch screens between the two, you can't stream a rented movie that you started watching on Apple TV to the iPad.

✔ **AV adapter cables:** Apple sells two $39 cables — one each for digital AV (HDMI) and composite video connections — that let you connect your iPad to a standard (composite) or high-definition (HDMI) television, projector, or other device that has an HDMI or composite video input. Apple also sells Lightning–to–digital AV and Lightning–to–VGA adapters at $49 each for use with the fourth-generation iPad and beyond.

If you have a more recent iPad, however, the appropriate digital AV (HDMI) adapter also lets you *mirror* the iPad screen on the connected TV or projector. So you can not only watch a movie or video but also view anything else that's on the iPad's screen: your Home screens, web pages, games, other apps, you name it.

Although the composite adapter has its cables built right in, the digital AV adapter doesn't include an HDMI cable, so you have to supply one. For more on accessories, check out Chapter 17.

Restricting Video Usage

If you've given an iPad to your kid or someone who works for you, you may not want that person spending time watching movies or television. You might want him or her to do something more productive, such as homework or the quarterly budget. That's where parental restrictions come in. Please note that the use of this iron-fist tool can make you unpopular.

Tap Settings⇨General⇨Restrictions⇨Enable Restrictions. You're asked to establish or enter a previously established passcode. Twice. Having done so, you can set restrictions based on movie ratings (PG, R, and so on) and regulate access to TV shows, also based on ratings. You can also restrict FaceTime usage or use of the camera (which when turned off also turns off FaceTime). For more on restrictions, flip to Chapter 15, where we explain the settings for controlling (and loosening) access to iPad features.

Deleting Video from Your iPad

Video takes up space — lots of space. After the closing credits roll and you no longer want to keep a video on your iPad, here's what you need to know about deleting it:

✏ To remove a downloaded video from the device — the flick remains in iCloud — tap Edit from the main Movies or TV Shows list screen, and tap the *x*-in-a-circle that appears on top of the movie poster. To confirm your intention, Apple asks whether you're sure you want to delete the video. If you're sure, tap Delete. (If you change your mind, tap Cancel.) To delete episodes of a TV series that you've watched, swipe from right to left on the episode name and then tap the red Delete button.

✏ If you delete a rented movie before watching it on your iPad, it's gone. You have to spend (more) loot if you hope to watch it in the future on the iPad.

Shooting Your Own Videos

The iPad 2 was the first iPad with a camera — um, two cameras, to be precise. The rear camera can record video up to the high-definition techie standard of 720p and at 30 frames per second (fps), or as *full-motion video.* Come again? That's a fancy way to say that the video ought to play back smoothly. The front camera can also perform at 30 fps, but the VGA *(video graphics array)* quality isn't quite as good.

Apple equipped later iPads with even better cameras. The 8-megapixel iSight camera on iPad Air 2 takes terrific stills (see Chapter 9) and lets you capture 1080p high-definition videos. Another bonus is that the camera has built-in video stabilization, which helps compensate for slightly jittery videographers. You can shoot video with the front-facing FaceTime camera as well, which includes a sensor that permits *HDR,* or *high dynamic range,* video. (Read Chapter 9 for more on HDR.) The iPad Pro shares the same camera specs as the Air 2.

Now that we've dispensed with that little piece of business, here's how to shoot video on the iPad:

1. **On the Home screen, tap the Camera icon.**

2. **Drag along the right edge of the screen until Video mode is selected.**

   The word *Video* is highlighted in yellow. On some models you can also choose Time Lapse or Slo-Mo. If either of your other options, Photo or Square, is selected, it will appear in yellow instead. (Read Chapter 9 for more on these options.)

   You can't switch from the front to the rear camera (or vice versa) while you're capturing a scene. So before shooting anything, think about which camera you want to use, and then tap the front/rear camera icon in the top-right corner of the screen when you've made your choice.

3. **Tap the red record button (labeled in Figure 8-9) to begin shooting a scene.**

   When you choose a non-video shooting format — Photo or Square — the round shutter button is white. In any case, while you're shooting a scene, the counter will tick off the seconds.

4. **Tap the red record button again to stop recording.**

   Your video is automatically saved to the All Photos album (labeled in Figure 8-9), alongside any other saved videos and digital stills that land in the Photos app.

Front/rear camera

Record

All Photos album

Figure 8-9: Lights, camera, action.

Going slow

If you have the iPad Air 2, iPad mini 4, or iPad Pro, you get another shooting benefit: the capability to capture video in slow motion, which we think is truly nifty. You'll love playing back in slow motion your kid's amazing catch in the varsity football game, just like the TV networks do to show off super plays by the pros.

When shooting in slow motion on the Air 2, the iSight camera records video at a high rate of 120 frames per second (fps) in 720p high-definition video. You get to select where to play back the video at quarter speed, as we show you in a moment.

But first things first: You have to grab the video before you can play it back. To shoot in slow motion, launch the Camera app and select Slo-Mo as your shooting format of choice. Shoot your slow-motion footage the same way you shoot at regular speeds. Note that the white circle surrounding the red shutter icon has teeny-tiny lines around it.

Tap the slow-motion video you want to watch. The video starts playing at normal speed, and then slows at a point determined by the phone. You can adjust this slow-motion section. Tap Edit and slide the vertical bars just above the frame viewer, as shown in Figure 8-10. (When the vertical lines are close, the video plays at a normal speed; when the lines are spread apart, the video plays slowly.) Note that when you play back a segment in slow motion, any accompanying audio is slowed too. Tap Revert to revert to the point at which the iPad arranged for the video to start going slow.

Figure 8-10: Adjusting your slow motion playback.

Going fast

The Time-Lapse camera feature on your iPad has the opposite effect of Slo-Mo, enabling you to capture a scene and play it back at a warped speed. (Unlike Slo-Mo, the Time-Lapse feature is on for all iPad models currently for sale.) Choose Time-Lapse the same way that you select other shooting modes, and then tap the record icon. The app captures photos at dynamically selected intervals. When you're ready to watch the sped-up sequence, tap play as you do with any other video.

Editing what you shot

We assume that you captured some really great footage, but you probably shot some stuff that belongs on the cutting room floor as well. No big whoop — you can perform simple edits right on your iPad. Tap the All Photos album in the lower-right corner of the Camera app to find your recordings, or tap the Videos album, Slo-Mo album, or Time-Lapse album, which Apple conveniently set up for you in the Photos app. Then:

1. **If the on-screen controls are not visible, tap a video recording.**

2. **Tap Edit.**

3. **Drag the start and end points along the frame viewer at the bottom of the screen to select only the video you want to keep.**

    Hold your finger over the section to expand the frame viewer to make it easier to apply your edits. Tap the play icon to preview your surgery.

4. **Tap Done and then tap Save as New Clip (as shown in Figure 8-11).**

    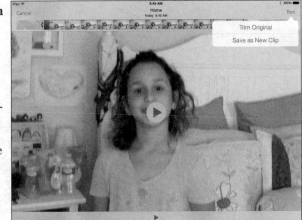

    This step creates a newly trimmed video clip; the original video remains intact. The new clip is stored in the All Photos, Videos, Slo-Mo, or Time-Lapse album.

    Tap *Cancel* to start over.

Figure 8-11: Getting a trim.

This method will let you edit footage captured only on an iOS device, not video from a digital camcorder or camera — even if you sync it to the iPad.

For more ambitious editing on the iPad, consider iMovie for iPad, a $4.99 app (free to purchasers of new iOS 7, iOS 8, and iOS 9 devices) resembling a bare-bones version of iMovie for Mac computers. Through iMovie, you can export your finished video to YouTube, Vimeo, CNN iReport, Facebook, iMovie Theater, or some other app. And iMovie for iPad lets you produce Hollywood-style movie trailers, just like on a Mac.

Any video edited with the iOS version of iMovie must have originated on an iOS device. You can't mix in footage shot with a digital camera or obtained elsewhere.

Sharing video

You can play back what you've just shot in portrait or landscape mode. And if the video is any good, you'll likely want to share it with a wider audience. To do so, open the All Photos or Videos album and tap the thumbnail for the video in question. Tap the share icon, and you can email the video (if the video file isn't too large), send it as a Message (see Chapter 5), or keep a copy in Notes.

And you have many other options: You can save the video to iCloud or share it in numerous other places, including Twitter, Facebook, Flickr, YouTube, Vimeo, and (if a Chinese keyboard was enabled) the Chinese services Youku and Tudou. You can also view your video as part of a slideshow (see Chapter 9) or, if you have an Apple TV box, dispatch it to a big-screen television via AirPlay.

Seeing Is Believing with FaceTime

We bet you can come up with a lengthy list of people you'd love to be able to eyeball in real time from afar. Maybe the list includes your old college roommate, or old college sweetheart, or your grandparents, who've long since retired to a warm climate.

That's the beauty of *FaceTime,* the video chat app. FaceTime exploits the two cameras built into the devices, each serving a different purpose. The front camera lets you talk face to face. The back camera shows what you're seeing to the person you're talking to.

To take advantage of FaceTime, here's what you need:

- **Access to Wi-Fi or cellular:** The people you're talking to need Internet access, too. On an iOS device, you need Wi-Fi or a cellular connection. If you want to go with the cell connection, you need at least a third-generation iPad running iOS 6. On a Mac, you need an upstream or downstream Internet connection of at least 128 Kbps. You also need at least a 1Mbps upstream and downstream connection for HD-quality video calls.

    Using FaceTime over a cellular connection can quickly run through your monthly data allotment and prove hazardous to your budget. However, you can do an audio-only FaceTime call, which can cut down significantly on your data usage.

- **FaceTime on recipient's device:** Of course you can do FaceTime video only with someone capable of receiving a FaceTime video call. That person must have an iPad 2 or later, an Intel-based Mac computer (OS X 10.6.6 or later), a recent-model iPod touch, or an iPhone 4 or later. (FaceTime first appeared on Apple's prized smartphone.)

Getting started with FaceTime

When you use FaceTime for the first time, after you tap the app's icon from the Home screen, you're required to sign in to FaceTime using your Apple ID, which can be your iTunes Store account, iCloud ID, or another Apple account. (You may have previously supplied this info when setting up your iPad.) If you don't have an account, tap Create New Apple ID to set one up in FaceTime.

You also must supply an email address or a phone number that callers use to call you from their own FaceTime-capable iPad, Mac, iPhone, or iPod touch.

If this is the first time you've used a particular email address for FaceTime, Apple sends an email to that address to verify the account. Tap (or click) Verify Now and enter your Apple ID and password to complete the FaceTime setup. If the email address resides in Mail on the iPad, you're already good to go.

If you have multiple email addresses, callers can use any of them for FaceTime. To add an email address after the initial setup, tap Settings➪ FaceTime➪Add Another Email. And phone numbers (for your iPhone) work too with iOS 6 or later.

In fact, it's often a good idea to allocate separate email addresses for FaceTime, assuming you have more than one Apple product that can take advantage of it. That way, a call to you when you're on your Mac, for example, won't ring on the iPad instead.

You can turn FaceTime on or off in Settings. However, if you don't turn off FaceTime, you don't have to sign back in when you launch the app.

Making a FaceTime call

Now the real fun begins — making a video call. (We say specifically "video call" because you can now also make FaceTime audio calls.) Follow these steps:

1. **Start the FaceTime app from the Home screen or by asking Siri to open the app on your behalf.**

   You can check out what you look like in a window prior to making a FaceTime call. So powder your nose and put on a happy face.

2. **Tap the Video tab.**

   Alternately, tap the Audio tab to make an audio-only FaceTime call.

3. **Choose someone to call:**

   - *Your contacts:* Tap the + icon to choose the name, and then tap the email address or phone number that the contact has associated with FaceTime.

   - *Someone new:* Tap the field in which to enter a name, email address, or number, and then tap the appropriate number in the list that appears. If this is the first time you're entering a number, you'll have the option to create a contact or add the number to an existing contact.

4. **If necessary, move the picture-in-picture window.**

   When a call is underway, you can see what you look like to the other person through a small picture-in-picture window, which you can drag to any corner of the video call window. The small window lets you know if your mug has dropped out of sight.

5. **(Optional) To toggle between the front and rear cameras, tap the camera icon (labeled in Figure 8-12).**

6. **Tap the End Call button when you're ready to hang up.**

While you're on a FaceTime call, the following tips will be handy:

- ✏ **Rotate the iPad to its side to change the orientation.** In landscape mode, you're more likely to see everybody at once.

- ✏ **Silence or mute a call by tapping the microphone icon.** Be aware that you can still be seen even though you're not heard (and you can still see and hear the other person).

- ✏ **Momentarily check out another iPad app by pressing the Home button and then tapping the icon for the app.** At this juncture, you can still talk over FaceTime, but you can no longer see the person. Tap the green bar at the top of the iPad screen to bring the person and the FaceTime app back in front of you.

How you look to the other person

Who you're talking to

Switch cameras   Mute

End call

Figure 8-12: Bob can see Ed, and Ed can see Bob (and Zeke the dog) in FaceTime.

Through the Split View feature added to the iPad through iOS 9, you can conduct and view a FaceTime video call while engaged in other activities on the iPad, provided you have an iPad Air 2, iPad mini 4, or iPad Pro.

Caller ID on FaceTime works just like caller ID on a regular phone call. You can choose the email address or phone number you want to display to someone when you call that person via FaceTime. Just tap the designated number under Caller ID in FaceTime settings.

Receiving a FaceTime call

Of course, you can get FaceTime calls as well as make them. FaceTime doesn't have to be open for you to receive a video call. Here's how incoming calls work:

- ✏ **Hearing the call:** When a call comes in, the caller's name (or email address) is prominently displayed on the iPad's screen, as shown in Figure 8-13, and the iPad rings.

✔ **Accepting or declining the call:** Tap Accept to answer the call or Decline if you'd rather not. If your iPad is locked when a FaceTime call comes in, answer by sliding the green Slide to Answer button to the right, or decline by doing nothing and waiting for the caller to give up. You can also tap Message to send a canned iMessage *(Sorry, I can't talk right now; I'm on my way; Can I call you later?)* or a custom message. Or you can tap Remind Me to be reminded in one hour that you may want to call the person back.

✔ **Silencing the ring:** You can press the sleep/wake button at the top of the iPad to silence the incoming ring. If you know you don't want to be disturbed by FaceTime calls before you even hear the ring, flip the side switch on the iPad to mute. You may have to head to Settings (see Chapter 15) to change the function of this switch from lock rotation to mute. In Settings (or Control Center), you can also turn on Do Not Disturb to silence incoming FaceTime calls.

Figure 8-13: Tap Accept to answer the call.

✔ **Blocking unwanted callers:** If a person who keeps trying to FaceTime you (yep, we're treating it as a verb) becomes bothersome, you can block him or her. Go to Settings⇨FaceTime⇨Blocked, and choose the person's name from your contacts. In the FaceTime app, you can block a caller who shows up on your caller list by tapping the *i*-in-a-circle next to the caller's name and then tapping Block This Caller.

✔ **Removing people from the call list:** If you don't want to block a caller but don't want the person clogging up your call list, tap Edit, tap the circle next to the person's name so that a check mark appears, and then tap Delete.

Although we heavily endorse the use of FaceTime, we'd be remiss if we didn't acknowledge other video-calling services that you can easily take advantage of on your iPad. The most notable are Microsoft-owned Skype and Google's Hangout, both of which we've used quite a bit.

With that, we hereby silence this chapter. But you can do more with the cameras on your iPad, and we get to that in Chapter 9.

Photography on a Larger Scale

*T*hroughout this book, we sing the praises of the iPad's vibrant multitouch display. You'd be hard-pressed to find a more appealing portable screen for watching movies or playing games. As you might imagine, the iPad you have recently purchased (or are lusting after) is also a spectacular photo viewer. Images are crisp and vivid, at least those that you shot properly. (C'mon, we know Ansel Adams is a distant cousin.)

What's more, you can shoot some of those pictures directly with your prized tablet. The reasons, of course, are the front and rear cameras built into the device. If you read Chapter 8, you already know you can put those cameras to work capturing video. In this chapter, you get the big picture on shooting still images.

Okay, we need to get a couple of things out of the way: The iPad may never be the most comfortable substitute for a point-and-shoot digital camera, much less a pricey digital SLR. As critics, we can quibble about the fact that no flash is included. And shooting can be awkward.

But we're here, friends, to focus on the positive. And having cameras on your iPad may prove to be a godsend when no better option is available. With the iPad Air 2, iPad mini 3, iPad mini 4, and iPad Pro, Apple has jazzed up the cameras to something splendid. For that matter, the cameras through the most recent iterations of the iPad generally have become pretty good. In Chapter 8, we tell you about the capability to capture full high-definition video up to what techies refer to as the 1080p standard.

In this chapter, we point out other optical enhancements in the most recent iPads. The newest iPad as of this writing, the iPad Pro, has an 8-megapixel iSight camera with backside illumination, an $f/2.4$ aperture, and a five-element lens. That's the same as the iPad mini 4 and iPad Air 2. The iPad Air and iPad mini 2 have 5-megapixel iSight cameras. Among other features, all these models have a hybrid infrared filter like what you'd find on an SLR, that helps lead to more uniform colors. Oh, and face detection makes sure the balance and focus are just right for up to ten faces on the screen.

Such features are photographer-speak for potentially snapping darn sweet pictures.

And we can think of certain circumstances — selling real estate, say, or shopping for a new home — where tablet cameras are quite convenient.

Apple has also made finding the pictures in your stash an easier task, too, with an organizational structure in iOS 7, iOS 8, and iOS 9 that arranges photos in the Photos app by collections, moments, and years.

Meanwhile, you're in for a real treat if you're new to *Photo Booth,* a yuk-it-up Mac program that is also on the iPad. That may be the best, or at least the most fun, use of the cameras yet.

We get to Photo Booth at the end of this chapter. But over the next few pages, you discover the best ways to make the digital photos on the iPad come alive, no matter how they managed to arrive on your machine.

Shooting Pictures

You can start shooting pictures on the iPad in a few ways. So we're going to cut to the chase immediately:

1. Fire up the camera itself. Choose one of the following:

- On the Home screen, tap the Camera app icon.
- From the lock screen, drag the Camera icon from the bottom-right corner in an upward motion.
- Drag Control Center up from the bottom of the screen and tap the Camera app icon.
- Ask Siri (read Chapter 14) to open the Camera app for you.

However you get here, your iPad has turned into the tablet equivalent of a Kodak Instamatic, minus the film, of course, and in a form factor that is obviously much bigger — way bigger on the 12.9-inch iPad Pro screen. But you're also effectively peering through one of the largest viewfinders imaginable if you have the near-10-inch display on what used to be the fullest-size iPad models. And yeah, the near-8-inch screen on the iPad mini provides a pretty sweet viewfinder as well.

If you're using a version of iOS prior to iOS 7 with your iPad, make sure the switch at the bottom-right corner of the screen is set to camera mode rather than video mode.

2. **Keep your eyes peeled on the iPad display, and use the viewfinder to frame your image.**

We marvel at the display throughout this book; the Camera app gives us another reason to do so.

3. **Select a shooting format:**

   • *Photo:* Think snapshot.

   • *Square:* This gives you a picture formatted to make nice with the popular Instagram photo-sharing app.

   • *Pano:* Short for panorama, this shooting mode lets you capture epic vistas.

   • *Video, Slo-Mo,* or *Time Lapse:* We kindly refer you to Chapter 8.

You move from one format to another by swiping up or down along the right edge of the screen so that the format you've chosen is highlighted in yellow.

4. **Snap your image by tapping the white round camera button.**

The button is at the middle-right edge of the screen whether you are holding the iPad in portrait mode or landscape mode (see Figure 9-1). As we show you in a moment, you'll be able to change the point of focus if necessary.

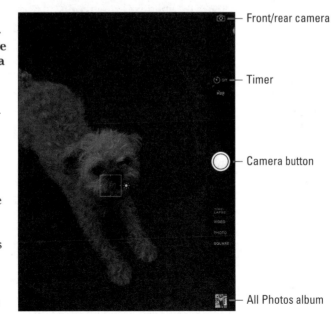

Front/rear camera

Timer

Camera button

All Photos album

Figure 9-1: Using the iPad as a camera.

The image you shoot lands in the Camera Roll album, in the lower-right corner of the screen. We explain what you can do with the images on the iPad later in this chapter.

Here are some tips for working with the Camera app:

- **Adjust the focal point.** Tap the portion of the screen in which you see the face or object you want as the image's focal point. A small rectangle surrounds your selection, and the iPad automatically adjusts the exposure and focus of that part of the image. The camera in the iPad can detect up to ten faces in a picture. Behind the scenes, the camera is balancing the exposure across each face. If you want to lock the focus and exposure settings while taking a picture, press and hold your finger against the screen until the rectangle pulses. AE/AF Lock will appear. Tap the screen again to make AE/AF Lock disappear.

  Next to the focus box is a sun icon. When that sunny exposure icon is visible, drag your finger up or down against the screen to increase or decrease the brightness in a scene. And you can lighten or darken scenes for both still photos and video.

- **Zoom in or out.** Tap the screen with two fingers and spread (unpinch) to zoom in or pinch to zoom out.

  The iPad has a 5X digital zoom, which basically crops and resizes an image. Such zooms are nowhere near as effective quality-wise as optical zooms on many digital cameras. Be aware that zooming works only with the rear camera still in camera mode; it doesn't work with the front camera or when you shoot video.

- **See grid lines to help you compose your picture.** Tap Settings➪Photos & Camera➪Camera and tap the Grid switch to turn it on (the switch turns green). Grid lines can help you frame a shot using the photographic principle known as the rule of thirds.

- **Toggle between the front and rear cameras.** Tap the front/rear camera icon (see Figure 9-1) in the upper-right corner of the screen.

  The front camera is of lower quality than its rear cousin. In the Air 2, however, the front camera is improved and more than adequate for the kinds of demands you put on it, including FaceTime and Photo Booth. You can say the same for older iPads.

- **Shoot in HDR.** To exploit *HDR (high dynamic range)* photography, tap the HDR icon. The HDR feature takes three separate exposures (long, normal, short) and blends the best parts of the three shots into a single image. In Settings (under Photos & Camera), you can choose to keep the normal photo along with your HDR result or just hang on to the latter.

- **Burst out.** In the blink of an eye, burst mode on the iPad can capture a burst of pictures — up to ten continuous images per second. Just keep your finger pressed against the camera button to keep on capturing those images. This feature works with the front FaceTime camera and the rear iSight camera.

✔ **Capture panoramas.** If you're traveling to San Francisco, you'll want a picture of the magnificent span that is the Golden Gate Bridge. In the Himalayas, you'd want a memento of Mount Everest. At a family reunion, you want that epic image of your entire extended clan. For just such moments, we recommend the panorama feature, which lets you shoot up to 240 degrees and stitch together a high-resolution image of up to 43 megapixels.

To get going, drag the screen so that Pano becomes your shooting mode of choice. The word *Pano* will be in yellow. Position the tablet so it's at the starting point and tap the camera button when you're ready. Slowly and steadily pan in the direction of the arrow. (Tap the arrow if you prefer panning in the opposite direction.) Try to keep the arrow just above the yellow horizontal line. When the task is complete, you can admire your handiwork.

✔ **Geotag your photos.** The iPad is pretty smart when it comes to geography. Turn on Location Services (in Settings under Privacy) and the specific location settings for the camera appear in Settings. Pictures you take with the iPad cameras are *geotagged,* or identified by where they were shot.

Think long and hard before permitting images to be geotagged if you plan on sharing those images with people from whom you want to keep your address and other locations private — especially if you plan on sharing the photos online.

✔ **Use the self-timer.** Many physical cameras have a self-timer that lets you be part of a picture, perhaps in a group setting with friends. The self-timer built into the Camera app adds this functionality to your iPad, whether you're using the front or rear camera. If anything, the addition of the self-timing feature might improve the quality of your selfies.

Tap the timer icon and choose 3 seconds or 10 seconds as the time interval between when you press the camera button and when the picture is captured. You'll see a countdown on the screen leading up to that moment, and then the iPad will capture a burst of up to ten images. (You can keep all ten photos, none, or a number in between.) To turn off the self-timer, tap the Off button. Couldn't be easier than that.

Of course, you're not always going to use your iPad to take pictures. Fortunately, you can add pictures to your prized tablet in several other ways. Alas, one of these methods involves buying an accessory. We zoom in in the following sections.

Syncing pix

We devote an entire chapter (see Chapter 3) to synchronizing data with the iPad, so we don't dwell on it here. But we'd be remiss if we didn't mention it in this chapter. (The assumption in this section is that you already know how to get pictures onto your computer.)

When the iPad is connected to your computer, click the Photos tab on the iPad Device page in iTunes on the Mac or PC. Then select a source from the Sync Photos From pop-up menu.

On a Mac, you can sync photos (and videos) via iPhoto software version 6.06 or later and Aperture 3.02 or later. On a PC, you can sync with Adobe Photoshop Elements 8.0 or later. Alternatively, with both computers, you can sync with any folder that contains pictures.

Connecting a digital camera or memory card

Almost all the digital cameras we're aware of come with a USB cable that you can use to transfer images to a computer. Of course, the iPad isn't a regular computer, and it isn't equipped with a USB port, nor does it have a memory card slot.

Instead, Apple sells an optional $29 iPad camera connection kit for the iPad 2 and the third-generation iPad, and separate ($29 each) Lightning–to–USB camera adapter and Lightning–to–SD card camera reader cables for more recent iPad models. These solutions work as follows:

1. **Connect your camera to your iPad, using one of the two connectors in the kit.**

   Two small connectors are included in the camera connection kit, and each fits into the iPad's dock connector at the bottom of the machine. One connector has a USB port; the other, an SD slot. If you have a fourth-generation iPad or later, use the Lightning–to–USB camera adapter for your camera and the Lightning–to–SD card camera reader to work with the card.

   If you're going the USB route, kindly use the cable that comes with your camera because no such cable comes with Apple's kit.

2. **Make sure that the iPad is unlocked.**

3. **If you haven't already done so, turn on the camera and ensure that it's set to transfer pictures.**

   Consult the manual that came with the camera if you're unsure which setting to use.

   The Photos app on the iPad opens and displays the pictures that you can import from the camera.

4. **Tap Import All to select the entire bunch, or tap the individual pictures you want to include if you'd rather cherry-pick.**

   A check mark appears next to each image you select. And that's pretty much it: The iPad organizes the pictures into albums and such, as we describe later in this chapter.

At this point, you're free to erase the pictures from your camera.

The SD card reader connector accommodates the SD memory cards common to so many digital camera models. The procedure works almost identically to the USB connector, except that you're inserting the SD gizmo into the dock or Lightning connector port rather than the USB connector mentioned previously. Just be careful to insert the SD gently to prevent any damage.

TECHNICAL STUFF The camera connection kit and the Lightning connectors support many common photo formats, including JPEG and Raw. The latter is a format favored by photo enthusiasts.

TIP We were surprised to discover that the USB connector in this kit can be used also with certain USB computer keyboards, MIDI keyboards, microphones, and even some USB memory card readers. No guarantee your USB device will be compatible, but it never hurts to try.

Saving images from emails and the web

You can save many of the pictures that arrive in emails or pictures that you come across on the web easily: Just press and hold down your finger against the image, and then tap Save Image when the menu pops up a second later. Pictures are stored in the All Photos album we get to shortly. You can also tap Copy to paste said image into another app on your device.

Tracking Down Your Pictures

So where exactly do your pictures live on the iPad? We just gave some of the answer away; the images you snap on the device first land in a photo album appropriately dubbed Camera Roll or sometimes All Photos.

In the Photos or Camera app — you can get to the former by tapping a thumbnail image in the latter — you'll also find pictures you've shared with friends and they've shared with you through the iCloud photo-sharing feature. The photos you imported are readily available too and are grouped in the same albums they were in on the computer.

Moreover, as part of iOS 8 or iOS 9, every picture you take with your iPad (and other iOS 8 or iOS 9 devices) can be stored in an iCloud photo library. You can access any of these pics if you have a Wi-Fi or cellular connection to the Internet. No more fretting about images hogging too much storage space on your tablet. What's more, the pictures are stored in the cloud at their full resolution in their original formats. (Apple will leave behind versions that are ideally sized for your tablet.)

You can still download to the iPad images that you want available when you're not connected to cyberspace.

In this section, we show you not only where to find these pictures but also how to display them and share them with others — and how to dispose of the duds that don't measure up to your lofty photographic standards.

Get ready to literally get your fingers on the pics (without having to worry about smudging them). Open the Photos app by tapping its icon on

Figure 9-2: All Photos tops your list of albums.

the Home screen or by going through the Camera app. Then take a gander at the trio of buttons at the bottom of the screen: Photos, Shared, Albums, as shown in Figure 9-2. We take these on one by one.

Choosing albums

Tapping Albums lists all the albums you have on your iPad, with your All Photos album (refer to Figure 9-2) at the upper left. Apple has kindly supplied additional premade albums: Panoramas, for all the panoramic scenes you've captured, Bursts, for your burst pictures, Selfies, Screenshots, Videos (shooting videos is described in Chapter 8), and Recently Deleted, to give you a chance to recover any images that were accidentally given the heave-ho. Apple also displays the number of days before those pictures are permanently gone.

Tap an album listing to open it. When you do, you see the minimalistic interface shown in Figure 9-3, which reveals the by-now-familiar All Photos album.

Browse the thumbnails until you find the picture or video you want, and then tap it. We soon show you all the cool things you can do from there.

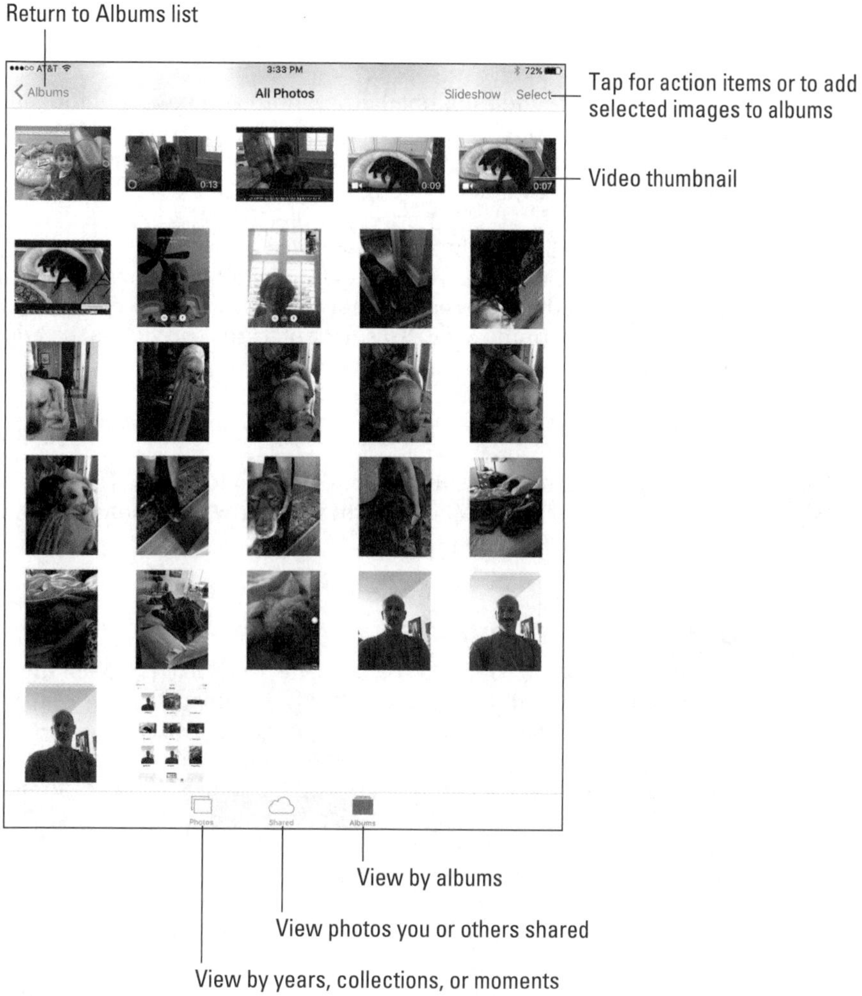
Return to Albums list
3:33 PM
Albums
All Photos
Slideshow
Select
Tap for action items or to add selected images to albums
Video thumbnail
View by albums
View photos you or others shared
View by years, collections, or moments

Figure 9-3: Digging into the All Photos album.

You'll know when a thumbnail represents a video rather than a still image because the thumbnail displays a tiny movie camera icon accompanied by the length of the video. Or you'll see a hatched circle, which represents video captured in slow motion or a time lapse, a topic reserved for Chapter 8.

Meanwhile, you can tell whether a photo is part of a burst binge in a couple ways. The first way is exposed here in the camera roll (or All Photos). The thumbnail that represents this sequence of shots will appear as though it's sitting on a stack of photos. (You'll see this thumbnail stack also when you come to collections view in the Photos app; we describe collections shortly.) Tap the thumbnail now. In the second way, the word Burst appears in the upper left of an image you've opened, with a numerical count of burst photos in parentheses.

If you can't locate the thumbnail for a photo you have in mind, flick up or down to scroll through the pictures rapidly, or use a slower dragging motion to pore through the images more deliberately. We're certain you'll find the one you're looking for soon enough.

To return to the list of albums, tap Albums at the upper-left corner of the screen. After backing out, you can create an album from the albums view by tapping the + in the upper-left corner (refer to Figure 9-2), typing a name for the album, and tapping Save. To select pictures (or videos) to add to your newly minted album, tap their thumbnails.

Shortly, we show you how to add pictures to an *existing* album.

Albums you create on the iPad reside only on the iPad. They can't be synced or copied to your PC or Mac, at least without work-arounds through a third-party app such as Dropbox.

Categorizing your pics

Placing pictures into photo albums seems to us like it's been the way of the world forever. But albums per se are not the only organizing structure that makes sense. As part of iOS 7, Apple cooked up a simple but ingenious interface for presenting pictures that is essentially a timeline of pictures, grouped by years, collections, and moments. iOS 8 and iOS 9 follow the same path.

Pictures categorized by years are indeed all the pictures taken in a given year. Can't be more straightforward than that.

The collections category is a subset within a year, such as your holiday pictures in Las Vegas. Within that grouping is another subset called moments — the pictures, say, that you took by the dancing fountains at the Bellagio Hotel.

Figure 9-4 shows side-by-side-by-side views of these groupings, which appear as a grid of Lilliputian thumbnails in the case of years — you can barely make out any of the pictures.

Tap the years view (Figure 9-4, left), and slightly bigger thumbnails appear as part of the collections view (Figure 9-4, center). Tap again, and the thumbnails get just a little bit bigger in the moments view (Figure 9-4, right).

Through all these views, you'll see location information headings that get a tad more specific as you move from years to collections to moments, assuming your iPad knows where the pictures were taken. (Location Services must be turned on under Privacy Settings for your iPad to know where these images were captured.) If you tap a place location, Apple will fire up a map and show you how many pictures were taken in that location, as revealed in Figure 9-5.

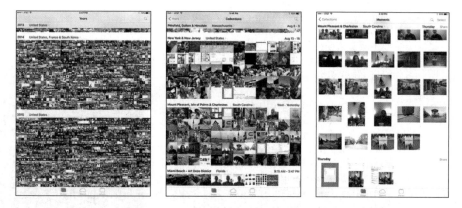

Figure 9-4: View your photos by years (left), collections (center), and moments (right).

To quickly skim all the pictures in the years view, press and drag your finger across the grid — as you do so, the thumbnails swell in size, one by one. Lift your finger and that last thumbnail takes over a chunk of the screen, ready for you to admire it, edit it, or share it.

You can also tap a thumbnail in moments view to see icons for sharing the picture, discarding it, and editing it, as shown in Figure 9-6. Tap again and those picture controls disappear and the picture is bordered on the top and bottom by black bars.

Your iPad shows all the pictures in your library in all the views. However, you can save some space by choosing compact summarized views in Collections and Years. To do so, go to Settings⇨Photos & Camera and make sure Summarize Photos is on by tapping the switch to make it green rather than gray, assuming it isn't already that way.

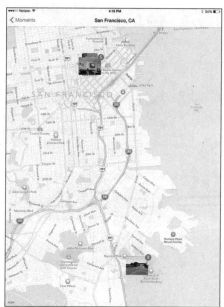

Figure 9-5: Finding pictures on a map.

Searching for pictures

Your iPad has one more feature to help you find a given photo among the thousands if not tens of thousands you've shot. You can search your entire photo library in the cloud. From the Photos app, tap the search icon, the one that resembles a magnifying glass.

Apple has kindly grouped some of your pictures into potentially helpful search categories: Nearby, Home, those taken from a specific time period or location, and Favorites, which are so designated each time you tap the heart icon above a chosen image. You can also consult a Recent Searches grouping. Or just type a search term with the on-screen keyboard, perhaps the date or the time a photo was taken or the location where it was shot.

Delete

Share   Edit

Figure 9-6: You can share, discard, or edit a photo.

Sharing your photos

Apple in its infinite wisdom recognizes that you might want to share your best images with friends and family and have those pictures automatically appear on those people's devices.

An impressive and aptly named solution called shared photo streams arrived on the iPad, iPod touch, and iPhone with iOS 6 (and a bit earlier on Macs running OS X Mountain Lion). It was modified in iOS 7 and is now referred to as iCloud photo sharing. (Somewhat confusingly, there is also My Photo Stream, a way to upload new photos and send them to your various iCloud devices.) The feature enables you to create albums of pictures and videos to share with other folks and lets you in kind receive photo streams that other people make available to you. Here's how:

1. **On the Home screen, tap Settings.**

2. **Tap Photos & Camera.**

3. **If the iCloud Photo Sharing option isn't on (green), tap it to turn it on.**

4. **Open the Photos app, and then tap the Shared tab.**

5. **Tap the + at the upper-left corner of the screen, and then type a name for your stream in the iCloud dialog that appears.**

   The name is your call, but we recommend something descriptive, along the lines of *My Trip to Paris* (and you should be so lucky).

6. **Tap Next and choose who will receive your stream, as shown in Figure 9-7.**

   You can type a phone number, a text address, or an email address, or choose one of your contacts by tapping the + in a circle in the To field of the iCloud pop-up window.

Cancel	**iCloud**	Create
To: Edward C Baig.		⊕

Figure 9-7: Inviting people to share your iCloud photos.

7. **Above the To field, tap Create.**

8. **Add photos as follows:**

   a. *Make sure the Shared icon is selected, and then tap the selected stream.*

   b. *Tap the + in a square. The Photos tab at the bottom of the display is selected, and then you can tap each photo you want to include.* You can choose from years, collections, or moments.

   c. *Tap Done.*

9. **(Optional) Enter a comment.**

10. **Tap Post.**

    The recipient will receive an email similar to the one in Figure 9-8 and can choose to sub-scribe to your shared album by tapping the button shown.

Subscribe to Edward Baig's "Trip to Paris"?

Figure 9-8: Inviting a friend to share pictures.

We recommend checking out the activity view at the top of the Shared tab. It provides a nice summary of photos you and your pals posted.

You can share photos and videos with pretty much anyone who has online access — people don't need to join iCloud. If you want to share your pictures with everyone, you can do so through a public gallery on iCloud.com. To do that, tap the share icon at the bottom of the Photos app and then tap the iCloud pictures in question. This time, tap People near the upper-right corner of the screen, and then flip the Public Website switch on (green).

If the people with whom you're sharing have their own iCloud accounts and have iOS 6 or later on a device or are using a Mac computer running OS X Mountain Lion, Mavericks, Yosemite, or El Capitan, they can not only glom onto your stream to view your photos but also leave comments about them. Don't worry — you have the power to remove snarky remarks.

If the people you're sharing with have iOS 7, iOS 8, or iOS 9, they can add their own photos and videos to the stream, provided doing so is okay with you. If it is, turn on the Subscribers Can Post switch. At your discretion, you can also receive notifications when your subscribers weigh in with a comment or add their own pictures or videos to the shared stream. After tapping the People tab, you can invite more people to view your stream.

If you're ultimately unhappy with the shared stream itself or the people with whom you're sharing it, you can kill the shared stream or kick those people off the list. To kill the stream, tap Shared, tap the Edit button, and tap the circled X that appears on the thumbnail image that represents the given stream. To remove a subscriber, tap the stream, tap People, and then tap the name of the person with whom you're sharing the stream. Scroll down to the bottom and tap Remove Subscriber. You'll be asked to tap a Remove button just to make sure or tap Cancel if you have second thoughts. If you do remove a subscriber, you can always re-invite the person later.

Admiring Your Pictures

Photographs are meant to be seen, of course, not buried in the digital equivalent of a shoebox. The iPad affords you some neat ways to manipulate, view, and share your best photos.

Maneuvering and manipulating photos

You've already found out how to find individual pictures in albums, via iCloud, and in years, collections, and moments groupings. You may already know (from previous sections in this chapter) how to display picture controls. But you can do a lot of maneuvering of your pictures without summoning those controls. Here are some options:

- **Skip ahead or view the preceding picture:** From a moments or album view, flick your finger left or right.

- **Switch from landscape or portrait mode:** The iPad's cool sensors are at work. When you turn the iPad sideways, the picture automatically reorients itself from portrait to landscape mode, as the images in Figure 9-9 show. Rotate the device back to portrait mode and the picture readjusts accordingly.

- **Zoom:** Double-tap to zoom in on an image and make it larger. Do so again to zoom out and make it smaller. Alternatively, on the photo, pinch your thumb and index finger together to zoom in and unpinch them to zoom out.

- **Pan and scroll:** This cool little feature was once practically guaranteed to make you the life of the party. Now it's commonplace if no less cool. After you zoom in on a picture, drag it around the screen with your finger, bringing front and center the part of the image you most care about. In this way, you can zoom in on Fido's adorable face as opposed to, say, the unflattering picture of the person holding the dog in his lap.

Figure 9-9: The same picture in portrait (left) and landscape (right) modes.

Launching slideshows

Those of us who store a lot of photographs on computers are familiar with running slideshows of those images. It's a breeze to replicate the experience on the iPad:

1. **Choose an album in the albums list.**

   To do so, tap the Photos icon from the Home screen or tap the Recently Added button in the Camera app.

2. **Do one of the following:**

   - *In the Photos app:* Select an album and tap Slideshow in the upper-right corner. You've designated every photo (and for that matter, video) in that album to be part of the slideshow.

   To cherry-pick the pictures you want to include in the slideshow, tap Select and then tap each image you want to include so that a check mark appears. Under this scenario, tap Add To and then add the chosen images to a new or an existing album. When that album is readily loaded, skip to the next step.

   - *In the Camera app:* Tap the image in the lower-right corner of the screen to display the most recent image you've shot, and find a picture to include in your slideshow. From there, follow the instructions for the Photos app to tap and choose other images for the slideshow or to choose an entire album.

3. **Tap Slideshow to start the slideshow, tap the screen, and then tap Options.**

4. **Choose a theme and the music (if any) that you'd like to accompany the slideshow.**

   You have five theme choices (Origami, Magazine, Dissolve, Ken Burns, and Push). Why not try them all, to see what you like? You can choose the music from your iTunes stash.

5. **Choose whether the slideshow should repeat rather than end automatically and determine the length between slides.**

   How long each slide plays is determined by how far you drag the slider that shows up in options from all the way to the left (a tortoise icon) to all the way to the right (a hare).

6. **Choose where you get to see the slideshow.**

   You can view the slideshow on the iPad itself or have it beamed wirelessly to an Apple TV, should you own one of Apple's set-top boxes. Tap the icon in the upper right to make that selection.

7. **Tap the play button to start the slideshow.**

Press Done when you're done watching. That's it! Enjoy the show.

Storing pictures in the (i)Cloud

As mentioned, through the iCloud service, any photo you take with the iPad or with another iOS 8 or iOS 9 device can be automatically stored in the cloud and pushed to another iPad, or your PC, Mac, iPhone, iPod touch, or Apple TV (third generation or later). The transfer is the antidote to the endless problem, "I've snapped a picture, now what?" Pictures are uploaded when your iCloud devices are connected to Wi-Fi.

What's more, you need no longer fret about storage space when using iCloud photo library. Apple used to store the last 1,000 pictures you took over a 30-day period in a special album — enough time, Apple figured, for all your devices to connect and grab those images, because a Wi-Fi connection was your only requirement. All the pictures you took remained on your PC or Mac, because those machines had more capacious storage. Thanks to iCloud photo library, the 1,000-picture limit on iOS devices no longer applies. Again, you can always manually move images from the shared album into other albums on your iPad or other iOS devices and computers, should you want to view those pictures when you don't have an Internet connection.

There's a catch to using the iCloud photo library: You have to pay for storage. You get 5GB of iCloud storage gratis, but shutterbugs will use that amount in a flash. You can get 50GB of storage for 99¢ a month, 200GB for $2.99 a month, and 1 terabyte for $9.99 a month.

Photos taken on the iPad aren't whisked to iCloud until you leave the Camera app. In that way, you get a chance to delete pictures that you'd rather not have turn up everywhere. But after you leave the Camera app, all the photos there are saved in the All Photos album (in the list of Albums in the Photos app), including pictures that arrived as email attachments that you saved as well as screen captures taken on the iPad. We found this last feature handy when writing this book, though Apple now also segregates screen captures in a dedicated album for such images.

You can save pictures in the All Photos album to any other album on the tablet. Start by tapping the Select button at the upper-right corner of the screen. Next, tap each photo you want to move. Tap the Add To button that shows up at the top of the screen and choose the new album destination for your chosen images.

If for some reason the pictures you snap on the iPad are not uploaded, go to Settings, scroll down and tap Photos & Camera, and make sure upload to My Photo Stream is turned on.

Editing and Deleting Photos

The iPad is never going to serve as a substitute for a high-end photo-editing program such as Adobe Photoshop. But you can dramatically (and simply) apply touch-ups and alter the composition of your pictures right from the Photos app.

To start, choose an image and tap Edit. You'll see the Edit Photo screen, as Figure 9-10 reveals.

The screen sports the following icons, from left to right:

Figure 9-10: Who says you can't improve the quality of the picture?

- **Auto-enhance:** Tapping the icon to the right of Cancel lets the iPad take a stab at making your image look better. Apple lightens or darkens the picture, tweaks color saturation, and more. Repeatedly tap the icon to turn this tool on or off. Tap Done if you like the result.

- **Rotate, straighten and crop:** Tapping this icon summons a number of additional icons and controls, as shown in Figure 9-11, top. You can

    - *Rotate the entire image counterclockwise.*

- *Straighten a crooked image or vice versa.* Rotate the numbered dial or wheel and watch the effect on the photo. Click Done when you're satisfied with how the image looks.

- *Crop the image.* Tap the crop icon, and choose among the various aspect ratio options. Press your finger against the image to drag the photo around a crop grid to get it just as you would like, pinching and unpinching as you see fit to get closer up or farther away. When you're satisfied with the result, tap Crop and then tap Save. Or tap Cancel to revert to the original.

✓ **Red-eye:** Tap this icon, in the upper-left corner of the screen, and then tap each red-eye you want to repair. The red-eye tool is visible only when you're trying to correct a photo with subjects who have a red-eye issue. (That's why you don't see this icon in Figure 9-10.)

✓ **Add a filter:** As Figure 9-11, center, shows, you can choose a filter — Mono, Tonal, Noir, Fade, Chrome, Process, Transfer, and Instant — after the fact. If you're not satisfied after applying a filter, tap None to go back to the original photo.

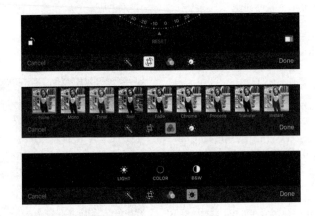

Figure 9-11: From straightening to cropping, you can make a good picture better.

✓ **Adjust light, color, B&W:** Apple provides numerous editing controls to adjust exposure, highlights, shadows, brightness, contrast, and black point (light); saturation, contrast, and cast (color); and intensity, neutrals, tone, and grain (B&W). For example, the controls shown in Figure 9-11, bottom, would let you ultimately change the look of a picture through the use of shadows, among other options.

To get at these, tap the fourth icon at the bottom of the display, which appears with other icons just to the left of the Done button. From there, tap Light, Color or B&W (as shown in Figure 9-11, bottom) to select the editing control you want to mess with. Then drag the slider at the bottom of the screen in either direction until you reach a level you're satisfied with — you see the effect on the image as you drag the slider. To fine-tune this even further, tap the icon with three horizontal lines and choose among your additional options. Had you tapped Light (as opposed to Color or B&W), tapping the icon with the horizontal lines would let you then choose a slider that adjusts the use of shadows. Tap Done when you're finished or Cancel to start over.

If you aren't satisfied with any of the edits that you've applied to your pictures, you can always tap Cancel followed by Discard Changes to restore the original.

Apple now allows third-party app makers to make their own filters and editing tools readily accessible from the Photos app.

Okay, so we told a tiny fib by intimating that photographs are meant to be seen. We should have amended that statement by saying that *some* pictures are meant to be seen. Others, you can't get rid of fast enough. Fortunately, the iPad makes it a cinch to bury the evidence:

1. **Tap the objectionable photograph.**

2. **Tap to display the picture controls, if they're not already displayed.**

3. **Tap the trash can icon.**

4. **Tap Delete Photo (or tap anywhere else to cancel, if you change your mind).**

    In an instant, the photo is mercifully disposed of. It's also deleted from the iCloud photo library across all your devices.

You may want to edit a photo that was not taken with your iPad. To do so, tap the photo, tap Edit, and then tap Duplicate and Edit. From there you'll be able to apply the aforementioned editing tools.

More (Not So) Stupid Picture Tricks

You can take advantage of the photos on the iPad in a few more ways. In each case, you tap the picture and make sure the picture controls are displayed. Then tap the share icon (shown in the margin) to display the choices shown in Figure 9-12. (Not all the options are visible in the figure.)

Figure 9-12: Look at what else I can do!

Here's a rundown of each choice:

- **AirDrop:** AirDrop is a neat wireless method for sharing photos, videos, or other files with folks who happen to be nearby and also have an iOS 7-, iOS 8-, or iOS 9-capable device or a Mac running Yosemite or El Capitan. You turn on the feature in Control Center (see Chapter 2) and choose whether to make your iPad discoverable to everyone or just contacts who are in the vicinity. Tap a photo to select it and then tap the photo or icon representing the person and the device with whom you are trying to share the image (refer to Figure 9-12). That person will receive an invitation to accept the photograph or reject it on his or her device. If the photo is accepted, the picture lands on the person's phone almost immediately.

- **Message:** Apple and your provider support picture messaging through MMS (Multimedia Messaging Service). Tap the Message option, and the picture is embedded in your outgoing message; you merely need to enter the phone number, email address, or name of the person to whom you're sending the picture. If that person is also using an iOS 5 or later device, the photo will be sent as an iMessage, which doesn't count against your texting allotment.

- **Mail:** Some photos are so precious that you just have to share them with family members and friends. When you tap Mail, the picture is embedded in the body of an outgoing email message. Use the virtual keyboard to enter the email addresses, subject line, and any comments you want to add — you know, something profound, such as "Isn't this a great-looking photo?" After tapping Send to whisk picture and accompanying message on their way, you have the option to change the image size (small, medium, or large) or keep the actual size. Consider the trade-offs: A smaller-sized image may get through any limits imposed by your or the recipient's Internet service provider or company. But if you can get the largest image through, you'll give the recipient the full picture (forgive the pun) in all its glory. (Check out Chapter 5 for more info on using email.)

- **Notes:** You can add your chosen image to the Notes app.

- **iCloud Photo Sharing:** You can post pics to a shared album.

- **Twitter:** Lots of people send pictures with their tweets these days. The iPad makes it a breeze. Tap Twitter and your picture is embedded in an outgoing tweet. Just add your words, sticking to Twitter's character limit of 140, and tap Post.

- **Facebook:** Lots (and we mean lots) of people also share photos on the world's largest social network. After your Facebook account is configured, you too can post there from your iPad.

- **Sina Weibo** and **Tencent Weibo:** If you've enabled a Chinese keyboard, you'll see options for China's own social networks.

- **Flickr:** The Yahoo!-owned service is another popular photo-sharing destination.

✔ **Save PDF to iBooks:** You can turn the image into a PDF that you can stash in the iBooks app.

✔ **Copy:** Tap to copy the image and then paste it into an email or elsewhere.

✔ **Slideshow:** We discuss slideshows earlier in this chapter. Here is another starting point for a slideshow, which as you know, can be accompanied by an optional musical soundtrack.

✔ **AirPlay:** Own an Apple TV set-top box? You can use AirPlay to stream photos from the tablet to the TV.

✔ **Save Image:** If you didn't shoot the image in question on your iPad but want to add it to the device, tap the Save Image option.

✔ **Hide:** Don't want the image to be seen (but don't want to delete it either)? Tap Hide and then tap Hide Photo. The selected pic will be hidden from the Moments, Collections, and Years views but still visible in Albums.

✔ **Assign to Contact:** If you assign a picture to someone in your contacts list, the picture you assign pops up whenever you receive a FaceTime call or Message from that person. Tap Assign to Contact. Your list of contacts appears on the screen. Scroll through the list to find the person who matches the picture of the moment. As with the Use as Wallpaper option (described next), you can drag and resize the picture to get it just right. Then tap Set Photo.

You can also assign a photo to a contact by starting out in Contacts. To change the picture you assigned to a person, tap his or her name in the contacts list, tap Edit, and then tap the person's thumbnail picture, which also carries the label Edit. From there, you can take another photo with the iPad's digital camera, select another photo from one of your albums, edit the photo you're already using (by resizing and dragging it to a new position), or delete the photo you no longer want.

✔ **Use as Wallpaper:** The Apple-supplied background images on the iPad can't measure up to pictures of your spouse, your kids, or your pet. When you tap Use as Wallpaper, you see what the present image looks like as the iPad's background picture. You're given the opportunity to move the picture around and resize it, through the now-familiar action of dragging or pinching against the screen with your fingers. You can even see how the picture looks against the time and date that appear on the lock screen. Another option is to take advantage of the Perspective Zoom setting, which lets you exploit a parallax animation effect in which the picture moves as you move the iPad. Tap the screen to toggle the setting on or off. When you're satisfied with what the wallpaper looks like, tap the Set button. Options appear that let you use the photo as wallpaper for the lock screen, the Home screen, or both, as shown in Figure 9-13. Per usual, you can also tap Cancel. (You find out more about wallpaper in Chapter 15.)

✔ **Print:** If you have an AirPrint-capable printer, tap Print to print the photo. You can choose how many copies of the print you want to duplicate.

More: Tapping here lets you post pictures to other sites with sharing plug-ins or extensions.

Sometimes you want to make decisions about multiple pictures at the same time, whether you're sharing them online, copying or printing them, adding them to a new album, or deleting them in bulk. Here's a convenient way to do so. Launch the Photos app and either tap a specific album in the app or open up to a moments view so that you see thumbnails of your pictures. Next, tap Select at the upper right, and then tap each thumbnail on which you're planning to take action, so that a check mark appears. As you do, the count for each picture you select increases. From here, you can tap the share icon (shown in the margin) to share pictures on a social network in bulk, email them,

Figure 9-13: Beautifying the iPad with wallpaper.

send them via a message, or copy or print them, as discussed previously. The options that appear may vary depending on how many pictures you've selected — for example, the number of photos you can email is limited.

You won't have to tap the share icon in every case to add pictures to a designated album or to delete them. After making your picture selections, look for Add To and the trash can icon at the top of the screen. Tap Add To and then, from the list that appears, tap the album where you want the pictures you've chosen to land. If you tap the trash can icon instead, you can dispose of the selected photos.

Entering the Photo Booth

Remember the old-fashioned photo booths at the local Five and Dime? Remember the Five and Dime? Okay, if you don't remember such variety stores, your parents probably do, and if they don't, their parents no doubt do. The point is that photo booths (which do still exist) are fun places to ham it up solo or with a friend as the machine captures and spits out wallet-size pictures.

With the Photo Booth app, Apple has cooked up a modern alternative to a real photo booth. The app is a close cousin to a similar application on the Mac. Here's how Photo Booth works:

1. **Tap the Photo Booth icon.**

   You get the tic-tac-toe-style grid shown in Figure 9-14.

2. **Point the front-facing camera at your face.**

   You see your mug through a prism of eight rather wacky special effects: Thermal Camera, Mirror, X-Ray, Kaleidoscope, Light Tunnel, Squeeze, Twirl, and Stretch. The center square (what is this, *Hollywood Squares?*) is the only one in which you come off looking normal — or, as we like to kid, like you're supposed to look. Some of the effects make you look scary; some, merely goofy.

   You can also use the rear camera in Photo Booth to subject your friends to this form of, um, visual abuse.

3. **Choose one of the special effects (or stick with Normal) by tapping one of the thumbnails.**

Figure 9-14: Photo booths of yesteryear weren't like this.

   Ed chose Mirror for the example shown in Figure 9-15 because, after all, two Eds are better than one. (Sorry, couldn't resist.) You can pinch or unpinch the image to further doctor the effect.

   If you're not satisfied with the effect you've chosen, tap the icon at the lower-left corner of the app to return to the Photo Booth grid and select another.

4. **When you have your bizarre look just right, tap the camera button on the screen to snap the picture.**

   Your pic lands (as do other pictures taken with the iPad cameras) in the All Photos album.

From the All Photos album or from right here in Photo Booth, pictures can be shared in all the usual places or deleted, which you might want to seriously consider, given the distortions you've just applied to your face.

Nah, we're only kidding. Keep the image and take a lot more. Photo Booth may be a blast from the past, but we think it's just a blast.

TIP

Before leaving this photography section, we want to steer you to the App Store, which we explore in greater depth in Chapter 11. Hundreds, probably thousands, of photography-related apps are available there, a whole host of them free. That's too many to mention here, but we know you'll find terrific photo apps just by wandering around the place. Head to the Photo & Video category to get started.

And there you have it. You have just passed Photography 101 on the iPad. We trust that the coursework was, forgive another pun, a snap.

Figure 9-15: When one coauthor just isn't enough.

Curling Up with a Good iBook

In This Chapter

▶ Getting the skinny on e-books

▶ Opening up to iBooks

▶ Reading books

▶ Shopping for iBooks

▶ Reading electronic periodicals

▶ Staying on top of News

Don't be surprised if you have to answer this question from an inquisitive child someday: "Is it true, Grandpa, that people once read books on paper?"

That time may still be a ways off, but it somehow doesn't seem far-fetched anymore. Apple is among the tech companies that are major proponents of the electronic-books revolution.

Don't get us wrong; we love physical books as much as anyone and are in no way urging their imminent demise. But we also recognize the real-world bene-fits behind Apple's digital publishing efforts — and those by companies such as Amazon (which manu-factures what is, for now, the market-leading Kindle electronic reader). As you discover in this chapter, the Kindle plays a role on the iPad as well.

For its part, the iPad makes a terrific electronic reader, with color and dazzling special effects, including pages that turn like those in a real book.

We open the page on this chapter to see how to find and purchase books for your iPad, and how to read them after they land on your virtual bookshelf. But first, we look at why you might want to read books and periodicals on your iPad.

Why E-Books?

We've run into plenty of skeptics who ask, "What's so wrong with the paper books that folks have only been reading for centuries that we now have to go digital?" The short answer is that nothing is wrong with physical books — except maybe that paper, over the long term, is fragile, and paper books tend to be bulky, a potential impediment for travelers.

On the other hand, when asked why he prefers paper books, Bob likes to drop one from shoulder height and ask, "Can your iPad (or Kindle) do that?"

Having said that, though, now consider the electronic advantages:

- **No more weight or bulk constraints:** You can cart a whole bunch of e-books around when you travel, without breaking your back. To the avid bookworm, this potentially changes the dynamic in the way you read. Because you can carry so many books wherever you go, you can read whatever type of book strikes your fancy at the moment, kind of like listening to a song that fits your current mood. You have no obligation to read a book from start to finish before opening a new bestseller just because that happens to be the one book you have in your bag. In other words, weight constraints are out the window.

- **Feel like reading a trashy novel?** Go for it. Rather immerse yourself in classic literature? Go for that. You might read a textbook, cookbook, or biography. Or gaze in wonder at an illustrated beauty. What's more, you can switch among the various titles and styles of books at will before finishing any single title.

- **Flexible fonts and type sizes:** With e-books, or what Apple prefers to call *iBooks,* you can change the text size and fonts on the fly — quite useful for people with less than 20/20 vision.

- **Get the meaning of a word on the spot:** No more searching for a physical dictionary. You can look up an unfamiliar word immediately.

- **Search with ease:** Need to do research on a particular subject? Enter a search term to find every mention of the subject in the book you're reading.

- **See all the artwork in color:** See your iBook the way it was meant to be seen. For example, the latest iBooks software from Apple lets you experience (within certain limits) the kind of stunning art book once reserved for a coffee table. Or you can display a colorful children's picture book. And the newest multitouch iBooks incorporate embedded videos, animations, 3D elements, narration, and more.

- **Get updates on books:** At least some e-books you might buy are updated — automatically.

✔ **Read in the dark:** The iPad has a high-resolution backlit display so that you can read without a lamp nearby, which is useful in bed when your partner is trying to sleep.

Truth is, this backlit story has two sides. The grayscale electronic ink displays found on Amazon's Kindle and several other e-readers may be easier on the eyes and reduce fatigue, especially if you read for hours on end. And although you may indeed have to supply your own lighting source to read in low-light situations, at least on some of the devices, those screens are easier to see than the iPad screen when you're out and about in bright sunshine. And some newer e-ink-type readers include displays that do light up.

You can *buy* an iBook by using iTunes on your Mac or PC, and you can now read that book on your Mac. You can also *read* iBooks on an iPhone, iPad, or iPod touch.

Beginning the iBook Story

To start reading iBooks on your iPad, you have to fetch the iBooks app in the App Store. (For more on the App Store, consult Chapter 11.)

As you might imagine, the app is free, and it comes with access to Apple's iBooks Store, of which we have more to say later in this chapter. For now, just know that the iBooks Store is an inviting place to browse and shop for books 24 hours a day. All the other books you end up purchasing for your iPad library turn up in the cover view shown in Figure 10-1 or in a view that lists your books by title.

The following basics help you navigate the iBooks main screen:

✔ **Change the view:** If you prefer to view a list of your book titles rather than use cover view, tap the change view icon at the upper-left corner of the screen (labeled in Figure 10-1). In cover view, you can sort the list by most recent, titles, authors, or categories, as shown in Figure 10-2.

✔ **Remove a book from view:** In cover view, tap Select, and then tap the book covers that you want to remove or tap Select All. Each selected book displays a check mark; tap a cover again to remove its check mark and thus deselect the book. When all the books you want to delete have check marks, tap Delete in the upper-left corner of the display. Apple asks you to tap a Delete This Copy button.

In list mode, as we like to call it, tap Select as well. This time, blank circles appear next to each title in the list. Tap the circle for each book you want to remove so that a check mark appears, and then tap Delete in the upper left. As before, you must confirm by tapping Delete This Copy.

As with other content you purchase from Apple, you can restore (download) any book you've purchased by tapping the Purchased icon at the bottom of the screen in the iBooks Store. The books you purchase from the iBooks Store land in iCloud. You'll know a book is in the cloud (as opposed to being downloaded onto your iPad) when you see the small iCloud icon. Tap that icon to download the book. If you prefer, you can hide books that are in iCloud from your iPad. Tap All Books, and then tap the Hide iCloud Books switch.

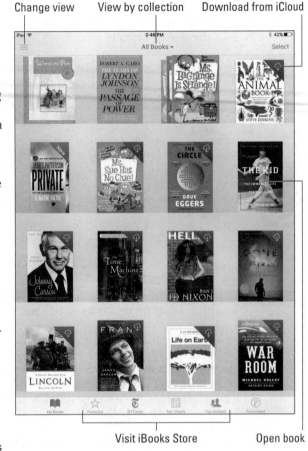

Change view   View by collection   Download from iCloud

Visit iBooks Store   Open book

Figure 10-1: You can read a book by its cover.

✔ **Organize books by collections:** If you have a vast library of e-books, you might want to organize titles by genre or subject by creating collections of like-minded works. You might have collections of mysteries, classics, biographies, children's books, how-to's, textbooks, even all the *For Dummies* books (we hope) you own.

Apple has created three collections on your behalf: books for all titles, audiobooks for the iPad equivalent of books on tape, and PDFs for the Adobe PDF files on your iPad. (Apple doesn't let you edit or remove the premade All, Books, Audiobooks, or PDFs collections.) To create, rename, or remove a collection of your own, tap All Books (refer to Figure 10-1) to show off your current list of collections and then choose from the following tasks:

- *Add a collection:* Make sure the My Books tab is selected at the bottom of the screen and then tap All Books at the top (you'll see a drop-down arrow). Tap + New Collection and type a name for the new collection.

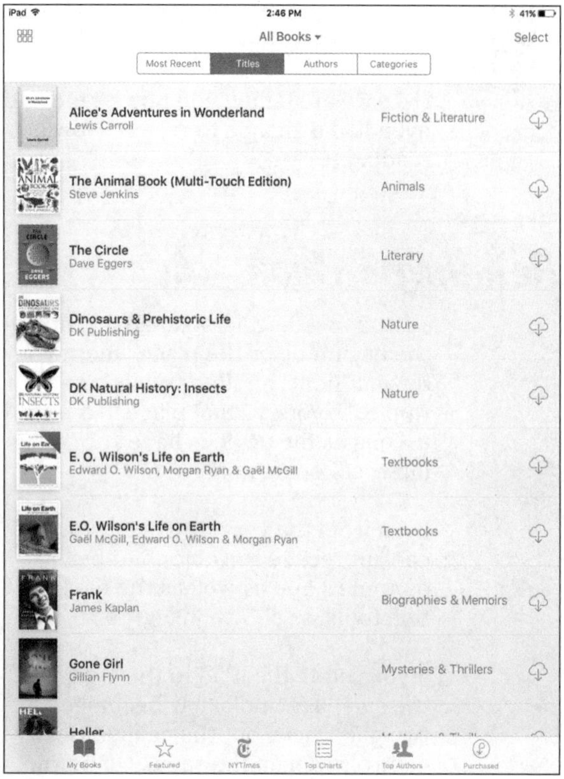

- *Delete a collection:* Tap Edit and the red circle, and then tap Delete to finish the

Figure 10-2: Sort a list of your books by most recent, title, author, or category.

job. If the collection contains books, you're asked whether you want to remove the contents of this collection from your iPad. If you choose not to remove them, they're returned to their original collections (Books, PDFs, or any other collection). Remember that you can't delete the premade All Books, Audiobooks, and PDFs collections.

- *Rename a collection:* Tap its name and type a new name. Again, you can't rename the All Books, Audiobooks, or PDFs collections.

- *Move a book or PDF to a new collection:* Go to the cover or list views, tap Select, tap each work you want to move, and then tap Move. Select the new collection for these titles.

A book can reside in only one collection at a time (aside from the All Books collection).

Here we are telling you how to move or get rid of a book before you've even had a chance to read it. How gauche. The next section helps you start reading.

Reading a Book

To start reading a book, tap it. The book leaps forward and opens to either the beginning or the place where you left off. (And you may have left off on an iPhone, an iPod touch, or another iPad because, through your Apple ID, your virtual place in a book is transported from device to device as long as the devices have an Internet connection.)

Even from the very title page, you can appreciate the color and beauty of Apple's app as well as the navigation tools, as shown in Figure 10-3.

If you rotate the iPad to the side, the one-page book view becomes a two-page view, but the navigational controls remain the same. On newer multitouch books, you may have a scrolling view of a book rather than the typical one-page view.

While you're lounging around reading, and especially if you're lying down, we recommend that you use the screen orientation lock (see Chapter 1) to stop the iPad from inadvertently rotating the display.

You can take advantage of the iPad's VoiceOver feature to have the iPad read to you out loud. The feature may not be quite like having Mom or Dad read you to sleep but can be a potential godsend for people with impaired vision. For more on the VoiceOver feature, consult Chapter 15.

Add bookmark

Table of contents/list   Search

Text size, fonts, brightness

Slider

Figure 10-3: Books on the iPad offer handy reading and navigation tools.

The VoiceOver feature is useful under certain circumstances. But we're not at the point where the iPad's loquacious virtual assistant Siri can read a book out loud. Maybe someday. For now, Siri can open the iBooks app, though. Read Chapter 14 for more on Siri.

Turning pages

You've been turning pages in books your entire life, so you don't want this simple feat to become a complicated ordeal just because you're reading electronically. Fear not; it's not.

You have no buttons to press. Instead, to turn to the *next* page of a book, do any of the following:

- **Tap or flick your finger near the right of the page.** The page turns in a blink.
- **Drag your finger near the right margin.** The page folds down as it turns, as if you were turning pages in a real book.
- **Drag down from the upper-right corner of the book.** The page curls from that spot. The effect is so authentic, you can make out the faint type bleeding from the previous page on the next folded-down page.
- **Drag up from the lower-right corner.** The page curls up from that spot.
- **Drag from the middle-right margin.** The entire page curls.

With the spilt multitasking feature added as part of iOS 9 (described in Chapter 2), be careful not to drag in from the right margin too close to the edge of the screen. Otherwise, you'll open a second app, rather than turn a page in the book.

To turn to the *previous* page in a book, tap, flick, or drag your finger in a similar fashion, except now do so closer to the left margin. You'll witness the same cool page-turning effects.

That's what happens by default anyway. Tap Settings⇨iBooks; you have the option to go to the next page instead of the previous page when you tap near the left margin. So tapping either margin would advance you to the next page.

You can also flick to scroll through a book vertically rather than turning pages in portrait view. Tap the font icon (little A and big A), and then flip the Scrolling View switch.

While in Settings, you can also flip switches that turn on (or off) full justification, leading to neat edges on both sides of a book that you're reading. There's also a setting to turn on auto-hyphenation.

Settings for audiobooks let you skip forward or back in the book you're listening to by intervals of 10, 15, 30, 45, or 60 seconds. To skip forward by the selected time interval when you've opened the audiobook, either tap the skip forward icon (which will reveal the time interval you selected) or swipe the book cover from right to left. To retreat by the selected time interval, tap the skip back icon or swipe from left to right.

You'll also note when listening to an audiobook that you can change the playback speed by 0.75x, 1.25x, 1.5x, or 2x. The default speed, of course, is 1x.

The iPad is smart, remembering where you left off. So if you close a book by tapping the Library button in the upper-left corner or by pressing the main Home button, you automatically return to this page when you reopen the book. It isn't necessary to bookmark the page (though you can, as we describe later in this chapter). The one proviso: You need an Internet connection when you close the book, because otherwise the server at Apple doesn't get the new bookmark info to pass on when you open the book on another device. And similarly, you need an Internet connection when you reopen the book to retrieve the information that was passed on.

Jumping to a specific page

When you're reading a book, you often want to go to a specific page. Here's how:

1. **If the page navigator controls aren't visible, summon them by tapping near the center of the page you're reading.**

   The controls are labeled in Figure 10-3.

2. **Drag your finger along the slider at the bottom of the screen until the chapter and page number you want appear.**

3. **Release your finger and — voilà! — that's where you are in the book.**

   Tap Back to Page *xx* at the bottom-left corner of the screen to return to your furthest point. Or tap Go to Page *xx* at the bottom right to return to a previous page you've read.

Going to the table of contents

Most books you read — on your iPad and elsewhere — have a table of contents. Here's how you use a table of contents on your iPad:

1. **With a book open on your iPad, tap the table of contents/list icon near the top of the screen (labeled in Figure 10-3).**

   The Table of Contents screen, as shown in Figure 10-4, appears.

2. **Tap the chapter, title page, or another entry to jump to that page.**

   Alternatively, tap the Resume button that appears at the upper-left corner of the screen to return to the previous location in the book.

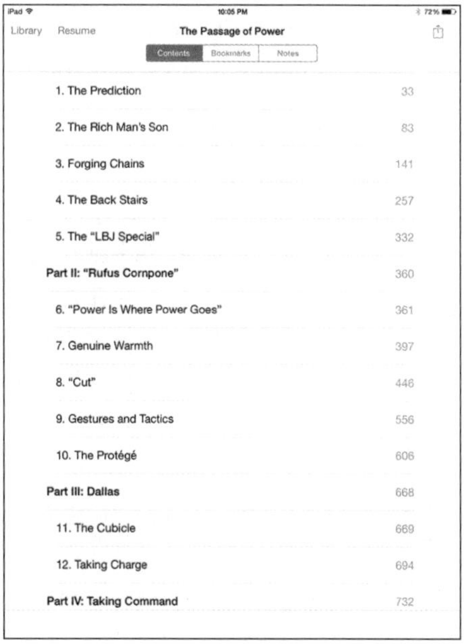

Adding bookmarks

Moving around to a particular location on the iPad is almost as simple as moving around a real book, and as we explain in the earlier section "Turning pages," Apple kindly returns you to the last page you were reading when you closed a book.

Figure 10-4: Perusing a table of contents.

Still, occasionally you want to bookmark a page so that you can easily return to it. To insert a bookmark somewhere, merely tap the bookmarks icon near the upper-right reaches of the screen. The bookmarks icon turns red, signifying that a bookmark is in place. Tap the ribbon if you want to remove the bookmark. Simple as that.

After you set a bookmark, here's how to find it later:

1. **Tap the table of contents/list icon (labeled in Figure 10-3).**

2. **Tap Bookmarks (if it's not already selected).**

   Your bookmark is listed along with the chapter and page citations, the date you bookmarked the page, and a phrase or two of surrounding text, as the example in Figure 10-5 shows.

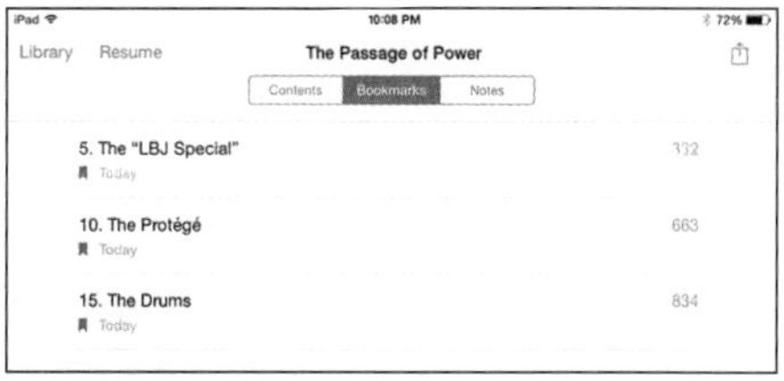

Figure 10-5: Finding the pages you bookmarked.

3. **Tap your desired bookmark to return to that page in the book.**

You can remove a bookmark from the bookmarks list by swiping your finger to the left along the bookmark and then tapping the red Delete button that appears.

Adding highlights and notes

In addition to setting bookmarks to jump to pages you want to read again, you can highlight words or passages on a page as well as add annotations or comments, which is handy for school assignments. Pardon the pun, but Apple is on the same page. Here's how to do both:

1. **Press and hold down against the text on a page. Then lift your finger to summon the Highlight and Note buttons.**

   These two buttons appear side by side, sandwiched along with Copy, Define, Share, and Search buttons, which we address in a moment.

   You see grab points along the highlighted word.

2. **(Optional) Refine the highlighted section by adjusting the grab points.**

3. **Tap one of the following to add a highlight or note:**

   • *Copy:* The word or passage you select can be pasted someplace else.

   • *Highlight:* The word or passage you selected is highlighted in color. You can read the highlight later by returning to the table of contents page in the same way that you find a bookmark. (See the preceding section and refer to Figure 10-5.)

   • *Note:* A Post-it–like note appears on the screen. Using the virtual keyboard, type your note.

After you add a highlight or note, the following tips are handy to know:

✔ **Remove a highlight or note.** Tap the highlighted text or note, and then tap the trash can icon on the toolbar that appears. When the Delete Highlight dialog appears, confirm your choice by tapping Delete. Alternatively, from the Notes section in the table to contents page, swipe your finger from right to left along an entry and then tap the red Delete button that appears.

✔ **Change the color of a highlight or note.** You can change the color from the default yellow to green, blue, pink, or purple. Touch the highlighted selection for a moment and then lift your finger. From the toolbar, tap the icon with the color that you prefer. You can underline a passage instead by tapping the icon with an underlined letter A. This icon is adjacent to the icons representing your color choices.

✔ **Share or print notes.** On the table of contents page, tap the share icon (shown in the margin) in the upper-right corner. Tap Mail to email your notes, or tap Print to print them (provided you have a compatible printer; see Chapter 2 for details about printing). You also have options to share via Message, or to post on Twitter, Facebook, or Sina Weibo, the Chinese social network (if a Chinese keyboard is enabled). We don't know how that will play politically in China. A third-party app sharing option may also present itself. Oh, and you can share notes in the iPad's own Notes app. So meta. Meanwhile, to see other possibilities for notes and iBooks generally, read the nearby sidebar "The iPad goes to school."

With iBooks, you can sync bookmarks and notes, as well as your collections across all your devices (Macs, iPhones, iPod touches, and of course your iPad). But if you don't want to do so, head to Settings and flip the switches to turn off these options. You also have the option to flip a switch that lets you allow books to access a publisher's content from the Internet.

The iPad goes to school

Apple has been pushing iPads in K-12 and higher education. As part of its vision for the iPad and with iBooks 2 and beyond, the company is throwing its considerable weight behind digital textbooks, works that include interactive captions, quizzes, 3D objects, and video. Apple even unveiled free software for the Mac called iBooks Author to encourage teachers and others to produce their own interactive books for learning.

In the meantime, among the early high school textbooks produced for the iPad are titles that cover algebra, environmental sciences, physics, and other subjects.

E. O. Wilson's *Life on Earth* is an especially rich interactive digital biology textbook like none you've seen, from 3D models of DNA to animated maps of global photosynthesis. The introduction to the book was made available for free, after which you were able to purchase additional chapters as they were released, at $1.99 apiece. Eventually, everything became free. (In general, publishers will have to work out pricing on most emerging textbooks.) Wilson's book could be viewed only by using iBooks 3.0 or later on an iPad running iOS 5.1 or later. (iBooks was up to iBooks 4.5 at the time of this writing.)

Meanwhile, if a book supports it, you can turn your notes into study cards — a great way for students to learn vocabulary or prepare for exams. (If the option is available, you'll see an icon that looks like a notepad just to the right of the Table of Contents button.) You can swipe the cards to move from one to another, or tap a card to see one side with glossary terms or material you've highlighted and the other with any notes you've supplied. You'll see an icon that looks like a small gear with a peace symbol inside it. Apple has the backing of such prominent textbook publishers as Houghton Mifflin Harcourt, McGraw-Hill, and Pearson. What's more, some third-party publishers such as Kno and Inkling are producing some interesting interactive textbooks.

According to Apple, hundreds of thousands of books in the iBooks Store can be used in school curriculums, including novels for English or social studies. A world of educational content is accessible also via the iTunes U app.

As you consider these various efforts, we understand if you wish you'd had an iPad with digital textbooks back when you were in school.

We should also point out that although educational materials are a main impetus behind iBooks, other books rich in audio, video, and other interactive materials take full advantage of Apple's latest software.

Changing the type size, font, and page color

If you want to change the way a page looks, begin by tapping the Aa icon at the top right of the screen. You can then change the following:

- **Typeface size:** Tap the uppercase *A* or the lowercase *a* to make the text larger or smaller, respectively.

- **Font:** Tap Fonts, and then tap the font style you want to switch to. Your choices at this time are Athelas, Charter, Georgia, Iowan, Palatino, San Francisco, Seravek, and Times New Roman. We don't necessarily expect you to know what these look like just by the font names — fortunately, you can examine the change right before your eyes. A check mark indicates the currently selected font style.

- **Scrolling:** If you prefer to scroll up or down to move from page to page, flip the Scrolling View switch.

- **Page color:** Tap White (the default), Sepia, or Night. You can also flip an Auto-Night Theme switch to have the iPad automatically choose the Night theme when you're reading in the wee hours without the lights on.

- **Brightness:** And speaking of light, you can raise or lower the brightness of the screen as you read by dragging the slider.

Searching inside and outside a book

If you want to find a passage in a book but can't remember where it is, try searching for it. Here's how:

1. **Tap the search (magnifying glass) icon.**

2. **Type your search term or page number on the virtual keyboard that slides up from the bottom.**

    All the occurrences in the book turn up in a window under the search icon, complete with a few lines of text and a page citation.

3. **Tap one of the items to jump to that portion of the book.**

    The words you were searching for are highlighted on that page.

You can also search the web (via Google or your chosen search engine) or Wikipedia, the online encyclopedia, by using the corresponding buttons at the bottom of the search results. If you do so, the iBooks app closes, and the Safari browser fires up Google or Wikipedia, with your search term already entered.

If you search Google or Wikipedia in this fashion, you are, for the moment, closing the iBooks app and opening Safari. To return to the book you're reading, you must reopen the app. Fortunately, you're brought back to where you left off in the book. And Google is still the search choice through iBooks, even if you selected another search engine in Safari.

Shopping for E-Books

We love browsing in a physical bookstore, and the experience of browsing Apple's iBooks Store is equally pleasurable. Apple makes it a cinch to search for books you want to read, and even lets you peruse a sample before parting with your hard-earned dollars. To enter the store from either the cover or library list view, tap one of the buttons at the bottom of the display: Featured, NYTimes, Top Charts, Top Authors, or Purchased. Of course the other My Books tab at the bottom of the screen brings you back to the library of books you already own. We explore these further shortly.

Meanwhile, a few things to keep in mind: The iBooks Store operates in 55 countries, but free iBooks are available in at least 155 countries as of this writing. More than one billion books have been downloaded. Not all books are available in all markets, of course. Some works — Jay-Z's memoir *Decoded,* to take a single example — are enhanced with video. Meanwhile, the store includes titles from major trade publishers: Hachette Book Group, HarperCollins, Macmillan, Penguin Group, Simon & Schuster, and Random House, as well as several independents. John Wiley & Sons, Inc., is also represented, of course.

Publishers, not Apple, set the prices. Many bestsellers in the joint cost $12.99, though some fetch $9.99 or less. *Dear Life* from Nobel Prize winner Alice Munro costs $8.99. Apple runs specials from time to time. Anne Hillerman's *Spider Woman's Daughter,* which once cost $15.99, was $6.99 at the time of this writing. Free selections are also available. Prices change all the time, so poke around for something you'll find pleasurable to read and then decide whether the book is worth buying for the price.

Just browsing the iBooks Store

You have several ways to browse for books in the iBooks Store. The top portion of the screen shows ever-changing ads for books that fit a chosen category (Mysteries & Thrillers in the example shown in Figure 10-6). But you can also browse Release Date in the particular category you have in mind. You can scroll to the left or right for more releases to peek at. Or tap See All for many more selections.

Figure 10-6: The featured page for Mysteries & Thrillers.

Look at the bottom of the screen. You see the following icons:

- **Featured:** This tab is where you've been hanging out so far in this chapter. Featured works are books being promoted in the store and may include popular titles or an author spotlight from the likes of *The Hunger Games* writer Suzanne Collins. You choose a given category to view (such as Fiction & Literature, Biographies & Memoirs, or Kids). In this Mysteries & Thrillers example, you'll see recent bestsellers, as well as authors whose names are in the spotlight. Swipe the featured books at the top of the screen for more choices. Do the same, if you want, for the Coming Soon sections, as well as sections not visible in the image (New & Notable, Rising Stars, and so on). Or tap See All for more selections. Scroll all the way to the bottom of the screen for links to check out your iTunes account information and redeem iTunes gift cards and gift certificates. You'll also find quick links, including iBooks on Facebook, Weekly Bestsellers Under $4, and Books Made into Movies. Are you a budding author? There's even a link to submit and sell your own books.

- **NYTimes:** Short for *The New York Times,* of course. These books make the newspaper's famous bestsellers lists, which are divided into fiction and nonfiction works. The top books in each list are initially shown. Scroll down to see more titles.

- **Top Charts:** Here Apple shows you the most popular books in the iBooks Store. You find lists for Paid Books and Free Books. Scroll down to see more of the top books in each category.

- **Top Authors:** Tapping the Top Authors icon lets you find books by poring through a list of popular authors, shown in a scrollable pane on the left half of the screen. Flick your finger up or down to scroll the list, or tap one of the letters in the margin to jump to authors whose name begins with that letter. When you tap an author's name, a list of his or her available titles appears in a scrollable pane on the right.

- **Purchased:** Tapping here shows you the books you've already bought, which you can download onto your iPad.

Searching the iBooks Store

In the upper-right corner of the iBooks Store is a search field, similar to the search field in iTunes. Tap the search field, and then use the virtual keyboard to type an author name or title to find the book you seek.

If you like freebies, search for *free* in the iBooks Store. You'll find tons of (mostly classic) books that cost nothing, and you won't even have to import them. See the section "Finding free books outside the iBooks Store," later in this chapter, for more places to find free books. By Apple's count, free content is distributed in 155 countries. Off the top of our heads, we can't remember how many countries are on Planet Earth, but it's fair to say that when it comes to digital books, Apple has most of them covered.

Deciding whether a book is worth it

To find out more about a book that you come across, you can check out the details page and other readers' reviews or read a sample of the book:

- **Find the book's details.** Tap its cover. An information screen appears with Details highlighted by default. You can see when the book was published, read a description, see the number of pages, and more.

- **Find ratings and reviews.** Tap Reviews to see the grades other readers bestowed on the book. If you've already read the book, throw in your own two cents by tapping Write a Review.

- **Find other books by the same author.** Tap Related to see the covers of other books written by the author. You can also check out other books that customers who bought this book also bought.

- **Share your interest in a book.** Tap the share icon in the upper-right corner of the information screen. You can then sing the praises of a book by tapping icons for Message, Mail, Notes, Twitter, and Facebook, as well as Chinese social networks Sina Weibo and Tencent Weibo (assuming you enabled a Chinese keyboard). You can also add the book to your Reminders app or tap Copy Link or Gift (if you're feeling generous).

The best thing you can do to determine whether a book is worth buying is to read a sample. Tap Sample, and the book cover almost immediately lands on your bookshelf. You can read it like any book, up until that juncture in the book where your free sample ends. Apple has placed a Buy button inside the pages of the book to make it easy to purchase it if you're hooked. The word *Sample* is plastered on the cover on the bookshelf to remind you that this book isn't yours — yet.

Buying a book from the iBooks Store

When a book meets or exceeds your lofty standards and you're ready to purchase it, simply do the following:

1. **Tap the price shown in the button on the book's information page.**

   Upon doing so, the dollar amount disappears, and the button carries a green Buy Book label. If you tap a free book instead, the button is labeled Get Book.

2. **Tap the Buy Book or Get Book button.**

3. **Enter your iTunes password (if you're prompted).**

   The book appears on your bookshelf in an instant, ready for you to tap it and start reading. You get an email receipt acknowledging your purchase via the same mail account in which you receive other receipts from iTunes for music, movies, and apps.

If you buy another book within 15 minutes of your initial purchase, you aren't prompted for your iTunes password again.

On the iPad Air 2, iPad mini 3,iPad mini 4, and iPad Pro with the Touch ID fingerprint scanner, you can authorize the purchase of a book by pressing your finger against the Touch ID scanner when prompted.

Buying books beyond Apple

The business world is full of examples in which one company competes with another on some level, only to work with it as a partner on another level. When the iPad first burst onto the scene in early April 2010, pundits immediately compared it to Amazon's Kindle, the market-leading electronic reader. Sure, the iPad had the larger screen and color, but the Kindle had a few bragging points too, including a longer battery life (up to about a month on the latest Kindle, versus about 10 hours for the iPad), a lighter weight, and a larger selection of books in its online bookstore.

But Amazon has long said that it wants Kindle books to be available for all sorts of electronic platforms, and the iPad, like the iPhone and iPod touch before it, is no exception. So we recommend taking a look at the free Kindle app for the iPad, especially if you've already purchased a number of books in Amazon's Kindle Store and want access to that wider selection of titles. On the iPad, you must purchase new Kindle books through the Safari (or another) browser, and not through the Kindle app.

The Barnes & Noble Nook app is also worth a look.

Competing against the iPad with smaller, less-expensive tablets are Barnes & Noble's Nook Tablet and Amazon's Kindle Fire, Kindle Fire HD, and Kindle Fire HDX. Google is doing the same with its Nexus tablets (with its Google Play Books app). And you can find numerous other players in the space.

You can find several other e-book–type apps for the iPad in the App Store. To name a few:

- CloudReaders from Cloud Readers (free)
- Kobo Reading App – Read Books and Magazines by Kobo
- Bluefire Reader from Bluefire Productions

See Chapter 11 for details about finding and downloading apps.

Finding free books outside the iBooks Store

Apple supports a technical standard called *ePub,* which is the underlying technology behind thousands of free public-domain books. You can import these to the iPad without shopping in the iBooks Store. Such titles must be *DRM-free,* which means that they're free of digital rights management restrictions.

To import ePub titles, you can download them to your Mac or PC, and then sync them to the iPad through iTunes. There are other methods. If you have Dropbox, for example, you can bring an ePub into your account, and from Dropbox you can share the title with iBooks. You can also email an ePub as an attachment.

You can find ePub titles at numerous cyberspace destinations, among them

- ✔ **Baen:** www.baen.com
- ✔ **Feedbooks:** www.feedbooks.com
- ✔ **Google Play:** http://play.google.com/store/books
- ✔ **Project Gutenberg:** www.gutenberg.org
- ✔ **Smashwords:** www.smashwords.com

(Note that not all the books at Google Play are free, and Google has a downloadable app.) Also, check out the free titles that you can find through the apps mentioned in the preceding section.

Reading Newspapers and Magazines

People in the newspaper business know that it's been tough sledding in recent years. The Internet has proved to be a disruptive force in media, as it has in so many areas. It remains to be seen what role Apple generally, and the iPad specifically, will play in the future of electronic periodicals or in helping to turn around sagging media enterprises. It's also uncertain which pricing models will make the most sense from a business perspective.

What we can tell you is that reading newspapers and magazines on the iPad is not like reading newspapers and magazines in any other electronic form. The experience is slick, but only you can decide whether it's worth paying the tab (in the cases where you do have to pay).

You can subscribe to or read a single issue of a newspaper or magazine on the iPad. There are several fine publishing apps worth checking out, including *USA TODAY* (where Ed works), *The Wall Street Journal, TIME* magazine, *The New York Times, The New Yorker, Reuters News Pro, BBC News, Vanity Fair,* and *Popular Science.* Sometimes you can read for free; sometimes you must play for your subscription. We also highly recommend fetching the free Zinio app, which offers more than 5,000 digital publications, including *Rolling Stone, The Economist, Consumer Reports, Forbes, Macworld, Car and Driver, Maxim, National Geographic Interactive, Spin,* and *Bloomberg Businessweek.* You can buy single issues of a magazine or subscribe, and you can sample and share some articles without a subscription.

In some cases, you have to pay handsomely or subscribe to some of these newspapers and magazines, which you find not in the iBooks Store but in the regular App Store, which we cover in Chapter 11. You also see ads (somebody has to pay the freight).

Meantime, if you like to read stuff from particular blogs or sites, consider the free Feedly news-gathering app, which you can fetch from the App Store.

The newest path to reading publications on your iPad is through the News app added with iOS 9. News essentially displaces the Newsstand folder that was available on your Home screen as a gathering place for your newspaper and magazine subscriptions.

News, however, is an app — not a special folder like Newsstand. It sports content from a gaggle of online and offline content producers, including some of the big name publishers visible in Figure 10-7. When you get started with the News app, you can choose the news sources and topics that you'd like to follow. Apple says you can choose from more than 1 million topics.

Figure 10-7: Many of the world's leading informational sources contribute to News.

After making your initial content selections, you'll receive a smorgasbord of news stories that are presumably of interest, all delivered in a handsome layout that loosely reminds us of one of our favorite third-party apps, Flipboard.

The News app was just getting started at the time of this writing, but Apple promises to refine the content it is sending your way as it gets to know your reading preferences over time.

In the meantime, you can search for content as well as share stuff you read, by tapping the now familiar share icon and choosing among a variety of sharing options.

However you choose to read on your iPad — through iBooks, electronic periodicals, or the new News app — your experience is likely to be rich, informative, and pleasurable.

Part IV
The iPad at Work

Find out what you can ask Siri at www.dummies.com/extras/ipad.

In this part . . .

- Learn how to shop 'til you drop in the App Store, an emporium replete with a gaggle of neat little programs and applications. Best of all, unlike most of the stores you frequent, a good number of the items can be had for free.

- Get down to business and explore staying on top of your appointments and people with Calendar and Contacts.

- Discover time- and effort-saving utilities such as Reminders, Notes, and Clock.

- Take control of your iPad with Notification Center and Control Center.

- Get to know Siri, your (mostly) intelligent assistant. She responds to your voice and can do some amazing tasks, including sending messages, scheduling appointments and reminders, searching the web, and playing a specific song or artist.

App-solutely!

In This Chapter

▷ Getting a handle on the different types of apps

▷ Searching for specific apps

▷ Getting apps onto your iPad

▷ Managing iPad apps

▷ Deleting and reviewing apps

*O*ne of the best things about the iPad is that you can download and install apps created by third parties, which is to say not created by Apple (the first party) or you (the second party). At the time of this writing, our best guess is that there are more than 1.6 million apps available and over 100 billion apps downloaded to date. Some apps are free, and other apps cost money; some apps are useful, and other apps are lame; some apps are perfectly well behaved, and other apps quit unexpectedly (or worse). The point is that of the many apps out there, some are better than others.

In this chapter, we take a broad look at apps that you can use with your iPad. You discover how to find apps on your computer or your iPad, and you find some basics for managing your apps. Don't worry: We have plenty to say about specific third-party apps in Chapters 18 and 19.

Tapping the Magic of Apps

Apps enable you to use your iPad as a game console, a streaming Netflix player, a recipe finder, a sketchbook, and much, much more. You can run three categories of apps on your iPad:

> ✔ **Apps made exclusively for the iPad:** This is the rarest kind, so you find fewer of these than the other two types. These apps won't run on an iPhone or iPod touch, so you can't even install them on either device.

✓ **Apps made to work properly on an iPad, iPhone, or iPod touch:** These so-called *universal apps* can run on any of the three device types at full resolution. What is the full-screen resolution for each device? Glad you asked. It ranges from 960 x 640 pixels for older iPhones and iPod touches to a whopping 2,732 x 2048 pixels for the iPad Pro. All other current iPads have 2,048 x 1536 pixels (except the first-generation iPad mini, which had but 1,024 x 768 pixels).

✓ **Apps made for the iPhone and iPod touch:** These apps run on your iPad but only at iPhone/iPod touch resolution (960 x 640) rather than the full resolution of your iPad (from 1,024 x 768 up to 2,732 x 2,048 pixels).

You can double the size of an iPhone/iPod touch app by tapping the little 2x button in the lower-right corner of the screen; to return it to its native size, tap the 1x button. Figure 11-1 shows you what an iPhone/iPod touch app looks like on an iPad screen.

Frankly, most iPhone/iPod apps look pretty good at 2x size, but we've seen a few that have jagged graphics and don't look as nice. Still, with 1.6 million apps to choose from, we're sure that you can find a few that make you happy.

Figure 11-1: iPhone/iPod touch apps run at a smaller size (left), but can be increased to double size (right).

You can obtain and install apps for your iPad in three ways:

- On your computer
- On your iPad
- By automatic download

To switch on automatic downloads on the iPad, tap Settings⇨App and iTunes Stores. Then tap the Automatic Downloads switch for Apps so that it turns green (on). After you do so, all apps you buy with iTunes on your computer or buy on other iOS devices will automagically appear on your iPad.

Consider also enabling automatic downloads for Music, Books, and Updates while you have App and iTunes Stores settings on your screen.

To use the App Store on your iPad, it must be connected to the Internet. Also, if you obtain an app on your computer, it isn't available on your iPad until you either sync the iPad with your computer or download the app from iCloud from the Purchased tab, covered later in this chapter. See Chapter 3 for details about syncing.

After you've obtained an app from the App Store on your computer or iPad, you can download it from iCloud to up to ten iOS devices (as long as you log in with your iCloud account or use Family Sharing).

But before you can use the App Store on your iPad or your computer, you first need an iTunes Store account. If you don't already have one, we suggest that you launch iTunes on your computer or the App Store or iTunes Store app on your iPad. Here's how:

- **On your computer:** Launch iTunes, click Sign In near the upper-left corner of the iTunes window, click Create Apple ID, and follow the on-screen instructions.
- **On your iPad:** Tap Settings⇨iTunes & App Store⇨Sign In⇨Create New Account and follow the on-screen instructions.

If you don't have an iTunes Store account, you can't download a single cool app — not even the free ones — for your iPad.'Nuff said.

Using Your Computer to Find Apps

Okay, start by finding cool iPad apps using iTunes on your computer. Follow these steps:

1. **Launch iTunes.**
2. **Click the iTunes Store tab near the top-center of the iTunes window.**

3. **Click the Apps icon (shown in the margin) near the top left of the iTunes window.**

   You're looking at the landing page of the iTunes App Store.

4. **Click the iPad tab near the top center of the iTunes window.**

   The iPad section of the iTunes App Store appears, as shown in Figure 11-2.

The default is to display all categories, which is what you see on the landing page. To look at a specific category of the App Store, press and hold All Categories (near the top right) and select a category from the drop-down menu.

Now you're ready to browse, search, and download apps, as we explain in the following sections.

Browsing the App Store from your computer

After you have the iTunes App Store on your screen, you have a couple of options for exploring its virtual aisles. Allow us to introduce you to the various "departments" available from the main screen. The main departments are featured in the middle of the screen, and ancillary departments appear on either side of them. We start with the ones in the middle:

- **Best New Apps:** This department displays seven icons in Figure 11-2. These apps are — what else? — the best new apps according to Apple's curators.

  Only seven icons are visible in Figure 11-2, but the Best New Apps department has more than that on most screens at most resolutions. Look for the See All link way over to the right of the words *Best New Apps* and click it to see *all* Best New Apps at once (20 Best New Apps were available the day the figure was captured). Or click and drag the scroll bar below the icons to see more. (If you don't see a scroll bar, hover the cursor over any item in Best New Apps and it will magically appear.)

- **Best New Games:** This department displays seven icons as well, representing the best new games available today. Again, you can see more of these icons by clicking the See All link or by dragging the scroll bar.

  The Best New Apps and Best New Games sections have appeared near the top of the iTunes App store for as long as we can remember. The other departments, such as More Amazing iOS 9 Apps and Share Your #Replay in Figure 11-2, are rotated regularly. In earlier editions of this book, the screen has displayed Previous Editors' Choices, What's Hot, Introducing Bundles, and Halloween Apps & Games. Regardless of what the department is called or its contents, all departments work the same: To see more items, click See All or drag the scroll bar.

Apps icon   iPad tab   App Store button

Search iTunes Store

Categories drop-down menu

Scroll bar

Figure 11-2: The iTunes App Store in all its glory (with the iPad tab selected).

Separating the Best New Apps and Best New Games departments from the More Amazing iOS 9 Apps and Share Your #Replay departments in Figure 11-2 is a row of rectangular advertisements (American Red Cross, Free App of the Week, Games, and Kids). Click an ad to learn more.

As you scroll down the page you'll find additional departments (Best New Game Updates, Popular Games, and Popular Apps in Figure 11-2) and two more rows of ads.

Apple has a habit of redecorating (or even reconfiguring) the iTunes Store every so often, so allow us to apologize in advance if the screen isn't exactly as described here when you visit.

Three additional departments appear on the right side of the window: Top Paid Apps, Top Grossing Apps, and our favorite, Top Free Apps. The number-one app in each department displays both its icon and its name; the next nine apps show text links only.

Using the search field in the iTunes Store

Browsing the screen is helpful, but if you know exactly what you're looking for, searching is faster. Follow these steps to search for an app:

1. **In the search field in the upper-right corner of the main iTunes window, type a word or phrase. Press Return or Enter to initiate the search.**

   In Figure 11-3, we searched for *photo.* You see results for the entire iTunes Store, which includes music, television shows, movies, and other stuff in addition to iPad apps.

Figure 11-3: We want to do cool stuff with our iPad camera, so we searched for *photo.*

2. **Click iPad Apps in the list of filters on the right (highlighted in blue in Figure 11-3) to limit your results to only iPad apps.**

One last thing: The little triangle to the right of each item's price (or free, download, or downloaded) button is another drop-down menu, as shown for the Pinterest app in Figure 11-3. This drop-down menu lets you send a link to it in an email to a friend (shown selected in Figure 11-3), share this item on Facebook or Twitter, or copy the product's link to the Clipboard so that you can paste it elsewhere.

Getting more information about an app in the iTunes Store

Now that you know how to find apps in the App Store, this section delves a little deeper and shows you how to find out more about an app that interests you.

To find out more about an app, just click its icon or text link. A details screen like the one shown in Figure 11-4 appears.

This screen tells you most of what you need to know about the app, such as basic product information and a narrative description, what's new in this version, the language it's presented in, and its system requirements. In the following sections, you take a closer look at the various areas on the screen.

Finding the full app description

Note the blue More link in the lower-right corner of the Description section in Figure 11-4; click More to see a longer description of the app.

Figure 11-4: The details screen for SketchBook Express for iPad, a nifty drawing and painting app.

Bear in mind that the app description on this screen was written by the app's developer and may be somewhat biased. Never fear, gentle reader: In an upcoming section, we show you how to find app reviews written by people who have used it (and, unfortunately, sometimes people who haven't).

Understanding the app rating

The SketchBook Express app is rated 4+, as you can see below the Free button in the upper-left corner of the screen shown in Figure 11-4. The rating means that the app contains no objectionable material. Here are the other possible ratings:

- **9+:** May contain mild or infrequent occurrences of cartoon, fantasy, or realistic violence; or infrequent or mild mature, suggestive, or horror-themed content that may not be suitable for children younger than the age of 9.

- **12+:** May contain infrequent mildly offensive language; frequent or intense cartoon, fantasy, or realistic violence; mild or infrequent mature or suggestive themes; or simulated gambling that may not be suitable for children younger than the age of 12.

- **17+:** May contain frequent and intense offensive language; frequent and intense cartoon, fantasy, or realistic violence; mature, frequent, and intense mature, suggestive, or horror-themed content; sexual content; nudity; or depictions of alcohol, tobacco, or drugs that may not be suitable for children younger than the age of 17. You must be at least 17 years old to purchase games with this rating.

Checking requirements and device support for the app

Last but not least, remember the three categories of apps we mention at the beginning of the chapter, in the "Tapping the Magic of Apps" section? If you look below the Information heading in Figure 11-4 (below the Description and What's New sections), you can see the requirements for this particular app. It says *Requires iOS 6 or later. Compatible with iPad.* Note that it doesn't mention the iPhone or iPod touch. That's because this app is in the first category of apps, those made exclusively for the iPad. Another clue that it falls into the first category is that it says *iPad Screenshots* above the two pictures shown in Figure 11-4. Finally, the app's name — SketchBook Express for iPad — should be a dead giveaway.

If the app belonged to the second or third category — apps made to work properly on an iPad, iPhone, or iPod touch, or apps made for the iPhone or iPod touch — the Information section would read *Compatible with iPhone, iPod touch, and iPad* rather than *Compatible with iPad.*

Now you're probably wondering how you can tell whether an app falls into the second or third category. The first clue is the little gray + sign next to the price, which appears for many of the apps shown in Figure 11-3. Apps with this symbol are universal and run at full resolution on iPhones and iPads. Another clue is to look at the screenshots. If you see *two* tabs — iPhone and iPad — after *Screenshots,* the app will work at the full resolution of an iPad, iPhone, or iPod touch. Conversely, if you only see one tab that says *iPhone Screenshots,* the app will run at iPhone/iPod touch resolution on your iPad.

One way to ensure that you look only for apps that take advantage of your iPad's big screen is to click the iPad tab on the front page of the App Store (shown earlier in Figure 11-2). All the apps displayed under the iPad tab are of the first or second type and are designed to take advantage of your iPad's larger screen.

Reading reviews

If you tap Ratings and Reviews (above the screenshots), you'll see reviews written by users of this app. Each review includes a star rating, from zero to five. If an app is rated four stars or higher, you're safe to assume that most users are happy with this app.

In Figure 11-4, you can see that this app has an average rating for the current version of 4 stars based on 389 user ratings. You can tap Ratings and Reviews to see the average rating for all versions (4 stars based on 2,380 user ratings for SketchBook Express). That means it's probably a pretty good app.

Finally, at the top of the Customer Reviews section and near the right side is a pop-up menu displaying Most Helpful (not shown in Figure 11-4). This menu lets you sort the customer reviews by your choice of Most Helpful, Most Favorable, Most Critical, or Most Recent.

Don't believe everything you read in reviews. Some people buy an app without reading its description, or they try to use it without following the included instructions. Then, when the app doesn't do what they expected, they give it a low rating. The point is, take the ratings and reviews with a grain of salt.

Downloading an app from the iTunes Store

When you find an app you want to try while browsing the App Store on your computer, just click the app's Free or Buy button. When you do so, you have to log in to your iTunes Store account, even if the app is free.

After you log in, the app begins downloading. When it's finished, it appears in the My iPad Apps section of your iTunes library, as shown in Figure 11-5.

Figure 11-5: Apps that you download appear in the Apps section of your iTunes library.

If an app costs money, you'll get a receipt for it via email, usually within 24 hours.

Downloading an app to your iTunes library is only the first half of getting it onto your iPad. After you download an app, you can sync your iPad so the app will be available on it. Chapter 3 covers syncing in detail. You can also get the app via the App Store's Purchased tab (described later in this chapter) or by enabling Automatic Downloads on the Settings app's Store pane on your iPad or the iTunes Preferences Store tab on your computer.

If you want apps to download to your iPad automatically, regardless of which device you used to purchase the app, you can set that up:

- **On a computer:** Connect your iPad via either USB cable or Wi-Fi. Launch iTunes and click the iPad button near the upper-right corner of the iTunes window. Click the Apps tab, scroll to the bottom, and enable the Automatically Sync New Apps check box.

- **On your iPad:** Tap Settings ⇨ iTunes and App Store. Then turn on the switch for Apps in the Automatic Downloads section.

You can enable Automatic Downloads for Music and Books on your iPad (but not in iTunes).

Updating an app from the iTunes Store

Every so often, the developer of an iPad app releases an update. Sometimes these updates add new features to the app, sometimes they squash bugs, and sometimes they do both. In any event, updates are usually good things for you and your iPad, so it makes sense to check for them every so often.

To do this in iTunes: Click the Apps icon to select it, as shown in Figure 11-5. Click the Updates tab. Then, to update all the apps at once, click the Update All Apps button in the lower-right corner of the screen. To update apps one by one, click the individual Update button for each app you want to update.

Note that if you hover the pointer over the Apps icon when updates are available, you'll see how many updates are waiting for you.

After you download an update this way, it replaces the older version in your iTunes library and on your iPad automatically the next time you sync. Or, if you've enabled automatic downloads for apps as described earlier in the chapter, the new app replaces the old app automatically the next time you're connected to the Internet.

Using Your iPad to Find Apps

Finding apps with your iPad is almost as easy as finding them by using iTunes. The only requirement is that you have an Internet connection of some sort — Wi-Fi or wireless data network — so that you can access the iTunes App Store and browse, search, download, and install apps.

Browsing the App Store on your iPad

To get started, tap the App Store icon (shown in the margin) on your iPad's Home screen. After you launch the App Store, you see five icons at the bottom of the screen, representing five ways to interact with the store, as shown in Figure 11-6. The first four icons at the bottom of the screen — Featured, Top Charts, Explore, and Purchased — offer four ways to browse the virtual shelves of the App Store. (We cover the fifth icon, Updates, a little later, in the "Updating an app from the App Store" section.)

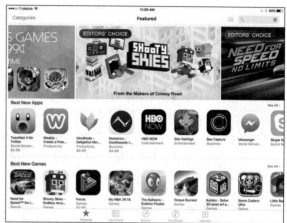

Figure 11-6: The icons across the bottom represent the five sections of the App Store.

Tap Categories in the top-left corner to browse apps in categories such as Books, Education, Games, Music, News, and Productivity, to name a few. Tap a category to see the apps it contains.

The Featured section is almost the same as the section of the same name on the landing page of the iTunes App Store (refer to Figure 11-2). Scroll down and you'll find the same ads and departments you'd see in iTunes on your computer.

The Top Charts section offers lists of the top paid and free apps, which correlate with the Top Free and Top Paid lists, respectively, on the right side of the screen in iTunes (as shown in Figure 11-2).

The Explore section is kind of cool. After granting it permission to use your current location, you'll find apps with local content, such as newspaper, television, and public transit apps. The feature is handy in your hometown but even more useful when you're out of town. (Note that Location Services must be enabled in Settings⇨Privacy for this feature to work.)

Finally, the Purchased section displays all your iPad apps — the ones currently installed on this iPad and any that you've purchased that aren't installed. To the right of each app, you see either Installed or iCloud (as shown in the margin). To install an uninstalled app, tap its iCloud button and then type your password.

Most pages in the App Store display more apps than can fit on the screen at once. For example, the Best New Apps section in Figure 11-6 contains more than the nine apps you can see. A few tools help you navigate the multiple pages of apps:

- ✓ **Swipe from right to left** to see more apps in a category.
- ✓ **Swipe up the screen** to see additional categories.
- ✓ **Tap the See All link** at the top right of most sections to (what else?) see all the apps in that section on the same screen.

Using the search field in the App Store

If you know exactly what you're looking for (or even approximately what you're looking for), rather than simply browsing, you can tap the search field in the upper-right corner of the iPad screen and type a word or phrase; then tap the Search key on the keyboard to initiate the search.

Finding details about an app in the App Store

Now that you know how to find apps in the App Store, the following sections show you how to find out more about a particular app. After tapping an app icon as you browse the store or in a search result, your iPad displays a details screen like the one shown in Figure 11-7.

The app description on this screen was written by the developer and may be somewhat biased.

Figure 11-7: Real Racing 3 is a free car racing game with awesome graphics and realistic physics.

The information you find on the Details tab for an app on your iPad is similar to that info on the iTunes screen on your computer. The links, rating, and requirements simply appear in slightly different places on your iPad screen. (See the section "Getting more information about an app in the iTunes Store," earlier in this chapter, for explanations of the main on-screen items.)

To read reviews from your iPad, tap the Reviews tab. If you scroll to the bottom of the page and see a More Reviews button (not visible in Figure 11-7), tap it to see (what else?) more reviews.

Downloading an app from the App Store

To download an app to your iPad (while using your iPad), follow these steps:

1. **Tap the blue price button (or the word *Get* or the download from iCloud icon) near the top of the app's details screen.**

   In Figure 11-7, you see the download from iCloud icon instead of a price because we purchased the game previously. Once tapped, the button transforms into a green Buy button.

2. **Tap the green Buy button.**

3. **When prompted, type your iTunes Store account password.**

   After you do, the App Store closes, and you see the Home screen where the new app's icon will reside. The new app's icon is slightly dimmed and has the word *Loading* below it, with a pie chart to indicate how much of the app remains to be downloaded (about one third, as shown in the margin).

4. **If the app is rated 17+, click OK on the warning screen that appears after you type your password to confirm that you're 17 or older before the app downloads.**

Downloading other content on your iPad

You may have noticed that the App Store app on your iPad offers nothing but apps. iTunes on your computer, on the other hand, includes sections for music, movies, TV shows, books, podcasts, and iTunes U.

On your iPad, you obtain music, movies, and TV shows with the iTunes Store app and read stories from newspapers and magazines in the News or Safari apps (both included with your iPad). To download books, podcasts, or iTunes U content, however, you'll need the iBooks, Podcasts, or iTunes U apps, which (curiously) are not included with your iPad out of the box.

The good news is that these apps are free in the App Store, so if you want to shop for books, podcasts, or iTunes U content on your iPad, you should probably go download one or more apps now.

All these apps work pretty much the same, so when you understand how to navigate the App Store app, you also know how to use all the store apps.

The app is now on your iPad, but it isn't copied to your iTunes library on your Mac or PC until your next sync unless you've enabled automatic downloads. If your iPad suddenly loses its memory (unlikely) or if you delete the app from your iPad before you sync (as we describe later in this chapter, in the section "Deleting an app"), that app is gone. That's the bad news. The good news is that you can download it again from the Purchased tab as described earlier in the chapter. Or the app will reappear spontaneously on your iPad if you've enabled automatic downloads.

Updating an app from the App Store

As we mention earlier in this chapter, every so often the developer of an iPad app releases an update. If an update awaits you, a little number in a circle appears on the Updates icon at the bottom of the iPad screen. Follow these steps to update your apps from your iPad:

1. **Tap the Updates icon if any of your apps needs updating.**

   If you tap the Updates icon and see (in the middle of the screen) a message that says *All Apps Are Up to Date,* none of the apps on your iPad requires an update at this time. If apps need updating, they appear with Update buttons next to them.

2. **Tap the Update button that appears next to any app to update it.**

   If more than one app needs updating, you can update them all at once by tapping the Update All button in the upper-right corner of the screen.

If you try to update an app purchased from any iTunes Store account except your own, you're prompted for that account's ID and password. If you can't provide them, you can't download the update.

Sometimes an update is worse than its predecessor. If you have mission-critical apps on your iPad, you probably shouldn't update them without careful consideration and research. And you'll want to disable Automatic Downloads for app updates. To do so, tap Settings⇨iTunes & App Store and then tap the Updates switch in the Automatic Downloads section so it's turned off (not green).

One last tip: If you download an app and it doesn't work properly, try deleting and redownloading it from the App Store. Doing so fixes the problem as often as not.

Working with Apps

Most of what you need to know about apps involves simply installing third-party apps on your iPad. However, you might find it helpful to know how to delete and review an app.

Deleting an app

The preinstalled apps that came on your iPad can't be removed, but you have two ways to delete any other app: in iTunes on your computer or directly from your iPad.

You can, however, hide certain preinstalled apps by choosing Settings⇨ General⇨Restrictions.

To delete an app in iTunes (that is, from your computer), click the Apps icon and then do one of the following:

- ✔ Click the app to select it and press the Delete or Backspace key on the keyboard.
- ✔ Click the app to select it and then choose Edit⇨Delete.
- ✔ Right-click the app and choose Delete.

After taking any of the actions in this list, you see a dialog that asks whether you're sure that you want to remove the selected app. If you click the Remove button, the app is removed from your iTunes library as well as from any iPad that syncs with your iTunes library.

Here's how to delete an app on your iPad:

1. **Press and hold any icon until all the icons begin to wiggle.**

2. **Tap the little *x* in the upper-left corner of the app that you want to delete.**

   A dialog appears, informing you that deleting this app also deletes all its data, as shown in Figure 11-8.

3. **Tap the Delete button.**

   You can't delete any of the bundled apps that came with your iPad.

4. **To stop the icons from wiggling, press the Home or sleep/wake button.**

Figure 11-8: Tap an app's little *x* and then tap Delete to remove the app from your iPad.

You also make icons wiggle to move them around on the screen or move them from page to page. To rearrange wiggling icons, press and drag them one at a time. If you drag an icon to the left or right edge of the screen, it moves to the next or previous Home screen. You can also drag two additional icons to the dock (where Safari, Mail, Photos, and Music live) and have a total of six apps available from every Home screen.

Friendly reminder: Rearranging your icons in iTunes is faster and easier than making them wiggle and move on the iPad. See Chapter 3 to find out how.

Writing an app review

Sometimes you love or hate an app so much that you want to tell the world about it. In that case, you should write a review. You can do this in two ways: in iTunes on your computer or directly from your iPad.

To write a review using iTunes on your computer, follow these steps:

1. **Navigate to the details page for the app in the iTunes App Store.**

2. **Click the Ratings and Reviews tab and then click the Write a Review button.**

   You may or may not have to type your iTunes Store password.

3. **Click the button for the star rating (1 to 5) you want to give the app.**

4. **In the Title field, type a title for your review, and in the Review field, type your review.**

5. **Click the Submit button when you're finished.**

   The Preview screen appears. If the review looks good to you, you're done. If you want to change something, click the Edit button.

To write a review from your iPad, follow these steps:

1. **Tap the App Store icon to launch the App Store.**

2. **Navigate to the details screen for the app.**

3. **Tap the Reviews tab and then tap the Write a Review link.**

   You probably have to type your iTunes Store password.

4. **Tap one to five of the stars at the top of the Write a Review screen to rate the app.**

5. **In the Title field, type a title for your review, and in the Review field, type your review.**

6. **Tap the Submit button in the upper-right corner of the screen.**

   Whichever way you submit your review, Apple reviews your submission. As long as the review doesn't violate the (unpublished) rules of conduct for app reviews, it appears in a day or two in the App Store, in the Reviews section for the particular app.

One final tip: You can configure the behavior of many apps in the Settings app. Scroll all the way down the list of settings and you'll find an alphabetical list of apps that have settings; tap an app in the list to see its settings.

People, Places, and Appointments

In This Chapter

▶ Understanding the calendar's different views and functions

▶ Mingling with contacts

We hate to break the news to you, but your iPad isn't all fun and games; it has a serious side. The iPad can remind you of appointments and help you keep all your contacts straight. If you purchased a new iPad (or iPhone or iPod touch) after October 22, 2013, you also received Numbers (a first-class spreadsheet), Pages (a terrific word processor), and Keynote (the best presentation program we know), as well as Photos, iMovie, and GarageBand.

In this chapter, we explore Calendar and Contacts, a pair of apps that aren't particularly flashy but can be remarkably useful. Space constraints prohibit us from covering the aforementioned productivity and lifestyle apps in this book, but check out our online coverage.

Working with the Calendar

The Calendar program lets you keep on top of your appointments and events (birthdays, anniversaries, and the like). You open it by tapping the Calendar icon on the Home screen. The icon is smart in its own right because it changes daily, displaying the day of the week and the date.

You can display five calendar views: by year, by month, by day, by week, and by a searchable list view that shows current and future appointments.

Tap one of the four tabs at the top of the screen — Day, Week, Month, or Year — to choose a view. There's a Today button in the lower-left corner of the screen, which returns you to the current date in any view. (Also at the bottom of the screen are the Calendars button and Inbox button, which we get to shortly.)

To get to list view, tap the search icon — a little magnifying glass — in the upper-right corner of the screen.

We take a closer look at these views in the following sections.

Year view

There's not much to the yearly view, but it does let you see the current calendar year with today's date circled in red. You can scroll up or down to see prior or future years, but that's about it; unfortunately, you still can't tell on which days you have appointments in year view. Boo. Hiss.

Month view

Tap any of the months visible in the yearly view to jump to that specific month, as shown in Figure 12-1. When your iPad is in month view, you can see which days have appointments or scheduled events. Tap a day to see the list of activities on the agenda for that day, which leads nicely into the next section.

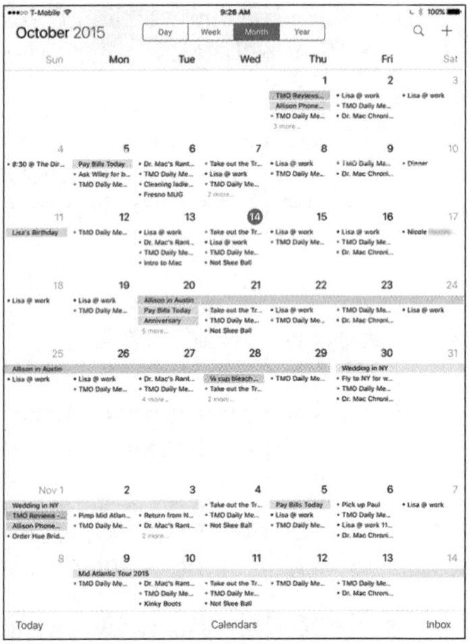

Day view

As we just mentioned, you have to tap a date to see what you have going on in a 24-hour period — though to see an entire day's worth of entries, you'll have to scroll up or down. You can swipe to the left to advance to the next day of the week and beyond; swipe to the right to retreat one or more days; or tap a day near the top of the screen to jump to it.

Figure 12-1: Month view.

In this day view, all-day events, birth-days, and events pulled from your Facebook account (if you provide your Facebook credentials) appear in a narrow strip above the timeline for the day, as shown for the all-day event *Wedding in NY* in Figure 12-2.

Your daily appointments span the entire time in which they've been scheduled on your calendar. For example, if an appointment runs from 11:45 a.m. to 12:45 p.m., that hour will be blocked off on the calendar like the *Confirm Flight* item shown in Figure 12-2.

You find out how to create calendar entries in a moment, but for now know that you can hold down on an event and drag it to a new time slot should your plans change. If you have overlapping appointments, you'll see more than a single entry claim a given time slot.

Calendars are color-coded according to the calendar in which you scheduled the appointment to help you distinguish an appointment you made on your travel calendar versus, say, a work, family, or Facebook calendar.

Week view

In week view, shown in Figure 12-3, you can see an entire week at a glance. The current day is circled in red. You can arrange to start your weekly view on any day of the week. Tap Settings ➪ Mail, Contacts, Calendars➪Start Week On, and then tap the day on which you want to start your week (Sunday is the default in the United States).

Figure 12-2: Day view.

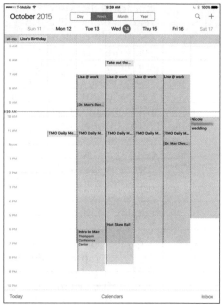

Figure 12-3: Week view.

TIP

Syncing calendars with your desktop

The iPad can display the color-coding you assigned in Calendar (formerly iCal) on a Mac. Cool, huh? If you're a Mac user who uses Calendar, you can create multiple calendars and choose which ones to sync with your iPad. What's more, you can choose to display any or all of your calendars on your iPad. Calendar entries you create on your iPad are synchronized with the calendar(s) you specified in the iTunes Info pane. You can also sync calendars with Microsoft Outlook on a Mac or Microsoft Outlook on a PC.

The best solution we've found is to use iCloud to keep calendars updated and in sync across all your iOS devices and computers. On the iPad, tap Settings⇨iCloud and make sure the Calendars switch is turned on (green).

One last thing: If you're a Mac user running OS X 10.9 Mavericks or later, iCloud is the *only* way you can sync calendar data, as we mention in Chapter 3.

List view

List view isn't complicated. You can get to this view by tapping the search (magnifying glass) icon in the upper-right corner of the screen. As you would expect, all your calendar appointments are listed chronologically, as shown in Figure 12-4. If you have a lengthy list, drag up or down with your finger or flick to rapidly scroll through your appointments. If you're looking for a specific calendar entry, you can search for appointments by typing the title, invitee names, location, or note in the search box above your list of entries (or employ Spotlight to help you search).

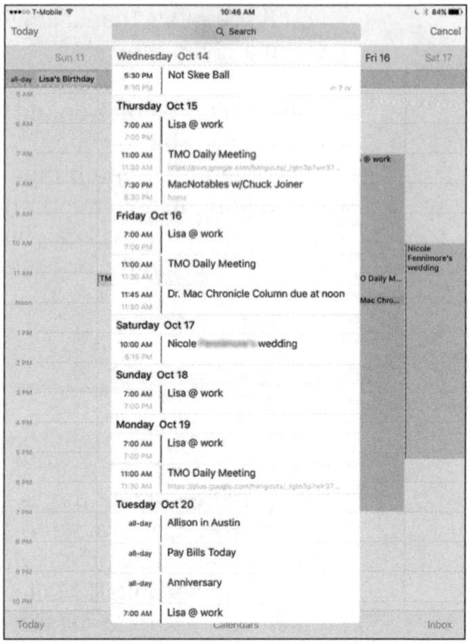

Tap any of the listings to get meeting or appointment details for that entry. If you tap a person's birthday, you see his or her contact information. Sorry, but you just ran out of excuses for not sending a card at least.

Figure 12-4: List view.

Adding Calendar Entries

In Chapter 3, you discover pretty much everything there is to know about syncing your iPad, including syncing calendar entries from your Windows machine (using the likes of Microsoft Outlook) or Mac (using Calendar or Outlook) or Google Calendars. And if you're syncing your calendar entries with iCloud, you can also manage your calendars at www.iCloud.com.

In addition, any calendar entries in Facebook can automatically show up in the Calendar app. You will have to visit Settings, enter your username and password, and then make sure the Calendar app in the Facebook setting is turned on.

In plenty of situations, you enter appointments on the fly. Adding appointments directly to the iPad is easy:

1. **On the Home screen, tap the Calendar icon, and then (optionally) tap the Year, Month, or Day view.**

2. **Tap the + icon in the upper-right corner of the screen.**

   The New Event screen appears, as shown in Figure 12-5.

3. **Tap the Title and Location fields in turn (second-generation iPads don't have a Location field) and type as much or as little information as you feel is necessary.**

   Tapping displays the virtual keyboard (if it's not already shown).

   If your iPad includes dictation or Siri, you can use either of those features to add a calendar entry. See Chapter 14 for more on dictation and Siri.

4. **To add start and end times:**

   a. Tap the Starts field.

   A carousel wheel, like the one shown for the Ends time in Figure 12-6, appears below the field you tapped.

   b. Choose the time the event starts.

   Use your finger to roll separate carousel controls for the date, hour, and minute (in 1-minute intervals)

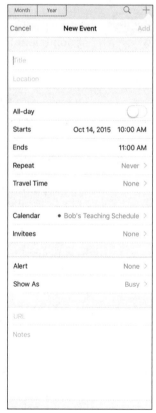

Figure 12-5: The screen looks like this just before you add an event to your iPad.

and to specify AM or PM. The process is a little like manipulating a combination bicycle lock or an old-fashioned date stamp used with an inkpad.

   c. *Tap the Ends field and choose the time the event ends.*

To enter an all-day milestone (such as a birthday), tap the All-Day switch to turn it on. (Green will be showing.) Because the time is no longer relevant for an all-day entry, you won't see Starts, Ends, or Time Zone options.

5. When you're finished, tap Add.

If your iPad comes equipped with Siri, we can't think of any easier way to add an entry. You can instruct Siri along the lines of "Set a lunch appointment for tomorrow at noon with the Smiths." Siri is pleased to comply.

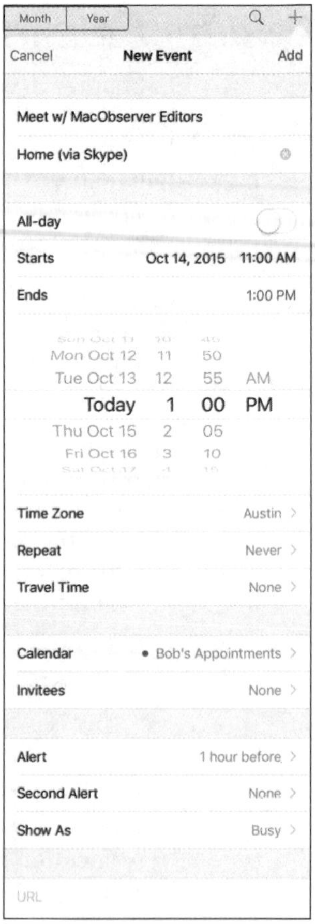

That's the minimum you have to do to set up an event. But we bet you want to do more. The Calendar app makes it easy:

- ✔ **Change the time zone.** If the correct location isn't already present, tap the Time Zone field and type the name of the city where the appointment is taking place.

- ✔ **Set up a recurring entry.** Tap the Repeat field. Tap to indicate how often the event in question recurs. This setting is good for everything from a weekly appointment, such as an allergy shot, to a yearly event, such as an anniversary.

The options are Every Day, Every Week, Every 2 Weeks, Every Month, and Every Year. Tap Never if you are planning to never repeat this entry again.

- ✔ **Add travel time to and from events.** Tap the Travel Time field and enable the Travel Time switch. A list of durations appears, ranging from five minutes to two hours. Tap a duration to specify your travel time.

- ✔ **Assign the entry to a particular calendar.** Tap Calendar, and then tap the calendar you have in mind (Home or Work, for example).

- ✔ **Invite people to join you.** Tap Invitees to specify who among your contacts will be attending the event.

Month	Year		Q	+
Cancel	**New Event**			Add

Meet w/ MacObserver Editors

Home (via Skype)   ⊗

All-day   ◯

Starts   Oct 14, 2015   11:00 AM

Ends   1:00 PM

Sun Oct 11	10	45	
Mon Oct 12	11	50	
Tue Oct 13	12	55	AM
Today	**1**	**00**	**PM**
Thu Oct 15	2	05	
Fri Oct 16	3	10	
Sat Oct 17	4	15	

Time Zone   Austin >

Repeat   Never >

Travel Time   None >

Calendar   ● Bob's Appointments >

Invitees   None >

Alert   1 hour before >

Second Alert   None >

Show As   Busy >

URL

Figure 12-6: Controlling the Starts and Ends fields is like manipulating a bike lock.

✔ **Set a reminder or alert for the entry.** Tap Alert and tap a time.

Alerts can be set to arrive at the actual time of an event, or 1 week before, 2 days before, 1 day before, 2 hours before, 1 hour before, 30 minutes before, 15 minutes before, or 5 minutes before the event. If it's an all-day entry, you can request alerts 1 day before (at 9:00 a.m.), 2 days before (at 9:00 a.m.), or 1 week before.

When the appointment time rolls around, you hear a sound and see a message like the one shown in Figure 12-7.

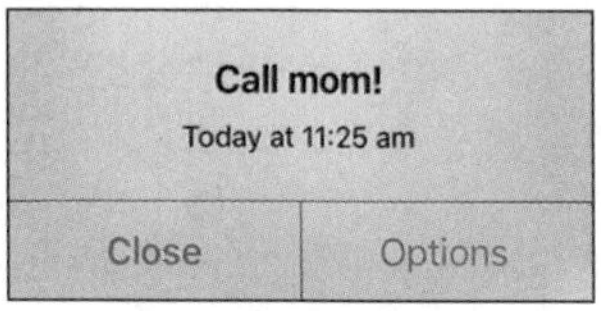

If you're the kind of person who needs an extra nudge, set another reminder by tapping the Second Alert field (which you'll see only if a first alert is already set).

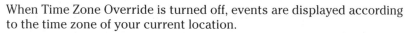

Figure 12-7: Alerts make it hard to forget.

✔ **Indicate whether you're busy or free by tapping Show As.** If you're invited to an event, you can tap Availability and then tap Free (if it's shown on your iPad).

✔ **Enter a web address.** Tap the URL field (at the bottom of the New Event screen) and type the web address.

✔ **Enter notes about the appointment or event.** Tap the Notes field (at the bottom of the screen) and type your note.

Tap Done after you finish entering everything.

Managing your calendars

When you have the hang of creating calendar entries, you can make the task much easier with these tips:

✔ **Choose a default calendar.** Tap Settings⇨Mail, Contacts, Calendars, and then flick the screen until the Calendar section appears. Tap Default Calendar and select the calendar that you want to show up regularly.

✔ **Make events appear according to whichever time zone you selected for your calendars.** In the Calendar settings, tap Time Zone Override to turn it on, and then tap Time Zone. Type the time zone's location, using the kcyboard that appears. If you travel long distances for your job, this setting comes in handy.

When Time Zone Override is turned off, events are displayed according to the time zone of your current location.

✔ **Turn off a calendar alert.** Tap Settings⇨Sounds, and then make sure that the selected alert tone is set to None. (You see only the last calendar alert sound that you selected. To see your other choices, tap Calendar Alerts.) You can also set default alert times for birthdays, all-day events, or certain other events. Tap Settings⇨Mail, Contacts, Calendars, and scroll down to Default Alert Times. For birthdays or other all-day events, you can choose to be alerted at 9:00 a.m. on the day of the event, at 9:00 a.m. one day before, at 9:00 a.m. two days before, or a week before. For other alerts, you can choose a default alert time at the time of event, 5 minutes before, 15 minutes before, 30 minutes before, 1 hour before, 2 hours before, 1 day before, 2 days before, or 1 week before the event.

✔ **Modify an existing calendar entry.** Tap the entry, tap Edit, and then make whichever changes need to be made.

✔ **Wipe out a calendar entry.** Scroll down to the bottom and tap Edit⇨ Delete Event. You have a chance to confirm your choice by tapping either Delete Event (again) or Cancel.

Letting your calendar push you around

If you work for a company that uses Microsoft Exchange ActiveSync, calendar entries and meeting invitations from coworkers can be *pushed* to your device so that they show up on the screen moments after they're entered, even if they're entered on computers at work. Setting up an account to facilitate this pushing of calendar entries to your iPad is a breeze, although you should check with your company's tech or IT department to make sure that your employer allows it. Then follow these steps:

1. **Tap Settings⇨Mail, Contacts, Calendars⇨Add Account.**

2. **From the Add Account list, tap Microsoft Exchange.**

3. **Fill in the email address, username, password, and description fields, and then tap Next.**

4. **If required, enter your server address on the next screen that appears.**

   The iPad supports something called the Microsoft Autodiscovery service, which uses your name and password to automatically determine the address of the Exchange server. The rest of the fields should be filled in with the email address, username, password, and description you just entered.

5. **Tap Next.**

6. **Tap the switch to turn on each information type that you want to synchronize using Microsoft Exchange.**

   The options are Mail, Contacts, Calendars, and Reminders. You should be good to go now, although some employers may require you to add passcodes to safeguard company secrets.

If you have a business-issued iPad and it is lost or stolen — or it turns out that you're a double agent working for a rival company — your employer's IT administrators can remotely wipe your device clean.

If you sync via iCloud, your calendar entries can also be pushed by tapping Settings⇨Mail, Contacts, Calendars⇨Fetch New Data and enabling the on/off switch for Push (green = on).

Displaying multiple calendars

By tapping the Calendars button at the bottom of the yearly, monthly, or daily view, you can choose the calendar or calendars to display on your iPad. Merely tap each calendar that you want to include so that a check mark appears next to it, as shown in Figure 12-8. To remove the check mark, tap again.

You can tap the Hide All Calendars button (not visible in Figure 12-8) when you don't want any calendars to be visible, or conversely tap Show All Calendars (also not visible in Figure 12-8) when you want your entire schedule to be an open book. You can also turn on Facebook events (in Settings) to display those in your calendar, as well as display birthdays, including those of the people you've friended on the social network.

Figure 12-8: Choosing the calendars to display.

From the Calendars listing, tap the *i*-in-a-circle for even more tricks. You can assign a color to your calendar, share the calendar with a given individual (tap Add Person to do so), make a calendar public (by flipping a switch), or delete the calendar.

Responding to meeting invitations

The iPad has one more important button in the Calendar app. It's the Inbox button, located at the bottom-right corner of the yearly, monthly, and daily views. If you partake in iCloud, have a Microsoft Exchange account, or have a calendar that adheres to the CalDAV Internet standard, you can send and receive a meeting invitation, though you also need a compatible email app that understands CalDAV and lets you not only receive but also respond to the invitation.

If you have any pending invitations, you'll see them when you tap the Inbox, which is separated into new invitations and invitations to which you've already replied. You can tap any of the items in the list to see more details about the event to which you've been invited.

Suppose that a meeting invitation arrives from your boss. You can see who else is attending the shindig, check scheduling conflicts, and more. Tap Accept to let the meeting organizer know you're attending, tap Decline if you have something better to do (and aren't worried about upsetting the person who signs your paycheck), or tap Maybe if you're waiting for a better offer.

And as we point out previously, you can also invite other folks to attend an event that you yourself are putting together.

Meantime, if you run into a conflict, why not ask Siri to change your schedule? For that matter, you can also call upon Siri to remind you when you have your next appointment. Visit Chapter 14 for more on this clever feature.

You can choose to receive an alert every time someone sends you an invitation. In the Calendar settings, tap New Invitation Alerts so that the switch is turned on.

As mentioned, if you take advantage of iCloud, you can keep calendar entries synchronized between your iPhone, iPad, iPod touch, and Mac or PC. When you make a scheduling change on your iPad, it's automatically updated on your computer and other devices, and vice versa. Choose iCloud from the Add Account screen to get started, assuming you didn't turn on iCloud when you first activated your iPad.

Subscribing to calendars

You can subscribe to calendars that adhere to the CalDAV and iCalendar (.ics) standards, which are supported by the popular Google and Yahoo! calendars and by the Mac's Calendar app. Although you can read entries on the iPad from the calendars you subscribe to, you can't create entries from the iPad or edit the entries that are already present.

To subscribe to one of these calendars, tap Settings⇨Mail, Contacts, Calendars⇨Add Account⇨Other. You then choose Add CalDAV Account or Add Subscribed Calendar. Next, enter the server where the iPad can find the calendar you have in mind, and if need be, a username, a password, and an optional description.

Finally, some apps, websites, and email messages will offer to add calendar events and subscriptions.

Sifting through Contacts

If you read the chapter on syncing (see Chapter 3), you know how to get the snail-mail addresses, email addresses, and phone numbers that reside on your Mac or PC into the iPad. Assuming that you went through that drill already, all those addresses and phone numbers are hanging out in one place. Their not-so-secret hiding place is revealed when you tap the Contacts icon on the Home screen. The following sections guide you from the main screen to whatever you want to do with your contacts' information.

Adding and viewing contacts

To add contacts from the Contacts app, tap the + icon at the top of the screen and type as much or as little profile information as you have for the person. Tap Add Photo to add a picture from your photo albums or collections (or to take a snapshot with your iPad camera). You can edit the information later by tapping the Edit button when a contact's name is highlighted.

A list of your contacts appears on the left panel of the screen, with the one you're currently viewing shown in gray; see Figure 12-9. On the right, you can see a mug shot of your contact, plus any info you have: phone number, email address, home and another address, and birthday (all blurred in Figure 12-9 to protect Jacob's privacy). You also find an area to scribble notes about a contact.

You have three ways to land on a specific contact:

Figure 12-9: A view of all contacts.

- ✓ **Flick your finger so that the list of contacts on the left side scrolls rapidly up or down,** loosely reminiscent of the spinning Lucky 7s and other pictures on a Las Vegas slot machine. Think of the payout you'd get with that kind of power on a one-armed bandit.

- ✓ **Slide your thumb or another finger along the alphabet on the left edge of the contacts list or tap one of the teeny-tiny letters** to jump to names that begin with that letter.

✔ **Start to type the name of a contact in the search field near the top of the contacts list. Or type the name of the place your contact works.** When you're at or near the appropriate contact name, stop the scrolling by tapping the screen.

When you tap to stop the scrolling, that tap doesn't select an item in the list. This may seem counterintuitive the first few times you try it, but we got used to it and now we really like it this way. Just think of that first tap as applying the brakes to the scrolling list.

You can change the way your contacts are displayed. Tap Settings⇨Mail, Contacts, Calendars. Then scroll down to Contacts settings on the right side of the screen, if it's not already visible. Tap Sort Order or Display Order, and for each one, choose the First, Last option or Last, First option to indicate whether you want to sort or display entries by a contact's first or last name.

Searching contacts

You can search contacts by entering a first or last name in the search field or by entering a company name.

You can locate people on your iPad without opening the Contacts app. Type a name in the Spotlight search field (see Chapter 2), and then tap the name in the search results. And if your iPad comes with Siri, you can not only ask her to find people for you but also have her compose and send them an email or iMessage, or call them via FaceTime video or audio chat.

If you're searching contacts with a Microsoft Exchange account, you may be able to search your employer's *global address list* (GAL for short). This search typically works in one of two ways:

✔ Tap the Groups button in the upper-left corner of the All Contacts screen and then tap the appropriate Exchange server name to find folks. Groups on your computer might reflect, say, different departments in your company, friends from work, friends from school, and so on.

✔ You can search an LDAP *(Lightweight Directory Access Protocol)* server. It strikes us that nothing is "lightweight" about something called an LDAP server, but we digress. Similarly, if you have a CardDAV account, you can search for any contacts that have been synced to the iPad.

Contacting and sharing your contacts

You can initiate an email from Contacts by tapping an email address under a contact's listings. Doing so fires up the Mail program on the iPad, with the person's name already in the To field. For more on the Mail app, we direct you to Chapter 5.

You can also share a contact's profile with another person. Tap the Share Contact button (you may have to scroll down to see it), and use the Mail or Messages app to send the contact's vCard, which is embedded in the body of a new Mail or Messages message. Just add an address and send it on its merry way. A *vCard,* in case you were wondering, is kind of like an electronic business card. You can identify it by its .vcf file format.

Finally, you can tap a contact's snail-mail address to launch the Maps app and see it pinned to a map.

Linking contacts

The people you know most likely have contact entries in more than one account, meaning that you might end up with redundant entries for the same person. The iPad solution is to *link* contacts. Find the contact in question, tap Edit, scroll to the bottom of the Edit screen, and tap Link Contact. Choose the related contact entry and then tap Link. It's worth noting that the linked contacts in each account remain separate and aren't merged.

Removing a contact

Hey, it happens. A person falls out of favor. Maybe he's a jilted lover. Or maybe you just moved cross country and no longer will call on the services of your old gardener.

Removing a contact is easy, if unfortunate. Tap a contact and then tap Edit. Scroll to the bottom of the Edit screen and tap Delete Contact. You get one more chance to change your mind.

And that, gentle reader, should be pretty much all you need to work with Contacts. Onward!

13

Indispensable iPad Utilities

*W*e'd venture to say that no one bought an iPad because of Notes, Clock, Reminders, or Game Center. Still, these apps help make the iPad indispensable on a daily basis.

In addition to the indispensable apps described in this chapter, we also demonstrate how to create a Wi-Fi hotspot no matter where you are (all iPads with 4G features except the second generation) and how to share with AirDrop.

Taking Note of Notes

Notes is an app that creates notes that you can save or send through email.

Notes received a major upgrade in iOS 9, with new features such as a "sketch with your finger" mode, checklists, and enclosures. In addition, many apps will allow you to save data directly to the Notes app (by tapping the share icon). Finally, all your notes are synced across all your enabled Apple devices via iCloud.

To create a note, follow these steps:

1. **On the Home screen, tap the Notes icon.**

2. **Tap the new note icon (shown in the margin) in the upper-right corner to start a new note.**

   The virtual keyboard appears.

3. **Type a note, such as the one shown in Figure 13-1.**

Figure 13-1 shows off a few of the new features in Notes: The list is formatted as a checklist, with a crudely drawn sketch at the bottom.

Other things you can do before you quit the Notes app include the following:

Text formatting

Checklist

Undo/redo/paste

Add photo or video

Finger sketch

Figure 13-1: The Notes app revealed.

✔ Tap the Notes or Folders button in the upper-left corner of the screen to see either a list of all your notes or — if you sync Notes with more than one account, such as iCloud, Google, or Yahoo! — folders for All Notes plus a separate folder for each service you sync with.

✔ When a list of notes is on-screen, tap a folder to see its contents, or tap a note to open and view, edit, or modify it. (**Hint:** The list is always visible when you hold your iPad in landscape mode with the longer edges parallel to the ground.)

- ↙ Tap the share icon at the top-right corner (and shown in the margin) to send the note using the Mail or Messages app (see Chapter 5 for more about Mail and iMessage), copy the note to the Clipboard (see Chapter 2 for the scoop on copy and paste), post the note to social media, assign the note to a contact, or print the note (see Chapter 2 for more about printing).

- ↙ Tap the trash icon near the top-right corner of the screen to delete the note.

When the keyboard is displayed, you can

- ↙ Tap the check mark icon above the top row of keys to create a checklist; select text before you tap it to change existing text into a check list.

- ↙ Tap the Aa icon above the top row of keys to format text as Title, Heading, Body, Bulleted List, Dashed List, or Numbered List. Select the text before you tap it to change its format.

- ↙ Tap the camera icon above the top row of keys to take a picture or select a picture from your Photos library and add it to this note.

- ↙ Tap the squiggly line icon above the top row of keys to sketch with your finger.

If you're using any iPad except the second-generation model, you can also use Siri to set up and dictate your note by speaking. (You hear more about Siri in Chapter 14.)

As with most iPad apps, your notes are saved automatically while you type them so that you can quit Notes at any time without losing a single character.

We'd be remiss if we didn't remind you one last time that you can sync Notes with your Mac and other devices via iCloud. We'd be remiss also if we didn't mention that unlike other sync functions, you don't enable Notes syncing in iTunes. Instead, you enable it in Settings⇨iCloud on your iPad and System Preferences⇨iCloud on your Mac.

And that's all she wrote. You now know what you need to know about creating and managing notes with Notes.

Remembering with Reminders

You can find lots of good to-do list apps in the App Store; if you don't believe us, search for *to-do list.* You'll find more than 100 offerings for the iPad. Many are free, but others sell (and sell briskly, we might add) at prices up to $30 or $40. Most of these third-party reminder apps have nothing to worry about from the Reminders app, although some people love it.

What you get for free is Reminders, a simple to-do list app for making and organizing lists, with optional reminders available for items in your lists.

Tap the Reminders icon on your Home screen, and you'll see something that looks like Figure 13-2.

Reminders on the right side of the screen in Figure 13-2 belong to a list called *BLTV Show,* as indicated by the list name highlighted on the left side of the screen and appearing at the top of the list.

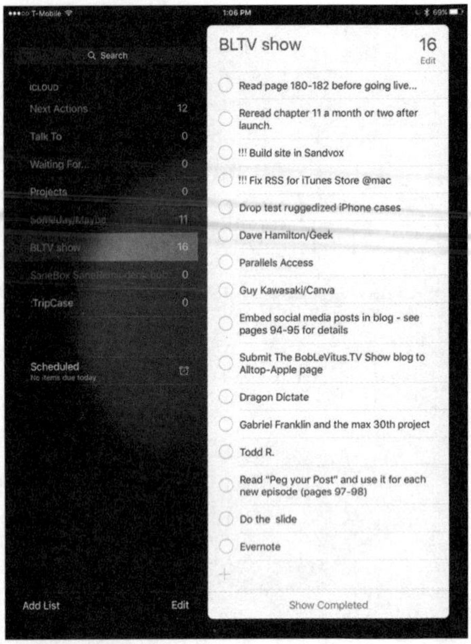

Figure 13-2: The Reminders app.

Working with lists

To create a list, tap Add List in the lower-left corner of the screen, type a name for the list on the virtual keyboard, and then tap Done. You can have as many or as few lists as you like.

To manage the lists you create, tap the Edit button at the bottom of the screen, shown in Figure 13-2. When you do, the left side of the screen goes into what we like to think of as edit mode, as shown in Figure 13-3.

From this screen, you can

- ✔ **Delete a list:** Tap the red minus sign for the list. The list's name slides to the left and reveals a red Delete button (see SaneBox SaneReminder in Figure 13-3).

  You can also delete a list without first tapping the Edit button by swiping the list's name from right to left. The red Delete button appears on the right; tap it to delete the list or tap anywhere else to cancel.

- ✔ **Reorder (move up or down) lists:** Press and hold your finger on the three horizontal lines (shown in the margin) to the right of a list's name in edit mode, and then drag the name up or down. When the list's name is where you want it, lift your finger. Note that the number of items in the list appears to the left of the three horizontal lines.

Setting up reminders

Reminders is a simple app, and the steps for managing reminders are equally simple. Here's how to remind yourself of something:

1. **On the Home screen, tap the Reminders app.**

2. **On the left side of the screen, tap the list to which you want to attach the reminder.**

   If you haven't created your own lists, you'll see the two default lists: Reminders and Scheduled. Otherwise, you'll see a list of all the reminder lists you've created.

   The virtual keyboard appears.

3. **Type a title for the new reminder.**

   You can dictate your reminder instead of typing it if you're using any iPad except a second-generation one. You can find out more about dictation in Chapter 14.

   The item appears in the current reminders list.

   At this point, your reminder is bare-bones; its date, repeat, and priority options have not been activated.

4. **Tap the reminder and then tap the little** *i*-in-a-circle to set the following options in the details overlay, as shown in Figure 13-4:

   • *Remind Me on a Day:* Tap if you want to specify a day and time for this reminder. If you have a 3G or 4G iPad, you can also set a location-based reminder. Just tap the At a Location switch (not shown in Figure 13-4 because this particular iPad is Wi-Fi only) to enable it, specify the location, and then choose When I Arrive, or When I Leave.

Figure 13-3: Tap the Edit button to create, delete, or reorder your lists.

Location-based reminders will suck your iPad battery dry faster than almost anything else. Remember to mark location-based reminders as completed by tapping their check boxes when you finish them. Otherwise, you will be reminded of something you've already done every time you pass that location and it will drain your iPad battery unnecessarily.

If you set a location-based reminder with an iPhone or iPad with 3G or 4G, or with the Reminders app in OS X Mountain Lion or later, the reminder syncs with your Wi-Fi-only iPad but without the location. In fact, you won't even see the At a Location switch if your iPad is Wi-Fi-only (as in Figure 13-4).

• *Repeat:* After you set a reminder, you'll notice that a Repeat button appears. Tap it if you want to set a second reminder for a different day or time.

• *Priority:* Tap to specify a priority for this reminder. You can select None, Low, Medium, or High.

• *List:* Tap if you want this reminder to appear in a list other than the one it currently appears in. Then tap the list to which you want to move this reminder.

• *Notes:* If you have anything else to add, tap the Notes field and type away.

5. **After you've set your options, tap the Done button in the upper-right corner of the details overlay.**

Choose the list you want your new reminder to appear on *before* you create it.

Details	Done

Our shiny new reminder

Remind me on a day	⬤
Alarm	Sun, 10/18/15, 2:00 PM
Repeat	Never ›

Remind me at a location	◯

Priority	None ! !! !!!
List	BLTV show ›
Notes	

Figure 13-4: Details for Our Shiny New Reminder.

Viewing and checking off reminders

After you create reminders, the app helps you see what you have and haven't done and enables you to do the following tasks:

- **Check off reminders.** You probably noticed that every reminder you create includes a hollow circle to its left. Tap the circle to indicate that a task has been completed. When you do, the words Hide (or Show) Completed appear at the bottom of the list. Tap these words to hide or show tasks you've completed in this list.

- **Search reminders.** To search for a word or phrase in all your reminders, completed or not, tap the search field at the upper left, type your word or phrase, and then tap the search icon (magnifying glass). Or swipe down from the middle of any Home screen to search for it with Spotlight.

- **Keep reminders on your Mac or PC.** You can create reminders on your Mac or PC with To Do items in iCal (Lion), Reminders (Mountain Lion or Mavericks), or Tasks in Outlook. And if you're using iCloud, your reminders will always be up to date on all your devices.

That's about it. The Reminders app isn't a bad effort. If it lacks a feature or two that you desire, check out the myriad third-party to-do list apps in the App Store.

Negotiating Notification Center

Notification Center, shown in Figure 13-5, drops down over whatever you're doing at the time so that you can easily see calendar entries, reminders, the weather forecast, and new email messages. Notification Center works regardless of which app you're using.

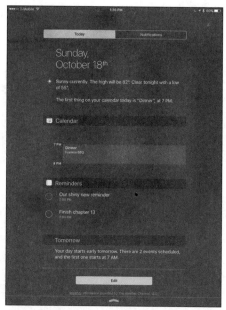

To summon Notification Center to the forefront of your iPad screen, all you need is the magical incantation — that is, a swipe from the top of the screen downward. Go ahead and give it a try. We'll wait.

Notifications also appear on the lock screen, as shown in Figure 13-6. Banner notifications are sweet, and we're particularly fond of sliding our finger to view a particular item. But we digress. You find out how to enable or disable banner and alert notifications for individual apps, but not until Chapter 15.

Figure 13-5: Notification Center in all its splendor.

Here's what you need to know about navigating Notification Center:

Figure 13-6: Notifications on the lock screen; slide your finger on one to open it.

- ✓ **Close Notification Center.** Swipe or flick upward the arrow that looks like a caret symbol (^) at the bottom of the list (refer to Figure 13-5).

- ✓ **Open a notification.** Tap the notification, and it opens in the appropriate program.

- ✓ **Clear a single notification.** Tap the little circle to the left of the notification and it disappears.

- ✓ **The Today and Notification tabs at the top of the screen provide different filters for your notifications.** Tap them to see the way each presents information. Note that some details, such as today's weather and the Tomorrow section, appear only on the Today tab.

TIP

You can switch between the Today and Notifications screens also by swiping from left to right and right to left.

✔ **Clear all notifications from a particular app.** Tap the Notifications tab at the top of the screen. (You can't use the Today tab to clear all notifications from a particular app.) Now tap the little x-in-a-circle to the right of the app's name (Reminders, Calendar, Messages, and such). The x turns into a Clear button. Tap the Clear button and all notifications from that app are cleared and the app's name disappears from Notification Center (but the name will reappear if the app needs to notify you again).

That's how to summon and use Notification Center. There's still a bit more to know — including how to change the notification settings for individual apps — but you have to wait until the chapter on settings (which happens to be Chapter 15).

Punching the Clock

Well, yes, most tablets do have a clock. But not every tablet has a *world clock* that lets you display the time in multiple cities on multiple continents. And not every device also has an alarm, a stopwatch, and a timer to boot.

So tap the Clock icon on your Home screen or in Control Center and see what the Clock app is all about.

World clock

Want to know the time in Beijing or Bogota? Tapping World Clock (in the Clock app) lets you display the time in numerous cities around the globe, as shown in Figure 13-7. When the clock face is dark, it's nighttime in the city you chose; if the face is white, it's daytime outside.

To add a city to the world clock, tap the + in the middle of the rightmost clock face (the one labeled Add),

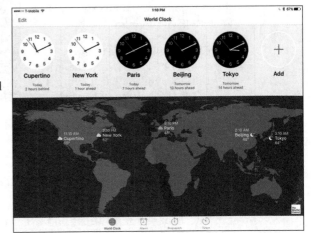

Figure 13-7: What time is it in Tokyo?

and then use the virtual keyboard to start typing a city name, as shown in Figure 13-8. (If you don't see the + clock face, you probably have six or more clocks. To see the rest of the clocks and the clock with the +, swipe the clocks from right to left.)

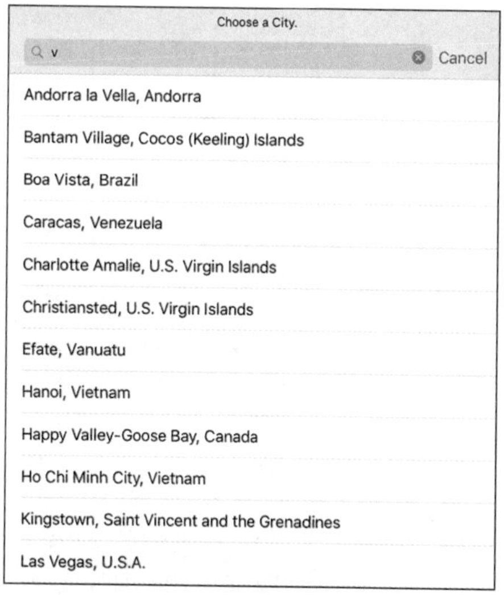

The moment you press the first letter, the iPad displays a list of cities or countries that begin with that letter. So, as Figure 13-8 shows, typing *v* brings up Andorra la Vella, Andora; Bantam Village, Cocos (Keeling) Islands; and Boa Vista, Brazil, among myriad other possibilities. You can create clocks for as many cities as you like, though only six cities at a time appear on-screen.

To remove a city from the list, tap Edit and then tap the red circle with the white horizontal line that appears to the left of the city you want to drop. Then tap Delete.

Figure 13-8: Clocking in around the world.

You can also rearrange the order of the cities displaying the time. Tap Edit, and then press your finger against the symbol with three horizontal lines to the right of the city you want to move up or down in the list. Then drag the city to its new spot.

Alarm

Ever try to set the alarm in a hotel room? It's remarkable how complicated setting an alarm can be, on even the most inexpensive clock radio. Like almost everything else, the procedure is dirt-simple on the iPad:

1. **Tap Clock on the Home screen or Control Center to display the Clock app.**

2. **Tap the Alarm icon at the bottom of the screen.**

3. **Tap the + button in the upper-right corner of the screen.**

4. **Choose the time of the alarm by rotating the wheel in the Add Alarm overlay.**

   This step is similar to the action required to set the time that an event starts or ends on your calendar.

5. **Tap Save when the alarm settings are to your liking.**

That's what you can do with a regular alarm clock. What's the big deal, you say? Well, you can do even more with your iPad alarm:

- **Set the alarm to go off on other days.** Tap Repeat and then tell the iPad the days you want the alarm to be repeated, as in Every Monday, Every Tuesday, Every Wednesday, and so on.

- **Choose your own sound.** Tap Sound to choose the tone that will wake you up. You can even use songs from your Music library and any custom tones stored on your iPad.

  Your choice is a matter of personal preference, but we can tell you that the ringtone for the appropriately named Alarm managed to wake Ed from a deep sleep.

- **Set the snooze to sleep in.** Tap Snooze on (showing green) to display a Snooze button along with the alarm. Tap the Snooze button to shut down the alarm for nine minutes.

- **Name your alarm.** If you want to call the alarm something other than, um, Alarm, tap the Label field and use the virtual keyboard to type another descriptor.

Simple stuff, really. But if you want really simple and have anything except a second-generation iPad, you can ask Siri to set the alarm for you. See Chapter 14 for how to use Siri.

You know that an alarm has been set and activated because of the tiny status icon (surprise, surprise — it looks like a clock) that appears on the status bar in the upper-right corner of the screen.

An alarm takes precedence over any tracks you're listening to on your iPad. Songs momentarily pause when an alarm goes off and resume when you turn off the alarm (or press the Snooze button).

When your ring/silent switch is set to Silent, *your iPad still plays alarms from the Clock app.* It stays silent for FaceTime calls, alert sounds, or audio from apps. But it *will* play alarms from the Clock app.

Although it seems obvious, if you want to actually *hear* an alarm, you have to make sure that the iPad volume is turned up loud enough for you to hear.

Stopwatch

If you're helping a loved one train for a marathon, the iPad Stopwatch function can provide an assist. Open it by tapping Stopwatch in the Clock app.

Just tap Start to begin the count, and then tap Stop when your trainee arrives at the finish line. You can also tap the Lap button to monitor the times of individual laps.

Timer

Cooking a hard-boiled egg or Thanksgiving turkey? Again, the iPad comes to the rescue. Tap Timer (in the Clock app) and then rotate the hour and minute wheels until the length of time you desire is highlighted.

 Tap the sounds icon (shown in the margin) near the bottom of the screen to choose the ringtone that will signify time's up.

After you set the length of the timer, tap Start when you're ready to begin. You can watch the minutes and seconds wind down on the screen, if you have nothing better to do. Or tap Pause to pause the countdown temporarily.

If you're doing anything else on the iPad — admiring photos, say — you hear the ringtone and see a *Timer Done* message on the screen at the appropriate moment. Tap OK to silence the ringtone.

Socializing with Social Media Apps

At first glance, the iPad appears light on social media support because Game Center is the only sign of social media on a new iPad. Still, iOS 9 is much more friendly to social media than it appears at first glance. Although your iPad doesn't come with official Facebook or Twitter apps, support for the two most popular social networks is baked right into iOS.

You can find free apps for these social media networks (and many others) in the App Store, but iOS 9 lets you install the Facebook and Twitter apps without even having to visit the App Store. Just tap Settings➪Facebook (or Twitter), and then tap the Install button to install the app you've chosen.

You don't necessarily need an app to participate in social networking. The networks we talk about in this section can be fully utilized using Safari on your iPad. And frankly, unlike the iPhone, where the Safari experience is hampered by the tiny screen and keyboard, the websites are eminently usable on your iPad. So, if you want to check them out and don't feel like downloading their apps, here are their URLs:

- ✔ **Facebook:** www.facebook.com
- ✔ **Twitter:** http://twitter.com

We'd be remiss if we didn't at least point out some of the niceties you get when you access one of these social media networks by using an app instead of a browser, so the following sections offer a few of our insights.

If you use Facebook or Twitter, the first thing to do, regardless of whether you intend to use the apps, is to tap Settings⇨Facebook and Settings⇨Twitter and provide your usernames and passwords. This will let you share photos, maps and directions, videos, URLs, and much more by tapping the share icon and then tapping the icon for Facebook or Twitter.

Facebook

The Facebook iPad app, as shown in Figure 13-9, makes it easy to access the most popular Facebook features with a single finger tap.

Note that the Facebook iPad app has a slick interface with quick access to many popular Facebook features, as shown on the left in Figure 13-9.

Figure 13-9: Bob's Facebook news feed, as shown in the Facebook iPad app (left) and Safari (right); you can use either (or both) to get your Facebook fix.

The biggest difference between Facebook on Safari versus the app may be that Safari can't provide push notifications for Facebook events such as messages, timeline posts, friend requests and confirmations, photo tags, events, or comments, whereas the iPad app does all that and more. Also, if you use Safari's private browsing mode, your login information will not be retained after you close the browser.

The bottom line is that there's nothing to prevent having the best of both worlds. So if you're a heavy Facebook user, consider using the Facebook iPad app for some things (such as push notifications and status updates) and Safari for others (such as reading your wall or news feeds).

Twitter

Twitter puts a slightly different spin on social networking. Unlike Facebook, it doesn't try to be all-encompassing or offer dozens of features, hoping that some of them will appeal to you. Instead, Twitter does one thing and does it well. That thing is letting its users post short messages, or *tweets,* quickly and easily from a variety of platforms, including web browsers, mobile phones, smartphones, and other devices.

Twitter users then have the option of following any other Twitter user's tweets. The result is a stream of short messages like the ones shown in Figure 13-10.

A tweet is 140 characters or fewer (including spaces). This tip, for example, is precisely 140 characters. Bottom line: Omit needless words.

Figure 13-10: The official Twitter iPad app through the eyes of Bob (@LeVitus).

Game Center

Game Center is the odd duck of the bunch. Unlike the other apps we cover in this section, Game Center has no website; you have to use the Game Center app that came with your iPad. And unlike the others, which are broad-based and aimed at anyone and everyone, Game Center is designed for a specific segment of the iPad (and iPhone and iPod touch) universe — namely, users who have one or more games on their iPads (or other devices).

Mac users can get in on the fun, too, as long as they're using Mountain Lion or later, which include a Game Center app similar to the one on your iPad.

Game Center acts as a match-up service, letting you challenge your friends or use its Auto-Match Invite Friend button to challenge a stranger who is looking for someone to play against.

Game Center supports thousands upon thousands of games these days, some of which are shown in Figure 13-11.

Figure 13-11: Some of the games with Game Center support.

The games include many top sellers, such as *Angry Birds, Real Racing 2 HD, Fairway Solitaire,* and Bob's current game obsession, the stunning *Real Racing 3.*

Sharing Your Connection (Personal Hotspot)

If you have a newer iPad (anything but a second-generation iPad), the personal hotspot is a feature that lets your iPad with Wi-Fi + 4G share its cellular high-speed data connection with other devices, including computers, iPod touches, and other iPads.

If your iPad is Wi-Fi only, feel free to skip this section — the Personal Hotspot option is available only on cellular iPads.

To enable your personal hotspot and share your cellular data connection with others, do the following:

1. **On the Home screen, tap Settings.**

2. **Tap Personal Hotspot.**

3. **Tap the Personal Hotspot switch to enable it (it will turn green).**

4. **Tap Wi-Fi Password and create or change the password for the Wi-Fi network you create.**

Now Wi-Fi, Bluetooth, or USB-enabled devices can join your hotspot network and share your iPad's cellular data connection.

Your personal hotspot network adopts your iPad's name, which is *Bob LeVitus's iPad* in Figure 13-12.

At the time we wrote this, most carriers offered support for personal hotspots in some or all of their data plans in the United States. Some don't, so check with your carrier if you don't see a Personal Hotspot option in the Settings app (and, of course, if your iPad has 4G).

Figure 13-12: Devices can join this network via Wi-Fi, Bluetooth, or USB by following the appropriate connection instructions.

Verizon doesn't charge extra for this feature, but the data used by connected devices counts against your monthly data plan allotment.

To see how much cellular data you're using, tap Settings⇨Cellular Data and scroll down until you see Cellular Data Usage, which displays your cellular usage for the current period as well as data used while roaming.

Dropping In on AirDrop

At various points when you're using your iPad, you encounter AirDrop, a fast, safe, and secure (through encryption) wireless method of sharing photos, videos, contacts, documents, and more with people you are close to physically.

You just tap the share icon (shown in the margin) in any app that offers one. AirDrop exploits both Wi-Fi and Bluetooth. No advanced setup is required.

To be part of an AirDrop exchange, you and the recipient must be using iOS 7 or later and have an iPhone 5 or later, a fourth-generation iPad or later, an iPad mini, a fifth-generation iPod touch, or a Mac running Yosemite or later.

Taking advantage of this clever feature involves three simple steps:

1. **Turn on the AirDrop feature (if it's not on already) in Control Center.**

   You have the option to make your device visible to Everyone (within the vicinity) or just to your contacts.

2. **Tap the share icon when it presents itself in an app and choose the file or files that you want to share.**

3. **Choose the recipients of those items by tapping the circle for the person, as shown in Figure 13-13.**

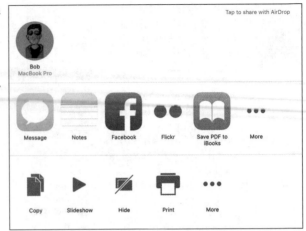

Figure 13-13: Tap Bob-in-a-circle to send the items to him.

Yes, you can choose more than one person. People in range who are eligible to receive the file are represented on your iPad by a circle. (The circles may even contain their pictures.)

The AirDrop process hath begun. The people on the receiving end will get a prompt asking them to accept the picture, video, or whatever it is you're offering them, as shown in Figure 13-14.

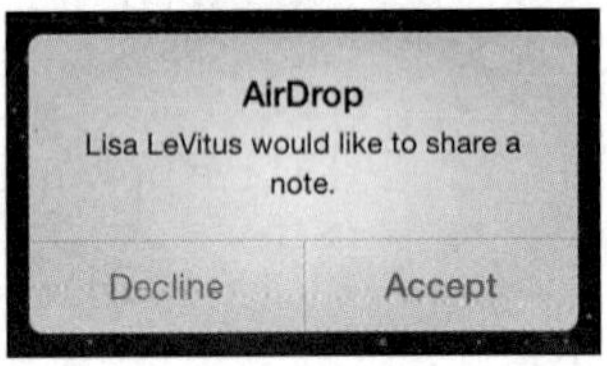

Assuming they take kindly to your offer and grant permission (by tapping Accept rather than Decline), the file lands on their devices in short order, where it is routed to its proper location. That is, a picture or video ends up in the Photos app, a contact in the Contacts app, and the Passbook pass in the Passbook app.

Figure 13-14: Bob is about to receive a note via AirDrop.

Taking iPad Controls Siri-ously

*H*ow could you not love Siri? The intelligent, voice-activated virtual personal assistant living like a genie inside the iPad minis and in iPads since the third generation not only *hear*s what you have to say but also attempts to figure out the intent of your words. Siri then does her darnedest to respond to your wishes. She — yes, it's a female voice (at least until you change it) — can help you dictate and send a message, get directions, call a friend, discover who won the ballgame, tell you when a movie is playing, ID the song playing in the background, arrange a wake-up call, search the web, find a decent place to eat, and lots more. Siri talks back, too, sometimes with humor and other times with attitude. When Ed told Siri he was tired, she responded with, "That's fine. I just hope you're not doing anything dangerous."

Siri isn't perfect. Sometimes Siri mishears us, occasionally more often than we'd like, and other times she doesn't quite know what we have in mind. But blemishes and all, we think she's pretty special — and she's become smarter along the way, much smarter with the move to iOS 9, in fact.

Come to think of it, we should probably stop referring to Siri as *she,* even though she, um, started that way. You can now choose a male or female voice to represent Siri — and yes, we'll resist making any other transgender references. We'll also resist saying much more about Siri until later in this chapter because we want to get to one of the most helpful features on your iPad, Control Center, which Apple correctly points out is merely a swipe away.

Controlling Control Center

As its name suggests, Control Center is a single repository for the controls, apps, and settings you frequently call upon. Indeed, you will almost certainly spend a lot more time in Control Center than in Settings.

To access Control Center, swipe up from the bottom of the screen — any screen. The beauty of Control Center is that it's always available when you need it.

Now, take a gander at Figure 14-1 to get an immediate handle on all the things that Control Center lets you get at right away.

We start the Control Center tour on the upper row and move from left to right. You see controls for any music (or video) you might be playing at the time,

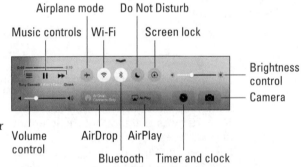

Figure 14-1: Control Center is merely a swipe away.

as shown in Figure 14-1. The song can be playing on the iPad's own Music app, or through a third-party app such as Spotify — which is, in fact, how the song is playing in this example. Next, you see icons for airplane mode (see Chapter 15 for more), Wi-Fi, Bluetooth, Do Not Disturb, the screen's orientation lock, along with a brightness control.

Drop down to the bottom row, and you have the volume control on the left. Next, you may see controls for AirDrop and AirPlay. The former is a way to share pictures, videos, and other files wirelessly with folks nearby who have recent iOS 7, iOS 8, or iOS 9 devices of their own and Bluetooth turned on. AirPlay is a way to stream music and movies wirelessly via Wi-Fi to Apple TVs and to compatible AirPlay-enabled speakers and receivers. We discuss AirPlay in greater depth in Chapter 8. And on the bottom right are icons for the timer (part of the Clock app) and the camera.

You can permit or deny access to Control Center on the lock screen in Settings. Go to Settings⇨Control Center⇨Access on Lock Screen. You can also allow or refuse access to Control Center from within apps. Go to Settings⇨Control Center⇨Access within Apps. Either way, Apple assumes that you'll use Control Center all the time. We agree.

Summoning Siri

When you first set up the iPad, you have the option of turning on Siri. If you did so, you're good to go. If you didn't, tap Settings⇨General⇨Siri, and flip the switch on so that green is showing.

You can call Siri into action in a few ways. The traditional way is to press and hold down the Home button until you hear a tone. Pretty simple, eh? Siri will then listen for your query, as shown in Figure 14-2. Start talking, and your question appears on-screen.

Go ahead, I'm listening...

You can also summon Siri by merely saying, "Hey Siri." And yes, this is Apple's answer to the "OK Google" voice command on Android devices. To take advantage of the Hey Siri feature, on iPads prior to iPad Pro, you have to connect your tablet to power. On the iPad Pro, you can use Hey Siri without plugging in your iPad. The feature applies to iPads running iOS 8 or later.

Siri also responds when you press a button on a Bluetooth headset.

Figure 14-2: Siri is eager to respond.

We should point out that having Siri turned on is a prerequisite to using dictation on your iPad, discussed later in this chapter.

What happens next is up to you. You can ask a wide range of questions or issue voice commands. If you didn't get your words out fast enough or you were misunderstood, tap the microphone icon at the bottom of the screen and try again.

Siri relies on voice recognition and artificial intelligence (hers, not yours). The voice genie responds in a conversational (if still ever-so-slightly robotic) manner. But using Siri isn't entirely a hands-free experience. Spoken words are supplemented by information on the iPad screen (as you see in the next section).

Making your iPad (and other computers) really smart

Chances are you haven't heard of WolframAlpha. But if you want to know the gross domestic product of France or find events that happened on the day you were born, WolframAlpha can deliver such facts. You don't search the web per se on WolframAlpha as you would using a service such as Google. WolframAlpha describes itself as a "new way to get knowledge . . . by doing dynamic computations based on a vast collection of built-in data, algorithms, and methods." It taps into knowledge curated by human "experts." So you can get nutritional information for peanut M&Ms or compute a growth chart for your 4-foot, 7-inch 10-year-old daughter.

There's a reason that Siri relies on this "computational knowledge engine," which was driven over a period of nearly 30 years by really smart guy Stephen Wolfram. We also recommend checking out the $2.99 WolframAlpha app for your iPad, which gives you broader access to the knowledge engine, beyond where Siri goes.

Just where does Siri get that information? By tapping into Location Services and seeking answers from the web using sources such as Bing, Wikipedia, Yelp, Yahoo!, Open Table, Twitter, and WolframAlpha, which you can learn more about in the nearby sidebar.

Through iOS 9, Siri assumes even more responsibility as the technology on your iPad that powers search. Ask Siri, for instance, to find all the videos you shot at your kid's graduation party and she'll oblige (at least if you tagged them correctly).

Siri on the iPad can open apps — Apple's own as well as third-party apps. Indeed, from your contacts, Siri might be able to determine who your spouse, coworkers, and friends are, as well as knowing where you live. You might ask, "How do I get home from here?" and Siri will fire up Maps to help you on your way. Or you can say, "Find a good Italian restaurant near Barbara's house," and Siri will serve up a list, sorted by Yelp rating. Using Open Table, Siri can even make a restaurant reservation.

If you ask about a favorite sports team, Siri will retrieve the score of the team's last game or the game in progress. And if you're rummaging through a longish email that you can't quite get through at the moment, you can have Siri set a reminder for you to follow up later in the evening.

Siri requires Internet access. A lot of factors go into accuracy, including surrounding noises and unfamiliar accents. And you also need to be comfortable with the fact that Apple is recording what you say.

Figuring Out What to Ask

The beauty of Siri is that there's no designated protocol you must follow when talking to her. Asking, "Will I need an umbrella tomorrow?" produces the same result as, "What is the weather forecast around here?" (See Figure 14-3.)

We think it's pretty darn cool that Siri teams up with one of our favorite apps, Shazam, to identify the name and artist of the musical track that's playing. Just ask Siri what song is playing and she'll name that tune (assuming that she indeed knows the song). When the song is properly identified, you even get a chance to buy it.

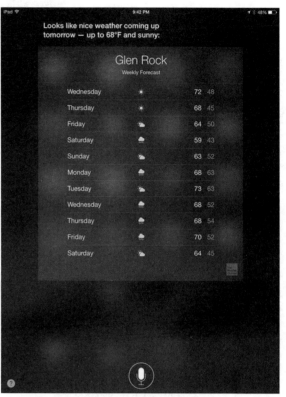

Figure 14-3: Siri can get you the weather.

If you're not sure what to ask, tap the *?*-in-a-circle to list sample questions or commands, as shown in Figure 14-4. You can tap any of these examples to see even more samples.

Here are some ways Siri can lend a hand . . . um, we mean a voice:

- **FaceTime:** "FaceTime *phone number* my wife."
- **Music:** "Play Frank Sinatra" or "Play Apple Music." "What song is this?" "Rate this song three stars."
- **Messages:** "Send a message to Nancy to reschedule lunch."
- **Calendar:** "Set up a meeting for 9 a.m. to discuss funding."
- **Reminders:** "Remind me to take my medicine at 8 a.m. tomorrow."
- **Maps:** "Find an ATM near here."
- **Mail:** "Mail the tenant about the recent rent check."

- ✔ **Photos:** "Show me the photos I took at Samuel's birthday party."

- ✔ **Stocks:** "What's Apple's stock price?"

- ✔ **Web search:** "Who was the 19th president of the United States?"

- ✔ **WolframAlpha:** "How many calories are in a blueberry muffin?"

- ✔ **Clock:** "Wake me up at 8:30 in the morning."

- ✔ **Sports:** "Who is pitching for the Yankees tonight?"

- ✔ **Trivia:** "Who won the Academy Award for Best Actor in 2003?"

- ✔ **Twitter:** "Send tweet, 'Going on vacation,' smiley-face emoticon" or "What is trending on Twitter?"

Figure 14-4: Siri can help out in many ways.

Correcting Mistakes

As we point out earlier, as good as Siri is, she sometimes needs to be corrected. Fortunately, you can correct her mistakes fairly easily. The simplest way is to tap the microphone icon and try your query again. You can say something along the lines of, "I meant tell me the weather in Botswana."

You can also tap your question to edit or fix what Siri thinks you said. You can make edits by using the keyboard or by voice. If a word is underlined, you can use the keyboard to make a correction.

Siri seeks your permission before sending a dictated message. That's a safeguard you come to appreciate. If you need to modify the message, you can do so by saying such things as, "Change Tuesday to Wednesday" or "Add: I'm excited to see you, exclamation mark" — indeed, *I'm excited to see you* and an *!* will be added.

Using Dictation

All iPads from the third generation on offer a dictation function, so you can speak to your iPad and the words you say are translated into text. It's easy and usually works pretty well. Even if you're a pretty good virtual-keyboard typist or use a Bluetooth keyboard (see Chapter 17), dictation is often the fastest way to get your words into your iPad.

You can enable dictation without enabling Siri and vice versa.

When you want to use your voice to enter text, tap the microphone key (see Figure 14-5) on the virtual keyboard that appears in the app you're using. Begin speaking right away. You'll see the wavy lines as you talk.

Microphone

Figure 14-5: Tap the microphone key to begin dictation; tap anywhere on-screen to end it.

The first time you tap the microphone key, a dialog appears asking if you want to enable dictation. Your humble authors are never shy about using our voices, so we happily agree. But why might you choose otherwise? Your voice input, contacts, and location are shared with Apple, which makes some people uncomfortable.

You can always enable or disable dictation later. Go to Settings ➪ General ➪ Keyboard and tap to turn the Enable Dictation switch on or off.

Dictation works only if you're connected to the Internet. If you're not connected, the microphone key will appear dimmed.

Some apps don't display the microphone key on the keyboard. If you don't see a microphone key, the app doesn't accept dictated input.

Tap Done to end the dictation. Older iPads may cogitate for a moment before your words magically appear. On the latest iPad models, words appear more quickly.

Here are a couple of ways you can improve your dictation experience:

✔ You can speak punctuation by saying it. So remember to say, "period," "question mark," or whatever at the end of your sentences. You can also insert commas, semicolons, dashes, and other punctuation by saying their names.

> ✔ The better your iPad hears you, the better your results will be:
>
> - A wired headset with a microphone is great when you have a lot of ambient noise nearby.
>
> - A Bluetooth headset may be better than the built-in microphone.
>
> - If you use the iPad's built-in mic, make sure the iPad case or your fingers aren't covering it.

When dictation is enabled, information is shared with Apple's servers. This hasn't stopped your authors from taking advantage of dictation, but if you have particular privacy concerns, it's helpful to keep this in mind.

Making Siri Smarter

From Settings, you can tell Siri which language you want to converse in. Siri is available in English (United States, United Kingdom, Canadian, Indian, New Zealander, Singaporean, or Australian), as well as versions of Chinese, Danish, Dutch, French, German, Italian, Japanese, Korean, and Spanish, Swedish, Thai, and Turkish.

You can also request voice feedback from Siri all the time, or just when you're using a hands-free headset. If you want, you can silence the feedback when the mute switch is on. You'll still get voice feedback if using the Hey Siri command.

In the My Info field in Settings, you can tell Siri who you are. When you tap My Info, your contacts list appears. Tap your own name in Contacts.

With iOS 7, iOS 8, and iOS 9, you can even choose whether Siri has either a male or female voice.

You can call upon Siri from the lock screen too. (That's the default setting, anyway.) Consider this feature a mixed blessing. Not having to type a passcode to get Siri to do her thing is convenient. On the other hand, if your iPad ends up with the wrong person, he or she would be able to use Siri to send an email or message in your name, post to Facebook, or tweet, bypassing whatever passcode security you thought was in place. If you find this potential scenario scary, tap Settings⇨Touch ID & Passcode on the iPad Air 2, iPad mini 3, iPad mini 4, and iPad Pro (Settings⇨Passcode on earlier models). Then enter your passcode and switch the Siri option under Allow Access When Locked from on (green is showing) to off (gray). You'll see the Allow Siri option under Touch ID & Passcode only if Siri is enabled in the first place. For more on Settings, read Chapter 15.

Part V
The Undiscovered iPad

Find out what other content you can download to your iPad at www.dummies.com/extras/ipad.

General

Display & Brightness

Wallpaper

Sounds

Passcode

Battery

Privacy

iCloud
baiged@mac.com

App and iTunes

Mail, Contacts,

Notes

Reminders

Messages

FaceTime

Maps

Safari

News

Music

Videos

In this part . . .

- Explore every single iPad setting that's not discussed in depth elsewhere in the book. By the time you finish reading Chapter 15, you'll know how to customize every part of your iPad that *can* be customized.

- Peruse our comprehensive guide to troubleshooting the iPad, which details what to do when almost anything goes wrong, complete with step-by-step instructions for specific situations.

- Gaze longingly at some of the iPad accessories we use and recommend, including carrying cases, physical keyboards, earphones and headphones, and speakers. No, this stuff's not included with your iPad, but we consider most of it essential just the same.

Setting You Straight on Settings

In This Chapter

▷ Getting the lowdown on Settings
▷ Taking off in airplane mode
▷ Preparing networks
▷ Brushing up on Bluetooth
▷ Uncovering usage statistics
▷ Setting up notifications
▷ Figuring out your location
▷ Seeking sensible sounds and screen brightness
▷ Keeping the clan together through Family Sharing
▷ Finding a lost iPad

Do you consider yourself a control freak? The type of person who has to have it your way? Boy, have you landed in the right chapter.

Settings is kind of the makeover factory for the iPad. You open Settings by tapping its Home screen icon; from there, you can do things such as change the tablet's background or wallpaper and specify the search engine of choice. You can also alter security settings in Safari, tailor email to your liking (among other modifications), and get a handle on how to fetch or push new data.

The Settings area on the iPad is roughly analogous to System Preferences on a Mac or the Control Panel in Windows, with a hearty serving of app preferences thrown in for good measure.

But you won't have to visit Settings in every case because Control Center grants you immediate access to some settings and controls that used to require a separate visit to the Settings complex, including airplane mode and display brightness, which we address in this chapter. But even with Control

Center, expect to make some tweaks in Settings from time to time. Because we cover some settings elsewhere in this book, we don't dwell on every setting here. (Nor do we describe every setting in the order in which Apple lists them.) But you still have plenty to digest to help you make the iPad your own.

Checking Out the Settings Screen

When you first open Settings, you see a display that looks something like Figure 15-1, with a scrollable list on the left side of the screen and a pane on the right that corresponds to whichever setting is highlighted in blue. We say "something like" because Settings on your iPad may differ slightly from what is shown here.

You must scroll down to see the entire list. Also, if you see a greater-than symbol (>) to the right of a listing, the listing has a bunch of options. Throughout this chapter, you tap the > symbol to check out those options.

As you scroll to the bottom of the list on the left, you come to all the settings that pertain to some of the specific third-party apps you've added to the iPad. (See Chapter 11.) These settings aren't visible in

Figure 15-1: Your list of settings.

Figure 15-1. Everybody has a different collection of apps on his or her iPad, so settings related to those programs will also be different.

Flying with Sky-High Settings

Your iPad offers settings to keep you on the good side of air-traffic communications systems. No matter which iPad you have — Wi-Fi only or a model with cellular — you have airplane mode.

Using a cellular radio on an airplane is a no-no. Wi-Fi is too, some of the time. But nothing is verboten about using an iPad on a plane to listen to music, watch videos, and peek at pictures. So how do you take advantage of the iPad's built-in music player (among other capabilities) at 30,000 feet, while temporarily turning off your wireless gateway to email and Internet functions? By turning on airplane mode.

To do so, merely tap Airplane Mode on the Settings screen to enable the setting. You'll know it's on rather than off when you see green instead of gray on the switch.

That act disables each of the iPad's wireless radios: Wi-Fi, cellular, and Bluetooth (depending on the model). While your iPad is in airplane mode, you can't surf the web, get a map location, send or receive emails, sync through iCloud, use the iTunes or App Store, or do anything else that requires an Internet connection. If a silver lining exists here, it's that the iPad's long-lasting battery ought to last even longer — good news if the flight you're on is taking you halfway around the planet.

✈ The appearance of a tiny airplane icon on the status bar at the upper-left corner of the screen reminds you that airplane mode is turned on. Just remember to turn it off when you're back on the ground.

 If in-flight Wi-Fi is available on your flight, which is increasingly the case, you can turn on Wi-Fi independently, leaving the rest of your iPad's wireless radio safely disabled. And it's a breeze to do by toggling the setting in Control Center.

Controlling Wi-Fi Connections

Wi-Fi is typically the fastest wireless network that you can use to surf the web, send email, and perform other Internet tricks on the iPad. You use the Wi-Fi setting to determine which Wi-Fi networks are available to you and which one to exploit based on its signal.

Tap Wi-Fi so that the setting is on, and all Wi-Fi networks in range are displayed, as shown in Figure 15-2.

 Tap the Wi-Fi switch off (gray) whenever you don't have access to a network and don't want to drain the battery. You can easily toggle Wi-Fi on and off in Control Center.

A signal-strength indicator can help you choose the network to connect to if more than one is listed; tap the appropriate Wi-Fi network when you

Figure 15-2: Check out your Wi-Fi options.

reach a decision. If a network is password-protected, you see a lock icon and need the passcode to access it.

When you are in a hotel, an airport, or at another location, you might still have to enter a password after joining even if the lock link is not present. And make sure you know where a network comes from before joining.

You can also turn the Ask to Join Networks setting on or off. Networks that the iPad is already familiar with are joined automatically, regardless of which one you choose. If the Ask feature is off and no known networks are available, you have to select a new network manually. If the Ask feature is on, you're asked before joining a new network. Either way, you see a list with the same Wi-Fi networks in range.

The iPad can also remember passwords for frequently used networks.

If you used a particular network automatically in the past but you no longer want your iPad to join it, tap the *i*-in-a-circle next to the network in question (in Wi-Fi settings) and then tap Forget This Network. The iPad develops a quick case of selective amnesia.

In some instances, you have to supply other technical information about a network you hope to glom on to. You encounter a bunch of nasty-sounding terms: DHCP, BootP, Static, IP Address, Subnet Mask, Router, DNS, Search Domains, Client ID, HTTP Proxy, and Renew Lease. (At least this last one has nothing to do with renting an apartment or the vehicle you're driving.) Chances are none of this info is on the tip of your tongue — but that's okay. For one thing, it's a good bet that you'll never need to know this stuff. What's more, even if you *do* have to fill in or adjust these settings, a network administrator or techie friend can probably help you.

Sometimes you may want to connect to a network that's closed and not shown on the Wi-Fi list. If that's the case, tap Other and use the keyboard to enter the network name. Then tap to choose the type of security setting the network is using (if any). Your choices are WEP, WPA, WPA2, WPA Enterprise, and WPA2 Enterprise. Again, the terminology isn't the friendliest in the world, but we figure that someone nearby can lend a hand.

If no Wi-Fi network is available, you have to rely on a cellular connection if you have capable models. If you don't — or you're out of reach of a cellular network — you can't rocket into cyberspace until you regain access to a network.

Getting Fired Up over Bluetooth

Of all the peculiar terms you may encounter in techdom, *Bluetooth* is one of our favorites. The name is derived from Harald Blåtand, a tenth-century Danish monarch, who, the story goes, helped unite warring factions. And, we're told, *Blåtand* translates to *Bluetooth* in English. (Bluetooth is all about collaboration between different types of devices — get it?)

Blåtand was obviously ahead of his time. Although we can't imagine that he ever used a tablet computer, he now has an entire short-range wireless technology named in his honor. On the iPad, you can use Bluetooth to communicate wirelessly with a compatible Bluetooth headset or to use an optional wireless keyboard. Such accessories are made by Apple and many others.

To ensure that the iPad works with a device, it typically has to be wirelessly *paired,* or coupled, with the chosen device. If you're using a third-party accessory, follow the instructions that came with that headset or keyboard so that it becomes *discoverable,* or ready to be paired with your iPad. Then turn on Bluetooth (on the Settings screen) so that the iPad can find such nearby devices and the device can find the iPad.

Bluetooth Pairing Request
Enter the code "6109" on "Edward Baig's Keyboard", followed by the return or enter key.

Cancel

In Figure 15-3, an Apple wireless keyboard and the iPad are successfully paired when you enter a designated passkey on the keyboard. You won't need a passkey to pair every kind of device, though. You can't, for example, enter a passkey when pairing the iPad with a wireless speaker. Bluetooth works up to a range of about 30 feet and doesn't require a line of sight.

Figure 15-3: Pairing an Apple wireless keyboard with the iPad.

You know Bluetooth is turned on when the Bluetooth icon (shown in the margin) is on the status bar. If the symbol is white, the iPad is communicating wirelessly with a connected device. If it's gray, Bluetooth is turned on in the iPad, *but* a paired device isn't nearby or isn't turned on. If you don't see a Bluetooth icon, the setting is turned off.

To unpair a device, select it from the device list and tap Forget This Device. We guess breaking up *isn't* hard to do.

The iPad supports stereo Bluetooth headphones, letting you stream stereo audio from the iPad to those devices.

The iPad can tap into Bluetooth in other ways. One is through *peer-to-peer* connectivity, so you can engage in multiplayer games with other nearby iPad, iPhone, or iPod touch users. You can also do such things as exchange business cards, share pictures, and send short notes. In addition, you don't even have to pair the devices as you do with a headset or wireless keyboard.

You can't use Bluetooth to exchange files or sync between an iPad and a computer. Nor can you use it to print stuff from the iPad on a Bluetooth printer (although the AirPrint feature handles that chore in some instances). That's because the iPad doesn't support any of the Bluetooth *profiles* (or specifications) required to allow such wireless stunts to take place — at least not as of this writing. We think that's a shame.

You may also see devices that communicate with the iPad through a flavor of Bluetooth called Bluetooth Low Energy or sometimes Bluetooth Smart or Bluetooth Smart Ready.

You can wirelessly share files also through AirDrop, as noted in Chapter 13 and elsewhere in this book.

Roaming among Cellular Data Options

You see another set of settings only if you have a cellular model iPad. The options appear on the right pane of the Settings screen when you highlight Cellular Data on the left:

- ✓ **Cellular Data:** If you know you don't need the cellular network when you're out and about or are in an area where you don't have access to the network, turn it off. Your battery will thank you later. But even if you have access to a speedy cellular network, be prudent; in a 4G environment where you can easily consume gobs of data, your data allowance may run out all too quickly.

- ✓ **Enable LTE:** LTE stands for Long Term Evolution. What it really stands for is speed. Turn Enable LTE on for the fastest possible cellular data connection if you're in range. The biggest disadvantage is that you can eat up data awfully fast.

- ✓ **Data Roaming:** You may unwittingly rack up lofty roaming fees when exchanging email, surfing with Safari, or engaging in other data-heavy activities while traveling abroad. Turn off Data Roaming to avoid such potential charges.

- ✓ **Account Information:** Tap View Account to see or edit your account information or to add more data.

- ✓ **Add a SIM PIN:** The tiny *SIM,* or *Subscriber Identity Module,* card inside your iPad with cellular holds important data about your account. To add a PIN or a passcode to lock your SIM card, tap SIM PIN. That way, if someone gets hold of your SIM, he or she can't use it in another iPad without the passcode.

   If you assign a PIN to your SIM, you have to enter it to turn the iPad on or off, which some might consider a minor hassle. And be aware that the SIM PIN is different from and may be in addition to any passcode you set for the iPad, as described later in this chapter.

- ✓ **Use Cellular Data For:** You can use your cellular connection for iCloud documents, iTunes, a Safari reading list, and certain third-party apps. You can see just how much data you're using on your apps and, if need be, shut down an app that's sucking up way too much. You can also decide whether or not to use cellular connections for FaceTime or for such system services as networking and Siri. Use the setting at the bottom of the Cellular Data panel to turn on the Wi-Fi Assist switch, which lets you automatically employ cellular data when your Wi-Fi connection is poor.

✓ **Cellular Data Usage:** This lists how much cellular data you've consumed for the current period. You also can see whether you're using up data while roaming. Overall, you'll know if you're closing in on your monthly data allowance.

An additional setting, Personal Hotspot, has been moved from the right pane to the left. Tap Personal Hotspot to share your iPad's data connection with any other devices you carry: perhaps a computer or smartphone. Just know that extra charges may apply and even if it doesn't you will rack up that much extra data. You or the owner of the device piggybacking on your Internet connection have to enter the designated password generated by the iPad for the Hotspot connection to make nice. You can use the hotspot feature via Wi-Fi or Bluetooth, or by connecting a USB cable. See Chapter 13 to find out how to use Personal Hotspot.

Managing Notifications

Through Apple's Push Notification service, app developers can send you alerts related to programs you've installed on your iPad. Such alerts are typically in text form but may include sounds as well. The idea is that you'll receive notifications even when the app they apply to isn't running. Notifications may also appear as numbered badges on their corresponding Home screen icon.

The downside to keeping push notifications turned on is that they can curtail battery life (although honestly, we've been pretty satisfied with the iPad's staying power, even when push notifications are active). And you may find notifications distracting at times.

You manage notifications on an app-by-app basis. To do so, tap Notifications on the left side of the Settings screen, as shown in Figure 15-4, and then tap the app you want to manage. All installed apps that take advantage of Notification Center (see Chapter 13) appear on the right side of the panel, as shown in Figure 15-4, with the enabled apps displayed in the upper section (Include) and disabled apps in the lower section (Do Not Include; not shown).

Tap any app to adjust its settings. Figure 15-5 shows notification settings for the Mail app (more specifically, Gmail). Some apps offer other options, including sound alerts, and other apps may offer fewer options, but we think you'll figure it out.

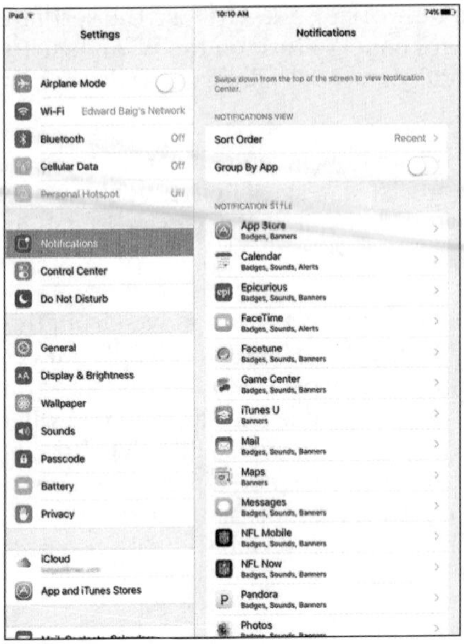

Figure 15-4: Notify the iPad of your notification intentions.

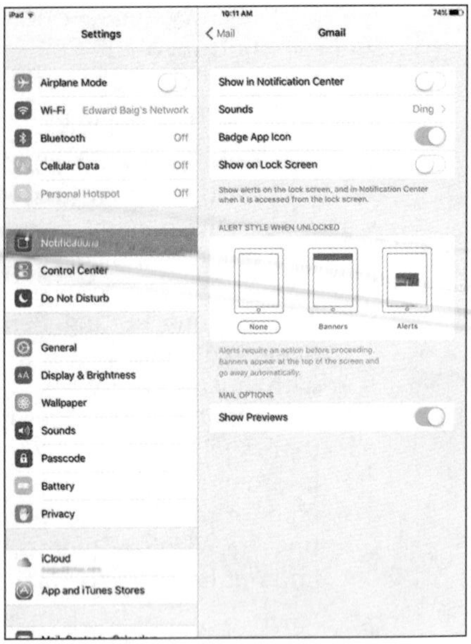

Figure 15-5: Notification settings for the Mail app.

To help you get started, here's a rundown of the options shown in Figure 15-5, starting at the top:

- ✔ **Show in Notification Center:** Enable or disable notifications for this app in Notification Center. Straightforward enough.

- ✔ **Sounds:** Choose the sound that accompanies notifications of new mail messages. (The Ding sound is selected in Figure 15-5.) You can choose from a lengthy list of sound and ringtone alternatives and tap each possible choice to hear it. Or select None if you're in the mood for quiet.

- ✔ **Badge App Icon:** Display the number of pending alerts on the app's icon on your Home screen.

- ✔ **Show on Lock Screen:** See notifications for this app when your iPad screen is locked.

- ✔ **Alert Style:** Select the style of alert you want to see:

  - *None:* Notifications won't appear spontaneously. They'll still be available in Notification Center (swipe down from the top of the screen; see Chapter 13) but won't interrupt your work (or play).

  - *Banners:* Display alerts as banners at the top of the screen and have them go away automatically.

  - *Alerts:* Display alerts that require action before proceeding.

✔ **Show Previews:** See the first part of the mail or iMessage as part of the notification in Notification Center.

Apps that don't take advantage of Notification Center can still offer notifications, but you'll have to scroll down to the Apps section on the left side of Settings and tap the app you want to alter. Note that the app you hope to fiddle with doesn't always appear in the Apps section of Settings. For that matter, many of the apps that do appear in the list don't offer notifications anyway.

The broader point we're trying to make is that we urge you to check out the settings for *all* the apps you see in this list. You'll never know about many useful options if you don't.

If you find you went overboard with notifications at first to the point where they become annoying or distracting, don't fret. You can always go back and redo any notifications you've set up.

Many of the notifications delivered in iOS 8 and iOS 9 are interactive, so you can respond to them on the spot. For example, you can reply to an incoming email or message without having to drop by the underlying app.

Here in Settings, you can also determine whether to sort notifications manually, sort them by the order in which they arrive, or group them by app. You can also choose whether to view Notification Center on the lock screen; to act upon your preference, you have to go to the Touch ID & Passcode or Passcode settings, which we get to shortly.

In iOS 8 and iOS 9, you can make a lot of modifications directly in Notification Center without paying a separate visit to Settings. In the today summary view, you get to choose whether to display traffic conditions, your calendar, reminders, and the tomorrow summary. You also have the capability to display compatible third-party widgets for apps you've installed on your iPad. To make such determinations, make sure the Today tab in Notification Center is highlighted and then tap Edit.

Apple understands that sometimes you don't want to be bothered by notifications or other distractions, no matter how unobtrusive they might be. The result is a feature aptly named Do Not Disturb. Flip the switch so the setting is turned on (green), and a moon icon appears in the status bar. Then you can rest assured that your alerts are silenced until you turn the setting off. Of course, it's even easier to turn this setting on or off in Control Center.

Controlling Control Center

We've already sung the praises of Control Center, the convenient utility that is no farther away than an upward swipe from the bottom of the screen. In Settings, you get to decide whether to make Control Center accessible from the lock screen and whether you can access it within apps. The switches for making these determinations are pretty straightforward.

Location, Location, Location Services

By using the onboard Maps or Camera apps (or any number of third-party apps), the iPad makes good use of knowing where you are. With Location Services turned on, your iPad has the capability to deliver traffic information and suggest popular destinations in your vicinity. And at your discretion, you can share your location with others.

iPads with cellular exploit built-in GPS to help determine your location. The Wi-Fi–only iPad can find your general whereabouts (by *triangulating* signals from Wi-Fi base stations and cellular towers).

If such statements creep you out a little, don't fret. To protect your right to privacy, individual apps pop up quick messages (similar to the warning presented by Maps, shown in Figure 15-6) asking whether you want them to use your current location. You can also turn off Location Services in Settings: Tap Privacy and then tap Locations Services to turn off the setting. Not only is your privacy shielded, but you also keep your iPad battery juiced a little longer.

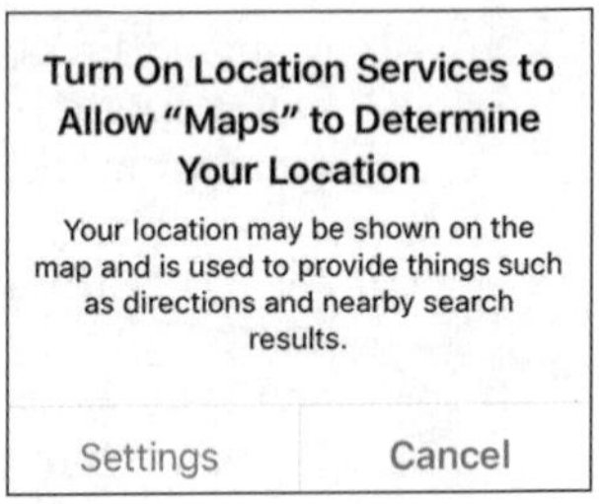

> **Turn On Location Services to Allow "Maps" to Determine Your Location**
>
> Your location may be shown on the map and is used to provide things such as directions and nearby search results.
>
> Settings   Cancel

Figure 15-6: Maps wants to know where you are.

Be aware as well that some apps will ask for access when you're in the midst of using them. Consider the request carefully before allowing such access.

While visiting the Privacy setting, you may want to consult the privacy listings for individual apps and functions on your iPad: Contacts, Calendars, Reminders, Photos, Bluetooth Sharing, Camera, Microphone, and HomeKit. If any third-party apps request access to these apps, they show up here.

You can also choose to share your location with family members and friends in the Messages and Find My Friends apps, and as part of Family Sharing.

From time to time on the iPad, you can land in the same destination multiple ways. For example, you can access the same privacy settings via the restrictions settings that we address later in this chapter.

Settings for Your Senses

A number of settings control what the iPad looks like and sounds like.

Display & Brightness

The brightness slider shown in Figure 15-7 appears when the Display & Brightness setting is highlighted. Who doesn't want a bright, vibrant screen? Alas, the brightest screens exact a trade-off: Before you drag the control to the max, remember that brighter screens sap the life from your battery more quickly.

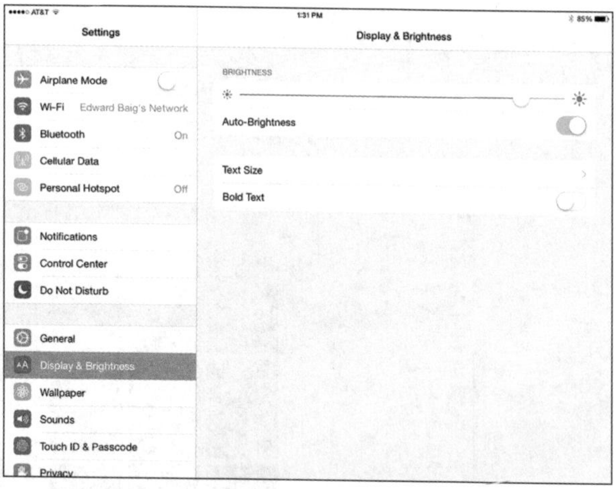

Figure 15-7: Sliding this control adjusts screen brightness.

 That's why we recommend tapping the Auto-Brightness switch so that it's on. The switch automatically adjusts the screen according to the lighting environment in which you're using the iPad — while at the same time being considerate of your battery. And the Auto-Brightness control is one reason to adjust the brightness here, as opposed to Control Center: Auto Brightness is not available in Control Center.

If the app you're spending time in supports dynamic type, you can adjust the type size by dragging a slider. Under Display & Brightness, you'll also find a switch for making text bold. If you choose to apply the Bold Text setting, you'll have to restart your iPad. You'll see similar options in the "Accessibility" section, later in this chapter.

Wallpaper

Choosing wallpaper is a neat way to dress up the iPad according to your aesthetic preferences. You'll find colorful dynamic animated wallpapers with floating bubbles that add a subtle dizzying effect. But stunning as they are, these images may not hold a candle to the masterpieces in your own photo albums (more about those in Chapter 9). And animations consume more power.

You can sample the pretty patterns and dynamic designs that the iPad has already chosen for you, as follows:

1. Tap Wallpaper and then tap Choose a New Wallpaper.

A list of your photo albums appears, along with Apple's own wallpaper.

2. **Tap Apple Wallpaper (Dynamic or Stills) or one of your own photo albums in the list.**

   We chose Stills to bring up the thumbnails shown in Figure 15-8 (left).

3. **Tap a thumbnail image.**

   That image fills the screen, as shown in Figure 15-8 (right).

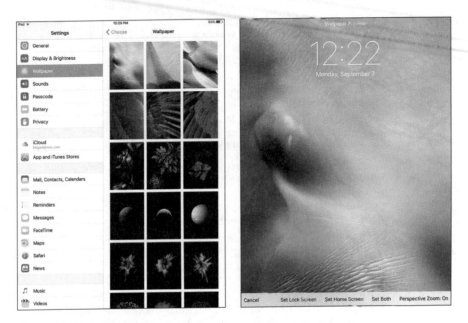

Figure 15-8: Choosing a majestic background.

4. **When an image is full-screen, choose among the following options, which appear at the bottom of the screen:**

   - *Set Lock Screen:* Your selected image is the wallpaper of choice when the iPad is locked.

   - *Set Home Screen:* The wallpaper decorates only your Home screen.

   - *Set Both:* Your image is the wallpaper for both the lock screen and the Home screen.

   - *Perspective Zoom:* Turn this motion effect on or off.

   - *Cancel:* Return to the thumbnail page without changing your Home or lock screen.

Sounds

Consider the Sounds settings area the iPad's soundstage. There, you can turn audio alerts on or off for a variety of functions: ringtones, text tones, new email, sent mail, calendar and reminder alerts, Facebook posts, tweets, and AirDrop. You can also decide whether you want to hear lock sounds and keyboard clicks.

You can alter the ringtone you hear for FaceTime calls and the text tones you hear for iMessages, and visit the iTunes Store to buy more text tones or ringtones, typically for $0.99 and $1.29 a pop, if you're not satisfied with those that Apple supplies. (Mac owners can create their own by using GarageBand, as can folks who use GarageBand on an iPad. And the app is now free for folks who purchase the latest iOS devices.) To set a custom tone for individuals in the Contacts app, tap the Edit button and then tap either the Ringtone or the Text Tone option.

To raise the decibel level of alerts, drag the ringer and alerts volume slider to the right. Drag in the opposite direction to bring down the noise. An alternative way to adjust sound levels is to use the physical volume buttons on the side of the iPad, as long as you're not already using the iPad's iMusic or Videos player to listen to music or watch video, respectively.

You can enable and disable the use of physical buttons to alter the volume by using the Change with Buttons switch, below the volume slider.

Exploring Settings in General

Certain miscellaneous settings are difficult to pigeonhole. Apple wisely lumped these under the General settings moniker. Here's a closer look at your options.

About About

You aren't seeing double. This section, as shown in Figure 15-9, is all about the About setting. And About is full of trivial (and not-so-trivial) information *about* the device. What you find here is straightforward:

✓ **Network you use (cellular models only):** AT&T, Sprint, T-Mobile, Verizon in the United States.

✓ **Number of songs stored on the device**

✓ **Number of videos**

✓ **Number of photos**

✓ **Number of apps**

✓ **Storage capacity used and available:** Because of the way the device is formatted, you always have a little less storage than the advertised amount of flash memory.

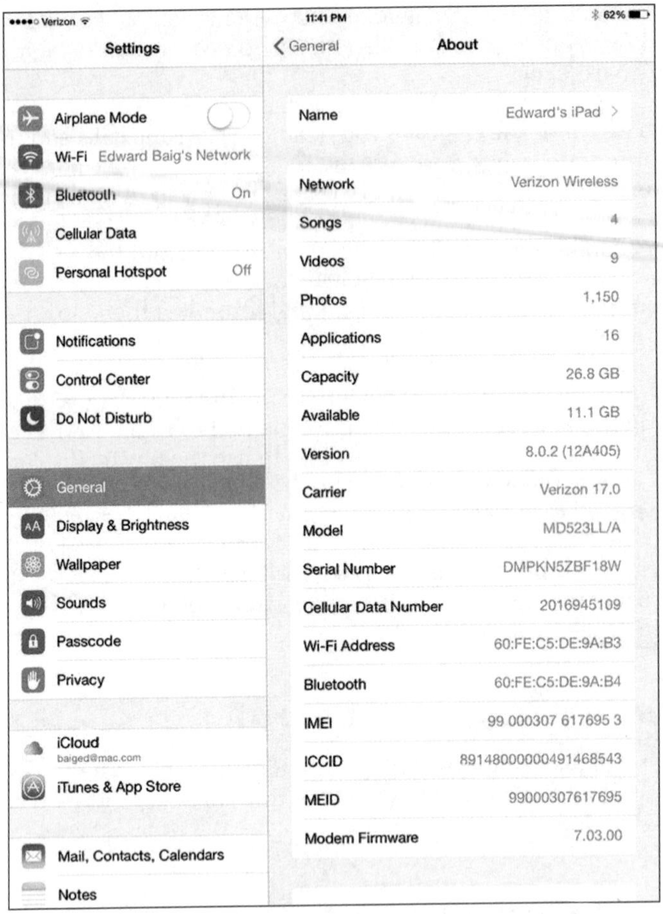

Figure 15-9: You find info about your iPad under About.

✔ **Software version:** As this book goes to press, we're up to version 9.1. But as the software is tweaked and updated, your device takes on a new build identifier, indicating that it's just a little bit further along than some previous build. In parentheses next to the version number, a string of numbers and letters, such as 13B143, tells you more precisely what software version you have. The number/letter string changes whenever the iPad's software is updated and is potentially useful to some tech-support person who might need to know the precise version.

✔ **Carrier (Wi-Fi + cellular versions only):** That's AT&T, Sprint, T-Mobile, or Verizon in the United States.

✔ **Serial and model numbers**

 ✔ **Cellular Data Number:** For billing purposes only.

 ✔ **Wi-Fi address**

 ✔ **Bluetooth address:** See the earlier section to find out more about this wireless feature.

 ✔ **IMEI, ICCID, and MEID:** These stand for *International Mobile Equipment Identifier, International Circuit Card Identifier,* and *Mobile Equipment Identifier,* respectively. They live up to their geeky acronyms by helping to identify your specific device.

 ✔ **Modern Firmware:** The version of your iPad's firmware, which is a combination of hardware and software that helps your iPad function as an iPad.

 ✔ **Legal Notices, License, Warranty, Regulatory RF Exposure, and Trusted Store:** You had to know that the lawyers would get in their two cents somehow. You find all the fine print here. And *fine print* it is because you can't unpinch to enlarge the text as you can elsewhere on the iPad (not that we can imagine more than a handful will bother to read this legal mumbo jumbo).

Software Update

The Software Update section is self-explanatory. When Apple unleashes an update, such as the ones that moved the device from iOS 7 to iOS 8 to iOS 9, you can find it here.

Siri

We love that Siri, the chatty personal digital assistant who can remind you whether to take an umbrella or clue you in on how the Giants are faring in the NFL, has found her way to the iPad from her original hangout spot on the iPhone 4s. You can talk to Siri by pressing and holding down the Home button and speaking out loud. Siri will talk back.

If your iPad is connected to power and running iOS 8 or iOS 9, you can also summon Siri without pressing the Home button. Instead, you can bark out the command, "Hey Siri." On the iPad Pro, you can summon Siri in this manner without connecting to power.

But sometimes, well — there's no way to say this kindly — you want Siri to shut up. To do that, just turn the Siri setting from on (green) to off. If you do disable Siri, be aware that the information she uses to respond to your requests is removed from Apple's servers. So if you call Siri back into duty later, it may take a little bit of time for the feature to resend information. Don't fret if you don't remember any of this. Apple reminds you ahead of your silencing Siri.

Other Siri settings to note:

- **Default language:** You can choose the language in which she will speak to you. The default is U.S. English.

- **Voice gender:** You can switch from a female to a male voice or vice versa.

- **Voice feedback:** You can select whether to always get voice feedback from Siri, as opposed to only when you're in a hands-free situation.

- **Your info:** And you can let Siri know who you are by choosing your name (if not already shown) in the My Info section of Siri settings. If for some reason you want to choose another name, you can do so from your list of contacts.

Spotlight Search

In Spotlight Search, you tell the iPad the apps that you want to search by flipping the switch for each one. There's also a switch here to turn on Siri Suggestions, a list of apps, people, locations, and such that would appear before you even enter a search query.

We address Search in Chapter 2 and Siri in Chapter 14. As a reminder, you can initiate a search on the iPad by dragging down from near the top of the screen. Such an action surfaces not only a search box but also any of the suggestions that Siri might supply.

Handoff & Suggested Apps

The Handoff feature lets you start a task (such as typing an email) on your iPad, on another iOS 8 or iOS 9 device, or on a Mac computer running OS X Yosemite or OS X El Capitan, and resume the task on another iPad, iOS 8 or iOS 9 device, or Mac. All the devices have to be running the identical iCloud account. On the tablet, you'll be able to resume with the app from your lock screen or app switcher. On a Mac, you'll see the appropriate app on the dock.

In the Suggested Apps section, you can flip on a setting to showcase installed apps or App Store suggestions relevant to your current location or based on your prior usage or both. Such suggestions appear on the lock screen and in the app switcher.

Multitasking

Three settings are found under Multitasking. Enable the Gestures option if you want to use four or five fingers to

- Pinch to the Home screen.

- Swipe up to the app switcher.

- Swipe left or right to switch among open apps.

By all means, enable this option if it isn't enabled. The gestures improve the multitasking experience, and we recommend that you give them a try. If you hate them, you know where to go to turn them off.

You'll also find a Multitasking setting to Allow Multiple Apps. Choose this to swipe from the right edge of the screen and pull in a temporary overlay of another app.

Another setting found here, called Persistent Video Overlay, enables you to continue to play a video in an overlay even after you press the Home button.

Accessibility

The Accessibility or Universal Access Features tools on your iPad are targeted at helping people with certain disabilities, but we encourage you to explore the various choices on your own, especially if you or a loved one have a particular area of need.

VoiceOver

The VoiceOver screen reader describes aloud what's on the screen. It can read email messages, web pages, and more. With VoiceOver active, you tap an item on the screen to select it. VoiceOver places a black rectangle around the item and either speaks the name or describes an item. For example, if you tap Display & Brightness, the VoiceOver voice speaks the words "Display and brightness button." VoiceOver even lets you know when you position the iPad in landscape or portrait mode and when your screen is locked or unlocked.

Within the VoiceOver setting, you have several options. For instance, if you turn on Speak Hints, VoiceOver may provide instructions on what to do next, along the lines of "Double-tap to open." You can drag a Speaking Rate slider to speed up or slow down the speech. You can also determine the kind of typing feedback you get: characters, words, characters and words, or no feedback. Additional switches let you turn on sound effects, change the pitch, and choose the default speech dialect. For example, you can choose an English dialect common to Australia, the United Kingdom, Ireland, or South Africa, along with, of course, the United States. You have additional speech choices from within these countries.

The voice you hear speaks in the language you specified in Language & Region settings, which we explain later.

You have to know a new set of finger gestures when VoiceOver is on, which may seem difficult, especially when you first start using VoiceOver. When you stop to think about it, this requirement makes a lot of sense because you want to be able to hear descriptions on the screen before you activate buttons. Different VoiceOver gestures use different numbers of fingers, and Apple recommends that you experiment with different techniques to see what works best for you. A VoiceOver Practice button is provided for this purpose.

Here are a few key gestures:

- ✔ **Tap:** Select the item.

- ✔ **Rotate two fingers:** This gesture has multiple outcomes that depend on how you set the rotor control gesture. To select your options, head to Settings⇨General⇨Accessibility⇨VoiceOver⇨Rotor. The rotor control gesture is similar to turning a dial: You rotate two fingertips on the screen. The purpose is to switch to a different set of commands or features. Suppose you're reading text in an email. By alternately spinning the rotor, you can switch between hearing the body of a message read aloud word by word or character by character. After you set the parameters, flick up or down to hear stuff read back. When you type an email, the flicking up and down gestures serve a different purpose: The gestures move the cursor left or right within the text.

- ✔ **Two-finger tap:** Stop speaking.

- ✔ **Two-finger swipe up:** Read everything from the top of the screen.

- ✔ **Two-finger swipe down:** Read everything from your current position on the screen.

- ✔ **Three-finger swipe up or down:** Scroll a page.

- ✔ **Three-finger swipe right or left:** Go to the next or previous page, respectively.

- ✔ **Three-finger tap:** Lets you know which page or rows are on the screen.

- ✔ **Four-finger flick up or down:** Go to the first or last part of the page, respectively.

- ✔ **Four-finger flick right or left:** Go to the next or previous section, respectively.

- ✔ **Double-tap:** Activate a selected icon or button to launch an app, turn a switch from on to off, and more.

- ✔ **Split tap:** For this gesture, you touch an item with one finger and tap the screen with another. When you touch an item, a voice identifies what you touched (for example, "Safari button" or "Notifications on button"). A tap with the second finger selects whatever was identified with the first finger (that is, "Safari button selected" or "Notifications on button selected"). Now you can double-tap to launch the button or whatever else was selected.

- ✔ **Double-tap, hold down for a second, and then add a standard gesture:** Tell the iPad to go back to using standard gestures for your next move. You can also use standard gestures with VoiceOver by double-tapping and holding down on the screen. You hear tones that remind you that standard gestures are now in effect. They stay that way until you lift your finger.

✔ **Two-finger double-tap:** Play or pause. You use the double-tap in the Music, YouTube, and Photos apps.

✔ **Three-finger double-tap:** Mute or unmute the voice.

✔ **Three-finger triple-tap:** Turn the display on or off.

Zoom

The Zoom feature offers a screen magnifier for those who are visually challenged. To zoom by 200 percent, double-tap the screen with *three* fingers. Drag three fingers to move around the screen. To increase magnification, use three fingers to tap and drag up. Tap with three fingers and drag down to decrease magnification.

You can tap a Zoom Controller switch for quick access to zoom controls.

The Zoom feature does have a downside: When magnified, the characters on the screen aren't as crisp (although the Retina display is still pretty sharp), and you can't display as much in a single view. You can also choose to zoom full screen or zoom only a window. And you can drag a slider to choose your maximum zoom level.

Larger Text

You can make text larger in the Mail, Contacts, Calendars, Messages, and Notes apps. Drag the slider from left to right or from the small *A* toward the larger *A*. You can turn on a Larger Accessibility Sizes switch to enlarge the text even more in certain supported apps. (You may recall the Text Size option we mention earlier when describing the Display & Brightness setting.)

Bold Text

Bold Text is another setting you first met in Display & Brightness. If you don't think the text on your iPad is bold or bright enough, turn on the Bold Text switch. As we noted, doing so (or turning it off again) requires that you restart your iPad.

Button Shapes

Turn the Button Shapes setting on, and the left-pointing arrow at the top-left corner of the Settings pane (next to General) disappears and the word *General* appears inside a pencil-shaped button.

Increase Contrast

The Increase Contrast setting is another effort to bolster legibility. You can reduce the transparency of the screen to improve the contrast on some backgrounds. You can darken colors. And you can reduce the intensity of bright colors. Play around with these options to see whether they make a difference.

Invert Colors

The colors on the iPad can be reversed to provide a higher contrast for people with poor eyesight. The screen resembles a film negative. (You remember, film, right?)

Grayscale

With the Grayscale setting, you can eliminate color and go gray.

Hearing Aids

The iPad can communicate with hearing aids through Bluetooth. And Apple has designed a Bluetooth technology for use with custom iPad hearing aids.

Subtitles and Captioning

Aimed at people who are deaf or hard of hearing, the Subtitles and Captioning setting lets you turn on a Closed Captions + SDH switch to summon closed-captioning or subtitles. You can also choose and preview the style for the subtitles and create your own subtitle style.

Audio Descriptions

Toggling the Audio Descriptions switch enables the iPad to automatically play audio descriptions when available.

Mono Audio

If you suffer hearing loss in one ear, the iPad's Mono Audio setting can combine the right and left audio channels so that both channels can be heard in either earbud of any headset you plug in. A slider control can adjust how much audio is combined and to which ear it is directed.

The iPad, unlike its cousins the iPhone and the iPod touch, doesn't come with earbuds or headphones. You have to supply your own.

Speak Selection

When the Speak Selection setting is on, the iPad speaks any text you select. You also find a slider control to adjust the speaking rate. And you can highlight words as they are spoken. You find this option under Speech, along with a Speak Screen button that when enabled lets you swipe down with two fingers from the top of the screen to hear the screen's content.

Speak Auto-Text

The Speak Auto-Text setting is also found under Speech. When this setting is on, the iPad automatically speaks autocorrections and capitalizations.

Reduce Motion

We think the parallax effect of icons and alerts is cool, but your neighbor may not agree. By turning on the Reduce Motion switch, you can reduce the parallax effect and be fairly confident that your wallpaper will remain still.

On/Off Labels

Throughout this book, you read that when certain switches are on, green appears. If you turn on the On/Off Labels switch, you'll still see green, but you'll also see a nerdy 1 when the setting or switch is turned on or a little 0 when the switch is off.

Guided Access

Parents of autistic kids know how challenging it can be to keep their child focused on a given task. The Guided Access setting can limit iPad usage to a single app and also restrict touch input on certain areas of the screen.

Switch Control

Several controls are represented under the Switch Control setting. The general idea is that you can use a single switch or multiple switches to select text, tap, drag, type, and perform other functions. However, turning on Switch Control changes the gestures you use to control your tablet and are presumably already familiar with. Switch Control makes use of different techniques. For example, the iPad can scan by or highlight items on the screen until you select one. Or you can choose to take advantage of scanning crosshairs to select a location on the screen. You can also manually move from item to item by using multiple switches, with each switch set to handle a specific action. We recommend poking around this setting to examine these and other options.

AssistiveTouch

Turn on the AssistiveTouch setting if you need to use an adaptive accessory, such as a joystick, because of difficulties touching the screen. When this setting is on, a movable dot appears; tap the dot to access certain features, such as Notification Center or Home. You can also create custom gestures through AssistiveTouch.

Touch Accommodations

Touch Accommodations, an iOS 9 addition, lets you customize the touch sensitivity of your iPad. For example, you can change the amount of time you must touch the screen before your touch is recognized. You can also change the duration in which the tablet treats multiple touches as a single touch. And you can enable a Tap Assistance option to allow any single finger gesture to perform a tap before a timeout period, which you can customize, expires.

Home-Click Speed

Tap the Home Button setting to choose a home-click speed. You can slow down the speed required to double or triple-click the Home button, which is next on the list of Accessibility options.

Accessibility Shortcut

Double-clicking the Home button launches multitasking. But you can set up the iPad so that triple-clicking the button (clicking three times really fast) turns on certain accessibility features. (This tool used to be called Triple-Click Home.) By doing so, you can turn on or off VoiceOver, Invert Colors, Grayscale, Zoom, Switch Control, and AssistiveTouch.

Storage & iCloud Usage

The About setting (covered earlier) gives you a lot of information about your device. But after you back out of About and return to the main General settings, you can find other settings for statistics on iPad usage under the Storage & iCloud Usage section:

- **Battery:** You almost always see a little battery meter in the upper-right corner of the screen, except for certain instances, such as when you watch videos and the top bar disappears. If you also want to see your battery life presented in percentage terms, make sure that the Battery Percentage setting is on. You can also see how much usage and standby time you've consumed since your last full charge. Usage (by percentage of battery used) can be displayed by app for the past 24 hours or the past 7 days.

- **iCloud:** This setting shows the amount of total and available storage. Tap Manage Storage to, well, manage your iCloud storage, taking note of all your iOS backups. If need be, you can buy more storage. Tap Change Storage Plan to get started. Under the pricing that was current at the time this book was written, you can pay $0.99 a month for 50GB, $2.99 a month for 200GB, or $9.99 a month for 1TB. You can also downgrade to a free 5GB plan.

- **Storage (for the device):** This option is found under iCloud settings. You can check out which apps on your iPad are hogging the most storage and delete those (from here) that you're no longer using.

Background App Refresh

Some apps continue to run in the background even when you're not actively engaged with them. If you flip the Background App Refresh switch (found under General settings) so that green is showing, you can allow such apps to update content when an active Wi-Fi or cellular connection is available. The potential downside to leaving this switch turned on is a hit on battery life.

As it turns out, your iPad is pretty smart about when to refresh apps. iOS detects patterns based on how you use your iPad. It learns when your tablet is typically inactive — at night perhaps when you're in slumberland. And in some cases, apps are refreshed when you enter a particular location.

You can also turn on or off Background App Refresh for any individual app listed under this setting. Flip the switch to make the determination for each given app.

Auto-Lock

Tap Auto-Lock in the General settings pane, and you can set the amount of time that elapses before the iPad automatically locks or turns off the display. Your choices are 15 minutes, 10 minutes, 5 minutes, or 2 minutes. Or you can set it so that the iPad never locks automatically.

If you work for a company that insists on a passcode (see the next section), the Never Auto-Lock option isn't in the list that your iPad displays.

Don't worry about whether the iPad is locked. You can still receive notification alerts and adjust the volume.

Restrictions

Parents and bosses may love the Restrictions tools, but kids and employees usually think otherwise. You can clamp down, er, provide proper parental guidance to your children or managerial guidance to your staff by preventing them (at least some of the time) from using the Safari browser, Camera, Siri & Dictation, FaceTime, AirDrop, iTunes Store, Apple Music Connect, iBooks Store, Podcasts, News, or Game Center. Or you might not let them install new apps or make purchases inside the apps you do allow — or (conversely) let them delete apps. When restrictions are in place, icons for off-limit functions can no longer be seen. Tap Enable Restrictions, set or enter your passcode — you have to enter it twice if you are setting up the passcode — and tap the switch next to each item in the Allow or Allowed Content lists that you plan to restrict. Their corresponding settings should be off (gray is showing rather than green).

You can also restrict the use of explicit language when you dictate text. An asterisk (*) replaces a naughty word.

Moreover, parents have more controls to work with. For instance, you can allow Junior to watch a movie on the iPad but prevent him from watching a flick that carries an R, NC-17, or some other rating. You can also restrict access to certain TV shows, explicit songs and podcasts, and apps based on age-appropriate ratings. In Game Center, you can decide whether your kid can play a multiplayer game or add friends. Apple lets you choose whether to let the kids read books with explicit sexual content. You can also restrict access to websites that have adult content.

Stop feeling guilty: You have your users' best interests at heart.

If guilt gets the better of you, you can turn off restrictions. Open the Restrictions setting by again typing your passcode. Then switch the setting on for each item you are freeing up. Tap Disable Restrictions. You have to enter your passcode one more time before your kids and office underlings return you to their good graces.

Under Restrictions settings, you'll find privacy controls as well. For example, you can impose restrictions on the use of Location Services, as well as Contacts, Calendars, Reminders, Photos, Bluetooth sharing, and more. (For these and additional privacy controls, visit the dedicated Privacy setting.)

And in this area, you can allow or restrict changes made to your accounts, cellular use, background app refreshes, even volume limits.

There's a lot here, and even if you're liberal about policing your kids' activities, we recommend you poke around and consider all your options.

Lock/Unlock

Use the Lock/Unlock setting to automatically lock and unlock your iPad when you close and open the clever iPad Smart Cover, Apple's Smart Case, or some other covers. If you set a passcode, you still have to enter it to wake the iPad from siesta-land.

Use Side Switch

You can use the Use Side Switch setting for one of two purposes: You can lock the rotation so that the screen orientation doesn't change when you turn the iPad to the side, or you can mute certain sounds. You get to make that choice through the Side Switch setting.

You won't see this setting on the iPad Pro since it doesn't have the side switch.

Date & Time

In our neck of the woods, the time is reported as 11:32 p.m. (or whatever time it happens to be). But in some circles, it's reported as 23:32. If you prefer the latter format on the iPad's status bar, tap the 24-Hour Time setting (under Date & Time) so that it's on (green).

This setting is just one that you can adjust under Date & Time. You can also have the iPad set the time in your time zone. Here's how:

1. Tap Date & Time.

You see fields for setting the time zone and the date and time.

2. **Tap the Time Zone field and make sure Set Automatically is turned off.**

   The current time zone and virtual keyboard are shown.

3. **Tap X to remove the city currently shown in the Time Zone field, and tap the letters of the city or country whose time zone you want to enter until the one you have in mind appears. Then tap the name of that city or country.**

   The Time Zone field is automatically filled in for that city.

4. **Tap the Set Date & Time field so that the time is shown; then roll the carousel controls until the proper time displays.**

5. **Roll the carousel controls to choose the proper month, day, and year until the correct date appears.**

6. **Tap General to return to the main Date & Time settings screen.**

You can also dispense with these settings and just have the iPad set the time automatically, based on its knowledge of where you happen to be. Just make sure to turn on the Set Automatically option.

Keyboard

Under Keyboard settings, you have the following options:

- **Auto-Capitalization:** Automatically capitalize the first letter of the first word you type after ending the preceding sentence with a period, a question mark, or an exclamation point. Auto-capitalization is on by default.

- **Auto-Correction:** The iPad takes a stab at what it thinks you meant to type.

- **Check Spelling:** The keyboard checks spelling while you type.

- **Enable Caps Lock:** All letters are uppercased LIKE THIS if you double-tap the shift key. (The shift key is the one with the arrow pointing up.) Tap shift again to exit caps lock.

- **Shortcuts:** By enabling this setting, the iPad's virtual keyboard will display a shortcut bar with controls to copy and paste the text you've selected text, or to make that text bold, italic, or underline. Don't confuse this Shortcuts setting with the "." Shortcut setting described later.

- **Predictive:** When enabled, the iPad keyboard will suggest certain words that you might want to type next. Tap a suggested word to accept it. You can also flip the Predictive switch on or off right from the keyboard itself.

✔ **"." Shortcut:** A period is inserted followed by a space when you double-tap the space bar. This setting is turned on by default; if you've never tried it, give it a shot.

You'll see another type of shortcut option, called Text Replacement, in which the keyboard presents a full phrase when you type a few letters. For example, typing the letters *omw* yields *On my way!* Tap the + under the Text Replacement setting to add a new phrase and the optional shortcut for that phrase. Saving a few letters is economical, don't you think?

You can choose to use an international keyboard (as we discuss in Chapter 2), which you enable from Keyboard settings. You can also enable the Split Keyboard option if you'd like to take advantage of this feature.

Apple gives you the power to substitute the default keyboard on your iPad for a custom alternative. Among the choices that you might consider are Swype, SwiftKey, Fleksy, and Adaptxt. For more on adding a third-party keyboard, consult Chapter 2.

Language & Region

The iPad is an international sensation. In the Language & Region section, you can set the language in which the iPad displays text, plus the date and time format for the region in question. You can choose a Gregorian, Japanese, or Buddhist calendar, too.

iTunes Wi-Fi Sync

We spend an entire chapter (Chapter 3, to be precise) on syncing. Just know that if you want to sync with iTunes on your computer when you're plugged into power and tapped into Wi-Fi, you can do it here.

VPN

After you tap VPN on the General settings screen, you see a control for VPN.

A *virtual private network,* or *VPN,* is a way for you to securely access your company's network behind the firewall — using an encrypted Internet connection that acts as a secure tunnel for data.

You can configure a VPN on the iPad by following these steps:

1. **Tap Settings⇨General⇨VPN⇨Add VPN Configuration.**

2. **Tap one of the protocol options.**

   The iPad software supports the protocols *IKEv2* (Internet Key Exchange) *L2TP* (Layer 2 Tunneling Protocol), *PPTP* (Point-to-Point Tunneling Protocol), and *IPSec,* which apparently provides the kind of security that satisfies network administrators.

3. **Using configuration settings provided by your company, fill in the appropriate server information, account, password, and other information.**

4. **Choose whether to turn on RSA SecurID authentication.**

   Better yet, lend your iPad to the techies where you work and let them fill in the blanks on your behalf.

After you configure your iPad for VPN usage, you can turn that capability on or off by tapping (yep) the VPN switch in Settings.

Reset

As little kids playing sports, we ended an argument by agreeing to a do-over. Well, the Reset settings on the iPad are one big do-over. Now that you're (presumably) grown up, think long and hard about the consequences before implementing do-over settings. Regardless, you may encounter good reasons for starting over; some of these are addressed in Chapter 16.

Here are your reset options:

✓ **Reset All Settings:** Resets all settings, but no data or media is deleted.

✓ **Erase All Content and Settings:** Resets all settings *and* wipes out all your data.

✓ **Reset Network Settings:** Deletes the current network settings and restores them to their factory defaults.

✓ **Subscriber Services:** Reprovisions (or refreshes) your account and resets your authentication code. It will not show up on all models.

✓ **Reset Keyboard Dictionary:** Removes added words from the dictionary. Remember that the iPad keyboard is intelligent. One reason why it's so smart is that it learns from you. So when you reject words that the iPad keyboard suggests, it figures that the words you specifically banged out ought to be added to the keyboard dictionary.

✓ **Reset Home Screen Layout:** Reverts all icons to the way they were at the factory.

✓ **Reset Location & Privacy:** Restores factory defaults.

Touch ID & Passcode

If you want to prevent others from using your iPad, you can set a passcode by tapping Touch ID & Passcode (or just Passcode on models without Touch ID) and then tapping Turn Passcode On. By default, you use the virtual keypad to enter and confirm a four-digit passcode. If you'd prefer a longer, stronger passcode, tap Change Passcode, and type your current passcode. Then tap Passcode Options, followed by Custom Alphanumeric Code, Custom Numeric

Code, or 6-Digit Numeric Code. Now enter and confirm your new passcode, which can be almost any combination of the letters, numbers, and symbols available on the standard virtual keyboard. You'll also be presented with the option to use your new passcode as your iCloud security code, which is used to protect the passwords you've stored in iCloud Keychain.

You can also determine whether a passcode is required immediately, after 1 minute, after 5 minutes, 15 minutes, 1 hour, or 4 hours. Shorter times are more secure, of course. On the topic of security, the iPad can be set to automatically erase your data if someone makes ten failed passcode attempts.

You can also change the passcode or turn it off later (unless your employer dictates otherwise), but you need to know the present passcode to apply any changes. If you forget the passcode, you have to restore the iPad software, as we describe in Chapter 16.

From the Touch ID & Passcode setting, you can determine whether to allow access to the today view, the notifications view, or Siri when the iPad is locked.

If you have an iPad Air 2, iPad mini 3, or iPad Pro, we strongly recommend that you at least try Touch ID, the clever fingerprint authentication scheme that not only lets you bypass the lock screen by pressing your thumb or another finger against the Home button, but also lets you purchase stuff in iTunes, the App Store, and the iBooks Store. You can also take advantage of the nascent Apple Pay mobile payments system but (as of this writing) only for certain online transactions — not physical retail stores as is possible with the iPhone 6, iPhone 6 Plus, iPhone 6s, and iPhone 6s Plus.

You can store up to five fingerprints (yours and people you trust with whom you share the iPad). Tap Add a Fingerprint and go through the training session that you likely encountered back when you set up your iPad (consult Chapter 2 for details). If the iPad doesn't recognize your finger, you see Try Again at the top of the screen. You get three wrong tries before you're forced to use a traditional passcode instead, at least for this session.

As an added security measure, a regular passcode is required the first time you try to get past a lock screen after restarting the tablet.

If you want to delete an authorized fingerprint, tap the listing for the finger in question, and then tap Delete Fingerprint. Excuse our French, but you've just given the finger to the finger.

Promoting Harmony through Family Sharing

Earlier under Restrictions, we show you how to impose an iron fist when it comes to permitting iPad usage at home. Now we're going to try and make everybody in the clan happy again. Visit iCloud settings and consider setting up Family Sharing with up to six members of your family. Adults and kids can partake, but one grown-up must take charge as the family organizer. We figure it might as well be you, the person reading this book. You'll be the person presenting your iCloud Apple ID username and password, and the one on the hook for paying for iTunes, iBooks, and App Store purchases. As the family organizer, you can turn on Ask to Buy so that you can approve (or deny) purchases or download requests from other members of your clan.

When Family Sharing has been implemented, you can all share a calendar, photos, reminders, and your respective locations. Family Sharing may also help find a missing device through the important Find My iPad feature, which we describe at the end of this chapter.

Should you leave Family Sharing, your account is removed from the group and you can no longer share content with everybody else. You won't be able to use DRM-protected music, movies, TV shows, books, or apps that another member purchased. And you won't be able to access the family calendar, reminders, or photos.

Family Sharing works with iOS 8 and iOS 9 devices, OS X Yosemite or OS X El Capitan on a Mac, and Find My Friends 3.0, Find My iPhone 3.1, and iCloud for Windows 4.0.

Settings for Social Media

Much as we all use our iPads to consume content, we also use it to exchange our own content — ideas, pictures and the like — with close intimates, colleagues, and yes, in some instances, people with whom we are trying to wield influence. The next set of settings is all about managing some of the most popular social networks and the people in our Contacts.

Twitter

In Twitter settings, you can add a new Twitter account and update your contacts so that Twitter uses their email addresses and phone numbers to automatically add their Twitter handles and photos. You also can choose yay or nay on whethcr you can use various apps with Twitter.

Facebook

Most of us know Facebook as a great service to help us stay in touch with relatives, associates, and old pals, rekindle relationships, and make new friends. But some people collect Facebook friends like baseball cards. If it seems like you're acquainted with all 1.49 billion-and-counting members of the mammoth social network, we know what you mean.

Fortunately, Apple kindly organizes your Facebook relationships on the iPad. If you turn on the Calendar and Contacts switches under Facebook settings on the iPad, your Facebook friends automatically populate your contacts list, complete with profile pictures as well as email addresses and phone numbers (if they made them public on Facebook). Birthdays and calendar appointments appropriately turn up in the Calendar app.

Think of these Facebook entries as live synced contact entries. If a person changes his or her phone number and email address on Facebook, that change will be reflected on your iPad, provided you have Wi-Fi or cellular coverage or the next time you do have coverage. And if your friends de-friend you — how cruel is that? — their contact info will disappear.

If the iPad can correctly match a Facebook friend entry with an existing contact entry, it will try to unify that contact under a single view. The Update All Contacts option under Facebook settings on the iPad serves a slightly different purpose. It tries to add Facebook profile information to contacts who are on Facebook but are not among your Facebook friends.

Flickr, Vimeo, Sina Weibo, Tencent Weibo

Yes, Flickr (online photo sharing), Vimeo (online video sharing), and Sina Weibo and Tencent Weibo (Chinese social networks if you've enabled a Chinese keyboard) get dedicated Settings areas from which you can enter your sign-in credentials to such services.

Sorting and displaying contacts

Do you think of us as Ed and Bob or Baig and LeVitus? The answer to that question will probably determine whether you choose to sort your contacts list alphabetically by last name or first name.

Tap Mail, Contacts, Calendars; scroll down to the Contacts section; and peek at Sort Order. Then tap Last, First or First, Last. You can determine whether you want to display a first name or last name first by tapping Display Order and then choosing First, Last or Last, First. You can also go with a short name to fit more names on the screen. You can choose a first name and last initial, first initial and last name, first name only, or last name only. If you prefer nicknames, you can choose those instead, when available.

In My Info, make sure your own name is chosen so that Siri knows where you live, among other reasons.

Find My iPad

We hope you never have to use the Find My iPad feature — though we have to say that it's darn cool. If you inadvertently leave your iPad in a taxi or restaurant, Find My iPad may just help you retrieve it. You need a free iCloud account and your iPad must be connected to a network of some kind.

Well, that's *almost* all you need. You'll have to turn on your account, so tap Settings⇨Mail, Contacts, Calendars, and then tap your iCloud account. Or tap Settings⇨iCloud. Either way, make sure Find My iPad is switched on.

Now, suppose you lost your tablet — and we can only assume that you're beside yourself. Follow these steps to see whether the Find My iPad feature can help you:

1. **Log on to your iCloud account at** www.icloud.com **from any browser on your computer.**

2. **Click the Find My iPhone icon.**

   If you don't see it, click the icon with a cloud in it that appears in the upper-left corner of the iCloud site. You see a panel with icons that are tied to various iCloud services, including Find My iPhone. (Yes, even though the feature is Find My iPad on the iPad, it shows up as Find My iPhone on the iCloud site. Don't worry; it'll still locate your iPad — and, for that matter, a lost iPhone or iPod touch, and even a Mac computer too.)

   Assuming that your tablet is turned on and in the coverage area, its general whereabouts turn up on a map (as shown in Figure 15-10) in standard or satellite view, or a hybrid of the two. In our tests, Find My iPad found our iPads quickly.

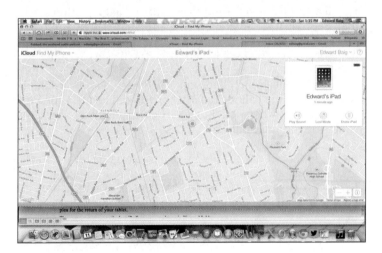

Figure 15-10: Locate a lost iPad.

Even seeing your iPad on a map may not help you much, especially if the device is lost somewhere in midtown Manhattan. Take heart.

3. **At the iCloud site, click the Lost Mode button.**

4. **Type a phone number at which you can be reached, as well as a plea to the Good Samaritan who (you hope) picked up your iPad.**

Apple has already prepared a simple message indicating that the iPad is lost, but you can change or remove the message and substitute your own plea for the return of your tablet.

The message appears on the lost iPad's screen, as shown in Figure 15-11.

 To get someone's attention, you can also sound an alarm that plays for two minutes, even if the volume is off. Tap Play Sound to make it happen. Hey, that alarm may come in handy if the iPad turns up under a couch in your house. Stranger things have happened.

Figure 15-11: An appeal to return the iPad.

We also recommend turning on the Send Last Location setting in Find My iPad because it automatically sends the tablet's location to Apple when the device's battery is critically low. That way, you still have a puncher's chance of getting back a lost iPad even when the battery is knocked out.

 Find My iPhone (which finds any iOS device) is now available as a free app. Another free app called Find My Friends will locate your friends on a map. Just hope that when you find a particular pal, he or she is not the one who snatched your missing iPad.

After all this labor, if the iPad is seemingly gone for good, click Erase iPad at the iCloud site to delete your personal data from afar and return the iPad to its factory settings. (A somewhat less drastic measure is to remotely lock your iPad by using a four-digit passcode.)

Meanwhile, the person who found (or possibly stole) your iPad cannot reactivate the device to use as his or her own, or to peddle, unless he or she successfully types in *your* Apple ID.

Even if you choose to erase the device remotely, it can still display a custom message with the information needed for someone to return it to you. If, indeed, you ever get your iPad back, you can always restore the information from an iTunes backup on your Mac or PC or iCloud.

We authors love a happy ending.

16

When Good iPads Go Bad

In This Chapter

▶ Fixing iPad issues

▶ Dealing with network problems

▶ Eliminating that sinking feeling when you can't sync

▶ Perusing the Apple website and discussion forums

▶ Sending your iPad to an Apple Store

▶ Finding your stuff on a repaired iPad

I n our experience, all Apple iOS devices — namely the iPad, iPhone, and iPod touch — are fairly reliable. But every so often, a good iPad might just go bad. We don't expect it to be a common occurrence, but it does happen occasionally. So, in this chapter, we look at the types of bad things that can happen, along with suggestions for fixing them.

What kind of bad things are we talking about? Well, we're referring to problems involving

- Frozen or dead iPads
- Wireless networks
- Synchronization of computers (both Mac and PC) or iTunes

After all the troubleshooting, we tell you how to get even more help if nothing we suggest does the trick. Finally, if your iPad is so badly hosed that it needs to go back to the mother ship for repairs, we offer ways to survive the experience with a minimum of stress or fuss, including how to restore your stuff from an iTunes or iCloud backup.

Resuscitating an iPad with Issues

Our first category of troubleshooting techniques applies to an iPad that's frozen or otherwise acting up. The recommended procedure when this happens is to perform the seven *R*s in sequence.

1. Recharge

2. Restart

3. Reset your iPad

4. Remove your content

5. Reset settings and content

6. Restore

7. Recovery mode

But before you even start those procedures, Apple recommends you take these steps:

1. **Verify that you have the current version of iTunes installed on your Mac or PC.**

   You can download the latest and greatest version here: `www.apple.com/itunes/download`.

2. **Verify that you're connecting your iPad to your computer using a USB 2.0 or 3.0 port.**

   If you encounter difficulties here, we implore you to read the paragraph in the next section that begins with this:

   > "*Don't* plug the iPad's dock connector or Lightning–to–USB cable into a USB port on your keyboard, monitor, or unpowered USB hub."

3. **Make sure that your iPad software is up to date.**

   To check with iTunes on your Mac or PC:

   a. *Connect the iPad to the computer, and then click the iPad icon in the row of icons below the toolbar.*

   If you connect more than one iDevice to this computer simultaneously, the button will say the number of devices (for example, *5 Devices*) rather than *iPad*. Click the button to display a drop-down list and select the device you want.

   b. *Click the Summary tab and then click the Check for Update button.*

To check with your iPad:

a. *On the Home screen, tap Settings.*

b. *In the Settings list on the left side of the screen, tap General.*

c. *On the right side of the screen, tap Software Update.*

If your iPad requires an update, you receive instructions for doing so. Otherwise, please continue.

If those three easy steps didn't get you back up and running and your iPad is still acting up — if it freezes, doesn't wake up from sleep, doesn't do something it used to do, or in any other way acts improperly — don't panic. The following sections describe the things you should try, in the order that we (and Apple) recommend.

If the first technique doesn't do the trick, go on to the second. If the second one doesn't work, try the third. And so on.

Recharge

If your iPad acts up in any way, shape, or form, the first thing you should try is to give its battery a full recharge before you proceed.

Don't plug the iPad's dock connector or Lightning–to–USB cable into a USB port on your keyboard, monitor, or an unpowered USB hub. You must plug the cable into one of the USB ports on your computer itself because the USB ports on your computer supply more power than the other ports. Although other USB ports *may* do the trick, you're better off using a built-in one on your computer.

If your computer is more than a few years old, even your built-in USB ports may not supply enough juice to recharge your iPad. It'll sync just fine; it just won't recharge. If you see *Not Charging* next to the battery icon at the top of the screen, use the included USB power adapter to recharge your iPad from an AC outlet rather than from a computer.

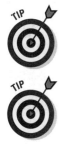

Most *powered* USB hubs, the kind you plug into an AC outlet, will charge your iPad just fine. But *passive* or *unpowered* hubs — ones that don't plug into the wall for power — won't cut it when it comes to charging your iPad.

If you're in a hurry, charge your iPad for a minimum of 20 minutes. We think a full charge is a better idea, but a charge of 20 minutes is better than no charge at all. And for faster charging in any circumstances, turn off your iPad while it charges, or put it in airplane mode at the very least.

Restart

If you recharge your iPad and it still misbehaves, the next thing to try is restarting it. Just as restarting a computer often fixes problems, restarting your iPad sometimes works wonders.

Here's how to restart your iPad:

1. **Hold down the sleep/wake button.**

2. **When the red slider appears, slide it to turn off the iPad and then wait a few seconds.**

3. **Hold down the sleep/wake button again until the Apple logo appears on the screen.**

4. **If your iPad is still frozen, misbehaves, or doesn't start, hold down the Home button for six to ten seconds to force any frozen applications to quit.**

5. **Repeat Steps 1–4 again.**

If your Home or sleep/wake button is acting up and you can't power down the usual way, try enabling Assistive Touch in Settings⇨General⇨Accessibility. A gray circle will appear on your screen; tap it and several options including on-screen versions of the Home and sleep/wake buttons appear. It may or may not help.

If these steps don't get your iPad back up and running, move on to the third *R:* resetting your iPad.

Reset your iPad

To reset your iPad, merely hold down the sleep/wake button and then hold down the Home button, continuing to keep both buttons down for at least ten seconds. When you see the Apple logo, release both buttons.

Resetting your iPad is like forcing your computer to restart after a crash. Your data shouldn't be affected by a reset — and in many cases, the reset cures whatever was ailing your iPad. So don't be shy about giving this technique a try. In many cases, your iPad goes back to normal after you reset it this way.

Sometimes you have to hold down the sleep/wake button *before* you hold down the Home button. If you press both at the same time, you might create a *screen shot* — a picture of whatever is on your screen at the time — rather than reset your iPad.

Unfortunately, sometimes resetting *doesn't* do the trick. When that's the case, you have to take stronger measures.

At this point, it's a good idea to back up your iPad's contents. On your iPad, go to Settings⇨iCloud⇨Storage & Backup and tap the Back Up Now button. Or connect your iPad to your computer and look in the Backup section of the Summary pane in iTunes, which also identifies when the last backup occurred.

Remove content

Nothing you've tried so far should have taken more than a few minutes (or 20 if you tried the 20-minute recharge). We hate to tell you, but that's about to change because the next thing you should try is removing some or all of your data to see whether it's causing your troubles.

To do so, you need to sync your iPad and then reconfigure it so that some or all of your files are *not* synchronized (which removes them from the iPad). The problem could be contacts, calendar data, songs, photos, videos, or podcasts. You can apply one of two strategies to this troubleshooting task:

 ✓ **If you suspect a particular data type** — for example, you suspect your photos because your iPad freezes whenever you tap the Photos icon on the Home screen — try removing that data first.

 ✓ **If you have no suspicions,** deselect every item and then sync. When you're finished, your iPad should have no data on it. If that method fixes your iPad, try restoring your data, one type at a time. If the problem returns, you have to keep experimenting to determine which particular data type or file is causing the problem.

If you're still having problems, the next step is to reset your iPad's settings and content.

Reset settings and content

Resetting involves two steps: The first one, resetting your iPad settings, resets every iPad *setting* to its default — the way the iPad was when you took it out of the box. Resetting the iPad's settings doesn't erase any of your data or media, so you can try this step without trepidation. The only downside is that you may have to go back and change some settings afterward. To reset your settings, tap the Settings icon on the Home screen and then tap General⇨Reset⇨Reset All Settings.

Be careful *not* to tap Erase All Content and Settings, at least not yet. Erasing all content takes more time to recover from (because your next sync takes a long time), so try Reset All Settings first.

Now, if resetting all settings didn't cure your iPad, you have to try Erase All Content and Settings. Read the next warning paragraph first. Then tap Settings⇨General⇨Reset⇨Erase All Content and Settings.

The Erase All Content strategy deletes everything from your iPad — all your data, media, and settings. Because all these items are stored on your computer — at least in theory — you should be able to put things back the way they were during your next sync. But you lose any photos or screen shots you've taken, as well as email, contacts, calendar events, playlists, and anything else you've created or modified on the iPad since your last sync.

After using Erase All Content and Settings, check to see whether your iPad works properly. If it doesn't cure what ails your iPad, the next-to-the-last *R,* restoring your iPad using iTunes, can help.

Restore

Before you give up on your poor, sick iPad, you can try to restore it. To restore, connect your iPad to your computer as though you were about to sync. But when the iPad icon appears in iTunes, click the Summary tab and then click the Restore button. This action erases all your data and media and resets all your settings.

If your computer isn't available, you can also trigger this step from your iPad by tapping Settings⇨General⇨Reset⇨Erase All Content and Settings.

If Find My iPad (Settings⇨iCloud⇨Find My iPad) is enabled, you'll see a message to disable it before you restore your iPad.

Because all your data and media still exist on your computer (except for photos or screen shots you've taken, as well as email, contacts, calendar events, playlists, and anything else you've created or modified on the iPad since your last sync, as noted previously), you shouldn't lose anything by restoring except possibly email or text messages sent or received since your last backup. Your next sync will take longer than usual, and you may have to reset settings you've changed since you got your iPad. But other than those inconveniences, restoring shouldn't cause you any additional trouble.

Performing a restore deletes everything on your iPad — all your data, media, and settings. You *should* be able to put things back the way they were with your next sync; if that doesn't happen, for whatever reason, you can't say we didn't warn you. That said, you may still be able to restore from an iTunes or iCloud backup as described in this chapter's thrilling conclusion, a scintillating section we call, "Dude, Where's My Stuff?"

Recovery mode

So, if you've tried all the other steps or you couldn't try some or all of them because your iPad is so messed up, you can try one last thing: Recovery mode. Here's how it works:

1. **Disconnect the USB cable from your iPad, but leave the other end of the cable connected to the USB port on your computer.**

2. **Turn off the iPad by holding down the sleep/wake button for a few seconds until the red slider appears onscreen, and then slide the slider.**

   Wait for the iPad to turn off.

3. **Hold down the Home button while you reconnect the USB cable to your iPad.**

   When you reconnect the USB cable, your iPad should power on.

    If you see a battery icon like the one shown in the margin, you need to let your iPad charge for at least 10 to 15 minutes. When the battery picture goes away or turns green instead of red, go back to Step 2 and try again.

4. **Continue holding down the Home button until you see the Connect to iTunes screen, and then release the button.**

   If you don't see the Connect to iTunes screen on your iPad, try Steps 1–4 again.

   If iTunes didn't open automatically already, launch it now. You should see a Recovery mode alert on your computer screen telling you that your iPad is in Recovery mode and that you must restore it before it can be used with iTunes.

5. **Use iTunes to restore the device, as we describe in the preceding section.**

Okay. So that's the gamut of things you can do when your iPad acts up. If you tried all this and none of it worked, skim through the rest of this chapter to see whether anything else we recommend looks like it might help. If not, your iPad probably needs to go into the shop for repairs.

Never fear, gentle reader. Be sure to read the "If Nothing We Suggest Helps" section, later in this chapter. Your iPad may be quite sick, but we help ease the pain by sharing some tips on how to minimize the discomfort.

Problems with Networks

If you're having problems with Wi-Fi or your wireless carrier's data network (Wi-Fi + 3G or 4G models only), this section may help. The techniques here are short and sweet — except for the last one, restore. Restore, which we describe in a previous section, is inconvenient and time-consuming, and entails erasing all your data and media and then restoring it.

First, here are some simple steps that may help:

✔ **Make sure that you have sufficient Wi-Fi or 3G or 4G signal strength, as shown in Figure 16-1.**

✔ **Try moving around.** Changing your location by as little as a few feet can sometimes mean the difference between great wireless reception and no wireless reception. If you're inside, try moving around even a step or two in one direction. If you're outside, try moving 10 or 20 paces in any direction. Keep an eye on the cell signal or Wi-Fi icon as you move around, and stop when you see more bars than you saw before.

✔ **Restart your iPad.** If you've forgotten how, refer to the "Restart" section, earlier in this chapter. As we mention, restarting your iPad is often all it takes to fix whatever is wrong.

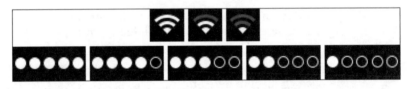

Figure 16-1: Wi-Fi (top) and 3G or 4G (bottom) signal strength from best (left) to worst (right).

If you have a Wi-Fi + 3G or 4G iPad, try the following:

✔ **Make sure that you haven't left your iPad in airplane mode, as we describe in Chapter 15.** In airplane mode, all network-dependent features are disabled, so you can't send or receive messages or use any of the apps that require a Wi-Fi or data-network connection (that is, Mail, Safari, Maps, and the iTunes and App Store apps).

✔ **Toggle airplane mode on and off.** Turn on airplane mode by swiping upward from the bottom of the screen to bring up Control Center and then tapping the airplane icon. Wait 15 or 20 seconds and then tap the airplane icon again to turn airplane mode off.

Toggling airplane mode on and off like this resets both the Wi-Fi and wireless data-network connections. If your network connection was the problem, toggling airplane mode on and off may correct it.

Apple offers two good articles that may help you with Wi-Fi issues. The first offers some general troubleshooting tips and hints; the second discusses potential sources of interference for wireless devices and networks. You can find them here:

http://support.apple.com/kb/TS3237

and here:

```
http://support.apple.com/kb/HT1365
```

If none of these suggestions fix your network issues, try resetting your network settings by tapping Settings➪General➪Reset➪Reset Network Settings.

Finally, if nothing else has fixed your issue, you can try restoring your iPad, as we describe previously in the "Restore" section.

Performing a restore deletes everything on your iPad — all your data, media, and settings. You should be able to put things back the way they were with your next sync. If that doesn't happen, well, consider yourself forewarned.

Sync, Computer, or iTunes Issues

The last category of troubleshooting techniques in this chapter applies to issues that involve synchronization and computer-iPad relations. If you're having problems syncing or your computer doesn't recognize your iPad when you connect it, here are some things to try.

We suggest that you try these procedures in the order they're presented here:

1. Recharge your iPad.

If you didn't try it previously, try it now. Go to the "Resuscitating an iPad with Issues" section, earlier in this chapter, and read what we say about recharging your iPad. Every word there also applies here.

2. Try a different USB port or a different cable if you have one available.

It doesn't happen often, but occasionally USB ports and cables go bad. When they do, they invariably cause sync and connection problems. Always make sure that a bad USB port or cable isn't to blame.

If you don't remember what we said about using USB ports on your computer rather than the ones on your keyboard, monitor, or hub, we suggest that you reread the "Recharge" section, earlier in this chapter.

3. Restart your iPad and try to sync again.

We describe restarting in full and loving detail in the "Restart" section, earlier in this chapter. You might also want to restart your computer at this point, just in case.

4. Reinstall iTunes.

Even if you have an iTunes installer handy, you probably should visit the Apple website and download the latest-and-greatest version, just in case. You can find the latest version of iTunes at `www.apple.com/itunes/download`.

More Help on the Apple Website

If you try everything we suggest earlier in this chapter and still have problems, don't give up just yet. This section describes a few more places you may find help. We recommend that you check them out before you throw in the towel and smash your iPad into tiny little pieces (or ship it back to Apple for repairs, as we describe in the next section).

First, Apple offers an excellent set of support resources on its website at `www.apple.com/support/ipad/setup`. You can browse support issues by category, search for a problem by keyword, read or download technical manuals, and scan the discussion forums.

Speaking of the discussion forums, you can go directly to them at `http://discussions.apple.com`. They're chock-full of useful questions and answers from other iPad users. If you can't find an answer to a support question elsewhere, you can often find it in these forums. You can browse by category or search by keyword. Either way, you find thousands of discussions about almost every aspect of using your iPad.

Now for the best part: If you can't find a solution by browsing or searching, you can post your question in the appropriate Apple discussion forum. Check back in a few days (or even in a few hours), and some helpful iPad user may well have replied with the solution. If you've never tried this fabulous tool, you're missing out on one of the greatest support resources available anywhere.

Last, but certainly not least, you might want to try a carefully worded Google search. You might just find the solution.

If Nothing We Suggest Helps

If you tried every trick in the book (this one) and still have a malfunctioning iPad, consider shipping it off to the iPad hospital (better known as Apple, Inc.). The repair is free if your iPad is still under its one-year limited warranty.

You can extend your warranty for as long as two years from the original purchase date, if you want. To do so, you need to buy the AppleCare Protection Plan for your iPad. You don't have to do it when you buy your iPad, but you must buy it before your one-year limited warranty expires. The retail price is $79, but we've seen it for a lot less, so it might pay to shop around.

Here are a few things you need to know before you take your iPad in to be repaired:

✐ *Your iPad may be erased during its repair,* so you should sync your iPad with iTunes before you take it in, if you can. If you can't and you entered data on the iPad since your last sync, such as a contact or an appointment, the data may not be there when you restore your iPad upon its return.

✐ Remove any accessories, such as a case or screen protector.

Although you may be able to get your iPad serviced by Best Buy or another authorized Apple reseller, we recommend that you take or ship it to your nearest Apple Store, for two reasons:

✐ **No one knows your iPad like Apple.** One of the Geniuses at the Apple Store may be able to fix whatever is wrong without sending your iPad away for repairs.

✐ **The Apple Store will, in some cases, swap out your wonky iPad for a brand-new one on the spot.** You can't win if you don't play, which is why we always visit our local Apple Store when something goes wrong (with our iPads, iPhones, iPods, and even our laptops and iMacs).

If you've done everything we've suggested, we're relatively certain that you're now holding an iPad that works flawlessly. Again.

That said, some or all of your stuff may not be on it. If that's the case, the following section offers a two-trick solution that usually works.

Dude, Where's My Stuff?

If you performed a restore or had your iPad replaced or repaired, you have one more task to accomplish. Your iPad may work flawlessly at this point, but some or all of your stuff — your music, movies, contacts, iMessages, or whatever — is missing. You're not sunk, at least not yet. You still have a couple of tricks up your sleeve.

✐ **Trick 1: Sync your iPad with iTunes and then sync it again.** That's right — sync and sync again. Why? Because sometimes stuff doesn't get synced properly on the first try. Just do it.

✐ **Trick 2: Restore from backup.** Click the Summary tab in iTunes and then click Restore Backup. If Find My iPad (Settings➪iCloud➪Find My iPad) is enabled, you'll first see a message to disable it before you restore your iPad. Then the Restore from Backup dialog appears and offers you a choice of backups, as shown in Figure 16-2. Select the one you want, click the Restore button, and let the iPad work some magic.

If you have more than one backup for a device, as Bob has for his iPhone 6s Plus in Figure 16-2, try the most recent (undated) one first. If it doesn't work or you're still missing files, try restoring from any other backups before you throw in the towel.

Figure 16-2: Select the appropriate backup and click the Restore button.

These backups include photos in camera roll, text messages, notes, contact favorites, sound settings, and more, but not media you've synced, such as music, videos, or photos. If media is missing, try performing Trick 1 again.

If you aren't holding an iPad that works flawlessly and has most (if not all) of your stuff, it's time to make an appointment with a Genius at your local Apple Store, call the support hotline (800-275-2273), or visit the support web page at www.apple.com/support/ipad.

17

Accessorizing Your iPad

nyone who has purchased a new car in recent years is aware that it's not always a picnic trying to escape the showroom without the salesperson trying to get you to part with a few extra bucks. You can only imagine what the markup is on roof racks, navigation systems, and rear-seat DVD players.

We don't suppose you'll get a hard sell when you snap up a new iPad at an Apple Store (or elsewhere). But Apple and several other companies are all too happy to outfit whichever iPad model you choose with extra doodads, from wireless keyboards and stands to battery chargers and carrying cases. So just as your car might benefit from dealer (or third-party) options, so too might your iPad benefit from a variety of spare parts.

The iPads preceding the fourth-generation feature the standard 30-pin dock connector that's been familiar to iPod and iPhone owners over the past decade. If you own either or both of these products, you also know that a bevy of accessories fit perfectly into that dock connector. Heck, you might even try to plug the battery chargers or other iPod or iPhone accessories you have lying around into the iPad. No guarantee that these will work, but they probably will. And you have nothing to lose by trying.

Note: In 2012, Apple switched to a new connector — the Lightning connector. Accessories compatible with the new connector have become pretty much ubiquitous, and there are dock connector–to–Lightning cables and adapters from Apple and others so you can use most older accessories with new iDevices.

One thing is certain: If you see a *Made for iPad* label on the package, the developer is certifying that an electronic accessory has been designed to connect specifically to the iPad and meets performance standards established by Apple. Just make sure that the connector matches the specific iPad model you have or that you have an available adapter. Note that not all adapters support video.

We start this accessories chapter with the options that carry the Apple logo and conclude with worthwhile extras from other companies.

Accessories from Apple

You've come to expect a certain level of excellence from Apple hardware and software, so you should expect no differently when it comes to various Apple-branded accessories. That said, you can find a variety of opinions on some of these products, so we recommend a visit to `http://store.apple.com`, where you can read mini-reviews and pore over ratings from real people just like you. They're not shy about telling it like it is. And by all means, check out the many price shopping comparison sites on the web to ensure that you're getting the best deal.

Casing the iPad

The thing about accessories is that half the time, you wish they weren't accessories at all. You wish they came in the box. Among the things we would have liked to see included with the iPad was a protective case.

Alas, it wasn't to be. No iPad has ever shipped with a case in the box, but you can find cases aplenty just the same. All you need is cash. You read about Apple's here and other cases later in this chapter.

Apple's iPad case, shown in Figure 17-1, is more cover than case, which is probably why it's called a *Smart Cover* instead of a *Smart Case.* Made specifically for iPads, it's ultra-thin and attaches magnetically. Flip the cover open (even just a little), and your iPad wakes instantly; flip it shut, and your iPad goes right to sleep. The case is available in numerous bright colors in polyurethane ($39–$49) or leather ($69). Bob says the aniline-dyed Italian leather on his Product Red Smart Cover is gorgeous and soft as butter.

Courtesy of Apple

Figure 17-1: Apple's Smart Cover for iPad.

Finally, there's the iPad Air 2 Smart Case, which combines a Smart Cover and a case to protect the back of your iPad Air 2. It's designed for the thinner profile of the Air 2. Like the Smart Cover, it too folds into a stand for reading, typing, or watching video. And because it's "smart," it automatically wakes and sleeps your iPad when you open and close it. The aniline-dyed leather case has a microfiber lining and is available in five bright colors for $79. A version for the iPad mini costs $69.

Whatever case you choose, make sure it is compatible with your favorite accessories.

Apple wireless keyboard

We think the various virtual keyboards that pop up just as you need them on the iPad are perfectly fine for shorter typing tasks, whether it's composing emails or tapping a few notes. For most longer assignments, however, we writers are more comfortable pounding away on a real-deal physical keyboard, and we suspect you feel the same way.

Fortunately, a physical keyboard for the iPad is an easy addition, and because it's the same keyboard that's been bundled with iMacs for years, you may even own one already.

The Apple wireless keyboard, shown in Figure 17-2, is a way to use a decent-enough aluminum physical keyboard without tethering it to the iPad. It operates from up to 30 feet away from the iPad via Bluetooth, the wireless technology we discuss in Chapter 15. Which leads us to ask, can you see the iPad screen from 30 feet away?

If you have an Apple TV connected to your HDTV, you can stream the screen of your iPad to the HDTV by using AirPlay. (See Chapter 8 for the details.) And the Apple wireless keyboard is great for using on the couch.

Courtesy of Apple

Figure 17-2: The Apple wireless keyboard.

As with many Bluetooth devices that the iPad makes nice with, you have to pair it to your tablet. Pairing is also discussed in Chapter 15.

The Bluetooth keyboard takes two AA batteries. It's smart about power management, too; it powers itself down when you stop using it to avoid draining those batteries. It wakes up when you start typing.

The Apple wireless keyboard is small and thin. If you carry a backpack, a briefcase, a messenger bag, or even a large purse, you almost certainly have enough room for a wireless keyboard.

And if your native tongue isn't English, you'll be happy to know that Apple sells versions of the wireless keyboard in numerous languages, each still $69.

Not all the function keys on the wireless keyboard, will, um, function on your iPad. They're there, though, because (as we note previously) Apple bundles the same keyboard with the iMac and sells it for other Macs.

Although we have tested a few third-party Bluetooth keyboards, the iPad ought to work fine with any keyboard that supports Bluetooth 2.1 + EDR technology. Bob is currently infatuated with his Logitech Ultrathin Keyboard Cover ($99), which includes iPad (and iPhone) specific keys, works like a Smart Cover to wake and sleep your iPad, and comes in an ultra-thin aluminum enclosure that looks great and matches the iPad perfectly. It's a little more expensive than the Apple wireless keyboard, but he says it's worth it.

Finally, you can connect many USB keyboards to your iPad with the iPad camera connection kit (for dock connector) or Lightning–to–USB camera adapter discussed in the following section.

Apple Smart Keyboard (for iPad Pro)

Apple built a special keyboard-and-cover combination for its large-display iPad Pro, the aptly named iPad Pro Smart Keyboard. The keyboard, which costs $169, is made from a sheet of durable custom-woven fabric that Apple says is laser ablated to form the shape of each key. At 4mm, it's really thin too.

The keyboard connects to the iPad Pro via the smart connector on the edge of the Smart Keyboard and on the side of iPad Pro. Making that connection is a tad tricky at first.

And beyond typing, you get the added benefit of using the Smart Keyboard as your Smart Cover.

Connecting a camera

iPads don't include a USB port or an SD memory card slot, which happen to be the most popular methods for getting pictures (and videos) from a digital camera onto a computer.

All the same, the iPad is a marvelous photo viewer. So, if you take a lot of pictures, Apple's $29 iPad camera connection kit, which we also discuss in Chapter 9, is worth considering for iPads that sport the 30-pin connector (iPad 2s and third-generation iPads). As a reminder, the kit consists of the two components shown in Figure 17-3, either of which plugs into the 30-pin dock connector at the bottom of older iPads. One sports a USB interface that you can use with the USB cable that came

Courtesy of Apple

Figure 17-3: iPad camera connection kit, Lightning–to–USB camera connector, and Lightning–to–SD card connector allow you to import images.

with your camera to download pictures. The other is an SD card reader that lets you insert the memory card that stores your pictures.

If you seek the same functionality for your iPad with a Lightning connector, the kit has been separated into two $29 items: a Lightning–to–USB camera connector and a Lightning–to–SD card connector.

Although the official line from Apple is that this USB adapter is meant to work with the USB cable from your digital camera, we tried connecting other devices. We were able to get an old Dell USB keyboard, readers for non–SD-type memory cards, USB speakers, MIDI keyboards, and more to work with it. But don't expect all your USB devices to be compatible: Some require more power than the iPad can provide, and others need software drivers that aren't available on the iPad. However, the adapter does work with many class-compliant USB devices, so if you have an adapter, there's no harm in giving it a shot.

We only hope that despite this helpful accessory, Apple will get around to adding a USB and an SD slot to iPads, but so far it hasn't happened, and we're not holding our breath.

Connecting an iPad to a TV or projector

The iPad has a pretty big screen for what it is, a tablet computer, and when it comes to the Retina display, we can't help but give it high praise. But that display is still not nearly as large as a living room TV or a monitor that you might see in a conference room or auditorium. To send iPad content to a bigger screen, you can choose from three connectors:

- ✔ **Digital AV adapter cable:** The most useful member of the Apple adapter family for most users is the Apple digital AV adapter ($39 for dock connector; $49 for Lightning connector). It uses HDMI, which is pretty much a standard on state-of-the-art HDTVs and other modern gear. And it comes with a nice bonus: You can mirror the display on your iPad on a big-screen TV, which is great for demos and presentations. Ed has used this adapter to, among other things, play *Angry Birds* on the bigger TV screen. Bob uses it to watch HD movies in hotel rooms. Both of us think it rocks. Be sure to get the Lightning–digital AV model for any iPad with a Lightning connector.

  You can wirelessly mirror the display of your iPad onto a large-screen TV as long as you're streaming to another Apple accessory called Apple TV. The streaming is accomplished through AirPlay, which we discuss in Chapter 8. Apple TV provides a lot of niceties in its own right, even if you don't own an iPad. (But if you don't, why are you reading this book?) For example, you can watch 1080p high-definition TV shows and movies; watch videos on Netflix, Hulu Plus, and Vimeo; listen to music from your iTunes library on a PC or Mac or iTunes Radio; and admire photos through iCloud. And the newest Apple TV models added an App Store, which includes a variety of games. But we digress. Let's move on to the adapters that work with older technology.

- ✔ **VGA adapter cable:** Projecting what's on the iPad's screen to a larger display is the reason behind the Lightning–to–VGA and dock connector–to–VGA adapter cables that Apple is selling for $49 and $29, respectively.

You can use them to connect your iPad to TVs, projectors, and VGA displays. What for? We told you: To watch videos, slideshows, and presentations on the big screen.

By today's standards, VGA (video graphics array) delivers low-resolution video output compared to the more advanced HDMI (high-definition multimedia interface).

Be sure to get the proper VGA adapter for your iPad model — choose the 30-pin dock connector or the Lightning cable as appropriate.

✔ **Composite AV cable:** You need this $39 cable to display iPad, iPhone, or iPod touch content on most standard-definition TVs, which we realize are becoming a disappearing breed. In any case, this cable connects the dock connector on the iPad to the composite video port of your TV via a yellow connector. You'll also need to hook up the red and white audio connectors to analog audio ports on your TV or AV receiver. *Note:* This adapter doesn't work with iPads with Lightning connectors — even with an adapter.

Keeping a spare charger

With roughly ten hours of battery life on the Wi-Fi–only iPad and nine hours on models with cellular access, a single charge can more than get you through a typical workday with your iPad. But why chance it? Having a spare charger at the office can spare you (!) from having to commute with one. The Apple iPad 12W USB power adapter sells for $19. Again, make sure to get the one with a Lightning cord if you have an iPad with that connector.

And if you're traveling abroad, consider the Apple World Travel Adapter Kit. The $29 kit includes the proper prongs and adapters for numerous countries around the globe, and it lets you juice up not only your iPad but also iPhones, iPod touches, and Macs.

Finally, if you have an old iPhone or iPod USB power adapter, or almost any other power adapter with a USB port, chances are good it'll work, though it may take longer to charge your iPad.

If you try to charge your iPad with an adapter that doesn't provide enough power, nothing bad will happen. Your iPad will merely charge much more slowly while it displays a *Not Charging* message instead of the battery-with-a-lightning-bolt icon you see when your iPad is connected to a charger with sufficient juice.

Apple Pencil for iPad Pro

Another iPad Pro–only accessory, the $99 Apple Pencil, is like a souped-up stylus that you can use to draw, doodle, or write on the screen. Press harder on the display to draw a thicker line; press more gently for a lighter line. And yes, the iPad Pro can detect whether you're using your finger or the Apple Pencil.

Apple says that the Apple Pencil battery can last about 12 hours and that you can get a half-hour of juice after charging the Pencil for just 15 seconds.

Apple has devised a cool way to pair the Pencil to your iPad. Just pull off the Pencil's cap to reveal a Lightning connector, which you plug into your iPad. Couldn't be any easier than that.

Listening and Talking with Earphones, Headphones, and Headsets

You've surely noticed that your iPad didn't include earphones or a headset. That's probably a blessing because the earphones and headsets Apple has included with iPods and iPhones since time immemorial aren't that good. In fact, Bob referred to them as "mediocre and somewhat uncomfortable" in almost every article he's written about the iPod or iPhone. Ed agrees. For what it's worth, iPhones and iPod touches now include Apple's redesigned — and much improved — EarPods.

Apple acquired a genuine headphone company, Beats, so Apple may leverage this purchase in some way and supply or at least make available top-notch Beats headphones. But as of this writing, the iPad still ships without headphones, so you get to select a pair of headphones, earphones, or a headset that suits your needs and your budget. That's good, right?

Wired headphones, earphones, and headsets

Search Amazon for *headphones, earphones,* or *headsets,* and you'll find thousands of each available at prices ranging from around $10 to more than $1,000. Or if you prefer to shop in a bricks-and-mortar store, Target, Best Buy, and the Apple Store all have decent selections, with prices starting at less than $20.

Much as we love the shopping experience at Apple Stores, you won't find any bargains there because Apple-branded products are rarely discounted. However, you can almost always find compatible non-Apple items such as headphones, earphones, and headsets cheaper somewhere else.

Earphones? Headphones? Headsets?

We refer to headphones and headsets several times and thought you might be wondering whether a difference exists and, if so, what it is. When we talk about *headphones* or *earphones*, we're talking about the things you use to listen to music. A *headset* adds a microphone so that you can use it for voice chatting, schmoozing with Siri, FaceTime video chatting, and (in the case of the iPhone or Internet VOIP services such as Skype) for phone calls. So headphones and earphones are for listening, and headsets are for both talking and listening.

Now you may be wondering whether earphones and headphones are the same. To some people, they may be, but to us, headphones have a band across the top (or back) of your head, and the listening apparatus is big and covers the outside of your ears. Think of the big fat things you see

covering a radio disk jockey's ears. Earphones (sometimes referred to as *earbuds*), on the other hand, are smaller, fit entirely in your ear, and have no band across the top or back of your head.

Headsets can be earphone style or, less commonly, headphone style. The distinguishing factor is that headsets always include a microphone. And some headsets are designed specifically for use with Apple i-products (iPhone, iPod, iPad) and have integrated play/pause and volume control buttons.

One last thing: Some companies refer to their earbud products as headphones, but we think that's confusing and wrong. So in this book, headphones are those bulky, outside-the-ear things, and earphones are teeny-tiny things that fit entirely in your ear.

With so many brands and models of earphones, headphones, and headsets available from so many manufacturers at so many price points, we can't possibly test even a fraction of the ones available today. That said, we've probably tested more of them than most people, and we have our favorites.

When it comes to headphones, Bob is partial to his SR60i from Grado, which is legendary for offering astonishingly accurate audio at an affordable price (around $80). He's tried headphones that cost twice, thrice, or even more times as much that he didn't think sounded nearly as good. Find out more at www.gradolabs.com.

Ed goes with sweet-sounding, albeit pricey (about $350) Bose QuietComfort 3 acoustic noise-canceling headphones and Monster Inspiration over-the-ear noise-canceling headphones (about $300).

For earphones and earphone-style headsets, Bob likes the Klipsch Image S4 headphones and S4i in-ear headset with mic and three-button remote. At around $79 and $99, respectively, they sound better than many similarly priced products, and better than many more-expensive offerings.

Bluetooth stereo headphones, earphones, and headsets

Neither of us has much experience with Bluetooth (wireless) stereo headphones and headsets, but we thought we'd at least plant the seed. The idea is that with Bluetooth stereo headphones, earphones, and headsets, you can listen to music wirelessly up to 33 feet away from your iPad. If this sounds good to you, we suggest that you look for reviews of such products on the web before you decide which one to buy. A search of Amazon for *stereo Bluetooth headset* brought up thousands of items, with prices starting as low as $11.99.

For what it's worth, Bob has been quite happy with his BlueAnt Pump HD Stereo Sportsbuds, a Bluetooth stereo headset he occasionally uses with his iPhone and iPad. He says they sound better and stay put in his ears better than other Bluetooth stereo headsets he's tried. They're also waterproof and sweat-proof. Last time he checked, they were going for around $40 at Amazon.com.

Listening with Speakers

You can connect just about any speakers to your iPad, but if you want decent sound, we suggest you look only at *powered* speakers, not *passive* (unpowered) ones. Powered speakers contain their own amplification circuitry and can deliver much better (and louder) sound than unpowered speakers.

Prices range from well under $100 to hundreds (or even thousands) of dollars. Most speaker systems designed for use with your computer, iPod, or iPhone work well as long as they have an auxiliary input or a dock connector that can accommodate your iPad.

Desktop speakers

Logitech (www.logitech.com) makes a range of desktop speaker systems priced from less than $25 to more than $300. But that $300 system is the Z5500 THX-certified 505-watt 5.1 digital surround system — surely overkill for listening to music or video on your iPad, which doesn't support surround sound anyway. The point is that Logitech makes a variety of decent systems at a wide range of price points. If you're looking for something inexpensive, you can't go wrong with a Logitech-powered speaker system.

Bob is a big fan of Audioengine (www.audioengineusa.com) desktop speakers. They deliver superior audio at prices that are reasonable for speakers that sound this good. Audioengine 5 is the premium product priced at $349 per pair; Audioengine 2 is its smaller but still excellent sibling priced at $199 per pair. They're available only direct from the manufacturer, but the company is so confident that you'll love them that it offers a free audition for the speaker systems. If you order a pair and don't love them, return them within 30 days for a full refund. Bob knows a lot of people who have ordered them, and so far no one has sent them back.

Bluetooth speakers

Like Bluetooth headsets, Bluetooth speakers let you listen to music up to 33 feet away from your iPad. They're great for listening by the pool or hot tub or anywhere else you might not want to take your iPad.

Both of us have written favorable reviews of the $149.99 wireless Jambox by Jawbone, a rechargeable speaker that offers very good sound despite being able to fit into the palm of your hand. You can connect via Bluetooth or its auxiliary stereo jack. A bonus: Jambox doubles as a decent-enough speaker-phone.

Jawbone has also introduced the Big Jambox. Quick quiz: What do you think that means? Right, a bigger version of the Jambox with bigger sound. Of course, at $299.99, it also carries a bigger price, and it's a bit less portable than its diminutive sibling. And because this isn't a one-size-fits-all society, Jawbone more recently introduced the Mini Jambox, which comes in multiple colors, and commands $129.99.

Ed also likes a big rival to the Big Jambox, the Bose SoundLink wireless mobile speaker, which fetches a similar price.

After reading Ed's review, Bob traveled with a Jawbone Jambox for years and liked it. Then he got the Ultimate Ears Boom wireless speaker/speakerphone ($199.99), of which he says, "blows the doors off the Jambox," and is the best-sounding $200 Bluetooth speaker he ever tested. And not wanting to be bested by Big Jambox, Ultimate Ears recently introduced Mega Boom ($299.99), which is (all together now) a bigger version of the Boom with bigger sound and Bob's current best-sounding pick at that price point.

AirPlay speakers

The newest type of speakers you might choose for your iPad support Apple's proprietary AirPlay protocol, which takes advantage of your existing Wi-Fi network to stream audio and/or video from your iPad (or other compatible iDevice) to a single AirPlay-enabled speaker or audio/video receiver.

The biggest differences between AirPlay and Bluetooth speakers are

✔ Bluetooth can stream music only in a compressed form; AirPlay can stream music (and video) uncompressed. So, a speaker with AirPlay should sound better than a similar speaker with Bluetooth.

- ✔ Bluetooth's range is roughly 30 feet; AirPlay's range is up to 300 feet. You can't extend Bluetooth's range; Wi-Fi range can easily be extended with inexpensive routers such as Apple's AirPort Express ($99).

- ✔ iTunes (on your computer) can use AirPlay to stream audio or video to multiple speakers or audio/video receivers, with individual volume controls for each device; Bluetooth streams to only one device at a time.

Docking your iPad with an extender cable

Because the iPad is much larger than an iPod or iPhone, you can't just dock the iPad into a speaker system designed for the smaller devices. All is not lost if you're partial to those speakers and still want to connect the iPad. CableJive (`http://cablejive.com`), RadTech (`www.radtech.us`), and others sell dock extender cables, which allow you to use your iPad with any docking device no matter how small its dock. Apple also sells a 30-pin-to–Lightning adapter cable, allowing you to connect an iPad to one of these speaker systems.

This type of cable doesn't work with S-video output, component video, or audio input jacks for recording.

Wrapping Your iPad in Third-Party Cases

Much as we like the Apple iPad case, other vendors offer some excellent and — as the sidebar "The refrigerator iPad?" points out — some very different options:

- ✔ **Abas:** Abas (`www.abas.net`) offers nice leather cases that won't set you back $689 like the Orbino crocodile-skin case we've seen.

- ✔ **Targus:** Targus (`www.targus.com`) has a full line of iPad cases in a variety of materials and prices. Most of them, including the leather portfolio, cost no more than $60.

- ✔ **Griffin Technology:** Griffin Technology (`www.griffintechnology.com`) also has a pretty good selection of iPad cases at reasonable prices.

- ✔ **iLuv:** iLuv (`www.i-luv.com`) is yet another case maker with a range of affordable cases fabricated from leather, fabric, and silicone, none of which costs more than $40.

- ✔ **Vario:** ZeroChroma (`www.zerochroma.com`) has Bob's current favorite Vario iPad (and iPhone) case ($69.95). The big attraction is the 16-angle rotating theater stand on the back that folds flush when not in use. Sweet!

- ✔ **BookBook:** The BookBook case from Twelve South (`www.twelvesouth.com`) looks like a fine vintage hardbound book but is actually a handsome iPad case and stand ($79.99).

The refrigerator iPad?

It figured that some outfit would produce a refrigerator magnet mount for your iPad, given how many people consult iPads in the kitchen for, among other reasons, recipes, reminders, and the weather. The company in question is Woodford Design (www.woodforddesign.com), and the result of its efforts is the aptly named FridgePad, a mount for the iPad. As long as your fridge door is made of steel or stainless steel, you can mount the iPad on a fridge vertically or horizontally and have full access to ports and buttons. FridgePad costs about $30 and comes in black or silver. We haven't tried it ourselves, but we watched a video that shows an iPad mounted in FridgePad withstanding repeated slams of a refrigerator door. The company claims the magnet is 25 times stronger than it needs to be.

✔ **LifeProof nüüd:** This case may be bulky and relatively expensive, but it is waterproof, dirtproof, snowproof, and shockproof. Bob says his second-generation iPad, which has been dropped several times and soaked in a spa more than once, would have died long ago without the LifeProof case (www.lifeproof.com). While connecting earphones or docking cables is more of a hassle than with most cases, and it's not cheap ($129.99), Bob says it's a lot cheaper than a new iPad. He's still using it today.

✔ **The iPad Bubble Sleeve:** From Hard Candy Cases (www.hardcandycases.com), the iPad Bubble Sleeve ($49.95) offers significantly better protection against bumps and scratches than any other case we've seen. If we expected our iPads to be exposed to moderate impacts, this case's rigid exterior and additional shock-absorbing rubber bumpers for the screen make it the case we'd choose.

But Wait . . . There's More!

Before we leave the topic of accessories, we think you should know about a few more products, namely, film protection products that guard your iPad's exterior (or screen) without adding a bit of bulk: the Griffin Technology A-Frame tabletop stand for your iPad, and 2-into-1 stereo adapters.

Protecting the screen with film

Some people prefer not to use a case with their iPads, and that's okay, too. But if you're one of those people (or even if you're not), you might want to consider protective film for the iPad screen or even the entire device. We've tried these products on our iPads in the past and have found them to perform as promised. If you apply them properly, they're nearly invisible, and they protect your iPad from scratches and scrapes without adding any bulk.

Bob recently discovered the joys of iVisor AG Screen Protector for iPad ($30) from Moshi (www.moshimonde.com) and says it's still the best screen cover he's tested to date. It's easy to apply, resists fingerprints better than Apple's oleophobic screen coating, and features patented technology for a bubble-free installation every time. The best feature, Bob believes, is that if it gets dirty, you just remove it, wash it under a faucet, air-dry it, and reapply it (bubble-free, of course).

Another option is from the aforementioned RadTech (www.radtech.us), which offers two types of Mylar screen protectors — transparent and anti-glare. These screen protectors are somewhat stiffer than the film products, and unlike film, they can be cleaned and reapplied multiple times with no reduction in performance. They effectively hide minor scratches, surface defects, and abrasions, and the hard Mylar surface not only resists scratches and abrasions but is also optically correct. Finally, they're reasonably priced at $19.95 for a pair of protectors of the same type.

Bob has also tested more traditional film products from InvisibleShield by ZAGG (www.zagg.com), BodyGuardz (www.bodyguardz.com), and Best Skins Ever (www.bestskinsever.com) and says, in a nutshell, they're more similar than they are different. If you want to protect your screen with film, get whichever has the price and warranty that suits your needs.

These skins can be tricky to apply (including the iVisor AG, which is the easiest of all to install). Follow the instructions closely, watch videos on the vendors' websites and YouTube, and take your time. If you do, you'll be rewarded with clear film protection that's nearly invisible yet protects your iPad from scratches, nicks, and cuts.

The last time we checked, Best Buy will apply these skins for you for less than $10, which may be a bargain compared to messing things up and having to buy another skin. Ask your favorite electronics retailer if it provides a similar service.

Standing up your iPad

The Griffin A-Frame ($39.99) is so unusual that we just had to include it. As you can see in Figure 17-4, it's a dual-purpose desktop stand made of heavy-duty aluminum. You can open it to hold your iPad in either portrait or landscape mode for video watching, displaying pictures (a great way to exploit picture frame mode, as we describe in Chapter 9), or even reading. In this upright mode, it's also the perfect companion for the Apple wireless keyboard (or any other Bluetooth keyboard for that matter). Or close the legs and lay it down, and it puts your iPad at the perfect angle for using the on-screen keyboard.

Courtesy of Griffin Technology

Figure 17-4: The Griffin A-Frame is a unique, dual-purpose tabletop stand for your iPad.

Soft silicone padding keeps your iPad from getting scratched or sliding around, and the bottom lip is designed to accommodate the charging cable in portrait mode. Furthermore, it works with many third-party cases, including Griffin's flexible and hard-shell cases, among others.

The iKlip (www.ikmulti media.com; $29.99) stand may not look as cool as Griffin's, but it's lightweight and folds flat, as shown in Figure 17-5. Bob says: "I love my iKlip Studio and rarely leave home without it."

Sharing your iPad with a 2-into-1 stereo adapter

A *2-into-1 stereo adapter* is a handy little device that lets two people plug their head-phones, earphones, or head-sets into one iPad (or iPod or iPhone, for that matter).

Courtesy of IK Multimedia

Figure 17-5: iKlip Studio is adjustable, portable, and easy to set up and use.

They're inexpensive (less than $10) and extremely useful if you're traveling with a friend by air, sea, rail, or bus. They're also great when you want to watch a movie with your BFF but don't want to risk waking the neighbors or roommates.

We call 'em *2-into-1 stereo adapters,* but that's not the only name they go by. Other names you might see for the same device include

- 3.5mm stereo Y-splitter
- ⅛-inch stereo 1-plug-to-2-jacks adapter
- ⅛-inch stereo Y-adapter
- 3.5mm dual stereo headphone jack splitter

You need to know only two things. The first is that ⅛-inch and 3.5mm are used interchangeably in the adapter world (even though they're not really the same).

Some measurements to keep in mind: ⅛ inch = 0.125 inch, whereas 3.5mm = 0.1378 inch. Not the same, but close enough for rock 'n' roll.

The second is that you want to make sure that you get a *stereo* adapter. Some monaural adapters work but pump the same sound into both ears, instead of sending the audio information for the left stereo channel to your left ear and the right stereo channel to your right.

In other words, you need a ⅛-inch or 3.5mm stereo adapter that has a single stereo plug on one end (to plug into your iPad) and two stereo jacks on the other (to accommodate two sets of headphones/earphones/headsets).

Test the adapter before you travel. Bob recently discovered that the one he had packed was much louder for one person than the other.

Part VI
The Part of Tens

In this part . . .

- ✔ Explore our ten favorite free apps in the iPad App Store. You'll find clever apps that serve as a superb way to enjoy digital comics, settle disputes over any movie, ever, and even help you identify the name of an unfamiliar song.

- ✔ Peruse our ten favorite not-for-free apps for the iPad, including one very addictive game and apps that let you create and mail picture postcards, make your own movies with Hollywood-style special effects, and control your Mac or PC remotely from your iPad.

18

Ten Appetizing and Free Apps

In This Chapter

▶ TripCase

▶ Shazam

▶ Flipboard

▶ Movies by Flixster

▶ IMDb Movies & TV

▶ Netflix

▶ Comixology

▶ Epicurious Recipes & Shopping List

▶ Evernote

▶ Pandora Radio

*K*iller app is familiar jargon to anyone who has spent any time around computers. The term refers to an application so sweet or so useful that just about everybody wants or must have it.

You could make the argument that the most compelling killer app on the iPad is the very App Store we expound on in Chapter 11. This online emporium has an abundance of splendid programs — dare we say killer apps in their own right? — many of which are free. These cover everything from food (hey, you gotta eat) to showbiz. Okay, so some rotten apples (aren't we clever) are in the bunch, too. But we're here to accentuate the positive.

With that in mind, in this chapter, we offer ten of our favorite free iPad apps. In Chapter 19, we tell you about our favorite iPad apps that aren't free but are worth every penny.

We show you ours, and we encourage you to show us yours. If you discover your own killer iPad apps, by all means, let us know — our email addresses are at the end of the Introduction to this book — so that we can check them out.

TripCase

We both travel more than most people and are somewhat set in our ways. Before a trip, we use our computers to print boarding passes, hotel and rental car details, and any other info we might need while in transit. The printouts are strictly analog, so they don't notify us (or anyone else) of gate changes or flight delays or cancellations. And, of course, they can't remind us to check in. Still, the system works reliably unless we lose our printed documents.

It may be old school, but it's the best we could do until recently. What we wished and hoped for was a single intelligent repository for travel-related information, one that was smart enough to alert us of gate changes, weather delays, flight cancellations, and the like, and one that was easy to configure, convenient to use, and free.

What we found is TripCase, which is all that and more. It's a free app (and website) that organizes details of each trip in one place, with reminders and flight alerts delivered directly to your iPad.

TripCase has a lot to like, but one thing we like best is that it's drop-dead simple to add your travel events — without copying and pasting or even typing. We merely forward our confirmation emails — for flights, hotels, rental cars, and other travel-related services — to trips@tripcase.com. TripCase parses the details, creates an itinerary, and sends us an email to confirm that our trip is ready to view in TripCase. We've forwarded confirmations from at least a half dozen travel providers, and TripCase has never failed to interpret them correctly. (And you can always enter details the old-fashioned way — by copying and pasting or typing.)

After TripCase has your info, you can view it in the TripCase app or in any web browser. The app is well-organized, with a timeline view of the itinerary (as shown in Figure 18-1), and details are but a tap away (as shown in Figure 18-2). TripCase also includes an action view with flight alerts, reminders, and other messages. Any way you look at it, TripCase does most of the work for you.

TripCase can even help you locate an alternate flight based on your original reservation should your flight be cancelled or delayed. And it reminds you to check in and print boarding passes 24 hours before each flight. Sweet!

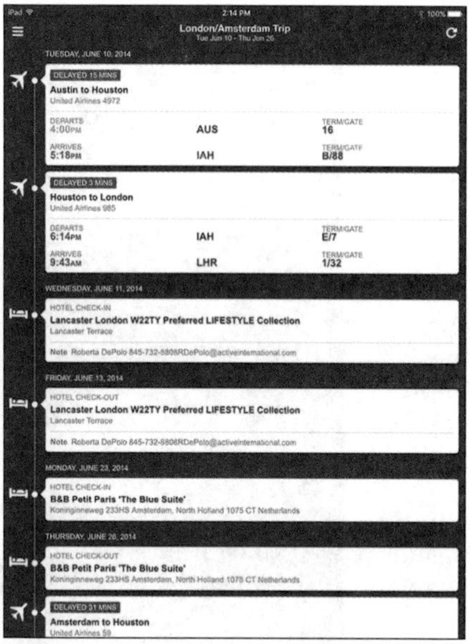

Figure 18-1: The timeline view shows you everything you need in the order you're likely to need it.

Figure 18-2: Tap any item in the timeline to see its details.

TripCase's motto is "stress-free travel." Although it may not make travel stress free — or increase the legroom in and around a cramped airline seat — it definitely makes travel less stressful.

Shazam

Ever heard a song on the radio or television, in a store, or at a club and wondered what it was called or who was singing it? With the Shazam app, you may never wonder again. Just launch Shazam and point your iPad's microphone at the source of the music. In a few seconds, the song title and artist's name magically appear on your iPad screen, as shown in Figure 18-3.

In Shazam parlance, that song has been *tagged*. Now, if tagging were all Shazam could do, that would surely be enough. But wait, there's more. After Shazam tags a song, you can

- Buy the song at the iTunes Store
- Watch related videos on YouTube

- Tweet the song on Twitter if you set up Twitter in Settings

- Read a biography, a discography, or lyrics

- Take a photo and attach it to the tagged item in Shazam

- Email a tag to a friend

Shazam isn't great at identifying classical music, jazz, show tunes, or opera, nor is it adept at identifying obscure indie bands. But if you use it primarily to identify popular music, it rocks (pun intended). It has worked for us in noisy airport terminals, crowded shopping malls, and even once at a wedding ceremony.

Oh, and one more thing: You can have Siri (with Shazam's assistance) identify a song for you even if you don't have the Shazam app installed.

Figure 18-3: Shazam can often identify obscure songs like this one by Todd Rundgren.

Flipboard

If imitation is (as the cliché goes) a form of flattery, Apple reaped high praise on Flipboard when it unleased a new News app as part of iOS 9. Apple's News seems to share much in common with Flipboard, the latter being a socially oriented personal magazine app that we're confident news and information junkies will like a lot.

To get started with Flipboard, tap the topics you're interested in: business, technology, sports, arts & culture, wine tasting, music, cute animals, and a lot more — over 30,000 topics in fact.

Flipboard then delivers articles based on your selections, all presented in a handsome, intuitive interface. Swipe left and right to move from page to page. Tap on the articles you want to read. Fine-tune the articles that Flipboard delivers by tapping a thumbs-up icon (more like this) icon or a thumbs-down one (less like this).

By choosing "weird" as one of his topics, Ed was able to read articles he was unlikely to stumble upon otherwise, including a story out of the Daily Mail in the UK that revealed "The weirdest things dentists have found in patients' mouths."

Trust us, you'll find articles in Flipboard that are a lot more appetizing than that one. As a bonus, you can link Flipboard to various social media accounts.

Movies by Flixster

We like movies, so we both use the Flixster app a lot. Feed it your zip code and then browse local theaters by movie, showtimes, rating, or distance from your current location. Or browse to find a movie you like and then tap to find theaters, showtimes, and other info, as shown in Figure 18-4. Another nice feature is the capability to buy tickets to most movies from your iPad with just a few additional taps.

Figure 18-4: Find out showtimes, watch the trailer, or get more info on the director or cast with a single tap.

We appreciate that we can read reviews, play movie trailers, and email movie listings to others with a single tap. We also enjoy the movie trailers for soon-to-be-released films and DVDs. Other free movie showtime apps are out there, but we like Flixster the most.

IMDb Movies & TV

While we're on the subject of the silver screen, we couldn't resist opening IMDb, shorthand for Internet Movie Database (owned by Amazon). And what a database it is, especially for the avid filmgoer. This vast and delightful repository of all things cinema is the place to go for complete cast/crew listings, actor/filmmaker bios, plot summaries, movie trailers, critics' reviews, user ratings, parental guidance, famous quotations, and all kinds of trivia.

You can always search for movies, TV shows, actors, and so on by typing a name in the search field at the top of the screen. You can also browse various menu choices to find current movies by showtimes, what's coming soon, or what's popular. You can browse TV recaps, too, or find people born on the day you happen to be looking and poking around the app. It's also fun to check out the Trending Celebrities on IMDb. The recent roster included Jaimie Alexander, Tom Hardy, Alexandra Daddario, Priyanka Chopra, Emilia Clarke, Johnny Depp, Leonardo DiCaprio, Marion Cotillard, Natalie Dormer, Michael Fassbender, Rooney Mara, among many others.

One piece of advice to movie buffs: Avoid IMDb if you have a lot of work to do. You'll have a hard time closing the curtain on this marvelous app.

Netflix

Flixster, IMDb, and now Netflix. You've no doubt detected a real trend by now, and that trend is indeed our affection for movies and TV shows. If you love TV and movies, too, you're sure to be a fan of the Netflix app. Over time, Netflix, the company that built its reputation by sending DVDs to subscribers through the mail, started streaming movies and TV shows over the Internet to computers, TVs, and other consumer electronics gear. You can now add the iPad to that list.

From the iPad, you have more or less instant access to thousands of movies on demand. And although these titles aren't exactly current blockbusters, we know you'll find plenty of films worth seeing. You can search by *genre* (classics, comedy, drama, and so on) and *subgenre* (courtroom dramas, political dramas, romantic dramas, and so on).

What's more, Netflix has started producing its own popular shows, including *House of Cards,* featuring Kevin Spacey, which Ed binged on, and *Orange Is The New Black.*

Although the app is free, as are the movies you choose to watch on the fly, you have to pay Netflix streaming subscription fees that start at $7.99 a month. You also need an Internet connection, preferably through Wi-Fi, although Netflix works on 3G and 4G models as well.

Remember what we've told you about streaming movies over 3G or 4G and be mindful of your data plan.

Comixology

The Comixology app is a fantastic way to read comic books on a 9.7-inch touchscreen. Its online store features thousands of comics and comic series from dozens of publishers, including Arcana, Archie, Marvel, Devil's Due, Digital Webbing, Red 5, DC Comics, and Zenescope, as well as hundreds of free comics.

Furthermore, many titles are clas-sics, like issue #1 of *The Amazing Spider-Man*. Released in 1963 for $0.12, a copy in excellent condition goes for at least $25,000 today! We're enjoying this out-of-print classic in pristine condition on our iPads, as shown in Figure 18-5, for a mere $1.99.

Other comics are priced from $0.99 per issue, though many issues of many series are available for free as a teaser.

Finally, this app provides a great way to organize the comics you own on your iPad so that you can find the one you want quickly and easily.

New releases are available every Wednesday, so visit the web store often to check out the latest and greatest offerings. Both the store and

Figure 18-5: Comixology is the best way to read comics on your iPad.

your personal comic collection are well organized and easy to use. And read-ing comics in Comixology is a pleasure you won't want to miss if you're a fan of comics or graphic novels.

Amazon bought this app (and its eponymous maker, Comixology) in 2013, and it's not as good as it used to be. The current version requires you to visit the Comixology website to buy comics, which you then download to the Comixology app. Before Amazon bought the Comixology app, it had its own built-in comic bookstore, which made buying a comic more convenient and straightforward. We hope Amazon will reconsider and bring back the in-app store someday. However, even with the convoluted buying process, we still don't know of anything that offers a better reading experience for comics and graphic novels.

Epicurious Recipes & Shopping List

We love to eat. But we're writers, not gourmet chefs, so we'll take all the help we can get when it comes to preparing a great meal. And we get a lot of that culinary assistance from Epicurious, which easily lives up to its billing as the "Cook's Companion." This tasty recipe app comes courtesy of Condé Nast Digital.

With more than 33,000 recipes to choose from, we're confident you'll find a yummy one in no time. From the Home screen, you can browse categories, often timed to the season. Around the time we were writing this book, recipe collection categories included Halloween Treats, Vegetarian Thanksgiving, Lunches Kids Love, and Cozy Brunch. To which we say, "Yum." Some recipes carry reviews.

If you tap Search in the instead, you can fine-tune your search for a recipe by food or drink, by main ingredient (for example, banana, chicken, pasta), by cuisine type, and by dietary consideration (low-carb, vegan, kosher, and so on), among other parameters.

When you discover a recipe you like, you can add it to a collection of favorites, email it to a friend, pass along the ingredients to your shopping list, summon nutritional information, or share it on Facebook and Twitter.

If you want to sync favorite recipes on your iPhone and iPad through a personal recipe box on Epicurious.com, you can now do so for free.

Bon appétit.

Evernote

Before we even talk about the Evernote iPad app, let's take a quick look at the problem Evernote resolves for us: storing our little bits of digital information — text, pictures, screen shots, scanned images, receipts, bills, email messages, web pages, and other info we might want to recall someday — and synchronizing all the data among all our devices and the cloud.

Evernote (www.evernote.com) is all that and more, with excellent free apps for iOS, Mac OS X, Android, and Windows, plus a killer web interface that works in most browsers.

You can create notes of any length on your iPad by typing, dictating, or photographing. You can add unlimited tags to a note, and create unlimited notebooks to organize your rapidly growing collection of notes.

You can even annotate images and PDFs in Evernote notes, using another free app from Evernote called Skitch, which we also recommend without hesitation.

Getting words and images into Evernote couldn't be much easier, but the info will be useless if you can't find it when you need it. Evernote won't let you down, with myriad options for finding and working with your stored data. In addition to the aforementioned tags and notebooks, Evernote offers searching and filtering (Tags and Notebooks) options to help you find the note you need, as shown in Figure 18-6.

Two other nice touches are worth noting:

- ✔ Notes are automatically tagged with your current location (as long as you create them on your iPad or other location-enabled device), so you can filter by Places.

- ✔ You can attach reminders to notes and receive notifications on the date and time you chose. Best of all, you'll be notified on your iPad as well as on your other iDevices, Macs, PCs, and on the Evernote website!

Our two favorite features are that Evernote syncs notes with all your devices and the cloud automatically and that everything we've mentioned so far — creating, organizing, and syncing notes — is free.

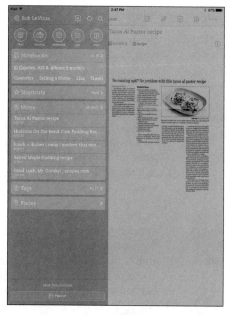

Figure 18-6: Evernote's main screen only hints at how easy it is to create and find notes.

Bob likes Evernote so much that he recently upgraded to the premium plan ($5/month or $45/year), primarily to increase his monthly upload limit from 60MB to 1GB and to get the capability to search for text in PDFs.

Pandora Radio

We've long been fans of Pandora on other computers and mobile devices, so we're practically delirious that this custom Internet radio service is available *gratis* on the iPad. And you can play Pandora music in the background while doing other stuff.

Pandora works on the iPad in much the same way that it does on a Mac or PC. In the box at the upper left, tap + Create Station and type the name of a favorite artist, song title, or composer via the iPad keyboard, and Pandora creates an instant personalized radio station with selections that exemplify the style you chose. Pandora will also suggest some stations you might like based on the stations you've already established, and you can browse genre stations.

Along the left panel of Figure 18-7, you see some of the eclectic stations Ed created. Tapping Shuffle at the top of the list plays musical selections across all your stations.

Suppose that you type *Beatles.* Pandora's instant Beatles station includes performances from John, Paul, George, and Ringo, as well as tunes from other acts.

And say that you type a song title, such as *Have I Told You Lately.* Pandora constructs a station with similar music after you tell it whether to base tunes on the Van Morrison, Rod Stewart, or another rendition.

Pandora comes out of the *Music Genome Project,* an organization of musicians and technologists who analyze music according to hundreds of attributes (such as melody, harmony, and vocal performances).

You can help fine-tune the music Pandora plays by tapping the thumbs-up or thumbs-down icon at the bottom of the screen associated with the music you've been listening to during the current session.

Figure 18-7: Have we told you lately how much we like Pandora?

Pandora also takes advantage of the generous screen real estate of the iPad to deliver artist profiles, lyrics, and more. (Refer to Figure 18-7.) You may see ads, too, unless you opt for Pandora One, a $4.99 a month premium upgrade that eliminates them. Pandora One adds other benefits as well, such as permitting you to more often skip music you don't like.

If you tap the share icon below an album cover of the currently playing song, you can write a message about the song, and then share it on Facebook or Twitter or email it. Other options in Pandora let you bookmark the song or artist that's playing or head to iTunes to purchase the song or other material from the artist directly on the iPad (if available). You can instantly create stations from artists or tracks or also indicate when you're tired of a track.

Before we leave the realm of the free apps, we'd like to remind you of an 11th freebie — a free app so wonderful that we wrote an entire chapter (Chapter 10) about it. The app is iBooks.

Ten Apps Worth Paying For

*I*f you read Chapter 18, you know that lots of great free apps are available for your iPad. But as the cliché goes, some things are worth paying for. Still, none of the ten for-pay apps we've chosen as some of our favorites are likely to break the bank. As you're about to discover, some apps in this list are practical, and some are downright silly. The common theme? We think you'll like carrying these apps around on your iPad.

Bill Atkinson PhotoCard

Who is Bill Atkinson? He had a hand (or both hands) in the first Macintosh computer, as well as in the MacPaint and HyperCard Mac applications. Today he's a world-renowned nature photographer, which brings us to his app. Bill Atkinson PhotoCard is a free app that lets you create gorgeous high-resolution postcards and send them via either email or the U.S. Postal Service.

But the reason we love it is that you can have printed postcards sent via USPS for $1.50 to $2.00 per postcard, depending on how many print-and-mail credits you purchase. The 8.25-x-5.5-inch postcards are, in a word, stunning. Printed on heavy glossy stock on a state-of-the-art HP Indigo Digital Press and then laminated for protection, they're as beautiful as any postcard you've ever seen.

You can use one of the 200 included Bill Atkinson nature photos, as shown in Figure 19-1, or you can use any picture in your Photos library. You can add stickers and stamps, as shown in Figure 19-1, and you can even add voice notes to emailed cards.

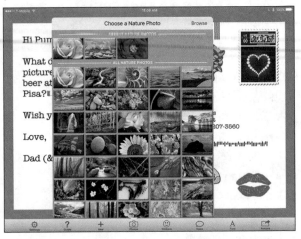

Figure 19-1: Your postcard can feature one of Bill Atkinson's gorgeous nature photos.

If you're still uncertain, download the app (it's free) and try it. Send an email postcard or two to yourself. After you've seen how gorgeous these cards can be and how easy the app is to use, we think you'll spring for some print-and-mail credits and take your iPad on your next vacation as Bob always does.

Words with Friends HD

This brings us to perhaps the only time in this entire book that your authors had a disagreement. Both of us love word games and puzzles, but Bob loves Words with Friends HD, whereas Ed prefers the real thing: namely, SCRABBLE.

Social media is all the rage these days, but most multiplayer iPad games are either boring or not particularly social. Words with Friends HD ($2.99), on the other hand, is the most social game Bob has found — and a ton of fun, too. It's kind of like playing SCRABBLE with a friend, but because it's turn-based, you can make a move and then quit the app and do other stuff. When your friend makes his next move, you can choose to be notified that it's your turn by sound, on-screen alert, and/or a number on the Words with Friends icon on your Home screen.

Bob says: "Try the free version (Words with Friends HD Free), and I'm sure you'll be hooked. Then challenge me if you like; my username is `boblevitus` (although I often have the maximum 20 games going, so keep trying if I don't accept your challenge right away)."

ArtStudio for iPad

Do you fancy yourself an artist? We know our artistic talent is limited, but if we were talented, ArtStudio for iPad is the program we'd use to paint our masterpieces. Even if you have limited artistic talent, you can see that this app has everything you need to create awesome artwork.

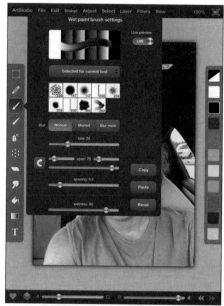

We were embarrassed to show you our creations, so instead we whipped up Figure 19-2, which shows just the options for just one of ArtStudio's tools (there are dozens and dozens more).

Here are just some of ArtStudio for iPad's features:

Figure 19-2: ArtStudio for iPad's Wet Paint Brush Settings and brush options.

- Offers 25 brushes, including pencils, a smudge tool, bucket fill, and an airbrush. Brushes are resizable and simulate brush pressure.

- Allows up to five layers with options, such as delete, reorder, duplicate, merge, and transparency.

- Provides filters, such as blur, sharpen, detect edges, and sepia.

Don't believe us? AppSmile.com (www.appsmile.com) rated it 5 out of 5, saying, "This is what Photoshop Mobile wishes it had been." SlapApp.com (www.slapapp.com) also rated it 5 out of 5 and said, "I've dabbled in quite a few painting and drawing apps and this one has 'em all beat by a long shot." And by all means, check out what talented artists can do with ArtStudio for iPad at www.flickr.com/groups/artstudioimages.

One last thing: The app was only $0.99 when we bought our copies — a special launch sale price. The price has gone up, but even at the new price, a whopping $4.99, it's still a heck of a deal for a thoughtfully designed and full-featured drawing and painting app.

Beware of rip-offs in the iTunes App Store, such as the similarly named Art Studio HD — For Your iPad. That one's a bad knock-off from developer Party Sub Productions that has garnered mostly 1-star ratings. Don't be fooled — the app you're looking for is ArtStudio for iPad, from Lucky Clan. Note that *Art* and *Studio* are run together to form a single word; if you search for the single word *ArtStudio*, you'll find it.

Pinball Crystal Caliburn II

Good pinball games require supremely realistic physics, and Pinball Crystal Caliburn II ($3.99) nails it. The way the ball moves around the table and interacts with bumpers and flippers is so realistic that you'll think you're at an arcade. The app is so realistic, in fact, that you can shake the table to influence the ball's movement.

Another hallmark of a great pinball game is great sound effects, and this game doesn't disappoint. The sounds the ball makes when it bounces off a bumper, is hit with a flipper, or passes through a rollover are spot-on and authentic.

If you like pinball, we think you'll love Pinball Crystal Caliburn II on your iPad. LittleWing (the developer) recently released an iOS version of its original pinball hit, Tristan, which also sports realistic physics and sounds and is also a lot of fun.

Art Authority for iPad

We've already admitted to being artistically challenged, but that applies only to making art. We both appreciate good art as much as the next person, or even more. That's why we're so enthusiastic about Art Authority, even at $9.99.

Art Authority is like an art museum you hold in your hand; it contains more than 90,000 paintings and sculptures by more than 1,000 of the world's greatest artists. The works are organized into period-specific rooms, such as Early (up to 1400s), Baroque, Romanticism, Modern, and American. In each room, the artworks are subdivided by movement. For

Figure 19-3: Exploring virtual art galleries with the iPad.

example, as Figure 19-3 shows, the Modern room has works of Surrealism, Cubism, Fauvism, Dadaism, sculpture, and several more.

You find period overviews, movement overviews, timelines, and slideshows, plus a searchable index of all 1,000+ artists and separate indices for each room.

Developer Open Door Networks includes an art near me feature, which lets you search for art in your vicinity. And the app has artwork and rooms optimized for the Retina display. And the art real size feature adds the perspective of understanding how big or small a work really is. Video has also been added for hundreds of major works. If you love art, check it out.

And let us point out a kid-friendly K-12 version with still close to 90,000 paintings and sculptures. It costs $7.99; "inappropriate" nudity for the youngsters has been eliminated.

Solar Walk

We like to gaze at the heavens, but we often have no clue what we're looking at. Solar Walk, a handsome animated 99-cents guide to the night sky from Vito Technology — refreshed to take advantage of the Retina display — will delight astronomy students and anyone fascinated by outer space, even if purists scoff that Pluto, no longer considered a planet, is included in the model of the solar system. (The official name of the app is Solar Walk — Solar System Planets, Orbits, and Moons with Pictures, Sounds and Lessons. Whew.)

From the start, you're taken on a virtual tour through the galaxy. You can search planets — Figure 19-4 shows Saturn — satellites, stars, and more. You can even travel through time and space with a time machine feature. Animated movies cover topics such as earth's cycles, solar eclipse, and the moon's phases.

Figure 19-4: Learning about beautiful Saturn in Solar Walk.

What's more, the app can exploit 3D, provided you supply your own *anaglyph*-style cyan-red 3D glasses. And if you hook the iPad up to a 3D TV using an HDMI adapter (see Chapter 17), you can get a true sense of the depth and sheer size of the solar system in 3D, while controlling what you see on the screen through the iPad.

Without 3D, you can use AirPlay to mirror what's on the iPad screen on the bigger TV screen, provided you have an Apple TV.

One thing we find frustrating: Solar Walk is heavy on in-app purchases. For example, you'll have to pay 99¢ to watch a movie on a solar eclipse or to watch an animation showing a repair of the Hubble telescope, though you can get a high-resolution bundle with numerous extras for $1.99,

Action Movie FX

With Action Movie FX, it's a breeze to add big-budget Hollywood-style special effects to video you shoot with your iPad. Action Movie FX comes from producer J. J. Abrams's Bad Robot Productions, best known for TV shows such as *Alias* and *Fringe* and feature films including *Star Trek* and *Super 8*. We expected the app to be pretty good, and it is — it may well be the most fun app we've ever used to make videos with an iPad.

The free version features eight big-budget movie effects, such as missile attack, avalanche, and meteor from outer space, as well as phaser fight and photon torpedoes from Abrams's epic theatrical release *Star Trek into Darkness*. In other words, Action Movie FX lets you add Hollywood-style special effects to your videos so you can "destroy" people, places, pets, and other stuff in a variety of fun and interesting ways.

Making a video with Action Movie FX couldn't be easier. Just launch the app, select the scene you want to use, tap Start, and shoot a minimum of five seconds of video. It's better if the footage is of someone or something that will remain still, unlike Bob's dog Zeke, the slightly blurry miniature vizsla in Figure 19-5.

When you've finished filming, you can adjust the timing as well as resize and reposition

Figure 19-5: An alien bursting out of Bob's dog.

the special effects. When you're satisfied with your creation, your masterpiece appears after a bit of processing; you can then share it, save it to your Camera Roll album, adjust its timing again, or shoot another video.

The free effects are great, but we found ourselves wanting more and have purchased most of the ten currently available FX packs, for $0.99 each. They're mostly great, but our absolute favorites are the Jet (shown in Figure 19-6) and Alien Burst (refer to Figure 19-5).

Figure 19-6: A jet taking out several vehicles on a quiet street.

The videos are HD, and look great in a text message or an email displayed on any device. The videos look fabulous on your iPad, but also look surprisingly good on a bigger display such as the one on a Mac, a PC, or an HDTV.

Finally, you just can't beat the price — your first eight effects are free. But we're betting that you'll like it enough to pop for one or more $0.99 FX packs. Either way, we're pretty sure you'll have as much fun as we have adding special FX to your videos.

Facetune for iPad

You don't really think those drop-dead gorgeous models are really that drop-dead gorgeous, now do you? They had "work done." And the portraits that show these men and women in their best light were doctored, touched-up, and made to look perfect.

The $4.99 Facetune app can make you look perfect, too — okay, we'll amend that to say it promises to make you look better. (As Bob and Ed know, you have to work with what you've got.)

After uploading a photo or taking pictures in the app with the camera on your iPad, you can tap the Facetune controls shown in Figure 19-7. Facetune smooths wrinkles, whitens teeth, heals zits, changes the contours of your face, gives you a full head of hair if

Figure 19-7: Facetune can make Ed look better.

you're lacking, and even defocuses the image to minimize imperfections in your face.

When you reach perfection, you can save the finished product to your Camera Roll album, share it by email, or post it on Facebook, Twitter, Tumblr, Messenger, or Flickr.

60 Minutes

As news junkies, we have long appreciated *60 Minutes,* CBS's venerable TV news magazine. CBS Interactive's $4.99 companion app to the series brings the latest *60 Minutes* segments to your iPad so that you can watch at your convenience. The *60 Minutes Overtime* segments, which provide weekly behind-the-scenes looks at how the various stories came together, are also available.

But the best part to us is the Previous+ section, which features more than 250 hand-picked stories, covering the 40-plus-year history of the show. Interview subjects include Coretta Scott King, Johnny Carson, George Steinbrenner (see Figure 19-8), Jodie Foster, Ronald and Nancy Reagan, Oprah Winfrey, and Barack Obama.

Figure 19-8: Bringing *60 Minutes* history to your iPad.

You can search shows by topic (newsmakers, politics, science, business, sports, entertainment, nature), by decade, and by correspondent, letting you zero in on some of the finest work from Ed Bradley, Harry Reasoner, and Mike Wallace. Andy Rooney is here too, as is the famous *60 Minutes* stopwatch.

Parallels Access

If you're like most of the iPad community, you mostly use your iPad for consumption: watching movies, listening to music, playing games, and browsing the web. You engage less often in productive activities on the iPad, mostly because it lacks a physical keyboard. (We're assuming here that you did not spring for an accessory keyboard for the iPad Pro or other iPads.) As a result, you still schlep a laptop with you on the road even though you also carry the iPad.

Parallels, a company best known for letting you run virtualized versions of Microsoft Windows on Macintosh computers, may eliminate the need to carry the extra machine. Its Parallels Access iPad app ties into a subscription service that lets you tap into your home or office PC remotely, whether it's a Windows PC or a Mac.

What sets Parallels Access apart from other apps that provide remote access to computers is that you can get to use *all* the programs that reside on your PC or Mac, including the proprietary software that your company may employ. Moreover, you can interact with those applications on the tablet as if each were designed for the iPad, and even use a browser running Adobe Flash on the iPad.

You start any PC or Mac desktop application on the iPad from a familiar looking launcher screen with icons for the apps you use most often. Such a screen is shown in Figure 19-9. You can add or remove icons to this launcher screen.

Figure 19-9: Parallels Access lets you run programs on a Mac or PC from the iPad.

Parallels, as the company puts it, "applifies" PC/Mac programs so that the software is modified on the tablet to display iPad-style buttons for actions such as copy, paste, and select. And touch gestures on the iPad substitute for mouse moves on your computer. For example, tapping is like clicking with a mouse; two-finger tapping is equivalent to a right-click. Hold your finger against the display in an Excel spreadsheet, say, and an iPad magnifying glass appears.

You can use your voice to dictate text remotely onto the home or office computer. And you can listen to music on the iPad that resides on your faraway computer, too — no, the folks back home or in the office will not hear what you're hearing; the app is set up so as not to disturb them.

Parallels Access can't completely make up for the lack of a physical keyboard on the iPad. But the on-screen Mac or Windows keyboards that appear in the app display any dedicated special keys unique to Mac or Windows keyboards.

The Parallels Access app is free to download, as is the agent program you must install on each Mac or PC that you choose to access. A Parallels Access subscription is $19.99 per year for an unlimited number of devices (iPads and iPhones running iOS 7 and higher, Android tablets and phones running Android 4 and higher, and Kindle Fire) and up to five computers (PCs running Windows 7, 8, 8.1, or 10, and Macs running Lion, Mountain Lion, Mavericks, Yosemite, or El Capitan).

Index

• U •

• V •

• W •